THE NEW
Beta Sigma Phi
Holiday Cookbook

Twelve Months of Festive Recipes

©Favorite Recipes Press, A Division of Heritage House MCMLXXXIV
Post Office Box 1408, Nashville, Tennessee 37202
Library of Congress Cataloging in Publication Data on page 191.

Dear Friends,

It's nice to hear that so many of you are willing to share your culinary secrets — because it's no secret that Beta Sigma Phis are the best cooks around! I can vouch for that, because it's been my pleasure to dine with members all over the world. And from Indonesia to Indiana, the menu has always been superb.

Perhaps you all are best during the holidays, when you can create a "Living Masterpiece" in your kitchens, and bring style and creativity to your family's table. Over 3,000 recipes were sent in by Beta Sigma Phis for the New Holiday Cookbook — and the experts at Favorite Recipes Press say these recipes are some of the best they have ever received from us. There's even a special "Gourmet Food Gifts" section for those of you who wish to wrap up your culinary talents and pass them on to secret sisters and other special friends — like me!

Add to that the excitement of the Sweepstakes and you have a fund-raising project that can also be a lot of fun for your members. Best of all, it's an easy way to support the Statue of Liberty service project — an effort that has all Beta Sigma Phis proud and participating! Together, we will make Lady Liberty's torch shine brighter than ever before.

Yours in Beta Sigma Phi,

Bill Ross

Bill Ross
President
Beta Sigma Phi International Executive Council

Recipes on pages 148 and 153.

Holidays for All Seasons	6
New Year's	9
St. Valentine's Day	23
St. Patrick's Day	35
Easter	47
Memorial Day	61
Independence Day	69
Labor Day	81
Halloween	93
Thanksgiving	107
Christmas	123
Gourmet Food Gifts	145
Special Occasions	157
Equivalent Chart	178
Metric Conversion Chart	179
Substitution Chart	180
Index	181
Ordering Information	193

Contents

Holidays for All Seasons

The calendar's full of celebrations! Holiday by holiday — month by month — there's an event or special occasion that inspires every good cook to entertain. And, now, it will be even easier and more fun with your all-new Beta Sigma Phi Cookbook, dedicated to making each holiday more fulfilling than ever.

From the first clink of New Year's champagne glasses to the nostalgic traditions of Christmas, in the pages that follow you'll discover a treasury of tempting recipes and party ideas to enjoy. Like the authentic Chinese New Year's recipes which will help you throw the most original New Year's party ever! And when Easter comes, discover how to make an edible Easter basket that also doubles as a centerpiece.

In addition to holiday fare, there are two additional sections you'll enjoy in your new Beta Sigma Phi cookbook: "Gourmet Food Gifts" — a selection of recipes for foods that make thoughtful gifts, not only at Christmas, but will be appreciated by a hostess any time of the year. And "Special Occasions" includes a score of recipes organized into clever party ideas. Just wait until you see the hearty soup recipes in the "Housewarming Soup Supper" . . . the choice of glorious desserts in the "Birthday Buffet" . . . the gourmet continental cuisine on "Grand Tour Sampler" . . . and picnic ideas so creative that even the ants will be surprised!

Selecting the right recipe for the occasion . . . enhancing it with simple food presentation tricks and creating an exciting mood with party decorations can turn even the simplest dish into a surprising treat. The following pages should help you do just that, giving even the most creative hostess a treasury of new ideas!

LET'S GIVE A PARTY!

Setting The Stage

Before party day ever arrives, imagine your rooms filled with people. Does the furniture arrangement lend itself to an easy traffic flow? If not, rearrange by removing ottomans and other small pieces of furniture that could turn your home into an obstacle course. Tuck lamp cords out of the way, remove knickknacks to open up spaces for snacks, and if there's a TV in the room, remove it to keep temptation out of sight! If cocktails are served, avoid "traffic jams" by setting up food tables separately from the bar.

If you're giving a large party in cold weather, you may want to clear a closet for coats or even rent a coatrack. A bed piled high with wraps is not only unattractive, but a sad sight for the first person who arrived.

For buffets, be sure to arrange the table setting for guests to pick up items as they need them. Don't fill their hands with silverware and a glass as they begin or you'll create balancing acts that are not only awkward, but dangerous to your carpet! For seated dinners, keep lights low, then brighten slightly as a signal it's time to eat. Flower centerpieces add a nice splash of color, but make sure the arrangement is not so tall that guests are peering through the petals to converse.

Enhance the mood with music. Pace the party with soft sounds as people first arrive to gayer music as the party evolves. Music selections should be planned in advance, tying it into the holiday whenever possible — such as famous love songs around Valentine's Day. But during the party, ask another family member to take charge of the music.

... A Host of Entertaining Ideas

Winding down the party is a matter of etiquette in itself. If guests must leave early, usher them quietly to the door so others don't think the party's over. However, if the night wears on much later than you intended, there are subtle ways to encourage guests to leave . . . brighten the lights a bit . . . stop serving drinks and offer fresh coffee instead . . . let the music stop. Only out of sheer desperation . . . resort to clearing the tables.

BE A STAR AT THE BAR!

One of the toughest challenges facing the Beta Sigma Phi hostess is getting guests to circulate through all parts of your home. Setting up the bar in an unusual spot is one way to remedy that problem. There's no reason why the bedroom, hallway or patio can't be converted into a creative bar.

To arrange a bedroom bar, clear off the dresser top and protect it with a heavy cloth or trays. Keep service simple and offer one type of glass for all beverages. Stash supplies of soda, ice, wine, etc. in an ice-filled bucket in the corner of the room.

If you're lucky enough to have a patio, lure guests outdoors to the bar set up on a picnic table, card table or even an ironing board covered with a checkered cloth. Fill a wheelbarrow or big galvanized tub with ice and use plastic cups for outdoor safety.

A few last words of advice. Buy more ice than you think you'll need; you can never have too much. Have a good assortment of nonalcoholic beverages on hand at all times. Don't worry about having enough glasses — mix and match is fine. And to make sure they're sparkling, rinse in soda water after washing to remove any soapy film. Finally, save yourself and your guests embarrassment by telling them in advance what drinks you're serving, rather than not having what's requested.

CREATIVE TOUCHES YEAR 'ROUND

Nothing can change "ho-hum" gatherings into truly festive celebrations easier than decorating with flair and originality. From the moment your guests enter your home, they should be able to sense the spirit and atmosphere of your party. Luckily, this can be accomplished easily — with the ingenuity for which Beta Sigma Phis are known.

SPRINGTIME parties are a natural for the clever Beta Sigma Phi hostess. Fill your home with flowers of the season. Place loose bunches of tulips, iris, daffodils or narcissus wherever color is needed. Cluster potted plants for an instant indoor garden. And don't forget the bathroom. Even a simple iris in a bud vase helps remind guests that springtime is here.

For Easter, bake the Easter basket cake from the recipe on page 58. Or create your own basket with a few handfuls of straw and plastic eggs. For a real party mixer, place a trivia question about each guest inside extra plastic eggs and hide them about the room. At the beginning of the party, invite guests to find an egg, open it and read their questions aloud. Finding out the answer is an excellent way to encourage mingling and a lot of fun at the end of the party when all answers are revealed.

Children love eating from their own Easter baskets. Fill one for each child with special holiday food and identify the baskets with personalized Easter eggs. They'll be thrilled!

When SUMMER comes, take the indoors outside! Have an "elegant" picnic complete with candlesticks, silver, good wine glasses and fine linens. Select a fancy menu and, when the

meal is over, bring out individual finger bowls for elegant wash-ups! For a more casual picnic, decorate with assorted wicker baskets filled with lush ferns and potted plants. Herbs and decorative weeds make a delightful centerpiece and smell wonderful!

When planning Beta Sigma Phi summertime menus, keep food light and healthful. For appetizers, cut up fruit in individual baskets carved from oranges. Or stuff cucumber halves. Dip drinks from a giant galvanized tub and serve them in mason jars. Guests love the unexpected!

AUTUMN is the perfect time for entertaining. With vacations over and children in school, cool weather seems to invite friendly gatherings. A harvest of fresh vegetables make colorful centerpieces. And so many fall vegetables are perfect food containers themselves. Hollowed-out pumpkins, acorn squash and eggplants hold anything from dips to a main course. And they're as pretty as they are useful! For the soup supper described later in your cookbook, hollow out large loaves of round, dark bread and place the soup bowl inside. Guests can actually nibble on the bread as they enjoy the soup!

Here are lovely decorating ideas to give Beta Sigma Phi homes a distinctive touch during the WINTER months — creative wreaths. You're limited only by your imagination! Select any of the "ingredients" listed below for a unique addition for your door or mantel.

- Bright red apples. Filled in with holly leaves and secured with wire, this wreath looks especially cheery on an outside door.
- Baby's breath. The beauty is in its simplicity. Place baby's breath in a straw-colored wreath and add glistening gold balls attached to pipe cleaners. Remove the balls after Christmas and enjoy this attractive wreath year-round!

Nuts. Glue an assortment of unshelled nuts including chestnuts, walnuts, hazelnuts, acorns and pecans on wreath form. Intermingle small pine cones attached with pipe cleaners. Finish by spraying with clear acrylic spray.

- For the holidays, glue wrapped candy, striped mints or any other hard candy such as lemon drops onto a wreath. Fill in with eucalyptus leaves and finish with a small pair of scissors hanging from a piece of yarn. Children love to snip off a piece of candy when they visit. Or, for the nutrition-conscious Beta Sigma Phi sister, wrap a small amount of trail mix in a clear wrap, leaving an end dangling so you can secure the "balls of health" with a staple to the wreath. A delicious alternative to candy!
- A braided rope wreath requires about 150 feet of one-inch rope. Cut it into 15 rope strands 90 inches long and divide the strands into three groups of five. (For easier handling as you braid, stitch each group of five at intervals with an upholstery needle and clear thread. Remove threads after braiding.) For Christmas, braid ropes covered with a holiday fabric or velvet. To make larger or smaller wreaths, simply adjust the length of strands.

The Christmas holidays conjure up a host of other decorating ideas as well. Use evergreens in large baskets for a delightful winter scent, adding color with apples and holly berries. Set the baskets in out-of-the-way corners or use as a table centerpiece. And for any winter gathering, you can't beat a cluster of candlesticks for mood enhancement. Use different-sized glass candlesticks for mood enhancement. Use different-sized glass candlesticks as a centerpiece or placed on an out-of-the-way corner table. For a truly unique centerpiece, fill a large glass bowl with pine cones and scatter small, colored Christmas balls throughout.

As you can see, creativity does not mean expense. And with this super collection of Beta Sigma Phi recipes, you can transform any gathering into a special event!

Recipes on pages 20 and 22.

New Year's Day

10 / New Year's

CHERYL'S HOT SPICED DRINK

1/2 pt. vodka
1 1/2 qt. cranberry juice
2 qt. apple juice
1/2 c. packed brown sugar
1/2 tsp. salt
4 cinnamon sticks
1 1/2 tsp. whole cloves

Pour vodka, cranberry and apple juices in large coffeepot. Combine remaining ingredients in basket of coffeepot. Perk using manufacturer's directions.

Lin Freeman
Zeta Zeta, Lafayette, Indiana

CHOCOLATE NOG PUNCH

1 pt. chocolate ice
  cream, softened
1 qt. eggnog, chilled
1/2 c. chocolate syrup
1 qt. club soda, chilled
1 c. whipped cream

Mix ice cream, eggnog and chocolate syrup in punch bowl. Stir in club soda gradually. Float whipped cream on surface. Garnish with chocolate shavings. Yield: 3 quarts.

R. Jeanette Beard
Sigma Iota, Adrian, Missouri

ORANGE BLOSSOMS

1 sm. can frozen
  lemonade concentrate,
  thawed
1 sm. can orange juice
1 orange juice can gin
1 egg white
1 tbsp. confectioners'
  sugar

Combine all ingredients and 6 ice cubes in blender container. Process until frothy. May use liquor of choice for gin.

Barbara C. Wojeck
Xi Beta Upsilon, Salamanca, New York

FROZEN STRAWBERRY DAIQUIRIS

1 10-oz. package frozen
  strawberries, thawed
4 oz. rum
1/2 sm. can pink
  lemonade concentrate
Sugar to taste

Combine all ingredients in blender container. Process until smooth. Add several ice cubes at a time. Process until slushy. May be frozen. Yield: 4-6 servings.

Sandi Davison
Preceptor Gamma Upsilon, Kansas City, Missouri

HOT ARTICHOKE DIP

1 14-oz. can artichoke
  hearts, drained,
  coarsely chopped
1 1/2 c. mayonnaise
2 7-oz. cans diced
  green chilies, drained
4 oz. Monterey Jack
  cheese, grated
1/2 c. Parmesan cheese
1 4-oz. jar diced
  pimento, drained

Mix first 5 ingredients. Add pimento, reserving 2 teaspoonfuls. Spoon into 1 1/2-quart baking dish. Sprinkle with reserved pimento and additional Parmesan cheese. Bake at 325 degrees for 30 minutes. Serve with chips. Yield: 5 cups.

Frances Woehler
Mu Iota, Marine City, Michigan

MICROWAVE SUPER BOWL CHALUPA DIP

1 1/2 lb. ground beef
1 17-oz. can refried
  beans
1 4-oz. can diced green
  chilies
3 to 4 c. shredded
  Cheddar cheese
1 7-oz. bottle of
  green taco sauce
1 1/2 bunches green
  onions, chopped
1 4-oz. can ripe
  olives, chopped
8 med. radishes, sliced
2 c. guacamole dip
1 8-oz. carton sour
  cream

Brown ground beef, stirring frequently. Mix in beans and chilies. Pat into greased 9 x 13-inch microwave dish. Sprinkle with cheese and taco sauce. Microwave, covered, on High for 8 to 10 minutes; cool. Decorate with concentric circles of remaining ingredients in order listed. Serve with tortilla chips. Yield: 10-12 servings.

Darlene Gross
Sigma Omicron, Edwards, California

PASSION PEA DIP

1/2 green pepper, finely
  chopped
6 jalapeno peppers,
  finely chopped
2 stalks celery, finely
  chopped
1 lg. onion, finely
  chopped
1 tsp. pepper
1 to 2 tbsp. Tabasco
  sauce
1/2 c. catsup
1 tbsp. salt
3 chicken bouillon cubes
1/4 tsp. each nutmeg,
  cinnamon
2 med. cans black-eyed
  peas
1/2 16-oz. can tomatoes
1 tsp. garlic powder
3 tbsp. flour
1/2 c. bacon drippings
2 slices bacon

Bring first 9 ingredients and spices to a simmer. Add black-eyed peas, tomatoes and garlic powder. Simmer for 30 minutes. Blend flour with 1 to 2 tablespoons water and bacon drippings. Add with bacon to hot mixture. Cook for 10 minutes, stirring frequently; remove bacon. Serve hot with tortilla chips. Yield: 4-6 servings.

Nancy Everhardt
Delta Nu, Johnson City, Tennessee

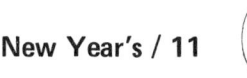

SPINACH DIP

1 c. mayonnaise
1 c. sour cream
1 sm. can chopped water chestnuts
1 tbsp. minced onion
1 pkg. frozen chopped spinach, thawed, drained
1 pkg. dry vegetable soup mix

Blend mayonnaise and sour cream. Mix in remaining ingredients; chill. Serve with bite-sized pieces of Hawaiian bread.

Jacqueline Shafar
Alpha Eta, Creston, Iowa

CURRY PATE

2 3-oz. packages cream cheese, softened
1 c. shredded sharp Cheddar cheese
1 tsp. Sherry
1/2 tsp. curry powder
1/4 tsp. salt
1/2 c. peach chutney
1 green onion, finely chopped

Beat first 5 ingredients until smooth. Spread 1/2 inch thick on serving plate. Chill until firm. Top with chutney and green onion. Serve with crackers.

Marcia Wilson
Xi Delta Epsilon, Brighten, Colorado

HOT MUSHROOM SPREAD

2 med. onions, chopped
1/4 c. butter
1 8-oz. package cream cheese, softened
1 lb. mushrooms, chopped
1/4 tsp. garlic salt
1/2 tsp. Worcestershire sauce

Saute onions in butter. Mix with cream cheese and remaining ingredients. Spread in baking dish. Bake at 375 degrees for 15 to 20 minutes. Serve with crackers or party rye bread. May be made ahead and reheated.

Diane Seiple
Preceptor Alpha Theta, Troy, Ohio

HOLIDAY SALMON LOG

1 16-oz. can salmon, drained
1 8-oz. package cream cheese, softened
1 tbsp. lemon juice
1 tbsp. grated onion
4 tsp. liquid smoke
1 tsp. pepper
1 tbsp. chopped parsley
1 c. chopped pecans

Mix first 6 ingredients until smooth. Shape into log. Wrap in foil. Freeze for 2 hours. Roll in parsley and pecans. Chill until serving time. Serve with French bread or crackers.

Marlene Baker
Preceptor Kappa, Chandler, Arizona

SURPRISE CHEESE LOG

1/4 c. mayonnaise
1 hard-boiled egg, chopped
3 tbsp. chopped green pepper
2 tbsp. each chopped onion, pimento
1 jalapeno pepper, seeded, chopped
1 tbsp. sugar
1/2 tsp. salt
1 16-oz. can chopped sauerkraut, drained
4 c. shredded Cheddar cheese
2 3-oz. packages cream cheese, softened
1 to 2 tbsp. milk

Mix first 8 ingredients. Stir in sauerkraut and Cheddar cheese. Shape into log. Blend cream cheese and milk. Spread over log. Chill for 4 hours or longer. Garnish with green pepper and pimento. Serve with crackers. Yield: 24 servings.

Shirley Kemp
Xi Alpha Chi, Iola, Kansas

RED SALMON PATE

1 lg. can red salmon
2 env. unflavored gelatin
1/2 c. mayonnaise
2 tbsp. lemon juice
1 tbsp. Worcestershire sauce
1/2 c. chili sauce
1/4 tbsp. pepper
1 tsp. dillweed (opt.)
1 7-oz. can tuna, drained
4 hard-boiled eggs, chopped
1/4 c. chopped onion
1/4 c. chopped stuffed olives

Drain salmon, reserving liquid. Dissolve gelatin in heated liquid. Blend with next 6 ingredients. Fold in salmon, tuna, eggs, onion and olives. Pour into fish-shaped mold. Chill until firm. Unmold on lettuce-lined plate. Yield: 12 servings.

Elizabeth B. Thompson
Preceptor Beta Eta, Bradenton, Florida

DILLED SHRIMP SPREAD

1 env. unflavored gelatin
1 can cream of mushroom soup
2 3-oz. packages cream cheese, cubed
1/4 c. thinly sliced green onions
2 tbsp. lemon juice
1/4 tsp. dillweed
1/2 lb. small fresh shrimp, cooked
1/2 c. each mayonnaise, sour cream
1/2 c. each chopped parsley, celery
1/4 tsp. hot pepper sauce

Soften gelatin in 3 tablespoons cold water. Mix with soup. Cook and stir until gelatin dissolves. Stir in cream cheese until melted; cool. Mix in remaining ingredients. Spoon into 6-cup mold. Chill, covered, for 4 hours; unmold. Serve with crackers. Yield: 8-10 servings.

Dorothy Decker
Xi Xi Zeta, Redwood City, California

12 / New Year's

MICROWAVE BACON POLES

10 slices bacon, cut in half lengthwise
20 garlic bread sticks

Wrap bacon around bread sticks. Place in paper towel-lined glass dish; cover with paper towel. Microwave on High for 3 minutes; turn sticks. Microwave for 2 to 4 minutes longer. Cool on paper towel until crisp. Yield: 20 servings.

Donna Guard
Mu Alpha, Garden City, Iowa

CHEESE AND OLIVE BALLS

1/4 lb. Cheddar cheese, grated, softened
1/4 c. butter, softened
1/4 tsp. paprika
3/4 c. flour
36 to 40 tiny stuffed Spanish olives

Blend cheese, butter and paprika. Mix with flour until smooth. Let stand, covered, for 15 minutes. Shape by teaspoonfuls into 1 1/2-inch circles. Wrap to enclose olives. Chill for 10 minutes. Bake at 375 degrees for 20 to 25 minutes. Yield: 36-40.

Bonnie D. Bond
Pi, Lutherville, Maryland

GOLDEN CHICKEN NUGGETS

4 chicken breasts, boned, skinned
1/2 c. bread crumbs
1/4 c. Parmesan cheese
2 tsp. MSG
1 tsp. each salt, basil, thyme
1/2 c. melted butter

Cut chicken into 1 1/2-inch squares. Mix bread crumbs, cheese and seasonings. Dip chicken in butter and in crumb mixture. Bake on foil-lined baking sheet at 400 degrees for 10 minutes.

Lisa Wallace
Epsilon Omega, Cullowhee, North Carolina

CHICKEN-NUT PUFFS

1 c. chicken broth
1/2 c. oil
1 tsp. celery seed
1 tbsp. parsley flakes
2 tsp. seasoned salt
1/8 tsp. cayenne pepper
2 tbsp. Worcestershire sauce
1 c. sifted flour
4 eggs
1 6-oz. jar boned chicken, finely chopped
1 c. finely chopped toasted almonds

Bring broth, oil, seasonings and Worcestershire sauce to a boil. Add flour. Cook over low heat until mixture forms smooth ball, stirring constantly; remove from heat. Beat in eggs 1 at a time. Stir in mixture of chicken and almonds. Drop by 1/2 teaspoonfuls onto greased baking sheet. Bake at 450 degrees for 10 to 15 minutes. Yield: 4 dozen.

Vam Erickson
Preceptor Gamma, Williston, North Dakota

ITALIAN BITES

1 loaf frozen bread, thawed
2 oz. pepperoni, thinly sliced
1 lb. spinach, cooked, drained
1 4-oz. package shredded mozzarella cheese
Salt and spices to taste
Parmesan cheese to taste

Roll bread dough on lightly greased baking sheet. Saute pepperoni. Layer spinach, pepperoni, mozzarella cheese, seasonings and Parmesan cheese in center of dough. Fold in edges; overlap to seal. Bake at 350 degrees for 20 to 25 minutes. Cut into 1-inch thick slices. Yield: 12 slices.

Jean A. Kask
Xi Alpha Epsilon, Enfield, Connecticut

SPECIAL COCKTAIL MEATBALLS

3 lb. ground beef
1/2 c. seasoned bread crumbs
4 tsp. horseradish
Garlic powder, pepper to taste
4 onions, finely chopped
1 tbsp. salt
1 1/2 c. tomato juice
1/4 c. butter
1/4 c. flour
3 c. beef broth
1 c. red wine
1/4 c. packed brown sugar
1/4 c. catsup
2 tbsp. lemon juice

Mix first 5 ingredients with half the onions, 2 teaspoons salt and tomato juice; shape into small balls. Bake at 450 degrees for 10 minutes until brown; drain. Saute remaining onions in butter. Blend in flour. Stir in broth, stirring until smooth. Add wine, brown sugar, catsup, lemon juice and 1 teaspoon salt. Simmer over low heat for 15 minutes. Add meatballs. Heat to serving temperature. Yield: 12 1/2 dozen.

Betty Carmichael
Preceptor Mu, Cherry Hill, New Jersey

HAM BALLS

1 egg
1 c. milk
1 c. graham cracker crumbs
2 lb. ground ham loaf mixture
1/2 c. tomato soup
1 1/2 c. packed brown sugar
1/4 c. vinegar
1 tsp. mustard

Mix egg, milk, graham cracker crumbs and ham loaf mixture. Shape into balls. Bake in 9 x 13-inch baking dish at 350 degrees for 45 minutes. Boil tomato soup with brown sugar, vinegar and mustard. Pour over ham balls. Bake for 20 minutes longer.

Marlys Reiland
Preceptor Theta, Eagle Grove, Iowa

TERIYAKI MEATBALLS

1 lb. ground chuck	1 tbsp. oil
1/4 c. chopped onion	2 tsp. Sherry
1/4 c. flour	2 tbsp. brown sugar
1 egg, slightly beaten	1/8 tsp. each ginger, MSG
1 tsp. salt	1 tsp. minced garlic
1/4 tsp. pepper	2 tsp. cornstarch
1/4 c. soy sauce	

Mix first 6 ingredients with 1 tablespoon soy sauce. Shape into 1-inch balls. Brown in oil; drain. Blend remaining ingredients, 3 tablespoons soy sauce and 1/2 cup water. Pour over meatballs. Simmer for 30 minutes. Yield: 4 dozen.

Esther Root
Tau Epsilon, New Richmond, Ohio

MICROWAVE CHEESY STUFFED MUSHROOMS

1/2 lb. ground beef	8 oz. mushrooms, stems removed
1/2 c. shredded mozzarella cheese	1/2 c. shredded Cheddar cheese
1/4 onion, chopped	

Cook ground beef until brown and crumbly; drain. Add mozzarella cheese and onion. Cook until cheese is melted. Spoon into mushroom caps. Sprinkle with Cheddar cheese. Microwave in glass dish on High for 2 minutes or until cheese melts.

Joyce Westphal
Kappa Zeta, Lenox, Iowa

CRAB AND SPINACH STUFFED MUSHROOMS

1 10-oz. package frozen chopped spinach, thawed, drained	2 to 3 lb. medium mushrooms, stems removed
1/2 lb. crab meat	2 to 3 tbsp. butter, softened
1 env. dry onion soup mix	1 c. grated Cheddar cheese
1 c. sour cream	
1/4 tsp. garlic powder	

Mix first 5 ingredients. Spoon into mushroom caps. Place on buttered baking sheet. Sprinkle with cheese. Bake, covered, at 350 degrees for 12 minutes. Yield: 3 dozen.

Judith Lein Brower
Delta Mu, Albany, Oregon

SESAME-CRAB ROLLS

1/2 lb. Velveeta cheese	20 slices bread, crusts trimmed
1/2 c. margarine	1 c. butter
2 6-oz. cans crab meat, drained	1 2-oz. can sesame seed

Melt cheese and margarine in double boiler; cool slightly. Add crab meat. Stir until cool. Flatten bread slices with rolling pin. Spread with crab meat mixture. Roll as for jelly roll. Dip in butter; roll in sesame seed. Freeze on baking sheet. Thaw for 15 minutes; cut into fifths. Broil for 5 minutes, turning once. Yield: 8 dozen.

Susan Claeys
Kappa, Sioux City, Iowa

STUFFED SNOW PEA PODS

2 1/2 c. finely chopped chicken	Salt and pepper to taste
1/4 c. each chopped onion, celery	1 6-oz. package frozen snow peas, thawed, drained
1/2 c. salad dressing	

Mix first 3 ingredients and seasonings. Spoon into pea pods. Chill. Yield: 2-3 dozen.

Janet Sanders
Preceptor Theta, Eagle Grove, Iowa

ASPARAGUS MOLD

1/2 tbsp. unflavored gelatin	1/2 tsp. salt
1 can madrilene consomme	1/8 tsp. pepper
1 tbsp. lemon juice	1 can cut asparagus, drained

Soften gelatin in 1/4 cup cold water. Dissolve in mixture of hot consomme, lemon juice, salt and pepper; cool. Fold in asparagus. Let stand until partially set. Pour into 3-cup mold. Chill for 5 to 6 hours or until set. Serve with mayonnaise. Yield: 6 servings.

Irene O'Daniel
Xi Alpha Epsilon, Atlanta, Georgia

ZUCCHINI AND ORANGE SALAD

6 med. zucchini	Italian-style salad dressing
1 med. onion, sliced	2 oranges, sliced
1 clove of garlic	Parmesan cheese

Cook zucchini in water until tender-crisp; drain. Slice 1/4 inch thick. Add onion, garlic and salad dressing. Chill, covered, for several hours. Drain; remove onion and garlic. Arrange zucchini and orange slices on lettuce-lined platter. Sprinkle with Parmesan cheese. Garnish with black olives. Yield: 6 servings.

Joanie Fletcher
Xi Alpha Sigma, Kelowna, British Columbia

CHINESE CABBAGE SALAD

1/2 sm. head each red, green cabbage, grated
4 green onions, chopped
2 tbsp. sugar
1/2 c. oil
3 tbsp. vinegar
1/2 tsp. pepper
1 tsp. each MSG, salt
1/2 pkg. Top Ramin seasoning mix
3 tbsp. sesame seed
1 pkg. Top Ramin noodles, broken
1/2 c. slivered almonds

Combine cabbage and onions. Mix sugar, oil, vinegar and seasonings. Pour over cabbage mixture. Add sesame seed, noodles and almonds just before serving. Yield: 10 servings.

Joan J. Egelston
Xi Beta Omega, Oak Harbor, Washington

CHINESE CHICKEN SALAD

Oil for deep frying
2 oz. rice sticks
1 sm. head lettuce, chopped
1/2 lb. chicken breast, cooked, shredded
2 tbsp. toasted sesame seed
4 green onions, shredded
2 tbsp. chopped toasted almonds (opt.)
1 tsp. each salt, MSG
1/2 tsp. pepper
3 tbsp. vinegar
2 tbsp. sugar
1/4 c. oil

Deep-fry rice sticks; drain. Combine with remaining ingredients just before serving.

Keiko Furusho
Upsilon Tau, Sebastopol, California

TACO SALAD

1 lb. ground beef
1 pkg. taco seasoning mix
1 head lettuce, chopped
1 green pepper, chopped
1 sm. onion, chopped (opt.)
4 tomatoes, chopped
2 c. shredded Cheddar cheese
2 sm. packages corn chips, crushed
California onion dressing

Brown ground beef. Mix with next 7 ingredients. Pour dressing over top. Yield: 6 servings.

Margie Shanafelt
Laureate Alpha, Centralia, Illinois

LONDON BROIL

1 3-lb. London broil
1/2 c. oil
6 tbsp. soy sauce
2 tbsp. Worcestershire sauce
1 tbsp. dry mustard
1 1/2 tsp. pepper
1/3 c. cider vinegar
1 tbsp. minced parsley
1 tsp. garlic salt
2 tbsp. lemon juice

Marinate London broil in mixture of remaining ingredients for 8 hours or longer. Broil for 8 to 10 minutes for medium-rare. Slice thinly. Yield: 6 servings.

Mary Ann Madar
Preceptor Beta Alpha, Elizabeth Township, Pennsylvania

SIMPLY ELEGANT STEAK AND RICE

1 1/2 lb. round steak, tenderized
1 1/2 tsp. oil
2 lg. onions, sliced into 1/2-in. thick rings
1 4-oz. can sliced mushrooms
1 can mushroom soup
1/2 c. dry Sherry
1 1/2 tsp. garlic salt
3 c. cooked rice

Slice steak into thin strips. Stir-fry in oil. Add onions. Saute until tender-crisp. Drain mushrooms, reserving liquid. Mix liquid with soup, Sherry and garlic salt. Pour over steak. Add mushrooms. Simmer, covered, for 1 to 1 1/2 hours. Serve over rice. Yield: 6 servings.

Jeanne K. Mahoney
Preceptor Alpha Mu, Battle Creek, Michigan

STIR-FRIED BEEF WITH BROCCOLI

1 lb. flank steak, partially frozen
2 tbsp. soy sauce
1 tbsp. Sherry
1 tsp. sugar
1 clove of garlic, minced
1 bunch broccoli, cut up
1 tbsp. salt
1 c. thinly sliced celery
1 tbsp. oil
1 tbsp. cornstarch
1 beef bouillon cube, crushed
1 tbsp. pimento strips (opt.)

Slice steak cross grain diagonally into short, very thin strips. Marinate in mixture of soy sauce, Sherry, sugar and garlic for 30 minutes. Cook broccoli in boiling salted water for 1 minute. Add celery. Cook for 1 minute longer; drain. Stir-fry steak in oil for 3 minutes. Stir in mixture of cornstarch, bouillon cube and 1/4 cup water. Cook for 1 minute, stirring constantly. Stir in broccoli, celery and pimento. Cook for 1 minute. Yield: 4 servings.

Sonia K. Grim
Preceptor Xi, Dallastown, Pennsylvania

BAKED CAVATINI

1 lb. ground beef
1 pkg. pepperoni, chopped
2 cans chopped mushrooms
2 green peppers, chopped
1 onion, chopped
1 med. can tomato sauce
2 jars pizza sauce
1 1-lb. package macaroni, cooked
1 lb. mozzarella cheese, shredded

Cook ground beef until brown and crumbly. Combine with next 7 ingredients and half the cheese. Pour into greased 11 x 15-inch baking dish. Top with remaining cheese. Bake at 350 degrees for 30 to 45 minutes. Yield: 8-10 servings.

Cindy Hardy
Xi Kappa Omicron, Crooksville, Ohio

FOOTBALL SPECIAL CHIMICHANGAS

1 1/2 lb. ground beef	1/2 tsp. salt
1 lg. onion, chopped	10 lg. flour tortillas
2 cloves of garlic, minced	1 sm. can chopped black olives
1 med. can refried beans	2 c. grated Cheddar cheese
1/2 c. chili salsa	Sour cream
1 tsp. chili powder	Green chili taco sauce

Brown ground beef with onion and garlic, stirring frequently. Stir in next 4 ingredients. Place 3/4 cup mixture in center of each tortilla. Sprinkle with olives and cheese. Roll to enclose filling, folding in sides. Brown in a small amount of oil. Top with sour cream and taco sauce. Yield: 10 servings.

Pat Myers
Upsilon Tau, Occidental, California

SHORTCUT LASAGNA

1 1/2 lb. ground chuck	1 16-oz. package lasagna noodles
1 tbsp. oil	
1 28-oz. can tomatoes	1 12-oz. carton cottage cheese
1 8-oz. can tomato sauce	1 8-oz. package shredded mozzarella cheese
2 env. spaghetti sauce mix	
2 12-oz. cans vegetable juice cocktail	1/4 c. Parmesan cheese
	Chopped parsley

Brown ground chuck in oil, stirring frequently. Stir in next 4 ingredients. Simmer for 10 minutes. Alternate layers of sauce, uncooked noodles, cottage cheese and mozzarella cheese in greased 9 x 13-inch baking pan until all ingredients are used, ending with sauce. Bake, tightly covered with foil, on jelly roll pan at 350 degrees for 1 hour. Let stand for 15 minutes. Sprinkle with Parmesan cheese and parsley. Yield: 12 servings.

Joyce Schomer
Pi Beta, Montgomery, Illinois

SPAGHETTI PIZZA

1 1/2 lb. ground beef	2 eggs, beaten
1/2 lb. spaghetti, cooked	2/3 c. milk
1 32-oz. jar spaghetti sauce	1 tsp. garlic powder
2 tsp. onion flakes	3 c. shredded mozzarella cheese

Cook ground beef until brown and crumbly; drain. Mix spaghetti with eggs and milk. Layer spaghetti mixture, sauce, ground beef, seasonings and cheese in greased 9 x 13-inch baking pan. Bake at 350 degrees for 30 minutes. Let stand for 5 to 10 minutes. Yield: 8-10 servings.

Evelyn Taylor
Beta Zeta, Jefferson, Iowa

ZITI BAKE

1 med. onion, diced	1 15-oz. carton ricotta cheese
1 clove of garlic, minced	
2 tbsp. oil	1/2 c. Parmesan cheese
2 15-oz. cans tomato sauce	
1 12-oz. can tomato paste	1 egg, beaten
	3/4 tsp. salt
2 tsp. brown sugar	1/4 tsp. pepper
1 tsp. oregano	1 16-oz. package ziti, cooked
1 bay leaf	
Parsley flakes	8 oz. mozzarella cheese, grated
1 lb. ground beef	

Saute onion and garlic in oil for 10 minutes. Add next 5 ingredients and 2 teaspoons parsley flakes. Simmer for 30 minutes. Brown ground beef, stirring frequently; remove from heat. Stir in next 6 ingredients, 1/4 cup parsley and half the sauce. Pour into 9 x 13-inch baking pan. Top with remaining sauce and mozzarella cheese. Bake at 350 degrees for 20 minutes. Yield: 8 servings.

Denise La Torre
Omicron, Great Bend, Kansas

CHIPPED BEEF AND EGG CASSEROLE

1/2 lb. dried beef	4 c. milk
3 slices bacon	Pepper to taste
Sliced mushrooms	16 eggs, beaten
1/2 c. margarine	1/4 tsp. salt
1/2 c. flour	1 c. evaporated milk

Saute first 3 ingredients in 1/4 cup margarine. Stir in flour, milk and pepper. Cook until thick, stirring constantly. Scramble eggs mixed with salt and milk in 1/4 cup margarine. Layer eggs and sauce alternately in buttered baking dish, beginning and ending with sauce. Chill until 1 hour before baking. Bake at 300 degrees until bubbly. Yield: 10-12 servings.

Patty Murphy
Xi Alpha Alpha, Greensboro, North Carolina

VEAL SCALLOPINI

1 1/2 lb. veal scallops, sliced 3/8 in. thick
Salt and pepper
Flour
7 tbsp. butter
3 tbsp. olive oil
1/2 c. dry Marsala
1/2 c. chicken broth
4 cloves of garlic, chopped
1 bay leaf
2 sprigs of parsley, chopped
1/2 tsp. each thyme, basil
1/4 lb. mushrooms, thinly sliced
2 c. milk
1/2 c. heavy cream
3/4 c. Parmesan cheese

Flatten veal to 1/4 inch. Season with salt and pepper to taste; coat with flour. Brown in 2 tablespoons butter and olive oil for 3 minutes on each side. Remove veal; drain off excess fat. Add wine, broth and 1/4 of the garlic. Boil for 1 to 2 minutes. Add veal and next 4 seasonings. Simmer for 10 to 15 minutes. Saute mushrooms and remaining garlic in 5 tablespoons butter. Stir in 5 tablespoons flour, milk, cream, cheese and 1 teaspoon each salt and pepper. Simmer for 15 minutes. Stir into veal mixture. Yield: 3 servings.

Angelina Guile
Preceptor Omicron, Westport, Washington

TOURTIERE

1 lb. lean ground pork
l lb. lean ground beef
1 onion, chopped
1 tsp. each cinnamon, salt
1/2 tsp. each sage, pepper
1/8 tsp. nutmeg
2/3 c. beef broth
1/3 c. cracker meal
1 unbaked 9-in. pie shell

Cook first 3 ingredients with seasonings until brown, stirring frequently. Add broth. Simmer for 20 minutes; drain. Mix in cracker meal until of meat loaf consistency, adding a small amount of additional broth if necessary. Spoon into pie shell. Bake at 450 degrees for 15 minutes. Bake at 350 degrees for 20 to 25 minutes. Yield: 4-6 servings.

Katie Fox
Omega, Whitefish, Montana

PORK MEDALLIONS WITH ARTICHOKE HEARTS AND APPLES

1 1/2 lb. boned pork loin, trimmed
Salt and pepper to taste
Flour
2 tbsp. clarified butter
1 Granny Smith apple, sliced
8 artichoke hearts, halved
1 tsp. minced shallot
1/8 tsp. minced garlic
2 oz. Cognac
2 oz. white wine
1 c. heavy cream

Slice pork into 8 medallions. Season with salt and pepper; coat with flour. Brown in butter over medium heat; remove. Stir in apple, artichoke hearts, shallot and garlic. Saute until lightly browned; remove from heat. Pour in Cognac; return to heat and ignite. Add wine and cream. Cook until thickened. Add pork. Cook for 1 to 2 minutes. Yield: 4 servings.

Cheryl Greenhawt
Beta Iota, Rawlings, Wyoming

BARBECUED PORK

3 lb. boneless pork
1 tbsp. salt
1/4 c. hoisin sauce
1 tsp. mein she sauce
1 tsp. 5-season herb powder
1/4 c. sugar
Dash each of MSG, garlic salt
1 tsp. red food coloring
1 tbsp. whiskey

Cut pork into 2 x 2 x 8-inch strips. Marinate overnight in mixture of remaining ingredients; drain. Place drapery pin in end of each strip. Suspend from oven rack over pan of water. Bake at 300 to 325 degrees for 1 to 1 1/4 hours. Cut into 1/4-inch strips. Serve with Chinese mustard sauce and toasted sesame seed.

Patricia A. Payne
Preceptor Alpha Alpha, Lake Oswego, Oregon

SWEET AND SOUR PORK

1 to 1 1/2 lb. lean pork, thinly sliced
1 tsp. salt
5 tsp. soy sauce
5 tsp. cornstarch
2 tbsp. oil
1/2 c. thin diagonal carrot slices
1/3 c. vinegar
1/3 c. sugar
1 8-oz. can pineapple chunks, drained
3 green onions, cut in 2-in. pieces
1 sm. green pepper, chopped

Marinate pork in mixture of salt, 2 teaspoons soy sauce and 2 teaspoons cornstarch for 20 minutes. Stir-fry in oil until pork turns white. Add carrot and 2 tablespoons water. Cook, covered, for 2 minutes. Mix vinegar, sugar, 1 tablespoon cornstarch, 1 tablespoon soy sauce and 1/2 cup water in saucepan. Cook until thick, stirring constantly. Add to pork with pineapple chunks. Bring to a boil. Stir in onions and green pepper. Cook for 30 seconds or until heated through. Serve with rice. Yield: 4 servings.

Valerie Beenken
Epsilon Rho, Mt. Pleasant, Iowa

FRUITED PORK ROAST

1 1/2 c. red Burgundy
1 tsp. each cloves, cinnamon
2 lg. cans pie apples
2 tbsp. Worcestershire sauce

New Year's / 17

1 5-lb. pork loin roast, boned
Salt and pepper to taste
1 pkg. pork stuffing mix

Combine first 5 ingredients and 1 cup water. Add roast. Marinate, covered, in refrigerator overnight. Remove apples; reserve marinade. Place half the apples on roast; roll to enclose and tie. Sprinkle with salt and pepper. Brown on all sides in a small amount of shortening. Roast in roasting pan at 350 degrees for 3 1/2 hours, basting frequently with marinade. Cool. Drain and thicken drippings. Prepare stuffing mix according to package directions, adding remaining apples. Press over roast. Bake for 20 minutes longer.

Cheryl Besel
Beta Iota, Rawlins, Wyoming

HOPPIN' JOHN

1 lb. dried black-eyed peas
1 lb. sausage
1 med. onion, chopped
1 c. rice, cooked
Salt, pepper and Tabasco sauce to taste

Bring peas with water to cover to a boil. Let stand, covered, for 20 minutes. Cook until tender. Brown sausage with onion; drain. Mix with peas and rice. Add salt, pepper and Tabasco sauce. Spoon into 9 x 12-inch baking dish. Bake at 400 degrees for 15 minutes. Yield: 10-12 servings.

Delilah Williams
Preceptor Gamma, Columbus, Mississippi

KRAUT-PORK PINWHEEL

1 1/2 lb. sausage
3/4 c. fine dry bread crumbs
2 eggs, slightly beaten
1 1/4 tsp. salt
Dash of pepper
1/2 tsp. Worcestershire sauce
2 c. chopped sauerkraut, drained
1/4 c. chopped onion

Mix first 6 ingredients. Pat into 9 x 13-inch rectangle on waxed paper. Mix sauerkraut and onion. Spread over sausage mixture. Roll as for jelly roll from narrow side. Place in baking dish. Bake at 350 degrees for 45 to 60 minutes. Yield: 6-8 servings.

Virginia Kirschner
Preceptor Alpha, Kendallville, Indiana

LAMB RIBLETS MONTEREY

1 c. chopped onion
2 lb. lamb riblets
1 tbsp. olive oil
1 clove of garlic, sliced
3 tbsp. each vinegar, lemon juice
2 tbsp. brown sugar
3/4 c. catsup
1 tsp. salt
1/8 tsp. pepper

Saute onion and lamb in olive oil until brown. Add remaining ingredients. Simmer, covered, for 1 hour. Yield: 3-4 servings.

Mandy Henningsen
Omega, Waterloo, Iowa

CHOP SUEY

1 lb. lean chop suey meat
1 med. onion, finely chopped
2 tbsp. shortening
1 1/2 c. chopped celery
1 16-oz. can bean sprouts, drained
2 16-oz. cans fancy mixed Chinese vegetables, drained
1 8-oz. can button mushrooms, drained
5 tbsp. soy sauce
2 tbsp. cornstarch

Saute meat and onion in shortening. Add celery and 2 cups water. Simmer for 1 hour. Stir in bean sprouts, mixed vegetables, mushrooms and enough water to almost cover. Simmer until heated through. Stir in mixture of soy sauce and cornstarch. Cook until thick, stirring constantly. Serve over rice. Yield: 6-8 servings.

Jeanette A. Fettig
Xi Gamma Xi, Logansport, Indiana

EASY DELICIOUS CHICKEN

1 lb. mushrooms, sliced
2 lb. boneless chicken breasts, skinned
1 1/2 c. white wine
1 jar gourmet mustard

Layer mushrooms and chicken in 9 x 13-inch baking dish. Pour blended wine and mustard over chicken. Marinate for 15 minutes. Bake at 350 degrees for 35 minutes. Serve with wild or herbed rice. Yield: 4 servings.

Susan Emsiek
Tri Alpha, Long Beach, California

SHREDDED ORIENTAL CHICKEN

2 chicken breasts, boned, skinned
4 tsp. cornstarch
8 tsp. soy sauce
1 1/2 tsp. salt
5 tbsp. dry white wine
1 egg white
1 tsp. oil
1 carrot, shredded
1 med. green pepper, shredded
1 green onion, sliced
1/2 tsp. ginger
1 tsp. sugar

Freeze chicken slightly. Cut into paper-thin strips. Mix with 2 teaspoons cornstarch, 2 teaspoons soy sauce, salt, 1 tablespoon wine and egg white. Stir-fry chicken in oil for 5 minutes or until white. Add vegetables. Stir-fry for 2 minutes. Add ginger and sugar. Blend 2 teaspoons cornstarch, 2 teaspoons wine and 2 tablespoons soy sauce. Stir into chicken mixture. Cook until evenly glazed, stirring constantly. Yield: 6 servings.

Betty S. Tipton
Laureate Nu, Olympia, Washington

CHICKEN AND VEGETABLE STIR FRY

1 tbsp. cornstarch
3 tbsp. soy sauce
2 tbsp. dry Sherry
1 tsp. each sugar, ginger
1/4 to 1/2 tsp. crushed red pepper
1 1/2 tsp. salt
3 chicken breasts, boned, cut into bite-sized pieces
3 med. zucchini, cut into bite-sized pieces
1 lb. small mushrooms
1/2 c. oil
1 6-oz. package frozen Chinese pea pods, thawed

Mix first 6 ingredients and 1 teaspoon salt. Add chicken. Marinate in refrigerator for 5 hours. Stir-fry zucchini and mushrooms with 1/2 teaspoon salt in oil until tender-crisp; remove. Add chicken and marinade. Stir-fry for 10 minutes. Add pea pods and zucchini mixture. Stir-fry until heated through. Serve with rice. Yield: 6 servings.

Colleen Carnaggio
Delta Theta, Harvard, Massachusetts

MANDARIN CHICKEN

1 fryer, boned
1/2 c. flour
1 tsp. each baking powder, soda
Cornstarch
Sugar
Salt
1 egg, slightly beaten
Several drops of yellow food coloring (opt.)
Oil for deep frying
Shredded lettuce
1 c. canned tomatoes
1/2 c. cider vinegar
1/2 c. chopped onion
Dash of cayenne
1/2 c. crushed pineapple
1/2 tsp. ginger
1 tbsp. soy sauce
1/2 c. chopped green pepper

Steam chicken pieces. Sift flour, baking powder, soda, 1/2 cup cornstarch, 1 teaspoon sugar and 1/2 teaspoon salt together. Add egg mixed with 2/3 cup ice water and food coloring; stir until just mixed. Float several ice cubes in batter. Dip chicken in batter. Deep-fry in oil until lightly browned; drain on paper towels. Cut into 1/2 to 1-inch thick slices. Arrange on lettuce-lined plates. Mix next 7 ingredients, salt to taste and 1 to 1 1/2 cups sugar. Bring to a boil. Simmer for 20 minutes. Stir in 1 tablespoon cornstarch blended with 1/4 cup water. Cook until thick, stirring constantly. Stir in green pepper. Let stand for 2 to 4 minutes. Pour over chicken. Yield: 4 servings.

Jan Lantz
Preceptor Zeta, Caldwell, Idaho

HEARTY TURKEY SOUP

1/4 c. chopped onion
1 stick margarine
4 c. chopped cooked turkey
6 c. broth
1 c. each chopped carrots, celery
1 10-oz. package frozen French-style green beans (opt.)
2 c. chopped potatoes
1 to 2 tsp. curry powder
1 tsp. oregano
2 tbsp. minced parsley
Salt and pepper to taste
3 1/3 c. half and half
6 tbsp. flour

Saute onion in margarine. Add turkey, broth, vegetables and seasonings. Simmer for 15 minutes. Stir in mixture of half and half and flour. Simmer until thickened, stirring constantly. Yield: 10 servings.

Geneva E. Murphy
Preceptor Alpha Sigma, San Angelo, Texas

CIOPPINO

1/2 lb. mushrooms, sliced
2 carrots, sliced
1 clove of garlic, crushed
1 onion, chopped
1/2 green pepper, chopped
2 tbsp. oil
1 can whole clams
1 15-oz. can tomato sauce
1 1/2 c. Chablis
Dash of lemon juice
Oregano, thyme, salt and pepper to taste
2 bay leaves
1 beef bouillon cube
1 lb. white fish, cut into 1-in. cubes
1 lb. shrimp
Lobster and crab (opt.)

Saute first 5 ingredients in oil. Drain clams, reserving juice. Add tomato sauce, clam juice, wine, 1 1/2 cups water, lemon juice, seasonings and bouillon cube. Simmer for 20 minutes. Add seafood. Simmer for 20 minutes. Yield: 4-6 servings.

Donna Faxon
Preceptor Alpha Epsilon, Tucson, Arizona

SUPER SHRIMP

3 slices bacon
1 sm. onion, chopped
2 tbsp. chopped parsley
1/2 green pepper, chopped
1 sm. stalk celery, chopped
1 tbsp. flour
2 c. canned tomatoes
1 8-oz. can tomato sauce
1 tsp. each salt, chili powder
1/2 tsp. pepper
1 bay leaf
2 lb. cooked shrimp
1 c. rice, cooked

Fry bacon; remove and crumble. Saute next 4 ingredients in bacon drippings. Stir in flour. Add tomatoes, tomato sauce and seasonings. Simmer for 45 minutes or until thickened. Stir in shrimp and bacon. Serve over rice. Yield: 6 servings.

Paula Linman
Xi Alpha Iota, Raleigh, North Carolina

CHINESE LOBSTER WITH NOODLES AND VEGETABLES

1 oz. dried mushrooms
8 oz. fresh noodles
Oil for deep frying
6 oz. lobster, thinly sliced
1 1/2 c. thinly sliced onions
1 8-oz. can bean sprouts
1 3-oz. can bamboo shoots, thinly sliced
Salt and pepper to taste
1 tsp. cornstarch
1 tsp. sweet and sour sauce

Soak mushrooms in hot water for 15 minutes; drain and slice thinly. Cook noodles in hot oil for 5 to 6 seconds until crisp; drain. Stir-fry mushrooms, lobster and next 3 ingredients with salt and pepper in a small amount of oil for 1 minute. Blend cornstarch with a small amount of cold water to make paste. Stir in 2 additional tablespoons water. Pour over lobster. Cook for 1 minute, stirring constantly. Stir in 1 teaspoon sweet and sour sauce. Serve over hot noodles with additional sweet and sour sauce.

Mildred M. Kaufman
Laureate Alpha Epsilon, Kitchener, Ontario, Canada

BAKED CAULIFLOWER ITALIANO

1 med. head cauliflower, broken into flowerets
1 tsp. salt
1 16-oz. can whole tomatoes
2 eggs, slightly beaten
1 can Cheddar cheese soup
1/4 c. grated Parmesan cheese
1 tsp. oregano

Bring cauliflower, salt and 1/2 cup water to a boil in covered saucepan. Simmer for 5 minutes; drain. Pour mixture of tomatoes and eggs over cauliflower in baking dish. Spoon soup over top. Sprinkle with cheese and oregano. Bake at 350 degrees for 30 minutes or until set. Yield: 8 servings.

Laura Lee Ford
Alpha Upsilon, Osage Beach, Missouri

POTATO-MUSHROOM SOUP

1 med. onion, finely chopped
1/4 lb. mushrooms, chopped
3 tbsp. butter
3 tbsp. flour
3 c. chicken broth
3 med. potatoes, chopped
2 c. milk
1 tsp. Worcestershire sauce
1 to 2 tbsp. chopped parsley
Salt and pepper to taste
Grated cheese

Saute onion and mushrooms in butter. Blend in flour. Add remaining ingredients except cheese. Bring to a boil. Simmer, covered, for 20 minutes or until potatoes are tender. Sprinkle cheese in serving bowls. Pour soup over cheese. Serve with hard bread or cheese croutons. Yield: 12-14 servings.

Patsy Woosley Clark
Xi Gamma Iota, Cabot, Arkansas

CHEESE SOUP

1/2 c. each chopped celery, onion
2 chicken bouillon cubes
1/2 c. chopped carrot
1 10-oz. package frozen mixed vegetables
1 1/4 c. chopped potatoes
1 can cream of chicken soup
1 1-lb. package Velveeta cheese, cubed

Simmer celery and onion in 2 cups water and bouillon cubes in covered saucepan for 20 minutes. Add vegetables. Cook for 30 minutes. Add soup and cheese. Heat until cheese melts, stirring constantly. May add chopped ham, chicken or turkey. Yield: 4 servings.

Muff Wallace
Xi Eta Zeta, Emmetsburg, Iowa

LENTIL SOUP

3 tbsp. oil
2 tbsp. flour
1 onion, chopped
3 cloves of garlic, crushed
Salt to taste
Pepper to taste
1 pkg. lentils
Chopped pork sausage
1/4 c. sour cream
Vinegar to taste

Combine oil, flour, onion, garlic and seasonings in pressure cooker. Cook until browned. Add lentils, sausage and enough water to fill 3/4 full. Cook for 3 to 4 minutes or to boiling point using pressure cooker instructions. Remove from heat. Let stand, covered, for 20 minutes. Stir in sour cream and vinegar. Yield: 3 quarts.

Lydia A. Dodson
Xi Kappa Nu, Masaryktown, Florida

GULLIVER'S SPINACH

3 slices bacon, finely chopped
1 sm. onion, finely chopped
3 tbsp. flour
1 c. milk
1/4 c. heavy cream
2 10-oz. packages frozen spinach, cooked, drained
1 tsp. salt
1/2 tsp. coarsely ground pepper (opt.)

Brown bacon with onion in saucepan. Stir in flour. Add milk and cream gradually. Simmer, until thickened, stirring constantly. Stir in spinach and seasonings.

Jackie Hamilton
Gamma Eta, Cleveland, Tennessee

WILD RICE SOUP

1 med. onion, chopped
1/2 green pepper, chopped
3 to 4 lg. mushrooms, sliced
1/2 c. butter, melted
1/2 to 2/3 c. flour
8 c. chicken broth
1/2 tsp. each salt, pepper
2 c. cooked wild rice
Chopped cooked chicken (opt.)
1 c. light cream
2 to 4 tbsp. white wine

Saute onion, green pepper and mushrooms. Blend butter and flour. Stir in hot chicken broth gradually. Mix in vegetables, seasonings, rice and chicken. Stir in cream and wine just before serving. Heat to serving temperature, stirring constantly. Do not boil. Yield: 8 servings.

Eleanor Snyder
Laureate Alpha, Williston, North Dakota

SCRAMBLED EGGS

1/4 c. melted butter
2 tbsp. chopped green onion
12 eggs
2/3 c. heavy cream
1 8-oz. package cream cheese, softened
1/2 tsp. lemon juice
1 tsp. salt

Combine butter and green onion in electric skillet. Add mixture of remaining ingredients. Cook to desired consistency; cover. Let stand on warm until serving time or 2 to 3 hours.

Colleen Liebhart
Gamma Phi, Brookfield, Missouri

HERB BREAD

2 brown and serve French rolls
1/2 c. butter, softened
1/4 c. Parmesan cheese
4 tsp. chopped parsley
1 tsp. oregano
1/4 tsp. garlic salt

Slice rolls almost to bottom. Mix remaining ingredients. Spread between slices and on top of loaves. Wrap in foil. Bake at 350 degrees for 15 minutes. Uncover tops. Bake for 15 minutes longer.

Patti Lochner
Delta Kappa, Ft. Myers, Florida

ORANGE JUICY MUFFINS WITH HONEY SPREAD

2 c. baking mix
1 egg
1 tsp. grated orange rind
2/3 c. orange juice
1/4 c. sugar
1/4 tsp. cinnamon
1/8 tsp. nutmeg
1/2 c. margarine, softened
1/2 c. honey

Combine first 4 ingredients and 2 tablespoons sugar. Beat for 30 seconds. Grease bottoms of muffin cups; fill 2/3 full. Sprinkle with mixture of sugar, cinnamon and nutmeg. Bake at 400 degrees for 15 minutes. Beat margarine and honey until fluffy. Serve with muffins. Yield: 1 dozen.

Gaye Tate
Zeta Gamma, Jasper, Alabama

YOGURT-POPPY SEED COFFEE CAKE

1 2-oz. package poppy seed
1 8-oz. carton yogurt
1 c. butter, softened
1 1/2 c. sugar
4 eggs, separated
2 c. plus 2 tbsp. sifted flour
2 tsp. soda
2 tsp. vanilla extract

Soften poppy seed in yogurt. Cream butter and sugar. Beat in egg yolks, yogurt and remaining ingredients. Fold in stiffly beaten egg whites. Bake in greased and floured tube pan at 375 degrees for 45 minutes. Top with confectioners' sugar or lemon glaze. Yield: 12-15 servings.

Sharon K. Kauffman
Beta Sigma, Ft. Morgan, Colorado

BRANDY-FRUIT SUPREME

1 lg. can each pears, peaches, pineapple, apricots
1 sm. can pitted dark cherries
15 macaroons, broken
1/2 stick butter, melted
1/2 c. packed brown sugar
1/2 c. dry Sherry

Mix drained fruit. Layer alternately with macaroons in baking dish. Pour mixture of butter, brown sugar and Sherry over layers. Bake, covered, at 350 degrees for 30 minutes. Serve over French vanilla ice cream. Yield: 10 servings.

Karen Seubert
Xi Beta Kappa, Glenwood Springs, Colorado

JUBILEE CHOCOLATE CAKE

3/4 tsp. soda
1 c. buttermilk
1 1/2 c. cake flour
Sugar
1/2 c. cocoa
Salt
1/2 c. oil
2 eggs, separated
1 1/2 c. cherry syrup
2 tbsp. cornstarch
2 16-oz. cans sweet pitted cherries, drained
1 tsp. grated orange rind
1/2 c. Kirsch
Vanilla ice cream

Dissolve soda in buttermilk. Combine flour, 1 cup sugar, cocoa and 1/2 teaspoon salt in mixer bowl. Beat in oil, buttermilk and egg yolks. Beat egg whites until foamy. Add 1/2 cup sugar gradually, beating until stiff. Fold into

New Year's / 21

batter. Bake in greased and floured 9 x 13-inch baking pan at 350 degrees for 30 minutes. Cool in pan on wire rack. Combine cherry syrup with 3 tablespoons sugar, cornstarch and dash of salt. Cook until thick, stirring constantly. Boil for 1 minute. Add cherries and orange rind. Cook until heated. Heat Kirsch over low heat. Pour over cherry mixture; ignite. Stir gently; ladle over scoops of ice cream and chocolate cake. Yield: 10-12 servings.

Photograph for this recipe on page 9.

BLACKBERRY JAM CAKE

Butter	1 c. sour cream
1 c. sugar	1 c. blackberry jam
4 eggs	1 c. packed brown sugar
2 c. flour	1/4 c. milk
2 tsp. soda	2 c. confectioners' sugar
Pinch of salt	

Cream 1 tablespoon butter and sugar. Beat in 3 eggs, 1 at a time. Beat in sifted flour, soda and salt alternately with remaining egg, sour cream and jam. Bake in 2 prepared 8-inch cake pans at 350 degrees for 40 to 45 minutes. Cook 1 stick butter and brown sugar for 2 minutes. Stir in milk. Bring to a boil; remove from heat. Beat in confectioners' sugar gradually, adding hot milk if necessary. Frost cooled cake.

Norma G. Bauer
Preceptor Beta Rho, Altamont, Illinois

RAISIN-ORANGE POUND CAKE

2 c. flour	Juice and grated rind of 1 orange
1 1/2 tsp. baking powder	2 eggs
1 tsp. salt	3/4 c. puffed Muscat raisins, coarsely chopped
1/2 tsp. cream of tartar	
1 3/4 c. sugar	1/4 c. orange juice
1/2 c. butter, softened	2 tsp. rum flavoring

Combine first 4 ingredients and 1 1/2 cups sugar. Add butter, orange rind, orange juice mixed with enough water to measure 1/2 cup and eggs. Beat for 2 minutes. Fold in raisins. Bake in greased and floured loaf pan at 350 degrees for 1 hour. Mix 1/4 cup sugar, 1/4 cup orange juice and rum flavoring. Pour over hot cake.

Marilyn E. Cadman
Xi Gamma, Lewiston, Maine

BABA AU RHUM

2 eggs, separated	2 tsp. baking powder
4 1/3 tbsp. sugar	2 slices each orange, lemon
2 1/3 tbsp. flour	1/2 c. dark rum

Beat egg yolks with 2 tablespoons sugar. Mix in flour, baking powder and stiffly beaten egg whites gradually. Bake in greased 8-inch square baking dish at 300 degrees for 20 minutes. Simmer 1 cup water, 7 teaspoons sugar and fruit slices for 2 to 3 minutes. Stir in rum. Pour over cake. Serve cold with custard in center. Yield: 8 servings.

Mary Gavin
Xi Delta, Bathurst, New Brunswick, Canada

RUM CAKE

1 c. chopped pecans	1/2 c. oil
1 box pudding recipe cake mix	1 c. dark rum
	1 c. sugar
1 sm. package vanilla instant pudding mix	1/2 c. butter

Sprinkle pecans in bottom of greased and floured tube pan. Mix cake mix, pudding, oil, 1/2 cup rum and 1/2 cup water. Bake at 325 degrees for 1 hour. Prick surface. Cool for 15 to 30 minutes. Boil sugar, butter and 1/4 cup water for 5 minutes, stirring constantly. Stir in 1/2 cup rum. Pour over cake.

Sandy Donnoe
Theta, Vincennes, Indiana

MACADAMIA-MOCHA SUPREME

1/2 c. chopped macadamia nuts	1 7-oz. jar marshmallow creme
1 9-in. chocolate wafer pie shell	1 12-oz. carton whipped topping
2 tbsp. coffee-flavored liqueur	

Sprinkle nuts onto pie shell, reserving 1 tablespoon. Mix liqueur, marshmallow creme and 2 tablespoons water. Fold in whipped topping. Pour into pie shell. Freeze. Sprinkle with reserved nuts. May substitute 1/4 cup coffee for liqueur. Yield: 6-8 servings.

Violet S. Voges
Preceptor Rho, New Braunfels, Texas

TIPSY PUDDING

3 egg yolks	1 tbsp. Sherry
1/4 c. sugar	6 slices sponge cake
1/8 tsp. salt	2 c. whipped cream
2 c. milk, scalded	1/2 c. chopped nuts

Beat egg yolks, sugar and salt. Add milk gradually. Cook in double boiler until thickened, stirring constantly; remove from heat. Stir in Sherry; cool. Pour over cake slices in serving dishes. Top with whipped cream and nuts. Yield: 6 servings.

Eleanor Hall
Preceptor Delta, Sulphur, Louisiana

CHOCOLATE LOVER'S CHEESECAKE

1 8 1/2-oz. package chocolate wafers, crushed	3 tbsp. flour
	4 oz. sweet chocolate, melted, cooled
1/3 c. melted margarine	3 eggs
1 1/4 c. sugar	2 tbsp. half and half
3 8-oz. packages cream cheese, softened	2 1/2 tsp. vanilla extract
	1/2 c. sour cream

Mix cookie crumbs, margarine and 1/4 cup sugar. Press into bottom and side of 9-inch springform pan. Beat next 3 ingredients and 1 cup sugar. Beat in eggs, 1 at a time. Blend in half and half and 2 teaspoons vanilla. Bake in prepared pan at 400 degrees for 10 minutes. Reduce temperature to 300 degrees. Bake for 55 minutes. Cool for 10 minutes before removing side from pan. Spread with mixture of sour cream and 1/2 teaspoon vanilla when cool. Yield: 16 servings.

Donetta Bantle
Alpha Nu, Stillwater, Oklahoma

CELEBRATION CHOCOLATE CHIP PIE

2 eggs, slightly beaten	1 c. miniature chocolate chips
1 c. sugar	
1/2 c. melted butter	1 9-in. unbaked pie shell
1 1/2 tsp. vanilla extract	
1/4 c. cornstarch	1/2 c. whipping cream
1 c. finely chopped pecans	2 tbsp. confectioners' sugar

Beat eggs and sugar. Add butter and 1 teaspoon vanilla; mix well. Blend in cornstarch. Stir in pecans and chocolate chips. Bake in pie shell at 350 degrees for 45 to 50 minutes. Cool for 1 hour. Whip cream with confectioners' sugar. Add 1/2 teaspoon vanilla. Beat until stiff peaks form. Serve with pie.

Photograph for this recipe on page 9.

ALMOST RHUBARB PIE

1 1/4 c. flour	3/4 tsp. salt
5 tbsp. confectioners' sugar	2 eggs, beaten
	2 c. finely chopped rhubarb
1/2 c. butter	
1 1/2 c. sugar	

Mix 1 cup flour, confectioners' sugar and butter until crumbly. Press into pie plate. Bake at 350 degrees for 15 minutes. Mix next 3 ingredients and 1/4 cup flour. Stir in rhubarb. Spoon into prepared plate. Bake at 350 degrees for 35 minutes or until set. Yield: 8 servings.

Joan Nosek
Preceptor Beta Epsilon, Cedar Rapids, Iowa

CHOCOLATE ICE CREAM ROLL

3/4 c. sll-purpose flour	1 c. sugar
	1 tsp. vanilla extract
1/4 c. cocoa	Confectioners' sugar
1 tsp. baking powder	1 pt. peppermint, pistachio or cherry ice cream, slightly softened
1/4 tsp. salt	
3 eggs	

Line 15 1/2 x 10 1/2 x 1-inch jelly roll pan with aluminum foil; grease well. Sift flour, cocoa, baking powder and salt together; set aside. Beat eggs in small mixer bowl on high speed for 3 to 5 minutes or until thick and lemon colored. Pour eggs into large mixer bowl. Beat in sugar gradually. Beat in 1/3 cup water and vanilla on low speed. Add flour mixture gradually, beating just until batter is smooth. Pour into prepared pan, spreading batter to corners. Bake in 375-degree oven for 12 to 15 minutes. Loosen cake from edges of pan; invert on towel generously sprinkled with confectioners' sugar. Remove foil; trim edges from cake. Roll hot cake and towel from narrow end; cool. Unroll cake. Spread ice cream over cake. Roll up; place seam side down on aluminum foil. Wrap and freeze for 4 hours or longer. Remove cake roll from freezer 15 minutes before serving. Unwrap; sprinkle with additional confectioners' sugar. Yield: 10-12 servings.

Jackie Soliday
Preceptor Alpha Phi, Wooster, Ohio

CHINESE-FRIED WALNUTS

4 c. walnuts	Oil for deep frying
1/2 c. sugar	Salt

Boil walnuts in 6 cups water for 1 minute. Rinse in hot water; drain. Combine with sugar in bowl; stir until sugar is dissolved. Deep-fry walnuts in oil for 5 minutes or until golden. Drain well in sieve. Sprinkle lightly with salt. Drain on paper towels. Store in airtight container.

Joan Williamson
Delta Sigma, Glendale, Arizona

BRANDIED CRANBERRIES

1 lb. fresh cranberries	4 tbsp. Brandy
2 1/3 c. sugar	

Spread washed cranberries in a 9 x 13-inch baking pan. Sprinkle evenly with 2 cups sugar. Cover tightly with foil. Bake at 350 degrees for 1 hour. Sprinkle cranberries with Brandy and 1/3 cup sugar, mixing well. Spoon cranberries into airtight container. Refrigerate or may be frozen. Serve over ice cream, fruit or pudding.

Maribeth Ramer
Alpha Lambda Phi, Spring, Texas

Recipes on pages 29 and 32.

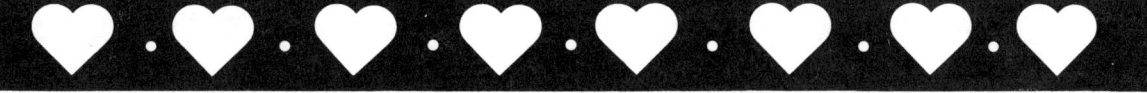

St. Valentine's Day

24 / St. Valentine's Day

PARTY PUNCH

1 lg. can frozen orange juice concentrate
1 46-oz. can pineapple juice
1 lg. package cherry gelatin
1/2 gal. orange sherbet
2 qt. lemon-lime soda

Blend juices and gelatin in punch bowl. Stir in sherbet and soda.

Doris Patterson
Xi Eta Psi, Collinsville, Illinois

SPARKLING FRUIT REFRESHER

1 6-oz. can frozen orange juice concentrate, thawed
1 6-oz. can frozen lemonade concentrate, thawed
2 drops of red food coloring
1 12-oz. bottle of ginger ale, chilled
1 16-oz. package frozen whole strawberries, thawed
1 pt. orange sherbet

Mix concentrates and 3 cups cold water in punch bowl. Stir in food coloring and ginger ale. Add strawberries. Float scoops of sherbet in punch. Serve immediately. Yield: 12 servings.

Sonya Matthies
Upsilon Psi, Elsmore, California

STRAWBERRY DAIQUIRIS

1 can frozen pink lemonade concentrate
1 lemonade can rum
3 tbsp. confectioners' sugar
1 pkg. frozen strawberries

Combine all ingredients in blender container. Fill with ice cubes. Process until smooth. May be stored in freezer.

Jewel Bonugli
Preceptor Theta Mu, Austin, Texas

SWEETHEART PUNCH

3/4 liter white wine
1 pt. frozen strawberries, thawed
1 qt. cranapple juice cocktail
1 bottle of club soda, chilled

Combine wine, strawberries and cranapple juice in punch bowl. Add soda just before serving. Yield: 24 servings.

Kathy Cosnerr
Epsilon Eta, Stromsburg, Nebraska

RED CINNAMON-APPLE SALAD

2 3-oz. packages lemon gelatin
1/2 c. red hot cinnamon candies
2 c. unsweetened applesauce
1 tbsp. lemon juice
Pinch of salt
1/2 c. chopped walnuts (opt.)
2 3-oz. packages cream cheese, softened
1/4 c. milk
2 tbsp. mayonnaise

Dissolve gelatin and candies in 3 cups boiling water; cool. Stir in applesauce, lemon juice and salt. Chill until partially set. Stir in walnuts. Spoon into mold. Blend cream cheese, milk and mayonnaise. Spread over top. Chill until set. Unmold onto lettuce-lined serving plate. Yield: 9-12 servings.

Ann D. Kroening
Preceptor Pi, Albuquerque, New Mexico

PINK CHERRY SALAD

1 can sweetened condensed milk
1 8-oz. carton whipped topping
1 sm. can crushed pineapple
1 c. coconut (opt.)
1 c. marshmallows
1 can cherry pie filling
1/2 c. chopped nuts

Mix sweetened condensed milk and whipped topping. Chill for 1 hour. Mix in remaining ingredients. Chill overnight. Stir just before serving. Yield: 15 servings.

Polly L. McLain
Gamma Theta, Evarts, Kentucky

PRETZEL SALAD

2 c. crushed pretzels
3/4 c. melted margarine
1 8-oz. package cream cheese, softened
1 c. sugar
2 c. whipped topping
2 pkg. strawberry gelatin
2 10-oz. packages frozen strawberries, thawed

Mix pretzels and margarine. Press into 7 x 11-inch baking pan. Bake at 350 degrees for 8 to 10 minutes; cool. Beat cream cheese and sugar. Stir in whipped topping. Spread over cooled crust; chill. Dissolve gelatin in 2 cups boiling water. Stir in strawberries. Pour over cream cheese layer. Chill until set. Yield: 12 servings.

Martha Kirby
Preceptor Gamma Iota, Monmouth, Illinois

RASPBERRY SALAD

2 pkg. frozen raspberries, thawed
2 3-oz. packages raspberry gelatin

St. Valentine's Day / 25

1 3-oz. package
  cream cheese,
  softened
1 9-oz. carton
  whipped topping
1/2 c. pecans

Drain raspberries, reserving juice. Add enough boiling water to juice to measure 2 cups. Dissolve 1 package gelatin in juice mixture. Combine with raspberries in 8 x 10-inch dish. Chill until set. Dissolve 1 package gelatin in 1 1/4 cups boiling water. Chill until partially set. Stir in cream cheese. Fold in whipped topping and pecans. Spread over congealed layer. Chill until set. Yield: 15 servings.

Judith Webb
Xi Alpha Delta, Oskaloosa, Iowa

VALENTINE SALAD

1/4 c. red hot
  candies
1 pkg. lemon gelatin
1 c. unsweetened
  applesauce
1 3-oz. package
  cream cheese,
  softened
2 tbsp. mayonnaise
2 tbsp. cream

Dissolve red hot candies in 1 cup boiling water. Mix with gelatin; stir until dissolved. Cool. Stir in applesauce. Pour half the mixture into mold; chill until set. Blend remaining ingredients. Spread over congealed mixture. Pour remaining gelatin over top. Chill until firm. Yield: 12 servings.

Patt Barnes
Xi Gamma Gamma, Arvada, Colorado

SPINACH AND STRAWBERRY SALAD

1 lb. fresh spinach, torn
1 c. fresh strawberries,
  sliced
1 c. fresh bean sprouts
1 c. seedless grapes, halved
1/4 c. crumbled
  crisp-fried bacon
1 c. oil
1/3 c. vinegar
1 med. onion, grated
3/4 c. sugar
1 tsp. Worcestershire
  sauce

Combine first 5 ingredients. Combine oil, vinegar, onion, sugar and Worcestershire sauce; beat well. Pour over salad; toss to coat. Yield: 6 servings.

Jeanne Garrison
Sigma Eta, Chesterfield, Missouri

BURGUNDY BEEF

2 lb. round steak, cut
  into 1/2-in. cubes
Meat tenderizer
3 med. onions, thinly
  sliced
1 clove of garlic
1/4 c. butter
2 cans beef gravy
1/2 tsp. salt
1/4 tsp. pepper
1/2 c. Burgundy
1/4 tsp. each
  marjoram, oregano
Sour cream

Sprinkle steak with meat tenderizer. Saute onion and garlic in butter until lightly browned. Remove onion; discard garlic. Brown steak in pan drippings. Stir in gravy, salt, pepper and sauteed onions. Simmer for 1 hour or until steak is tender. Stir in Burgundy and seasonings. Simmer for 15 minutes. Stir in sour cream. Serve over rice or noodles. Yield: 6 servings.

Brenda Whittington
Delta Iota, West Frankfort, Illinois

CHERRY-ALMOND PORK

1 3 to 4-lb. pork roast
Salt and pepper to taste
1 16-oz. jar cherry
  preserves
1/4 tsp. cinnamon
2 tbsp. light corn syrup
1/4 c. red wine vinegar
1/4 c. slivered almonds

Season roast with salt and pepper to taste. Bake at 300 to 325 degrees for 2 hours; drain. Bring next 4 ingredients to a boil, stirring frequently. Simmer for 2 minutes. Stir in almonds. Pour over roast. Bake for 30 minutes longer, basting frequently. Yield: 6-8 servings.

Susie Harbers
Xi Upsilon Psi, Yoakum, Texas

LOVE AND KISSES CHICKEN

1 lg. chicken breast,
  boned, halved
2 tbsp. butter
1/4 c. Brandy
4 sheets phyllo
  pastry
3 tbsp. unsalted
  butter, melted
1/4 c. chopped walnuts
Freshly grated nutmeg
Cinnamon
1 to 2 tsp. Dijon
  mustard
1/3 c. chicken
  bouillon
1/4 c. apple juice
1/2 c. whipping
  cream
1 med. apple, peeled,
  sliced

Brown chicken in butter over medium heat for 10 minutes. Warm 2 tablespoons Brandy in small saucepan. Ignite and pour over chicken. Remove from heat; shake gently until flames subside. Add remaining Brandy; stir to coat well. Remove chicken. Brush phyllo sheets with melted butter, stack and cut in half lengthwise. Place 1 chicken breast at end of each half. Top with walnuts, nutmeg and cinnamon. Roll to enclose chicken, tucking ends under. Bake on baking sheet at 400 degrees for 20 to 25 minutes. Stir mustard into pan drippings. Stir in bouillon and apple juice. Simmer for 5 minutes. Stir in whipping cream. Cook over medium heat until slightly thickened. Add apple slices. Serve with chicken. Yield: 2 servings.

Mary Murkin
Epsilon Omega, Mission, British Columbia, Canada

CHICKEN AND MUSHROOM CREPES

2 1/2 c. milk
3 eggs
Flour
1 tsp. salt
Butter, melted
3/4 lb. mushrooms, sliced
1 c. chicken broth
2 egg yolks
1 c. shredded Swiss cheese
3 c. chopped cooked chicken
Chopped parsley

Mix 1 1/2 cups milk, eggs, 2/3 cup flour, 1/2 teaspoon salt and a small amount of butter. Chill, covered, for 2 hours. Cook crepes using manufacturer's directions for crepe pan. Saute mushrooms in a small amount of butter; remove. Blend 1/4 cup flour, 1/2 teaspoon salt and a small amount of additional butter into pan drippings. Stir in mixture of chicken broth, egg yolks and 1 cup milk. Cook until thickened, stirring constantly. Stir in cheese. Combine 1/2 cup sauce with 1/4 cup mushrooms for topping. Mix remaining mushrooms and chicken with sauce. Place 1/3 cup on each crepe. Roll to enclose filling; place in 9 x 13-inch pan. Top with reserved mushroom sauce and parsley. Bake at 325 degrees for 20 minutes. Yield: 6 servings.

Suzy Wickstrom
Alpha Pi, Missoula, Montana

CRANBERRY CHICKEN MICHELE

1 6-oz. package Stove Top stuffing for pork
1/4 c. butter
6 to 8 chicken breasts, boned
Salt and pepper to taste
1 16-oz. can whole cranberry sauce
1 env. dry onion soup mix
1 8-oz. bottle of low-calorie Russian dressing

Prepare stuffing mix according to package instructions using butter and 1 1/2 cups water. Spoon into center of each chicken breast; fold to enclose stuffing. Place in 9 x 9-inch baking dish. Season with salt and pepper. Bake at 350 degrees for 30 minutes. Combine remaining ingredients. Spoon over chicken. Bake for 30 minutes longer. Yield: 6-8 servings.

Michele Hunt
Beta Beta, Ft. Myers, Florida

SEAFOOD LASAGNA

1 c. chopped onion
2 tbsp. butter
1 8-oz. package cream cheese, softened
1 1/2 c. cottage cheese
1 egg, beaten
1 to 2 tsp. basil
1/2 tsp. salt
1/8 tsp. pepper
1/3 c. milk
2 cans cream of mushroom soup
1/3 c. white wine
1 lb. shrimp, cooked
1 5 1/2-oz. can crab meat
8 lasagna noodles, cooked
1/4 c. Parmesan cheese
1/2 c. grated Cheddar cheese

Saute onion in butter until tender. Mix cream cheese with the next 5 ingredients in bowl. Stir in sauteed onion. Mix milk, soup, wine, shrimp and crab meat. Layer half the noodles, cream cheese mixture and seafood mixture in 9 x 13-inch baking dish. Repeat layers. Top with Parmesan cheese. Bake at 350 degrees for 45 minutes. Sprinkle with Cheddar cheese. Let stand for 5 minutes before serving.

Wendy Roney
Delta Kappa, Mississauga, Ontario, Canada

MOTHER'S CINNAMON APPLES

1 c. red cinnamon candies
1/2 c. sugar
Several drops of red food coloring
4 c. sliced apples

Melt candies in 1 cup boiling water. Stir in sugar and food coloring. Add apples. Simmer for several minutes until apples are red. Yield: 4-6 servings.

Michele Kennedy
Lambda Rho, Troy, Michigan

BEETS WITH PINEAPPLE

2 tbsp. brown sugar
1 tbsp. cornstarch
1/4 tsp. salt
1 9-oz. can pineapple tidbits
1 tbsp. butter
1 tbsp. lemon juice
1 16-oz. can sliced beets, drained

Mix first 3 ingredients in saucepan. Stir in pineapple. Cook until thick, stirring constantly. Stir in remaining ingredients. Cook for 5 minutes or until heated through. Yield: 4 servings.

Christa Belknap
Alpha Delta, Knoxville, Iowa

CHERRY-NUT-CREAM CHEESE LOAF

1 8-oz. package cream cheese, softened
1/2 c. sugar
9 tbsp. flour
2 eggs
1 pkg. cherry-nut quick bread mix

Mix cream cheese, sugar and 1 tablespoon flour. Beat in 1 egg. Mix 1 slightly beaten egg with 1 cup water. Add to bread mix with 1/2 cup flour; mix well. Spoon 2/3 batter into greased and floured 5 x 9-inch loaf pan. Spread cream cheese mixture over batter. Top with remaining batter. Bake at 375 degrees for 45 to 55 minutes; cool. Refrigerate, wrapped in foil, overnight.

Jill Burg
Zeta Epsilon, Carbondale, Colorado

CHERRY CREPES

3/4 c. flour
5 tbsp. sugar
1/2 tsp. salt
1 c. milk
2 eggs, beaten
2 tbsp. oil
1/4 c. lemon juice
12 oz. cream cheese, softened
1 1/2 tsp. grated lemon rind
1 can cherry pie filling

Mix flour, 1 tablespoon sugar and salt. Make a well in center. Pour in milk, eggs and oil; beat until smooth. Bake crepes in pan using manufacturer's instructions. Beat 3 tablespoons lemon juice, cream cheese, 1/4 cup sugar and lemon rind until fluffy. Spoon 2 tablespoonfuls in center of each crepe; roll to enclose filling. Place seam side down in 9 x 13-inch baking dish. Heat pie filling and remaining lemon juice in saucepan. Pour over crepes. Bake at 400 degrees until heated through. Yield: 18 servings.

Teresa Cecil
Xi Gamma Mu, Albany, Georgia

CHERRY CRUNCH

1 c. flour
3/4 c. oats
1 c. packed brown sugar
1 tsp. cinnamon
1/2 c. melted butter
4 c. cherries, drained
1 c. sugar
2 tbsp. cornstarch
1 tsp. vanilla extract

Mix flour, oats, brown sugar, cinnamon and butter until crumbly. Press half the mixture in greased 9-inch baking pan. Top with cherries. Mix remaining ingredients with 1 cup water in saucepan. Cook until thickened, stirring constantly. Pour over cherries. Top with remaining crumbs. Bake at 350 degrees for 1 hour. Serve warm with ice cream or whipped cream. Yield: 8 servings.

Julia L. Martin
Xi Eta Alpha, Hugoton, Kansas

CHERRY PUDDING CAKE

1 c. cherry juice
2 eggs
2 tbsp. butter, softened
2 c. sugar
Flour
2 tsp. soda
Salt
2 c. sour cherries, drained
1/2 c. chopped nuts
2 c. packed brown sugar

Beat cherry juice with eggs and butter. Beat in sugar, 2 cups flour, soda and 1/2 teaspoon salt. Stir in cherries and nuts. Pour into ungreased 9 x 13-inch baking pan. Bake at 350 degrees for 50 minutes. Mix brown sugar, 3 heaping tablespoons flour, pinch of salt and 2 cups water in saucepan. Cook until thickened. Spread on cake. Chill overnight before serving. Yield: 15 servings.

Arlean Jensen
Laureate Alpha Pi, Los Altos, California

CHOCOLATE-STRAWBERRY MOUSSE

6 sq. semisweet chocolate
1 tbsp. shortening
1 10-oz. package frozen strawberries, thawed
1 1/2 env. unflavored gelatin
1/4 c. sugar
2 egg whites
1 c. heavy cream, whipped

Melt chocolate and shortening in double boiler. Coat inside of 12 foil muffin cups with chocolate. Chill until firm. Coat with chocolate again; chill. Puree strawberries. Combine with gelatin and 2 tablespoons sugar in saucepan. Cook over low heat until gelatin is dissolved, stirring frequently. Place in container of ice water; stir until mixture begins to thicken. Beat egg whites until foamy. Add remaining 2 tablespoons sugar 1 tablespoon at a time, beating until soft peaks form. Fold whipped cream into strawberry mixture. Fold in egg white mixture. Remove foil gently from chocolate cups. Pipe mousse through decorating tube into cups.

Jacklyn Young
Beta Epsilon, Fairview, Montana

POTS DE CREME

1 c. semisweet chocolate chips
2 egg yolks
3 tbsp. Brandy
1 1/4 c. light cream, scalded

Place ingredients in blender container. Process until smooth. Pour into individual serving dishes. Chill for 3 hours or longer. Yield: 6 servings.

Melissa Levinsky
Preceptor Beta Omega, Meadville, Pennsylvania

MACAROON DESSERT

12 coconut macaroons
1 tbsp. unflavored gelatin
2 eggs, separated
1 c. sugar
2 c. milk
1/4 tsp. salt
1/2 tsp. almond extract
1/2 c. chopped nuts (opt.)
1/2 pt. whipping cream, whipped
Maraschino cherries

Arrange macaroons in 9 x 12-inch pan. Soften gelatin in 1/4 cup water. Mix egg yolks, sugar, milk, gelatin and salt in saucepan. Bring to a boil, stirring constantly. Stir in flavoring. Pour over stiffly beaten egg whites. Stir in nuts. Pour over macaroons. Chill in refrigerator overnight. Cut into squares; invert on serving plate. Top with whipped cream and cherry. Yield: 12 servings.

Doris Busby
Xi Preceptor, Baxter Springs, Kansas

LACY DESSERT BASKETS

3/4 c. quick-cooking oats
1/3 c. flour
1/4 tsp. baking powder
2 tbsp. milk
2 tbsp. light corn syrup
1 1/4 c. sugar
Butter
2 eggs
1 tsp. vanilla extract
1/3 c. currant jelly
1 12-oz. package frozen raspberries, thawed, well drained
2 1/2 tbsp. red wine

Mix first 5 ingredients, 1/2 cup sugar and 6 tablespoons melted butter. Drop 4 well-spaced tablespoonfuls onto 4 well-greased baking sheets. Spread batter into 3-inch circles. Bake at 375 degrees for 6 minutes; cool for 30 seconds. Shape around inverted 6-ounce custard cup to form baskets. Remove when cool. Cream 1/2 cup softened butter and 3/4 cup sugar in mixer bowl. Add eggs 1 at a time, beating for 5 minutes after each addition. Stir in vanilla. Spoon 1/3 cup into each basket. Melt jelly in saucepan. Stir in raspberries and wine. Chill, covered, in refrigerator. Spoon over filling. May add 1 ounce melted unsweetened chocolate to filling and top with whipped cream and chocolate sprinkles. Yield: 16 servings.

Marilyn K. Price
Preceptor Sigma, Ft. Washington, Maryland

SNOWFLAKE PUDDING WITH RASPBERRY SAUCE

1 env. unflavored gelatin
1 c. sugar
1/2 tsp. salt
1 1/4 c. milk
1 tsp. vanilla extract
2 c. whipping cream, whipped
1 1/3 c. flaked coconut
1 10-oz. package frozen raspberries, crushed
1 1/2 tsp. cornstarch
1/2 c. currant jelly

Mix gelatin, sugar, salt and milk in saucepan. Cook over medium heat until gelatin and sugar dissolve, stirring constantly. Chill until partially set. Fold in vanilla, whipped cream and coconut. Spoon into 9 x 13-inch dish. Chill until firm. Combine remaining ingredients in saucepan. Cook over medium heat until thickened, stirring constantly; strain. Chill in refrigerator. Serve over pudding. Yield: 12-15 servings.

Janet A. Jensen
Xi Iota, Belle Fourche, South Dakota

MARGUERITES

3 egg whites
1 c. sugar
1 tsp. vanilla extract
3/4 c. saltines, crushed
1/2 c. chopped pecans
Vanilla ice cream
Strawberries, crushed

Beat egg whites until soft peaks form. Add 1/2 cup sugar with vanilla gradually, beating until stiff. Fold in mixture of saltines, pecans and 1/2 cup sugar. Shape into tart shells in greased muffin cups. Bake at 350 degrees for 25 minutes; cool. Place scoop of ice cream in each tart shell. Freeze. Top with strawberries. Yield: 12 to 18 servings.

Jean L. Kuhn
Xi Iota, Wyoming, Michigan

MERINGUES

4 egg whites
1/2 tsp. cream of tartar
Pinch of salt
1 c. sugar
1 tsp. flavoring
Several drops of food coloring (opt.)
1 qt. ice cream
8 to 10 oz. fresh strawberries

Beat egg whites, cream of tartar and salt until soft peaks form. Add sugar gradually, beating until stiff. Stir in flavoring and food coloring. Shape into 4-inch hearts on brown paper, forming edges higher than the center. Bake at 250 degrees for 50 to 60 minutes; cool. Spoon ice cream and sweetened strawberries into cooled Meringues. Yield: 12-14 servings.

Helen Moor
Laureate Epsilon, Indianapolis, Indiana

VALENTINE MERINGUE SHELLS

6 egg whites
1 1/2 tsp. lemon juice
2 c. sugar
Frozen strawberries
Whipped cream

Beat egg whites until frothy. Beat in lemon juice. Add sugar gradually, beating until stiff. Shape 2 tablespoons mixture into shells on brown paper. Place in 400-degree oven; turn off heat. Let stand in closed oven overnight. Spoon strawberries into meringue. Top with whipped cream.

Louise J. Ferguson
Zeta Eta, Tillamook, Oregon

STRAWBERRY DELIGHT

1 c. flour
1/2 c. butter, melted
1/4 c. packed brown sugar
1/2 c. chopped pecans
1 10-oz. package frozen strawberries, thawed
1 c. sugar
2 tsp. lemon juice
2 egg whites
1 c. whipping cream, whipped
Sliced fresh strawberries (opt.)

Mix first 4 ingredients in 8-inch square baking pan. Bake at 350 degrees for 20 minutes, stirring occasionally; cool. Beat frozen strawberries, sugar, lemon juice and egg whites in mixer bowl at high speed for 10 minutes or until stiff peaks form. Fold in whipped cream. Press 2/3 of the crumb

St. Valentine's Day / 29

mixture into 9-inch springform pan. Spoon in strawberry mixture. Sprinkle with remaining crumbs. Freeze until firm. Garnish with fresh strawberries. Yield: 8-10 servings.

Tricia Smith
Zeta Phi, St. Marys, Georgia

STRAWBERRY PIZZA

2 sticks margarine	1 lg. carton whipped topping
2 c. flour	2 c. sugar
1 c. chopped pecans	6 tbsp. cornstarch
1 8-oz. package cream cheese, softened	6 tbsp. strawberry gelatin
3 c. confectioners' sugar	2 qt. strawberries

Melt margarine; mix with flour and pecans. Press into pizza pan. Bake at 250 degrees for 35 to 40 minutes; cool. Beat cream cheese with confectioners' sugar. Fold in whipped topping. Spread over crust, forming a raised outer edge. Bring sugar, cornstarch and 2 cups water to a boil in saucepan. Cool slightly. Stir in gelatin and strawberries. Spoon over cream cheese layer. Chill until set. Garnish with additional whipped topping.

Kathy Reynolds
Xi Alpha Eta, Cleveland, Mississippi

STRAWBERRY SHORTCUT CAKE

2 c. strawberries with juice	1 1/2 c. sugar
1 3-oz. package strawberry gelatin	1/2 c. shortening
	3 tsp. baking powder
1 c. miniature marshmallows	1 c. milk
	3 eggs
2 1/4 c. flour	1 tsp. vanilla extract
	1/2 tsp. salt

Combine strawberries and gelatin in bowl; set aside. Grease bottom of 9 x 13-inch baking pan. Arrange marshmallows in pan. Combine remaining ingredients in mixer bowl; mix until moistened. Beat at medium speed for 3 minutes. Pour over marshmallows. Spoon strawberry mixture over top. Bake at 350 degrees for 45 to 50 minutes. Yield: 12 servings.

Judy Blanc
Lambda, Boise, Idaho

HEAVENLY CHOCOLATE MOUSSE-FILLED CAKE

1 pkg. angel food cake mix	2 1/2 c. whipping cream
	3 tsp. vanilla extract
Red food coloring	1/4 c. confectioners' sugar
2 tsp. unflavored gelatin	
1/3 c. cocoa	2/3 c. semisweet chocolate chips
2/3 c. sugar	

Prepare cake using package directions, adding 3 or 4 drops of food coloring to stiffly beaten egg white portion of batter. Place baked cake on serving plate. Slice 1-inch layer from top. Remove center of cake, leaving 1-inch thick shell. Soften gelatin in 2 tablespoons cold water. Stir cocoa into 1/3 cup boiling water in saucepan. Cook over low heat until smooth and thickened, stirring constantly. Add gelatin, stirring until dissolved. Remove from heat; mix in sugar. Cool to room temperature. Whip 1 1/2 cups cream with 2 teaspoons vanilla until stiff peaks form. Beat in chocolate gradually on low speed just until blended. Chill for 30 minutes. Spoon into cake shell. Replace top. Whip 1 cup cream with confectioners' sugar, 1 teaspoon vanilla and 2 or 3 drops food coloring until stiff. Frost cake. Chill in refrigerator. Melt chocolate chips in double boiler over hot water. Spread 1/8 inch thick on wax paper-lined baking sheet. Chill for 5 to 8 minutes or until chocolate begins to set. Cut heart shapes with cookie cutter. Do not remove. Chill overnight. Peel hearts from paper. Arrange on cake.

Photograph for this recipe on page 23.

CHERRY CHOCOLATE CAKE

1 tsp. each soda, salt	1 c. chopped walnuts
	1 c. semisweet chocolate chips
3/4 c. sugar	
3/4 c. oil	1 can cherry pie filling
2 eggs	
2 tsp. vanilla extract	1 c. confectioners' sugar
2 c. flour	
1 tsp. cinnamon	2 tbsp. milk

Blend soda, salt and next 6 ingredients. Stir in walnuts, chips and pie filling. Bake in bundt pan at 350 degrees for about 1 hour. Glaze with mixture of confectioners' sugar and milk. Yield: 15 servings.

Kathleen Hamlin
Preceptor Eta Psi, San Diego, California

MARASCHINO CHERRY CAKE

2 1/4 c. sifted flour	1/4 c. maraschino cherry juice
1/2 tsp. salt	
1 1/3 c. sugar	1/2 c. egg whites
1 tbsp. baking powder	1/4 c. chopped walnuts
1/2 c. shortening	16 maraschino cherries, chopped
1/2 c. milk	

Mix sifted dry ingredients, shortening, milk and cherry juice in mixer bowl. Beat at medium speed for 2 minutes. Add egg whites. Beat for 2 minutes longer. Fold in walnuts and cherries. Bake in prepared 8 x 10-inch pan at 350 degrees for 30 to 35 minutes.

Cheryl Noder
Xi Lambda Alpha, Bradford, Illinois

CHERRY GELATIN CAKE

1 20-oz. can crushed pineapple
1 pkg. white cake mix
1 3-oz. package cherry gelatin
4 eggs, slightly beaten
2/3 c. oil
1 c. shredded coconut
1 c. chopped pecans
4 c. whipped topping
1 can cherry pie filling

Drain pineapple, reserving juice. Combine cake mix, gelatin, eggs, oil and 1/3 cup water in mixer bowl; beat until well blended. Stir in pineapple, coconut and pecans. Spoon into greased and floured 10 x 14-inch baking pan. Bake at 350 degrees for 45 minutes. Pierce hot cake with fork. Pour pineapple juice over cake; chill. Frost with mixture of whipped topping and pie filling. Chill overnight.

Shirley Strosaker
Xi Lambda Omicron, Orange, California

CHERRY-NUT PARTY CAKE

1/2 c. shortening
3/4 c. sugar
3 eggs
2 1/4 c. sifted cake flour
1 tbsp. baking powder
1/2 tsp. salt
1/4 c. maraschino cherry juice
1/2 c. milk
1/2 c. chopped maraschino cherries
1/2 c. pecan pieces
2 c. sweetened whipped cream
Cherry halves
Pecan halves

Cream shortening and sugar until fluffy. Beat in eggs 1 at a time. Add sifted dry ingredients alternately with mixture of cherry juice and milk, beating well after each addition. Fold in cherries and pecans. Bake in greased and floured 9-inch cake pans at 375 degrees for 25 to 30 minutes. Cool in pans for 5 minutes before turning onto rack to cool completely. Spread whipped cream between layers and over top and side of cake. Decorate top with cherry and pecan halves. Yield: 16 servings.

Glenda L. King
Xi Alpha Xi, Tempe, Arizona

WALNUT-CHERRY CAKE

1 c. coarsely chopped walnuts
1 pkg. white cake mix
1/2 tsp. vanilla extract
6 drops of red food coloring
1 8-oz. container whipped topping
1 21-oz. can cherry pie filling

Chop 3/4 cup walnuts medium fine. Prepare cake mix using package directions, adding vanilla and 3/4 cup walnuts. Bake in two 9-inch cake pans using package directions. Cool in pan for 10 minutes before inverting on rack to cool completely. Stir food coloring into whipped topping. Spoon 1-inch ring around top of each layer. Fill centers with pie filling. Stack layers. Spread whipped topping on side. Sprinkle with 1/4 cup walnuts. Chill before serving. Yield: 12 servings.

Kathi Grieser
Beta Iota, Ogden, Utah

FRIENDSHIP CAKE

2 1/3 c. sugar
4 1/3 c. flour
2 1/3 c. milk
3 eggs
1 1/2 tsp. cinnamon
1/2 tsp. salt
2 tsp. baking powder
2/3 c. oil
2 tsp. vanilla extract
1 1/2 tsp. soda
1/2 c. chopped nuts (opt.)
1 8-oz. can crushed pineapple, drained (opt.)
1/2 c. chopped apples (opt.)
1/2 c. coconut (opt.)
1/2 c. raisins (opt.)

Mix 1/3 cup sugar, 1/3 cup flour and 1/3 cup milk in large bowl. Let stand, covered, for 5 days, stirring each day. Do not refrigerate. Add 1/2 cup sugar, 1 cup flour and 1 cup milk on 5th day; mix well. Let stand, covered, for 5 days, stirring each day. Add 1/2 cup sugar, 1 cup flour and 1 cup milk on 10th day; mix well. Remove 3 cups mixture to give to 3 friends who will proceed with these directions as if from the second day. Place remaining batter in large bowl. Beat in 1 cup sugar, 3 eggs and 2 cups sifted flour. Add remaining ingredients; mix well. Bake in greased bundt pan at 350 degrees for 50 minutes. Yield: 12 servings.

Deborah Gerkin
Gamma Kappa, Cape Canaveral, Florida

SWEETHEART CAKE

2 1/2 c. sifted cake flour
1 1/2 c. sugar
3 1/2 tsp. baking powder
1 1/2 tsp. salt
Shortening
3/4 c. milk
1/4 c. maraschino cherry juice
2 1/2 tsp. almond extract
2 tsp. vanilla extract
4 egg whites
Maraschino cherries
1/2 c. chopped walnuts
2 tbsp. butter
4 c. confectioners' sugar
9 tbsp. heavy cream, scalded
Several drops of red food coloring

Sift flour, sugar, baking powder and 1 teaspoon salt into mixer bowl. Cut in 1/2 cup shortening until crumbly. Mix milk and cherry juice. Stir 3/4 of the mixture into dry ingredients. Add 2 teaspoons almond and 1 teaspoon vanilla flavoring. Beat for 2 minutes. Add remaining milk mixture and egg whites. Beat for 2 minutes. Stir in 18 chopped cherries and walnuts. Bake in greased and floured pans at 375 degrees for 20 to 25 minutes. Mix 2 tablespoons shortening, butter, 1/2 teaspoon almond flavoring, 1 teaspoon vanilla and 1/2 teaspoon salt. Beat in 1/2 cup confectioners' sugar. Add cream alternately with remaining confectioners' sugar, mixing well after each addition. Stir in food coloring and chopped cherries if desired. Spread over cooled cake. Yield: 8-12 servings.

Ruth Ann Eccles
Delta, Des Moines, Iowa

RED VELVET CAKE

2 eggs, beaten	1 1-oz. bottle of
1 1/2 c. sugar	red food coloring
1 1/2 c. oil	2 3-oz. packages
1 tsp. vinegar	cream cheese,
2 1/2 c. flour	softened
1 tsp. soda	2 c. confectioners'
1 c. buttermilk	sugar
2 tsp. vanilla extract	

Mix first 4 ingredients. Beat in sifted flour and soda. Stir in buttermilk gradually. Add 1 teaspoon vanilla and food coloring. Bake in 9 x 13-inch pan at 350 degrees for 30 minutes. Beat remaining ingredients with 1 teaspoon vanilla until smooth. Spread on cooled cake. Yield: 12-14 servings.

Vivian T. Howard
Zeta Iota, Savannah, Georgia

STRAWBERRY-SOUR CREAM CAKE

Flour	1 16-oz. package
1 tsp. soda	frozen strawberries
1/3 tsp. salt	in juice, thawed,
1 1/4 c. sugar	drained
1 c. shortening	2 tbsp. strawberry juice
3 eggs	1/2 c. butter, softened
1/2 c. sour cream	2 c. confectioners'
2 tsp. vanilla extract	sugar

Sift 2 cups flour, soda, salt and sugar into mixer bowl. Add 1/2 cup shortening, eggs, sour cream and 1 teaspoon vanilla. Beat at low speed for 3 minutes. Beat at high speed for 3 minutes. Fold in strawberries. Spoon into 2 greased and floured 8-inch cake pans. Bake at 350 degrees for 30 to 40 minutes. Cool in pans for 10 minutes before removing to rack to cool completely. Mix 1/2 cup shortening, 3 tablespoons flour, 1 teaspoon vanilla and remaining ingredients in mixer bowl. Beat for 7 minutes. Frost cooled cake. Garnish with mint leaves and fresh strawberries.

Peggy Garrett
Delta Nu, Naples, Florida

WHITE CUSTARD CAKE

1 c. sugar	1 tsp. vanilla
2 tbsp. flour	extract
1/2 tsp. salt	2 c. whipped topping
2 c. milk, scalded	1 angel food cake,
4 eggs, separated	thinly sliced
1 pkg. unflavored gelatin	Flaked coconut

Blend sugar, flour and salt into hot milk. Stir a small amount of hot mixture into beaten egg yolks; stir egg yolks into hot mixture. Cook until thick, stirring constantly. Stir in gelatin softened in 1/2 cup cold water. Cook until smooth, stirring constantly; remove from heat. Stir in vanilla; cool. Fold in stiffly beaten egg whites and 1 cup whipped topping. Layer half the cake slices and half the custard in 9 x 13-inch cake pan; repeat layers. Chill overnight. Spread 1 cup whipped topping over custard. Sprinkle with coconut. Garnish with fresh strawberries.

Peggy Barnes
Xi Sigma Omicron, San Antonio, Texas

CHERRY CUPCAKES

2 8-oz. packages cream	1 tsp. vanilla extract
cheese, softened	24 vanilla wafers
3/4 c. sugar	1 21-oz. can cherry
2 eggs	pie filling
1 tbsp. lemon juice	Whipped topping

Beat first 5 ingredients until fluffy. Place 1 vanilla wafer in foil-lined muffin cups. Fill 2/3 full with cream cheese mixture. Bake at 375 degrees for 15 to 20 minutes. Top with pie filling and whipped topping. Yield: 2 dozen.

Theo Clark
Alpha Alpha, Rockford, Illinois

STRAWBERRY CUPCAKES

1 pkg. white cake mix	1 c. frozen
3 tbsp. flour	strawberries with
1 3-oz. package	juice, thawed
strawberry	1 stick margarine,
gelatin	softened
3/4 c. oil	1 box confectioners'
4 eggs, beaten	sugar

Combine first 5 ingredients in mixer bowl. Beat at medium speed for 2 minutes. Add 1/2 cup strawberries. Beat for 1 minute longer. Fill paper-lined muffin cups 2/3 full. Bake at 325 degrees for 20 minutes. Cream margarine. Add confectioners' sugar and 1/2 cup strawberries alternately, mixing well after each addition. Frost cooled cupcakes. Yield: 2 dozen.

Sharon Vollmer
Zeta Zeta, Lafayette, Indiana

32 / St. Valentine's Day

CHOCOLATE FLUTED KISS CUPS

1 8-oz. milk chocolate candy bar
1 tbsp. melted shortening (opt.)
1 c. creamy peanut butter
1 c. confectioners' sugar
1 tbsp. butter, softened
24 milk chocolate kisses

Melt chocolate bar in top of double boiler over hot water. Place 24 pleated miniature paper liners in miniature muffin cups. Coat liners with chocolate using pastry brush. Thin chocolate with shortening if necessary. Chill for 20 minutes. Spread chocolate over thin spots. Chill overnight. Remove liners. Combine peanut butter, confectioners' sugar and butter in small mixer bowl. Beat until smooth. Spoon into chocolate cups. Chill, covered, in refrigerator. Top with kisses. Yield: 2 dozen.

Photograph for this recipe on page 23.

CHOCOLATE TRUFFLES

1/2 c. heavy cream
1/3 c. sugar
6 tbsp. butter
2 c. miniature semisweet chocolate chips
1 tsp. vanilla extract
1 tbsp. shortening
Finely chopped nuts
Shaved chocolate
Confectioners' sugar

Combine heavy cream, sugar and butter. Bring to a boil; remove from heat. Add 1 cup chocolate chips immediately. Stir until chips are melted; add vanilla. Pour into bowl. Let stand until cool; stir occasionally. Chill, covered, for several hours. Melt 1 cup chocolate chips and shortening. Shape chilled mixture in 1/2-inch balls. Roll in chopped nuts, shaved chocolate or confectioners' sugar or coat with melted chocolate. Yield: 3 dozen.

Photograph for this recipe on page 1.

STRAWBERRIES

1 can sweetened condensed milk
2 c. shredded coconut
1 lg. package strawberry gelatin
Sugar
Slivered almonds
Several drops of green food coloring

Mix condensed milk, coconut and gelatin. Shape by teaspoonfuls into strawberries. Tint sugar and almonds with green food coloring. Dip end of strawberry into sugar and place almond stem in each. Chill in refrigerator.

Joanne Sturges
Eta Beta, Longwood, Florida

CHERRY CHEESECAKE

2 c. graham cracker crumbs
Sugar
6 tbsp. butter, softened
4 eggs
1 1/2 tsp. vanilla extract
3 8-oz. packages cream cheese, softened
2 tsp. lemon juice
1 c. sour cream
1 can cherry pie filling

Mix cracker crumbs, 3 tablespoons sugar and butter. Press onto bottom and up side to within 1 inch of top of springform pan. Beat eggs until fluffy. Beat in 1 cup sugar gradually. Add 1 teaspoon vanilla, cream cheese and lemon juice; mix well. Pour into prepared crust. Bake at 375 degrees for 30 to 35 minutes. Cool for 1 hour. Combine sour cream, 2 tablespoons sugar and 1/2 teaspoon vanilla. Spread over cheesecake. Bake at 400 degrees for 15 minutes; cool. Chill in refrigerator. Top with pie filling. Yield: 12-16 servings.

Deb Tornholm
Epsilon Iota, Clarinda, Iowa

CHOCOLATE LOVER'S CHEESECAKE

1 1/2 c. miniature semisweet chocolate chips
11 oz. cream cheese, softened
1/3 c. sugar
1/4 c. butter, softened
2 tsp. vanilla extract
3/4 c. chopped pecans
1 1/2 c. whipping cream
1 4-oz. milk chocolate bar
2 tbsp. confectioners' sugar
Semisweet chocolate curls

Melt chocolate chips in double boiler. Combine cream cheese, sugar and butter in large mixer bowl; beat until smooth. Add 1 1/2 teaspoons vanilla. Beat in melted chocolate and pecans. Whip 1 cup heavy cream in bowl until stiff peaks form. Fold into chocolate mixture. Spoon into foil-lined 5-cup heart-shaped mold. Chill until firm. Unmold onto serving tray; peel off foil. Chill in refrigerator. Melt milk chocolate bar in 2 tablespoons water in double boiler. Stir occasionally. Cool slightly. Spread over mold. Combine remaining 1/2 cup cream, confectioners' sugar and 1/2 teaspoon vanilla in small mixer bowl. Beat until stiff peaks form. Frost sides of mold. Chill until serving time. Decorate with chocolate curls.

Photograph for this recipe on page 1.

MARASCHINO CHERRY BARS

Butter, softened
2 1/3 c. flour
1/3 c. sugar
2 eggs, slightly beaten
1 c. packed brown sugar
1/2 tsp. vanilla extract
1 1/2 tsp. baking powder
1/2 tsp. salt
1/2 c. chopped nuts
1 10-oz. jar maraschino cherries, drained, chopped
3 to 4 tbsp. cherry juice
2 1/2 c. confectioners' sugar
2 to 3 tbsp. flaked coconut

St. Valentine's Day / 33

Cut 3/4 cup butter into mixture of 2 cups flour and sugar until crumbly. Press into 9 x 13-inch baking pan. Bake at 350 degrees for 12 to 15 minutes. Mix 1/3 cup flour, eggs and next 6 ingredients. Spoon into crust. Bake at 350 degrees for 20 to 25 minutes; cool. Mix cherry juice, confectioners' sugar and 2 tablespoons butter. Spread over top. Sprinkle with coconut. Yield: 4 dozen.

Barbara Dunthorn
Kappa, Pocatello, Idaho

CHERRY BARS

1 c. flour	1 c. sugar
2 tbsp. confectioners' sugar	1 1/2 tsp. maraschino cherry juice
1/2 c. butter, softened	
Pinch of salt	1/2 c. coconut
2 eggs, beaten	1/2 c. chopped nuts

Mix flour, confectioners' sugar, butter and salt until crumbly. Spread in 8 x 11-inch pan. Mix eggs with remaining ingredients. Pour over crumb mixture. Bake at 350 degrees for 20 minutes. Yield: 15-20 servings.

Lois Heinis
Eta Alpha, Quincy, California

CHEESECAKE COOKIES

1 1/3 c. packed brown sugar	4 eggs
2 c. chopped walnuts	4 tbsp. lemon juice
4 c. flour	4 tbsp. milk
1 1/3 c. margarine, melted	4 tsp. vanilla extract
1 c. sugar	Several drops of red food coloring
4 8-oz. packages cream cheese, softened	1 can cherry pie filling

Mix brown sugar, walnuts and flour. Stir in margarine until crumbly. Press into large shallow baking pan. Bake at 350 degrees for 12 to 15 minutes. Cream sugar and cream cheese. Beat in eggs and next 4 ingredients. Bake at 350 degrees for 25 minutes; cool. Cut into squares. Top with pie filling.

Sylvia J. Ziegler
Xi Gamma Lambda, Flint, Michigan

CRUNCHY KISS COOKIES

1/2 c. light corn syrup	1 tsp. vanilla extract
1/4 c. packed light brown sugar	2 c. crisp rice cereal
	1 c. slightly crushed cornflakes
1 c. creamy peanut butter	36 milk chocolate kisses

Combine corn syrup and brown sugar. Bring to a boil, stirring constantly; remove from heat. Blend in peanut butter and vanilla. Stir in rice cereal and cornflakes. Shape into balls by teaspoonfuls. Press chocolate kisses into centers, shaping mixture into circles. Store in covered container. Yield: 3 dozen.

Photograph for this recipe on page 1.

HEART-SHAPED COOKIES

1 3/4 c. sifted flour	2/3 c. shortening
3/4 tsp. soda	1 egg
1 tsp. salt	1/2 tsp. vanilla extract
1 c. packed brown sugar	1 1/2 tsp. lemon extract
1/3 c. sugar	1 1/2 c. oats

Sift flour, soda and salt into bowl. Beat in sugars, shortening, egg, flavorings and 1 tablespoon water. Mix in oats. Roll out on floured surface to 1/8-inch thickness. Cut with heart-shaped cookie cutter. Bake on greased cookie sheet at 350 degrees for 10 to 12 minutes. Yield: 2 dozen.

Lynn M. Hittle
Alpha Tau, Lafayette, Indiana

VALENTINE BUTTER COOKIES

1/2 c. butter, softened	2 tsp. cream of tartar
1/2 c. shortening	1 tsp. soda
1 c. sugar	1 1/2 tsp. vanilla extract
3 eggs	Red decorator sugar crystals
3 1/2 c. flour	

Cream butter, shortening and sugar. Beat in eggs 1 at a time. Blend in mixture of flour, cream of tartar and soda. Stir in vanilla. Chill for 2 hours. Roll out on floured surface to 1/4-inch thickness. Cut with heart-shaped cookie cutter. Sprinkle with decorator crystals. Bake on ungreased cookie sheet at 425 degrees for 6 to 8 minutes. Store in airtight container. Yield: 5 1/2 dozen.

Nell Absher
Xi Beta Phi, Lilburn, Georgia

VALENTINE SWEETHEARTS

1 c. margarine, softened	2 tsp. vanilla extract
1 1/2 c. sugar	1/2 tsp. each baking powder, salt
2 eggs	
2 tbsp. milk	3 c. flour

Cream margarine and sugar. Mix in eggs, milk and vanilla. Add baking powder and salt. Mix in flour gradually. Chill overnight. Roll out on floured surface. Cut with heart-shaped cookie cutter. Bake on greased baking sheet at 350 degrees for 8 to 10 minutes. Yield: 4 dozen.

Kathy Steele
Kappa Nu, Linton, Indiana

34 / St. Valentine's Day

KISS COOKIES

1 c. butter, softened
1 c. creamy peanut butter
1 c. sugar
1 c. packed brown sugar
2 eggs
2 tsp. vanilla extract
1/4 c. milk
3 1/2 c. flour
2 tsp. soda
1 tsp. salt
2 10-oz. packages chocolate kisses

Cream butter, peanut butter and sugars. Stir in eggs, vanilla and milk. Mix in combined dry ingredients. Chill dough for 1 to 4 hours. Shape into 1-inch balls. Bake on cookie sheet at 375 degrees for 10 to 12 minutes. Press kiss in center of hot cookies immediately. Remove cookies to rack to cool overnight. Yield: 4 dozen.

Rebecca L. Carter
Alpha Iota, Lewiston, Idaho

HONEY COOKIES

3/4 c. honey
1/2 stick butter
2 eggs
3/4 c. sugar
1/2 c. finely chopped almonds
1/3 c. finely chopped candied citron
1 tbsp. grated lemon rind
4 1/2 c. sifted flour
1 tsp. soda
1 tsp. cinnamon
1/2 tsp. nutmeg
3 1/2 c. confectioners' sugar
1/4 c. milk
1 tsp. shortening
1 egg white
1/4 tsp. cream of tartar

Bring honey and butter to a boil; cool to lukewarm. Beat eggs until light. Beat in sugar gradually. Stir in warm honey mixture gradually. Fold in almonds, citron and lemon rind. Stir in sifted flour, soda, cinnamon and nutmeg gradually. Chill, covered, overnight. Roll out dough 1/4 at a time, on lightly floured surface to 1/4 inch thick. Cut with cookie cutter. Place 1 inch apart on lightly greased cookie sheet. Bake at 350 degrees for 10 minutes. Cool on wire racks. Blend 2 cups confectioners' sugar, milk and shortening. Frost cookies. Beat egg white with cream of tartar until soft peaks form. Add 1 1/2 cups confectioners' sugar gradually, beating until stiff. Pipe through writing tip of decorator tube to decorate as desired. Decorate with marzipan roses.

Betty Behrend
Preceptor Alpha Xi, Atchison, Kansas

PINK PEPPERMINT PIE

1 6-oz. package semisweet chocolate chips, melted
Milk
2 1/2 c. miniature marshmallows
1/4 tsp. peppermint flavoring
1/4 tsp. salt
1/8 tsp. red food coloring
1 c. whipping cream, whipped
1 baked 9-in. pie shell

Melt chocolate chips with 1/3 cup milk in double boiler over low heat, stirring frequently; set aside. Combine next 4 ingredients with 1/2 cup milk in double boiler. Cook until marshmallows are melted, stirring constantly. Pour into bowl. Chill until slightly thickened. Fold in whipped cream. Spread half of mixture in pie shell. Dollop half the chocolate mixture on top. Swirl through chocolate with knife. Repeat layers. Chill until set.

Nicki Lynn Brennemann
Epsilon Kappa, Hyannis, Nebraska

STRAWBERRY CHIFFON PIE

2 eggs, separated
1/2 c. milk
1 env. unflavored gelatin
1/2 c. sugar
3/4 c. pureed fresh strawberries
1 c. strawberry yogurt
1 tsp. lemon juice
4 drops of red food coloring
1 graham cracker pie shell

Beat egg yolks with milk in saucepan. Stir in gelatin and 1/4 cup sugar. Let stand for 1 minute. Cook over low heat for 5 minutes or until gelatin dissolves, stirring constantly. Add strawberry puree, yogurt, lemon juice and food coloring to gelatin mixture; beat well. Chill until thick, stirring occasionally. Beat egg whites until soft peaks form. Add 1/4 cup sugar gradually, beating until stiff. Fold into strawberry mixture. Spoon into pie shell. Chill until set. Garnish with whole strawberries.

Sara Sapp
Beta Iota, Rawlins, Wyoming

STRAWBERRY MARGARITA PIE

1 1/3 c. graham cracker crumbs
1/4 c. sugar
1/4 c. melted butter
1 can sweetened condensed milk
3 tbsp. Tequila
3 tbsp. Triple Sec
1/4 c. lime juice
1/2 c. frozen strawberries with juice, thawed
2 c. whipping cream, whipped

Combine first 3 ingredients. Press into 9-inch pie plate. Beat condensed milk, Tequila, Triple Sec and lime juice in mixer bowl at medium speed for 3 minutes. Add strawberries. Beat at low speed for 1 minute. Fold in whipped cream. Pour into prepared pie shell. Freeze overnight. Let stand in refrigerator for 30 minutes before serving. Garnish with additional whipped cream and strawberries. Yield: 8 servings.

Ann Sample
Xi Alpha Omicron, Albuquerque, New Mexico

Recipe on page 39.

St. Patrick's Day

St. Patrick's Day

EASY IRISH CREAM

3 eggs, beaten
1 can sweetened condensed milk
1 16-oz. carton nondairy creamer
3 tbsp. chocolate syrup
1/4 tsp. coconut extract
1 1/3 c. whiskey

Blend all ingredients. Chill before serving.

Carole Batterton
Xi Iota Zeta, Galesburg, Illinois

HANGING-OF-THE-GREENS PUNCH

1 3-oz. package lime gelatin
1 6-oz. can pineapple juice
1 8-oz. bottle of lemon juice
3/4 oz. almond flavoring
1 1/2 c. sugar
1 32-oz. bottle of ginger ale
1 32-oz. bottle of club soda
Several drops of green food coloring (opt.)

Prepare gelatin according to package directions. Combine with remaining ingredients; stir until sugar dissolves. Pour over ice in punch bowl. Yield: 1 gallon.

Marlaine Marie Loftin
Alpha Upsilon Pi, Portland, Texas

MERRY LIME COOLER

1 qt. lime sherbet, softened
1 c. pineapple juice
1 qt. vanilla ice cream, softened
1 c. 7-Up

Blend first 3 ingredients. Stir in soda just before serving. Yield: 8-10 servings.

Barbara C. Nelson
Preceptor Rho, Ogden, Utah

SHAMROCK PUNCH

1 48-oz. can unsweetened pineapple juice
2 c. sugar
2 pkg. unsweetened lemon-lime drink mix
1 tsp. almond flavoring

Blend all ingredients in gallon container. Fill with water; chill.

Debra Sharpe
Epsilon Nu, Statesboro, Georgia

ST. PATRICK'S PUNCH

1 3-oz. package lime gelatin
1 6-oz. can frozen lemonade concentrate
2 c. pineapple juice
1 liter ginger ale, chilled

Dissolve gelatin in 1 cup boiling water. Stir in 2 cups cold water, concentrate and juice. Add ginger ale just before serving. Yield: 15-20 servings.

Barbara A. Bradford
Preceptor Phi, Gainesville, Georgia

VODKA LIME SLUSH

1 12-oz. can each frozen lemonade, limeade concentrate
2 c. vodka
2 c. sugar
7-Up

Mix concentrates, vodka and sugar with 9 cups water in freezer container. Freeze until slushy. Stir soda into each serving.

Dianne Whitten
Preceptor Gamma, Castle Rock, Washington

HOT ASPARAGUS CANAPES

1 3-oz. package blue cheese, softened
1 8-oz. package cream cheese, softened
1 egg, beaten
20 thin slices bread, trimmed
20 spears cooked asparagus
1/2 lb. butter, melted

Mix first 3 ingredients until smooth. Flatten bread with rolling pin. Spread with cheese mixture. Place 1 asparagus spear on each slice. Roll to enclose spear; fasten with toothpick. Dip in butter; place seam side down on baking sheet. Freeze partially. Slice into 3 sections. Store in freezer. Bake on baking sheet at 400 degrees for 15 minutes. Yield: 60 servings.

Kaye Lewis
Xi Beta Upsilon, Salamanca, New York

AVOCADO DIP

4 avocados, mashed
1 8-oz. package cream cheese, softened
1 tsp. lemon juice
3 tbsp. picante sauce
1/2 tsp. salt

Beat all ingredients until smooth. Serve with tortilla chips. Yield: 2 cups.

Sandy Torrance
Lambda Omicron, Wynnewood, Oklahoma

REUBEN TRIANGLES

1 16-oz. can chopped sauerkraut, drained
1 12-oz. can corned beef, flaked
1/2 c. shredded Monterey Jack cheese
1/2 c. taco sauce
2 tbsp. sliced green onion
1/2 tsp. crawawy seed
3 10-count cans refrigerator biscuits

Mix first 6 ingredients. Roll biscuits to 4-inch circles on lightly floured surface. Spoon filling in center of each circle. Moisten edge with water. Fold up to form triangle; pinch to seal. Bake on greased baking sheet at 400 degrees for 10 minutes. May freeze and reheat at 400 degrees for 10 minutes. Yield: 30 servings.

Lucy Carey
Beta Upsilon, Ames, Iowa

SPINACH BALLS

1 1/2 sticks butter, softened
6 eggs, beaten
1 c. Parmesan cheese

2 pkg. frozen chopped spinach, thawed, well drained
2 c. cheese and garlic-flavored croutons

Beat butter, eggs and Parmesan cheese. Stir in spinach and croutons. Chill for 1 hour. Shape into 2-inch balls. Bake on baking sheet at 375 degrees for 15 minutes. May freeze balls before baking. Yield: 2 dozen.

Dora E. Benavides
Nu, Huntsville, Alabama

SPINACH TORTILLA DELIGHT

2 pkg. frozen chopped spinach, thawed, well drained
6 green onions, chopped
1 pkg. ranch-style salad dressing mix

1 c. mayonnaise
1 jar real bacon bits
1 c. sour cream
10 lg. tortillas

Mix first 6 ingredients. Spread on tortillas; roll to enclose filling. Chill, wrapped in plastic wrap, overnight. Let stand at room temperature for 15 minutes before serving.

Judy Burt
Xi Sigma Pi, San Diego, California

VEGGIE SANDWICH SPREAD

1 10-oz. package frozen chopped spinach, thawed, well drained
1 pkg. Knorr's dry vegetable soup mix
1/2 c. chopped onion

1 c. salad dressing
1 8-oz. can water chestnuts, chopped
1 c. sour cream
Sandwich bread, trimmed

Mix first 6 ingredients. Chill overnight. Spread on bread to serve. Yield: 4 cups.

Ruth E. Meyers
Alpha Mu, Angola, Indiana

CHICKEN SALAD IN MELON RINGS

4 c. chopped cooked chicken
3 tbsp. lemon juice
1 c. sliced celery
1/3 c. chopped onion
1 2-oz. jar sliced pimento, drained
1/2 c. mayonnaise

1/4 c. chopped roasted almonds
1 c. seedless green grapes
1 tsp. salt
1/2 tsp. pepper
2 cantaloupes
Lettuce

Sprinkle chicken with lemon juice. Add next 8 ingredients; toss to mix. Chill, covered, in refrigerator. Slice ends off cantaloupes. Slice each cantaloupe crosswise into 3 rings. Place each on lettuce-lined serving plate. Spoon chicken salad into ring. Garnish with additional grapes. Yield: 6 servings.

Linda Arelene Whorley
Xi Beta Upsilon, Kingsport, Tennessee

CORNED BEEF SALAD

1 3-oz. package lime gelatin
2 tbsp. vinegar
1 12-oz. can corned beef, flaked
2 med. stalks celery, chopped

1 sm. onion, finely chopped
2 hard-boiled eggs, chopped
1 c. mayonnaise
2 tsp. horseradish
1/2 tsp. salt

Dissolve gelatin in 1 cup boiling water. Add vinegar. Chill for 1 hour or until partially set. Stir in remaining ingredients. Pour into 6 1/2-cup ring mold. Chill until set. Invert onto lettuce-lined serving plate. Yield: 8 servings.

Letitia Norman
Xi Iota, Belle Fourche, South Dakota

MINT SALAD

1 3-oz. package lime gelatin
1 sm. can crushed pineapple
1 c. miniature marshmallows

1 10-oz. carton whipped topping
1 8-oz. pkg. butter mints, crushed

Sprinkle gelatin over pineapple and marshmallows in bowl; mix well. Chill for several hours. Fold in remaining ingredients. Chill overnight. May be frozen. Yield: 6-8 servings.

Bonnie Bailey
Laureate Delta, Jefferson City, Missouri
Paula Schmidt
Theta Rho, San Marcos, California

38 / St. Patrick's Day

GRAPEFRUIT-AVOCADO SALAD

1 avocado, sliced
1 grapefruit, sectioned
Lettuce
1/3 c. sugar
1/4 tsp. salt
1 tsp. each dry mustard, poppy seed, paprika
1/3 c. honey
5 tbsp. vinegar
1 tbsp. lemon juice
1 c. oil

Arrange avocado and grapefruit on bed of sliced lettuce. Mix next 8 ingredients in bowl. Beat oil in gradually. Spoon over salad. Chill until serving time. Yield: 4 servings.

Jane C. Davis
Delta Zeta, Troy, Alabama

SPINACH SALAD

1 c. mayonnaise
1/2 tsp. salt
1/2 tsp. Tabasco sauce
2 tsp. vinegar
1/2 c. each finely chopped celery, onion
2 10-oz. packages frozen chopped spinach, thawed, drained
3 hard-boiled eggs, chopped
1 c. grated Cheddar cheese

Mix first 4 ingredients. Stir in celery, onion, spinach, eggs and cheese. Chill overnight.

Edythe Shelton
Laureate Eta, Salina, Kansas

CORNED BEEF AND CABBAGE

1 4-lb. corned beef brisket
8 sm. onions
4 potatoes, peeled, quartered
8 med. carrots
Caraway seed
1 med. head cabbage, cut into wedges

Cover brisket with cold water in stock pot. Simmer, tightly covered, for 3 1/2 hours or until tender; skim. Add onions, potatoes and carrots. Sprinkle with caraway seed. Simmer, covered, for 20 minutes; remove brisket to warm platter. Add cabbage. Simmer for 10 to 15 minutes or until vegetables are tender.

Judith C. Stevens
Xi Kappa Iota, McHenry, Illinois

DUBLIN DINNER

4 c. thinly sliced potatoes
1/2 tsp. salt
1 sm. head cabbage
1/2 c. mayonnaise
1 tbsp. mustard
1 tbsp. French salad dressing
1 12-oz. can corned beef, cut into 6 slices

Boil potatoes with salt in 1 cup water in covered skillet for 5 minutes. Push potatoes to center. Cut cabbage into 6 wedges. Place around potatoes. Simmer for 10 minutes or until tender; remove from heat. Combine mayonnaise, mustard and salad dressing. Arrange corned beef over potatoes. Pour half the dressing over corned beef. Serve with remaining dressing. Yield: 6 servings.

Helen McKenna
Xi Delta Phi, Kane, Pennsylvania

CORNED BEEF MIXTURE

1 12-oz. can corned beef
3 hard-boiled eggs
6 green onions with tops, finely chopped
4 cloves of garlic, finely chopped
1 med. dill pickle, finely chopped
1 stalk celery with leaves, finely chopped
2 jalapeno peppers, finely chopped
3 tbsp. chopped fresh parsley
1 tsp. crushed red pepper
Pinch of tarragon
1 tsp. horseradish
1 tbsp. prepared mustard
Mayonnaise
Paprika

Mash corned beef and eggs. Mix in next 8 ingredients. Stir in horseradish, mustard and enough mayonnaise to moisten to desired consistency. Shape into ball. Sprinkle with paprika. Chill overnight. Serve with crackers. Yield: 8 servings.

Ruby Allday
Phi, Long Beach, Mississippi

CRUSTY CORNED BEEF CASSEROLE

2 12-oz. cans corned beef, flaked
2 16-oz. cans cut green beans
2 tbsp. prepared mustard
1 c. chili sauce
1 10-oz. package corn bread mix
1/2 c. chopped ripe olives

Mix corned beef and next 3 ingredients. Spread in 8 x 12-inch baking dish. Prepare corn bread mix using package directions, adding olives. Spoon over corned beef mixture. Bake at 400 degrees for 40 minutes. Yield: 6-8 servings.

Ruth B. Scrimgeour
Preceptor Beta, Seattle, Washington

WHISKEY-GLAZED CORNED BEEF

6 to 7 lb. corned beef
1 clove of garlic
2 bay leaves
4 whole cloves
4 white peppercorns
3/4 c. blended whiskey
1/4 c. orange juice
3/4 c. packed brown sugar
1 tsp. mustard
1 lg. head cabbage, cut into 12 wedges

St. Patrick's Day / 39

Combine first 5 ingredients with 1/2 cup whiskey and enough water to cover in stock pot. Simmer, covered, for 3 to 4 hours or until tender; remove corned beef to roasting pan. Strain and reserve stock. Score fat. Heat orange juice, brown sugar, mustard, 2 tablespoons stock and 1/4 cup whiskey until blended, stirring constantly. Pour over corned beef. Bake at 400 degrees for 30 minutes, basting every 10 minutes. Simmer cabbage in remaining stock for 10 minutes or until tender. Serve with parsley-buttered new potatoes. Yield: 12 servings.

Naomi Champa
Xi Zeta Iota, Fairview Park, Ohio

BAIRD BEANS

1 1/8 c. pinto beans	1 lg. can tomatoes
Salt	1 tsp. (scant) chili
1 tsp. shortening	powder
1 to 1 1/2 lb. ground beef	1 tsp. sugar
1/2 onion, chopped	Pepper to taste

Boil beans with 1 teaspoon salt in about 3 cups water for 2 minutes; remove from heat. Let stand, covered, for 1 hour. Drain, leaving water to cover. Stir in shortening. Bring to a boil. Simmer, loosely covered, for 1 hour. Brown ground beef with onion, stirring frequently. Add to beans with remaining ingredients. Cook for 1 hour longer. Serve with fried potatoes. Yield: 6 servings.

Shari Baird
Xi Gamma, Cheyenne, Wyoming

STUFFED GREEN PEPPERS

1/2 lb. ground beef	12 oz. Monterey Jack
1 tbsp. oil	cheese, grated
1 lg. onion, chopped	2 tbsp. minced parsley
6 med. tomatoes, chopped	1 clove of garlic, minced
8 lg. green peppers, seeded	1/4 tsp. each basil, oregano
3 c. pinto beans, drained	1 tsp. salt
	1/4 tsp. pepper

Brown ground beef in oil; remove. Saute onion and tomatoes in pan drippings. Parboil green pepper in salted water for 3 minutes; drain. Mix remaining ingredients with ground beef, onion and tomatoes. Fill green pepper with mixture. Arrange close together in baking pan. Bake, covered, at 325 degrees for 30 minutes. Yield: 8 servings.

Sarah Barton
Alpha Kappa, Pascagoula, Mississippi

STUFFED CABBAGE ROLLS

1 lg. head cabbage, parboiled, drained	1/2 lb. ground beef
	1 lb. ground pork
1/2 c. rice	1/2 tsp. salt
1 egg	1/4 tsp. pepper
1 lg. onion, chopped	1 c. tomato juice
1 tbsp. chili powder	2 tsp. bacon drippings

Remove cabbage leaves. Mix next 8 ingredients. Place a small amount on each cabbage leaf; tuck ends in and roll to enclose filling. Place seam side down in baking pan. Chop remaining cabbage and place on top. Pour mixture of tomato juice, bacon drippings and 1/4 cup water over cabbage. Bake at 325 degrees for 1 1/2 hours. Yield: 6 servings.

Suzanne Bell
Xi Iota Gamma, Lufkin, Texas

LIMERICK HAM DINNER

1 3-lb. smoked boneless ham	2 16-oz. cans whole white potatoes
1 1/4 tsp. Tabasco sauce	1/2 c. minced parsley
6 whole cloves	1/4 c. prepared horseradish
1 clove of garlic	1/4 tsp. salt
1 bay leaf	1/2 c. whipping cream, whipped
1 tsp. celery seed	
1 3 1/2-lb. cabbage, cut into wedges	1 tbsp. chopped chives (opt.)

Place ham in large kettle with water to cover. Stir in 1 teaspoon Tabasco sauce, cloves, garlic, bay leaf and celery seed; cover tightly. Simmer for 1 3/4 hours or until tender. Remove to platter; keep warm. Boil cabbage, covered, in cooking liquid for 8 minutes or until tender-crisp. Heat potatoes. Drain; roll in parsley. Arrange with ham and cabbage on serving platter. Combine horseradish, 1/4 teaspoon Tabasco sauce and salt. Fold in whipped cream. Turn into serving dish; sprinkle with chives. Serve with ham.

Photograph for this recipe on page 35.

CROCK•POT IRISH STEW

2 lb. boneless lamb, cubed	4 med. potatoes, peeled, quartered
2 tsp. salt	1 sm. bay leaf
1/4 tsp. pepper	1/4 c. quick tapioca
2 med. carrots, cut into 1/2 in. slices	1 10-oz. package frozen peas
2 sm. onions, thinly sliced	

Sprinkle lamb with salt and pepper. Alternate layers of lamb, carrots, onions and potatoes in Crock·Pot. Add bay leaf, tapioca and 2 cups water. Cook, covered, on High for 1 hour. Cook on Low for 8 to 10 hours. Add peas. Cook for 1 to 2 hours longer. Yield: 4 servings.

Kathleen Garrett
Epsilon Lambda, Jackson, Michigan

40 / St. Patrick's Day

ST. PAT'S CHICKEN

1 2 1/2 to 3 1/2-lb. chicken, cut up
1/4 c. oil
1 sm. onion, chopped
1/2 clove of garlic, minced
2 8-oz. cans tomato sauce
1 green pepper, cut into strips
1/2 tsp. salt
1/4 tsp. pepper
1 c. Burgundy
6 oz. spaghetti, broken, cooked

Brown chicken in oil; remove. Saute onion and garlic in pan drippings. Stir in tomato sauce, green pepper, salt and pepper. Add chicken. Simmer, covered, for 1 hour. Add Burgundy. Simmer for 10 minutes longer. Serve over spaghetti. Yield: 6-8 servings.

Barbara P. Fowler
Laureate Theta, Richland, Washington

GOURMET STUFFED CORNISH HENS

10 slices bacon
1 12-oz. can beer
1 8-oz. package seasoned stuffing mix
4 Cornish game hens
Salt and pepper to taste

Cook 6 slices bacon until crisp; drain on paper towel and crumble. Mix 1 cup beer with bacon drippings. Add stuffing mix and crumbled bacon; toss to moisten. Sprinkle hens with salt and pepper. Stuff with stuffing mixture. Place breast side up in baking pan. Top each with 1 slice bacon. Bake at 475 degrees for 15 minutes or until lightly browned. Reduce temperature to 350 degrees. Baste with beer. Bake for 30 minutes or until tender, basting frequently with remaining beer. Yield: 4 servings.

Norma Mathis
Preceptor Epsilon Alpha, Hanford, California

BROCCOLI WITH PARMESAN

1 onion, minced
6 tbsp. margarine
1/4 c. flour
2 c. milk
1 egg yolk
1 c. Parmesan cheese
1/2 tsp. salt
1/8 tsp. pepper
2 1/2 lb. broccoli, cooked
1/2 c. bread crumbs

Saute onion in 1/4 cup margarine. Stir in flour. Add milk gradually. Cook until thickened, stirring constantly. Add a small amount of hot mixture to egg yolk; stir egg yolk into hot mixture. Stir in cheese, salt and pepper. Pour half the sauce into 2-quart baking dish. Arrange broccoli on top. Cover with remaining sauce. Sprinkle with bread crumbs. Dot with 2 tablespoons margarine. Bake at 400 degrees for 20 minutes. Yield: 8 servings.

Claire Hebert
Preceptor Delta, Sulphur, Louisiana

IRISH-BRAISED CABBAGE

1 med. head Savoy cabbage, quartered
1/4 c. chopped onion
2 tbsp. butter
2 lg. tomatoes, peeled, seeded, chopped
1 tbsp. flour
1 c. chicken bouillon
Salt and pepper to taste
2 tsp. finely chopped parsley
1/4 c. sour cream

Pour boiling water over cabbage. Let stand for 10 minutes. Drain and pat dry. Place in casserole. Saute onion in butter. Add tomatoes. Stir in flour and bouillon. Bring to a boil, stirring constantly. Add seasonings. Spoon over cabbage. Bake, covered, at 375 degrees for 30 minutes, basting occasionally. Stir several tablespoons sauce from cabbage into sour cream. Pour over cabbage. Bake for 10 to 15 minutes longer.

Terry Walker
Xi Pi, Pittsburg, Kansas

CHICKEN-FLAVORED COLCANNON

1 lb. potatoes, cooked, peeled
1/2 c. evaporated skim milk
1 tbsp. margarine
Salt to taste
White pepper to taste
2 env. instant chicken broth mix
2 c. shredded cabbage
3/4 c. shredded leeks

Mash potatoes with milk, margarine and seasonings. Prepare chicken broth using package instructions. Add cabbage and leeks. Cook until tender; drain. Stir into potato mixture. Bake in greased 1-quart casserole at 350 degrees for 20 minutes. Yield: 4 servings.

Nancy Kimmel
Xi Epsilon Psi, Terre Haute, Indiana

VEGETABLE CASSEROLE

1 pkg. frozen French-style green beans
1 pkg. frozen peas, cooked
1 pkg. frozen fordhook lima beans
1 can water chestnuts
1 1/3 c. mayonnaise
1 med. onion, grated
1 tsp. mustard
1 tsp. Worcestershire sauce
1/4 tsp. Tabasco sauce
Juice of 1/2 lemon
Garlic powder and salt to taste
2 hard-boiled eggs, grated

Cook green beans, peas and lima beans until just tender; drain. Mix remaining ingredients except eggs. Stir into vegetables. Bake in 2-quart casserole at 350 degrees for 25 minutes. Top with grated eggs. Bake for 5 minutes longer. Yield: 8-10 servings.

Oneta Gentry
Xi Alpha Mu, Birmingham, Alabama

St. Patrick's Day / 41

COLCANNON

6 scallions with tops, chopped
1/2 c. milk
1 tsp. MSG
3 tbsp. butter
1 env. instant mashed potatoes
2 c. shredded cooked cabbage
Salt to taste

Simmer scallions in milk until tender. Add 1 1/2 cups water, MSG and 2 tablespoons butter. Bring to a boil; remove from heat. Beat in mashed potatoes until fluffy. Stir in cabbage and salt. Pour 1 tablespoon melted butter over top. Yield: 4 servings.

Carol D. Drumluk
Gamma Iota, Rome, New York

POTATO SOUP

2 sticks margarine, melted
3/4 c. flour
1 1/2 tbsp. pepper
11 c. milk
6 med. potatoes, cooked, mashed
2 lb. Velveeta cheese, grated

Blend margarine, flour and pepper in saucepan. Stir in 3 cups milk. Cook until thickened, stirring constantly. Stir in remaining milk. Bring to a boil. Cook for 5 minutes; remove from heat. Stir in potatoes and cheese. Yield: 32 servings.

Sharen Nichols
Alpha Chi Eta, Round Rock, Texas

NOODLES WITH PESTO SAUCE

1 c. chopped parsley
1 tbsp. basil leaves
1 tsp. salt
1/8 tsp. white pepper
2 cloves of garlic, crushed
1/2 c. olive oil
2 tbsp. butter
3/4 c. Parmesan cheese
1/4 c. finely chopped walnuts
1 8-oz. package noodles, cooked

Mix all ingredients except noodles. Pour over noodles in bowl; toss lightly. Yield: 4 servings.

Susan Thomas
Epsilon Mu, Cavan, Ontario, Canada

HOT MUSTARD

1/4 c. sugar
1/4 c. dry mustard
2 tbsp. flour
Dash of salt
1/3 c. vinegar
1 16-oz. jar mustard

Mix first 4 ingredients in bowl. Stir in 3 tablespoons boiling water to make a thick paste. Blend in vinegar and mustard. Chill in airtight container overnight. Serve with corned beef or ham. Yield: 2 cups.

Jane Koehn
Laureate Alpha Zeta, Jacksonville, Florida

AVOCADO BREAD

1 stick butter, softened
3/4 c. sugar
2 eggs
3/4 c. mashed avocado
1 tsp. lemon juice
1/3 c. milk
2 c. flour
1 tsp. baking powder
1/2 tsp. soda
1/4 tsp. salt
1/2 c. coarsely chopped almonds

Cream butter and sugar. Mix in eggs and avocado. Mix lemon juice and milk. Add to avocado mixture alternately with sifted dry ingredients, beating well after each addition. Stir in almonds. Bake in greased loaf pan at 350 degrees for 1 hour.

Lynn Reves
Theta Theta, Altus, Oklahoma

HOLIDAY IRISH BREAD

1/2 box raisins
1 c. chopped nuts
2 c. sugar
1 tsp. each cinnamon, allspice, nutmeg
2 sticks margarine
2 eggs, beaten
3 c. flour
1 tsp. soda

Bring first 3 ingredients, spices, margarine and 2 cups water to a boil over low heat. Cool to room temperature. Mix in eggs, flour and soda. Bake in 2 greased loaf pans at 300 degrees for 2 hours. Yield: 12 servings.

Kathy Gibbons
Preceptor Zeta, Redford, Michigan

IRISH FRECKLE BREAD

2 pkg. dry yeast
1 c. warm potato water
1/2 c. lukewarm mashed potatoes
1/2 c. sugar
5 1/4 c. flour
1 tsp. salt
2 eggs, beaten
1/2 c. margarine, melted
1 c. raisins
1/2 c. golden raisins (opt.)

Dissolve yeast in potato water. Beat in potatoes, 2 tablespoons sugar and 1 cup flour. Let rise, covered, for 30 minutes or until bubbly. Stir dough down. Mix in 6 tablespoons sugar, salt and 1 cup flour. Mix in eggs, margarine and raisins. Stir in enough remaining flour to make soft dough. Knead on lightly floured surface until smooth and elastic. Place in greased bowl, turning to grease surface. Let rise, covered, until doubled in bulk. Shape into 4 loaves. Place 2 side by side in each of 2 greased 5 x 9-inch loaf pans. Let rise until doubled in bulk. Bake at 350 degrees for 35 to 50 minutes or until bread tests done. Cool on wire rack. Yield: 2 loaves.

Katie Dvorak
Xi Lambda Xi, Clarendon, Texas

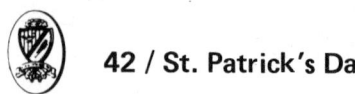

IRISH BROWN BREAD

1 1/2 c. stone-ground
  whole wheat flour
1/2 c. wheat germ
1 c. self-rising flour
1/4 tsp. salt
1 tsp. soda
2 c. buttermilk
Melted butter

Mix first 4 ingredients. Make a well in center. Stir in mixture of soda and buttermilk. Place dough in lightly greased 8-inch round baking pan. Cut shallow cross on top. Bake at 400 degrees for 1 hour. Cool in pan on rack for 5 minutes. Brush with melted butter. Remove from pan to cool completely.

Maureen U. Fitzgerald
Xi Gamma Lambda, Falls Church, Virginia

QUICK IRISH SODA BREAD

6 tbsp. shortening
2 c. baking mix
1 tbsp. sugar
1/2 c. raisins
1 tbsp. caraway seed
3/4 c. milk

Cut shortening into biscuit mix until crumbly. Mix in next 3 ingredients. Stir in milk. Bake in greased 9-inch pan at 375 degrees for 30 minutes. Yield: 6 servings.

Jean Vincent
Preceptor Iota Nu, Ukiah, California

WHOLE WHEAT SODA BREAD

1 c. all-purpose flour
2 tbsp. brown sugar
1 tsp. soda
1/2 tsp. salt
1/4 c. margarine
2 c. whole wheat flour
1/3 c. oats
1 1/2 c. buttermilk

Combine all-purpose flour, brown sugar, soda and salt. Cut in 2 tablespoons margarine until crumbly. Mix in whole wheat flour and oats. Stir in buttermilk and 2 tablespoons melted margarine. Knead on floured surface 10 times. Shape into ball. Place in greased 9-inch pie plate. Slash cross on top. Bake at 375 degrees for 40 to 50 minutes. Cool slightly before serving.

Mary Charles
Preceptor Theta Xi, Pleasanton, California

SHAMROCK ROLLS

1 cake yeast
1/2 c. mashed potatoes
1/4 c. shortening
1/4 c. sugar
1 1/2 tsp. salt
1 c. milk, scalded
1 egg, beaten
4 to 4 1/2 c. sifted
  flour
Melted butter

Soften yeast in 1/4 cup warm water. Mix next 5 ingredients; cool. Stir in yeast mixture and egg. Add 2 cups flour. Mix in remaining flour gradually. Knead on floured surface for 6 to 8 minutes. Let rise, covered, until doubled in bulk. Punch dough down. Let rise for 10 minutes longer. Shape into rolls. Place in greased pan. Let rise until doubled in bulk. Bake at 400 degrees for 10 to 12 minutes. Brush with butter. Yield: 2 dozen.

Diane Lindburg
Delta Chi, Prineville, Oregon

FROZEN MINT MALLOW

20 chocolate sandwich
  cookies, crushed
1/4 c. butter, melted
32 marshmallows
1/2 c. milk
1/2 c. Creme de Menthe
1 pt. whipping cream

Combine cookie crumbs with butter. Reserve 1/4 cup for topping. Press remaining crumbs into bottom of 9-inch springform pan. Melt marshmallows with milk in double boiler. Stir in Creme de Menthe. Chill until slightly thickened. Whip cream until slightly thickened. Add marshmallow mixture gradually, beating until stiff. Pour into prepared pan. Sprinkle with reserved crumbs. Freeze. Yield: 6-8 servings.

Jackie Corker
Delta Kappa, Mississauga, Ontario, Canada

GRASSHOPPER CREPES

2 eggs
1/2 c. flour
1 tbsp. each sugar,
  cocoa
2/3 c. buttermilk
3 tbsp. Vandermint
  Liqueur
2 tbsp. melted butter
1/4 c. milk
1 10-oz. package
  miniature
  marshmallows
1/4 c. green Creme
  de Menthe
2 c. whipping cream,
  whipped
2 drops of green food
  coloring

Beat eggs until frothy. Beat in dry ingredients alternately with buttermilk. Mix in 1 tablespoon Vandermint Liqueur and butter. Chill for 1 hour. Make 8-inch crepes, using 3 tablespoons batter for each, according to directions with crepe pan. Combine milk and marshmallows in double boiler. Heat until marshmallows are melted; cool. Beat in remaining Vandermint Liqueur and Creme de Menthe. Fold in whipped cream and food coloring. Chill in refrigerator. Spoon filling onto crepes and fold over to enclose filling. Chill until serving time. Garnish with additional whipped cream and grated chocolate. Yield: 8-10 servings.

Barbara Ashton
Preceptor Xi, Sherwood Park, Alberta, Canada

MINTED ANGEL ALLEGRETTI

1 pkg. angel food
  cake mix
2 1/4 c. miniature
  marshmallows
1/2 c. milk
1/4 c. green Creme de
  Menthe
1/4 tsp. salt

St. Patrick's Day / 43

6 drops of green
   food coloring
1 pt. whipping cream,
   whipped
1 1-oz. packet
   premelted
   unsweetened
   chocolate

Prepare and bake cake mix according to package directions; cool. Split into 3 layers. Melt marshmallows with milk, stirring until blended; cool. Stir in Creme de Menthe, salt and food coloring. Fold in whipped cream. Spread 1 cup frosting between each layer. Spread remaining over top and side of cake. Drizzle chocolate around edge. Chill until serving time. Yield: 16 servings.

Suzanne Williams
Pi Beta, Diamond Bar, California

IRISH MINT DESSERT

1 6-oz. package
   lime gelatin
1/4 tsp. peppermint
   extract
4 1/2 oz. whipped
   topping
8 chocolate mint
   cookies, crumbled

Dissolve gelatin in 2 cups boiling water. Stir in 2 cups cold water and flavoring. Chill for 1 1/2 hours or until partially set. Pour 1 1/3 cups gelatin into 5 x 9-inch loaf pan. Chill for 5 minutes. Blend whipped topping into remaining gelatin. Spoon 1/3 of the topping mixture over gelatin layer. Sprinkle with half the cookie crumbs. Repeat layers. Chill until firm. Yield: 10-12 servings.

Vickie Thomas
Gamma Delta, Weiser, Idaho

MARGO'S MINT MARVEL

1 3-oz. package lime
   gelatin
1 3-oz. package
   chocolate pudding
   mix
1 1/3 c. milk
1/2 tsp. peppermint
   extract
1/2 c. butter, melted
1 box chocolate
   wafers, crushed
1 c. sugar
1 8-oz. package
   cream cheese,
   softened
1 8-oz. carton
   whipped topping

Dissolve gelatin in 1 cup boiling water; cool. Cook pudding with milk until thick. Stir in peppermint extract; cool. Mix butter and chocolate wafer crumbs; reserve 1/3 cup for topping. Press remaining crumb mixture into 9 x 13-inch pan. Cream sugar and cream cheese. Stir in gelatin. Fold in whipped topping. Pour half the mixture into crust. Chill until set. Spread pudding over top. Spread remaining gelatin mixture over pudding. Sprinkle with reserved crumbs. Chill until set. Yield: 12-16 servings.

Margo Laughlin
Preceptor Iota Sigma, Los Osos, California

IRISH MIST CREAM

4 eggs, separated
2 tbsp. honey
2 1/2 c. milk, scalded
7 tsp. unflavored gelatin
1/2 c. Irish Mist liqueur
1 1/2 c. whipping cream,
   whipped

Blend egg yolks and honey. Stir in a small amount of hot milk; stir egg yolks into hot milk. Simmer until thick, stirring constantly. Do not boil. Soften gelatin in a small amount of warm water. Stir into yolk mixture; cool. Blend liqueur with 3/4 of the whipped cream. Fold in stiffly beaten egg whites. Stir into yolk mixture. Pour into 2-quart serving bowl. Chill for 2 hours or longer. Top with remaining whipped cream. Yield: 6-8 servings.

W. Marie Hickey
Laureate, Charlottetown, Prince Edward Island, Canada

IRISH TRIFLE

1 10-oz. can sliced
   peaches
1 3-oz. package peach
   gelatin
1/3 c. Sherry
1 8-in. sponge cake,
   cut into 1-in. cubes
1 1/2 c. milk
1/2 c. light cream
1 sm. package vanilla
   instant pudding mix
1 pkg. whipped topping
   mix
Green food coloring

Drain peaches, reserving juice. Add enough cold water to juice to measure 1 cup. Dissolve gelatin in 1 cup boiling water; add peach juice. Chill until partially set. Sprinkle Sherry over cake cubes in serving bowl. Arrange peaches over cake. Spoon gelatin mixture over top. Chill until set. Beat milk, cream and pudding mix for 1 to 2 minutes or until well blended. Spoon over congealed layer. Chill for 30 minutes. Top with whipped topping tinted with food coloring. Yield: 8 servings.

Sally Funderburk
Xi Pi, Gainesville, Georgia

FROZEN LEMON DESSERT

3 c. vanilla wafer crumbs
1/2 c. butter, melted
6 eggs, separated
1 can sweetened condensed
   milk
1 6-oz. can frozen
   lemonade concentrate
1 pt. whipping cream,
   whipped
3/4 c. sugar

Mix vanilla wafer crumbs with butter. Press into 9 x 13-inch baking dish. Combine beaten egg yolks with condensed milk; beat well. Beat in frozen lemonade. Fold in whipped cream. Pour over crust. Beat egg whites until soft peaks form. Add sugar gradually, beating until stiff. Spread over filling. Brown lightly under broiler. Chill for 1 hour. Freeze until firm. Yield: 20-22 servings.

Ruth Ferguson
Preceptor Iota, Boulder, Colorado

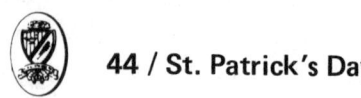

PISTACHIO ICE CREAM DESSERT

45 butter crackers, crushed
1 stick margarine, melted
3 pkg. pistachio instant pudding mix
2 1/4 c. milk
1 1/2 qt. vanilla ice cream, softened
12 to 16 oz. whipped topping
4 to 5 med. Heath candy bars, chilled, finely crushed

Mix cracker crumbs and margarine. Press into bottom of 9 x 13-inch baking pan. Beat pudding mix and milk until well blended. Add ice cream; beat until smooth. Pour into pie shell. Chill. Spread whipped topping over top. Sprinkle with crushed candy. Chill in refrigerator overnight. May be frozen. Yield: 12-15 servings.

Irene G. Berghoff
Laureate Alpha Kappa, Bethalto, Illinois

CREME DE MENTHE CAKE

1 pkg. white cake mix
Green Creme de Menthe
1 jar fudge ice cream topping
1 tbsp. white Creme de Cacao
1 12-oz. carton whipped topping

Prepare cake mix according to package directions, adding 1/4 cup Creme de Menthe. Bake in 9 x 13-inch baking pan according to package directions. Spread fudge topping over warm cake; Blend 3 tablespoons Creme de Menthe and Creme de Cacao into whipped topping. Spread over cake. Yield: 15 servings.

Myrt Combs
Laureate Eta, Coeur d'Alene, Idaho

PISTACHIO CAKE

1 pkg. white cake mix
3 eggs
1 c. oil
1 c. chopped walnuts
1 c. club soda
2 pkg. pistachio instant pudding mix
2 env. whipped topping mix
1 1/2 c. milk

Beat first 5 ingredients and 1 package pudding mix for 2 to 3 minutes. Bake in greased 9 x 12-inch pan at 350 degrees for 40 minutes. Beat 1 package pudding mix, whipped topping mix and milk until stiff. Spread on cake. Yield: 12 servings.

Shirley Flournoy
Laureate Lambda, Likely, California

MINT CAKE

1 c. chocolate chips
Milk
2 c. graham cracker crumbs
1/2 tsp. vanilla extract
2 1/2 c. confectioners' sugar
1/2 c. chopped walnuts
1/4 c. butter, softened
1 tsp. peppermint extract
Several drops of green food coloring

Melt chocolate chips with 1/2 cup milk over low heat. Mix in cracker crumbs, vanilla, 1/2 cup confectioners' sugar and walnuts. Press into buttered 8 x 9-inch pan. Mix butter, 2 cups confectioners' sugar, peppermint extract, food coloring and 2 tablespoons milk. Spread on cake. Chill until serving time. Yield: 24 servings.

Freeda Sanderson
Pi, Killarney, Manitoba, Canada

IRISH KISSES

3 egg whites
1/4 tsp. cream of tartar
1 tsp. vanilla extract
1/4 tsp. peppermint extract
Dash of salt
1 c. sugar
36 chocolate kiss candies
Green sugar crystals

Beat egg whites with next 4 ingredients until soft peaks form. Add sugar gradually, beating until stiff. Drop by tablespoonfuls 1 1/2 inches apart on ungreased cookie sheet. Press candy kiss into top of each cookie. Bring meringue up and over candy with spatula, covering completely; swirl top. Sprinkle with sugar crystals. Bake at 275 degrees for 30 minutes. Remove to rack to cool. Yield: 3 dozen.

Deena Swink
Eta Tau, Dongola, Illinois

RUSSIAN MINTS

1 c. margarine, softened
2 c. sifted confectioners' sugar
4 sq. unsweetened chocolate, melted
4 eggs
1 tsp. peppermint flavoring
2 tsp. vanilla extract
Vanilla wafers
1 c. whipping cream, whipped
Chopped nuts
Cherries

Cream margarine and sugar. Blend in chocolate. Beat in eggs and flavorings. Layer vanilla wafer, chocolate mixture, whipped cream and nuts in lined muffin cups. Top with cherry. Freeze until firm. Yield: 2 dozen.

Sue Ferguson
Preceptor Beta, Houston, Texas

PISTACHIO-ALMOND CHEESECAKE

1 c. flour
Confectioners' sugar
1/2 c. margarine, softened
1/4 c. ground almonds
1 8-oz. package cream cheese, softened
4 c. whipped topping
2 pkg. pistachio instant pudding mix
2 1/2 c. milk

Mix flour, 2 tablespoons confectioners' sugar, margarine and almonds. Press into 9 x 13-inch cake pan. Bake at 350 degrees until lightly browned; cool. Blend 2/3 cup confectioners' sugar and cream cheese. Fold in 2 cups whipped topping. Spread over cooled crust. Beat pudding mix with milk in mixer bowl until thick. Spread over cream cheese layer. Spread remaining 2 cups whipped topping over top. Garnish with slivered almonds.

Elaine Cooper
Alpha Mu, Sherwood Park, Alberta, Canada

IRISH CREAM CHEESECAKE

1 1/2 c. graham cracker crumbs	1/2 c. milk
Sugar	3 8-oz. packages cream cheese, softened
6 tbsp. melted butter	3 eggs
1 sm. package French vanilla instant pudding mix	1 c. sour cream
	3/4 c. confectioners' sugar
Irish cream liqueur	

Mix graham cracker crumbs, 1/2 cup sugar and butter. Press into bottom and 2 1/2 inches up side of greased springform pan. Blend pudding, 1/3 cup sugar, 1 cup liqueur and milk. Cook until thickened and bubbly. Spoon into bowl to cool. Beat cream cheese until fluffy. Beat in eggs. Beat in pudding mixture. Pour into crust. Bake at 375 degrees for 50 minutes. Blend 1 tablespoon liqueur, sour cream and confectioners' sugar. Spread over top. Bake for 2 minutes longer.

Barbara Bernhard
Xi Omega, Carson City, Nevada

IRISH SHAMROCK COOKIES

1/4 c. butter, softened	1 egg
1 sm. package pistachio instant pudding mix	1 tbsp. sugar
	Confectioners' sugar frosting, tinted green
1 1/3 c. baking mix	

Cream butter and pudding mix. Add baking mix, egg and sugar; mix well. Roll on lightly floured board to 3/8-inch thickness. Cut with shamrock-shaped cookie cutter. Bake on lightly greased cookie sheet at 350 degrees for 9 to 10 minutes. Cool on wire racks. Top with frosting. Yield: 1 1/2 dozen.

Jane Cervantes
Beta Lambda, Dayton, Ohio

BLARNEY STONES

2 c. sugar	4 tsp. baking powder
4 eggs, separated	1 tsp. vanilla extract
2 c. flour	Melted butter
Half and half	Green food coloring (opt.)
2 boxes confectioners' sugar	2 1/2 to 3 pkg. crushed peanuts

Cream sugar and egg yolks until fluffy. Beat in flour and baking powder alternately with 1 cup boiling water. Fold in stiffly beaten egg whites and vanilla. Bake in 9 x 13-inch baking pan at 325 degrees for 45 minutes; cool. Cut into 1 1/2-inch squares. Mix enough melted butter and half and half with confectioners' sugar to make of spreading consistency. Stir in food coloring. Frost squares on all sides. Roll in peanuts. Yield: 3 1/3 dozen.

Vera V. Spencer
Xi Gamma Omicron, Wichita, Kansas

CREME DE MENTHE BARS

3 sticks margarine	1 tsp. vanilla extract
1 c. sugar	1 can chocolate syrup
4 eggs	2 c. confectioners' sugar
1 c. flour	2 tbsp. Creme de Menthe
1/2 tsp. salt	1 1/2 c. chocolate chips

Cream 1 stick margarine and sugar. Beat in eggs. Stir in next 4 ingredients. Bake in ungreased 10 x 15-inch pan at 350 degrees for 30 minutes; cool. Blend 1 stick melted margarine, confectioners' sugar and Creme de Menthe. Spread over first layer. Chill until firm. Melt remaining stick of margarine with chocolate chips. Spread over top. Cut into bars to serve. Yield: 40 servings.

Alice M. Hoelzer
Alpha Zeta, Sandusky, Ohio

GRASSHOPPER SQUARES

4 3/4 c. confectioners' sugar	1/2 tsp. peppermint extract
1 c. butter, softened	1 3-oz. package cream cheese, softened
2 sq. unsweetened chocolate, melted	1 tsp. vanilla extract
1 1/2 c. flour	6 drops of green food coloring
1/2 tsp. baking powder	Chocolate decorator candies
1/4 tsp. salt	
4 tbsp. milk	

Cream 3/4 cup confectioners' sugar and 3/4 cup butter. Stir in chocolate. Mix in flour, baking powder, salt, 1 tablespoon milk and 1/4 teaspoon peppermint extract. Press into greased 9 x 13-inch baking pan. Bake at 325 degrees for 15 to 25 minutes; cool. Blend 4 cups confectioners' sugar, cream cheese, 1/4 cup butter, 3 tablespoons milk, vanilla, 1/4 teaspoon peppermint flavoring and green food coloring. Spread over top. Sprinkle with chocolate candies. Chill in refrigerator. Yield: 4 dozen.

Debby Brabander
Omicron, Great Bend, Kansas

46 / St. Patrick's Day

MINT SWIRL BROWNIES

5 tbsp. butter, softened
1 3-oz. package cream cheese, softened
3/4 c. sugar
2 eggs
2/3 c. flour
1/2 tsp. baking powder
1/4 tsp. salt
1/3 c. chopped nuts
2 sq. unsweetened chocolate
1/2 tsp. peppermint extract
Several drops of green food coloring
1 c. confectioners' sugar
1/2 tsp. vanilla extract

Cream 1/4 cup butter, cream cheese and sugar. Beat in eggs. Stir in combined flour, baking powder and salt. Spoon half the batter into another bowl. Stir nuts and 1 square melted chocolate into half the batter. Drop by tablespoonfuls in a checkerboard pattern into greased 9 x 9-inch baking pan. Stir peppermint flavoring and food coloring into remaining batter. Drop by tablespoonfuls into empty spaces; swirl with knife. Bake at 350 degrees for 15 to 20 minutes; cool. Melt 1 square chocolate and 1 tablespoon butter over low heat, stirring constantly. Stir in confectioners' sugar and vanilla until crumbly. Add about 2 tablespoons boiling water, or enough to make of pouring consistency. Pour over brownies. Yield: 2 dozen.

Cathy Thompson
Delta Tau, Thomaston, Georgia

CHOCOLATE-LIME SWIRL PIE

25 to 30 chocolate wafers
3 tbsp. melted butter
1 3-oz. package lime gelatin
1/4 c. sugar
1 tsp. grated lemon rind
1/4 c. lemon juice
10 drops of green food coloring
1 c. evaporated milk, partially frozen

Reserve 12 wafers. Crush remaining wafers. Mix crumbs and butter; reserve 1/4 cup for topping. Press remaining crumbs into 9-inch pie plate. Line side with reserved whole wafers. Dissolve gelatin and sugar in 3/4 cup boiling water. Mix in lemon rind, half the lemon juice and food coloring. Chill until partially set. Beat evaporated milk until stiff. Add 2 tablespoons lemon juice. Beat until very stiff. Fold in gelatin mixture. Spoon into crust. Sprinkle reserved crumbs over top. Chill until firm.

Jacqueline Craig
Preceptor Beta, Pointe Claire, Quebec, Canada

DIVINE GRASSHOPPER PIE

1 1/2 c. chocolate cookie crumbs
1/4 c. melted butter
3 c. miniature marshmallows
1/2 c. milk
1/4 c. Creme de Menthe
3 tbsp. Creme de Cacao
1 1/2 c. whipping cream, whipped
Several drops of green food coloring (opt.)

Mix cookie crumbs and butter. Press into bottom and side of 9-inch pie plate. Bake at 350 degrees for 10 minutes; cool. Melt marshmallows with milk, stirring constantly. Stir in liqueurs. Chill until thickened. Fold into whipped cream. Stir in food coloring. Spoon into crust. Garnish with chocolate shavings or additional chocolate cookie crumbs. Yield: 6-8 servings.

Martha Bein
Xi Zeta Lambda, Aurora, Illinois

DAIQUIRI PIE

1 8-oz. package cream cheese, softened
1 can sweetened condensed milk
1 6-oz. can frozen limeade concentrate, thawed
1/3 c. light rum
Several drops of green food coloring
1/2 pt. whipping cream, whipped
1 baked 9-in. pie shell

Beat cream cheese in mixer bowl until fluffy. Add condensed milk and limeade concentrate; beat until smooth. Stir in rum and food coloring. Fold in whipped cream. Pour into cooled pie shell. Freeze for 4 hours or chill for 2 hours. Garnish with lime twists. Yield: 6-8 servings.

Benetta Sanders
Xi Kappa, Winnemucca, Nevada

FROSTY MINT ICE CREAM PIE

1 pkg. devil's food cake mix
3/4 c. chocolate fudge frosting
1/4 c. oil
1 1/2 qt. mint-chocolate chip ice cream, softened

Combine cake mix, frosting, oil and 3/4 cup water in mixer bowl. Beat at low speed until moistened. Beat at high speed for 2 minutes. Spoon into 2 well-greased 9-inch round baking pans. Bake at 350 degrees for 25 to 30 minutes; cool completely. Spread ice cream in center of each, leaving 1/2-inch rim around sides. Freeze for 2 hours.

Carol Singleton
Delta Omega, Danville, Kentucky

HEAVENLY HOT FUDGE SAUCE

1 stick butter or margarine
1 1/4 c. sugar
4 tbsp. cocoa
1 can Milnot

Melt butter or margarine in heavy skillet. Add sugar and cocoa, stirring constantly. Add Milnot slowly, stirring constantly. Bring to a boil. Pour over ice cream.

Carol Collier
Xi Delta Mu, Connersville, Indiana

Recipes on pages 48, 50, 53 and 57.

Easter

ORANGE JULIUS

1 6-oz. can frozen orange juice concentrate
1 c. milk
1/2 c. sugar
1/2 tsp. vanilla extract
10 to 12 ice cubes

Process all ingredients in blender container with 1 cup water for 30 seconds or until smooth.

Terry Utterback
Theta Rho, New Hampton, Iowa

EASTER CHEESE MOLD

1 16-oz. package dry curd cottage cheese
1/3 c. butter, softened
2 tbsp. milk
3/4 c. finely chopped M and M's plain chocolate candies

Combine all ingredients in mixer bowl. Beat at medium speed until blended. Place in oiled 1-quart mold. Chill for 2 hours or overnight. Unmold on plate. Spread on celery, carrots, apples or warm bread.

Photograph for this recipe on page 47.

APRICOT SALAD

1/2 c. sugar
1 20-oz. can pineapple
1 3-oz. package apricot gelatin
5 tbsp. milk
1 8-oz. package cream cheese, softened
1 4-oz. carton whipped topping

Bring sugar and pineapple to a boil. Stir in gelatin; cool until partially set. Whip milk and cream cheese. Fold cream cheese mixture and whipped topping into gelatin. Chill in refrigerator for several hours. Yield: 10-12 servings.

Mim Nichol
Xi Zeta Lambda, North Aurora, Illinois

EASTER SALAD

2 pkg. lemon gelatin
Green food coloring
1 20-oz. can crushed pineapple
1 env. whipped topping mix, prepared
1 8-oz. package cream cheese, softened
1 tbsp. lemon juice
3/4 c. sugar
2 tbsp. flour
2 egg yolks
Coconut (opt.)

Prepare gelatin using package directions, tinting with food coloring. Drain pineapple, reserving juice. Stir pineapple into gelatin. Chill until set. Mix whipped topping and cream cheese until well blended. Spread on gelatin layer. Add enough water to pineapple juice to measure 1 cup. Combine with next 4 ingredients. Cook until thick; cool. Spread over cream cheese layer. Sprinkle with coconut. Yield: 12-15 servings.

Joetta J. Shain
Xi Tau, Charlestown, Indiana

CARROT SALAD

1/2 lb. carrots, grated
3/4 c. chopped black walnuts
3/4 c. chopped raisins
1/2 c. mayonnaise
1 tsp. sugar
1 tbsp. lemon juice

Mix carrots, walnuts and raisins. Blend mayonnaise, sugar and lemon juice. Add to carrot mixture, stirring to coat. Yield: 6 servings.

Peggy Roemer
Laureate Delta, Louisville, Kentucky

FROZEN FRUIT CUP

2 10-oz. packages frozen sliced strawberries, thawed
2 20-oz. cans crushed pineapple
6 bananas, sliced
1 16-oz. can mandarin oranges
2 6-oz. cans frozen orange juice concentrate, thawed
1/3 c. lemon juice

Combine all fruits and juices. Fill individual molds full. Freeze; thaw for 30 to 60 minutes before serving. Yield: 25 servings.

Ivy Subacz
Preceptor Alpha Beta, Kalamazoo, Michigan

FROSTED SALAD

2 sm. packages lemon gelatin
2 c. 7-Up
1 20-oz. can crushed pineapple
2 c. miniature marshmallows
2 lg. bananas, sliced
2 c. pineapple juice
1 c. sugar
1/4 c. flour
2 eggs, slightly beaten
1/4 c. butter
1 8-oz. package cream cheese, softened
1 env. whipped topping mix, prepared
1 c. chopped nuts
1 c. shredded coconut

Dissolve gelatin in 2 cups boiling water. Stir in 7-Up. Chill until partially set. Fold in pineapple, marshmallows and bananas. Chill until set. Simmer pineapple juice, sugar, flour and eggs until thick. Stir in butter; cool. Stir in cream cheese; chill. Fold in whipped topping. Spread over gelatin layer. Sprinkle with nuts and coconut. Chill before serving. Yield: 15 servings.

Kerry L. Myers
Gamma Psi, Gary, West Virginia

GUMDROP SALAD

1 lb. gumdrops
1 lb. red Tokay grapes, seeded, cut into halves
1 pkg. miniature marshmallows
1 med. can crushed pineapple, drained
1 c. chopped nuts
Juice of 1 lemon
3/4 c. pineapple juice
2/3 c. sugar
1 tsp. vinegar
1/4 c. flour

Mix first 5 ingredients. Measure lemon juice; add equal amount of water. Blend with pineapple juice, sugar and vinegar. Bring to a boil. Stir in flour. Cook until thickened, stirring constantly; cool. Pour over gumdrop mixture; mix well.

Beverly J. Steele
Xi Alpha Alpha, Havana, Illinois

LIME-LEMON GELATIN SALAD

1 20-oz. can fruit cocktail, chilled
1 8-oz. can fruit cocktail, chilled
1 sm. can sliced pineapple, chilled
1 sm. can grapefruit sections, chilled
2 3-oz. packages lime gelatin
2 bananas, sliced
2 oranges, sectioned, sliced
6 or 7 marshmallows, chopped
Chopped nuts
1/2 pt. whipping cream, whipped

Drain fruit, reserving juice. Add enough water to reserved juice to measure 1 1/2 cups liquid. Dissolve gelatin in 2 cups boiling water. Stir in reserved juice mixture. Chill until partially set. Fold in fruits, marshmallows and nuts. Fold in whipped cream. Pour into serving bowl. Chill until set.

Isabel Eichner
Xi Xi Zeta, San Francisco, California

SPRING PARTY SALAD

1 3-oz. package lime gelatin
1 9-oz. can crushed pineapple
1/2 c. pineapple juice
1 c. grated Cheddar cheese
1/3 c. finely chopped nuts
1/2 pt. whipping cream, whipped

Dissolve gelatin in 1 cup boiling water. Stir in pineapple and juice. Chill in refrigerator until partially set. Fold in cheese, nuts and whipped cream. Pour into individual molds. Yield: 11 servings.

Peggy Callahan
Laureate Gamma, Santa Ana, California

CARMEN'S SHRIMP SALAD

1 can chicken noodle soup
1 8-oz. package cream cheese
1 3-oz. package lemon gelatin
1/2 c. mayonnaise
1 c. chopped celery
1/2 c. chopped green onions
1/2 c. diced chopped pimento
1 can shrimp

Heat soup and cream cheese, stirring constantly until well blended. Stir in gelatin dissolved in 1/2 cup boiling water and mayonnaise; cool. Add remaining ingredients. Pour into mold. Chill until set.

Lori Mooney
Upsilon, Weiser, Idaho

SHRIMP SALAD

1 4 1/2-oz. can shrimp
4 hard-boiled eggs, chopped
1/2 tsp. salt
Pinch of pepper
2 tbsp. pickle relish
1 tbsp. finely chopped green onions and tops
2 tbsp. finely chopped celery center ribs
3 tbsp. salad dressing

Mash shrimp. Mix with remaining ingredients. Chill before serving. Yield: 2 servings.

Alma Louise Klitzing
Laureate Alpha Epsilon, Altamont, Illinois

ELEGANT STANDING RIB ROAST

1 tbsp. each lemon-seasoned pepper, paprika
2 tbsp. each seasoned salt, onion salt
3/4 tbsp. garlic salt
1 standing rib roast, boned, tied
Oil

Combine seasonings. Sprinkle a small amount over roast. Rub with oil. Pat remaining seasonings onto roast. Place in roasting pan. Roast in preheated 375-degree oven for 1 hour. Turn off oven. Let stand in closed oven for several hours. Turn oven to 375 degrees. Roast for 1 hour.

Toni Ruda
Xi Theta Phi, Manchester, Missouri

HAM LOAF

1 lb. each ground cured ham, pork
1 1/2 lb. ground beef
1/2 c. bread crumbs
3/4 c. milk
1/2 tsp. salt
Pinch of pepper

Mix all ingredients. Shape into loaf in baking pan. Pour 1/2 cup boiling water around loaf. Bake at 325 degrees for 1 1/2 hours. Yield: 10-12 servings.

Kathryn Cook
Eta Epsilon, Beecher City, Illinois

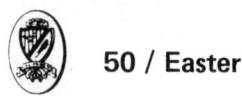

EASTER BREAKFAST CASSEROLE

8 slices toast, buttered, cubed
3 c. chopped ham
1 lb. American cheese, cubed
6 eggs, beaten
3 c. milk
3/4 tsp. each dry mustard, salt
Crushed potato chips

Arrange toast cubes in buttered 9 x 13-inch pan. Layer ham and cheese over top. Mix eggs, milk and seasonings. Pour over cheese layer. Chill overnight. Sprinkle with potato chips. Bake at 350 degrees for 1 hour. Cool for 10 minutes. Yield: 12-15 servings.

Darlene Beyer
Xi Beta Omicron, Hays, Kansas

GRAN'S EASTER BRUNCH EGGS

12 hard-boiled eggs, cut in half
1/4 tsp. salt
Pinch of pepper
1 tsp. prepared mustard
1 6 1/2-oz. can deviled ham
1 can cream of mushroom soup
1/2 c. milk
1 6-oz. can mushrooms

Remove yolks from eggs; mash. Mix with salt, pepper, mustard and half the ham. Spoon into egg whites. Place in baking dish. Mix remaining ingredients. Pour over eggs. Bake at 350 degrees for 20 minutes. Yield: 6 servings.

Pat Vehlewald
Delta Delta Eta, Kernville, California

HAM BALLS AND SAUCE

1 lb. ground ham
1/2 lb. each ground pork, beef
1 c. fine cracker crumbs
2 tbsp. chopped onions
2 tbsp. dried green pepper
1/4 tsp. salt
1/4 tsp. pepper
2 eggs
1 c. milk
1 8-oz. can tomato sauce
3 tbsp. vinegar
1 tsp. dry mustard
1 c. packed brown sugar

Mix first 9 ingredients. Add milk gradually. Shape into large balls. Brown lightly. Place in 6 x 9-inch baking dish. Mix remaining ingredients. Pour over meatballs. Bake at 350 degrees for 1 hour; baste occasionally. Yield: 8 servings.

Patricia M. Livingston
Gamma Kappa, Cocoa, Florida

UPSIDE-DOWN HAM LOAF

3 tbsp. brown sugar
Pineapple slices
1 1/2 lb. ground cured ham
1 lb. ground chuck
1 c. cracker crumbs
1 tbsp. dry mustard
2 eggs, beaten
1 1/2 c. milk
Maraschino cherries

Sprinkle bottom of 8 x 11-inch casserole with brown sugar. Arrange pineapple slices on top. Mix next 6 ingredients. Press mixture firmly into prepared dish. Bake, covered, at 250 degrees for 1 3/4 hours; uncover. Bake for 15 minutes longer. Invert onto serving plate. Place cherry in center of each pineapple slice. Yield: 12-16 servings.

Nancy J. Middleton
Preceptor Gamma Chi, Liberty, Missouri

ORANGE-GLAZED HAM

1 5 to 7-lb. smoked picnic ham
Whole cloves
1/2 c. packed light brown sugar
1/4 c. frozen orange juice concentrate, thawed
1 tbsp. prepared mustard

Place ham fat side up on rack in roasting pan. Bake at 350 degrees for 1 hour. Remove skin, leaving collar at bone. Score into diamond pattern; insert cloves. Spoon mixture of brown sugar, juice concentrate and mustard over ham. Bake to 135 degrees on meat thermometer, basting several times. Garnish with curly endive and orange slices. Yield: 8-10 servings.

Photograph for this recipe on page 47.

LEG OF LAMB WITH SALSA

1 5 to 6-lb. leg of lamb
1/4 c. butter, softened
2 oz. dried red chilies
2 cloves of garlic
1/4 c. olive oil
2 c. pulque
2 onions, chopped
8 sm. pickled green chilies
Grated Parmesan cheese

Bake lamb at 325 degrees for 1 1/2 to 2 hours. Spread with butter. Bake for 10 to 15 minutes longer. Process red chilies, garlic, oil and pulque in blender container until smooth. Pour over lamb slices to serve. Top with onions and green chilies. Sprinkle with cheese. May substitute half water, half tequila for pulque. Yield: 8 servings.

Phoebe Richards
Preceptor Upsilon, Montclair, California

MARINATED PORK ROAST

1 4 to 5-lb. loin pork roast
1/2 c. each soy sauce, Sherry
1 tbsp. dry mustard
1 tsp. each ginger, thyme
2 cloves of garlic, crushed

Place roast in plastic bag. Add mixture of remaining ingredients; seal bag. Marinate for 2 to 3 hours at room temperature or overnight in refrigerator; remove from bag. Bake in 9 x 13-inch baking pan at 325 degrees for 2 hours. Baste with marinade. Bake for 1 hour longer or to 175 degrees on meat thermometer, basting occasionally. Yield: 6-8 servings.

Cathy Reavis
Iota Rho, Sapulpa, Oklahoma

BREAKFAST STRATA

1/3 c. chopped green onions
1/2 c. sliced mushrooms
1 1/2 c. milk
Salt and pepper to taste
1/3 c. melted margarine
8 eggs, beaten
1 lb. bacon crisp-fried, crumbled
2 1/2 c. croutons
2 c. grated Cheddar cheese
Paprika

Saute green onions and mushrooms. Beat milk, seasonings and margarine into eggs gradually. Add sauteed mixture. Layer bacon, croutons and 1 1/2 cups cheese in baking dish. Pour egg mixture over top. Sprinkle with 1/2 cup cheese and paprika. Bake at 325 degrees for 1 to 1 1/4 hours. Yield: 10-12 servings.

Diane Campbell
Laureate Beta Upsilon, Chico, California

HOLIDAY BRUNCH LASAGNA

1 c. chopped onion
1/3 c. bacon drippings
1/3 c. flour
1/2 tsp. salt
1/4 tsp. pepper
3 c. milk
1 c. sour cream
12 lasagna noodles, cooked
1 lb. bacon, crisp-fried, crumbled
12 hard-boiled eggs, sliced
2 c. shredded Swiss cheese
1/4 c. grated Parmesan cheese
Chopped parsley (opt.)

Saute onion in bacon drippings. Blend in flour, salt and pepper. Add milk gradually. Cook until thickened, stirring constantly. Blend in sour cream. Spoon small amount of sauce in 9 x 13-inch baking dish. Alternate layers of 4 noodles, bacon, eggs, Swiss cheese and sauce until all ingredients are used. Top with additional bacon. Sprinkle with Parmesan cheese and parsley. Bake at 350 degrees for 25 to 30 minutes. Let stand for 10 minutes before serving. Yield: 12 servings.

Shirley S. MacNitt
Preceptor Rho, Singer Island, Florida

CHICKEN-FRUIT SANDWICH

4 slices cooked chicken
4 slices buttered toast
1/2 sm. onion, chopped
1 1/2 c. chopped celery
2 tbsp. each salt, pepper
1 1/2 c. mayonnaise
1 16-oz. can pears, drained, sliced
1 1/2 c. shredded Cheddar cheese
Paprika

Arrange chicken slices on toast Mix next 5 ingredients. Spread over chicken. Top with pear slices. Sprinkle with cheese and paprika. Bake at 350 degrees for 10 minutes. May substitute turkey for chicken. Yield: 4 servings.

Elaine Reinke
Alpha Delta, Hettinger, North Dakota

CHICKEN BREASTS WITH PROSCIUTTO

3 lg. whole chicken breasts, split, boned, skinned
Italian-flavored Shake and Bake mix
3/4 lb. mushrooms, thinly sliced
3 tbsp. butter
1/4 c. light cream
1/2 c. dry white wine
3 thin slices prosciutto
3 thin slices process Swiss cheese

Coat chicken with Shake and Bake mix using package directions. Bake at 400 degrees for 20 minutes. Saute mushrooms in butter until lightly browned. Stir in cream and wine. Pour over chicken. Top with ham and cheese slices. Bake for 5 minutes. Yield: 3 servings.

Anita Zieman
Zeta Delta, Greeley, Colorado

SHRIMP MELTS

2 tbsp. chopped onion
1 tbsp. margarine
1 1/2 tbsp. flour
1 tsp. dry mustard
1 c. milk
1 can shrimp, drained
4 English muffins, split, toasted, buttered
1 c. grated Cheddar cheese

Saute onion in margarine; remove from heat. Blend in flour and mustard. Add milk gradually. Cook until thickened, stirring constantly. Add shrimp. Spread on muffin halves. Sprinkle with cheese. Broil until cheese melts. Garnish with watercress and radish roses. Yield: 8 servings.

Joan G. Routt
Preceptor Alpha Sigma, San Angelo, Texas

MICROWAVE LENTEN TUNA WEDGES

2 eggs, slightly beaten
1 1/2 c. cooked rice
6 green onions, chopped
2 7-oz. cans tuna
1/2 c. melted butter
1/4 tsp. thyme
1 c. fine bread crumbs

Mix eggs, rice, onions and tuna. Stir in remaining ingredients. Spoon into lightly greased 9-inch glass pie plate; cover with waxed paper. Microwave on High for 9 to 11 minutes, turning once. Yield: 6-8 servings.

Sharon Kay Pilkington
Lambda Eta, Ann Arbor, Michigan

BEETS WITH ORANGE SAUCE

1 tbsp. butter, melted
1/4 c. packed brown sugar
2 tbsp. flour
3/4 c. orange juice
1/4 c. slivered orange rind
2 1/2 c. chopped cooked beets
Dash of paprika
1/8 tsp. salt
Juice of 1 lime

Blend butter, brown sugar and flour in double boiler. Stir in orange juice and rind. Cook until thickened. Simmer for 5 minutes, stirring constantly. Add beets and seasonings. Cook for 30 minutes. Stir in lime juice. Yield: 6 servings.

Shirley M. Chontos
Xi Iota Xi, Vallejo, California

BROCCOLI CASSEROLE

6 slices bacon, chopped
1/4 c. chopped onion
1 can cream of mushroom soup
1 5-oz. can water chestnuts, sliced
2 pkg. frozen chopped broccoli, cooked
1/2 tsp. salt
Pepper to taste

Fry bacon until crisp. Add onion. Saute until tender. Stir in soup and water chestnuts. Add broccoli, salt and pepper. Bake in 1 1/2-quart casserole at 325 degrees for 30 minutes. Yield: 8 servings.

Kathleen Lewis
Sigma Omega, Willits, California

MICROWAVE BROCCOLI DELISH

1 sm. onion
Margarine
1 c. chopped Velveeta cheese
1 clove of garlic, minced
1 can mushroom soup
1 can mushrooms
1/2 c. slivered almonds
2 pkg. frozen chopped broccoli, cooked, drained
3/4 c. Grape Nuts

Saute onion in margarine. Add next 5 ingredients. Mix with broccoli. Spoon into buttered glass casserole. Sprinkle with mixture of Grape Nuts and 1/4 cup margarine. Microwave on High for 10 to 12 minutes. Yield: 8-10 servings.

Sandra Johnson
Xi Phi, Chickasha, Oklahoma

BRUSSELS SPROUTS PROVENCAL

1 med. onion, chopped
1 clove of garlic, minced
1 tbsp. oil
1 c. chopped tomatoes
1 16-oz. can tomatoes
1 tsp. basil
Salt and pepper to taste
1 lb. Brussels sprouts, cooked, drained
1/2 c. grated Swiss cheese (opt.)

Saute onion and garlic in oil until onion is tender. Mix in tomatoes and seasonings. Simmer for 8 to 10 minutes, stirring occasionally. Add Brussels sprouts. Simmer for 2 to 3 minutes. Sprinkle with cheese to serve. Yield: 4 servings.

Doris Daley
Preceptor Eta Phi, Chadron, Nebraska

CARROT RING

2 lb. carrots, cooked, mashed
1 c. evaporated milk
3 tbsp. butter
2 tsp. salt
2 tbsp. onion juice
2 eggs
1 tbsp. flour
Dash of paprika
2 c. peas, cooked

Process all ingredients except peas in blender container until smooth. Spoon into greased 8-inch ring mold. Place in pan of water. Bake at 350 degrees for 1 hour. Unmold onto serving plate. Fill center with peas. Yield: 6 servings.

Marian I. Shank
Laureate Beta, Lancaster, Pennsylvania

NUTTY CARROTS

5 c. 3-inch carrot sticks
1 1/2 tsp. salt
1/2 c. melted butter
2 tsp. honey
1/4 tsp. pepper
2 tbsp. lemon juice
1/4 tsp. grated lemon rind
1/2 c. coarsely chopped walnuts

Cook carrots with 1/2 teaspoon salt in 1 1/2 cups water until just tender; drain. Heat next 5 ingredients and 1 teaspoon salt. Pour over carrots. Sprinkle with walnuts. Yield: 8 servings.

Sharon K. Kauffman
Beta Sigma, W. Morgan, Colorado

SAUCY CELERY CASSEROLE

4 c. thinly sliced celery
1/4 c. margarine
2 tbsp. flour
1/4 tsp. salt
1 c. milk
1 c. shredded American cheese
1 can mushrooms
2 tbsp. chopped green pepper

Saute celery in margarine until tender-crisp. Stir in flour, salt and milk. Cook until thick, stirring constantly. Add 3/4 cup cheese, mushrooms and green pepper. Cook until cheese is melted, stirring constantly. Bake in 1-quart casserole at 350 degrees for 20 minutes. Sprinkle with remaining cheese. Yield: 6 servings.

Betty Laughlin
Gamma Gamma, Blackwell, Oklahoma

CORN FREMONT

2 c. cream-style corn
1 c. cracker crumbs
2/3 c. grated American cheese
1/4 c. chopped onion
1/2 c. chopped celery
1 tsp. salt
1/4 tsp. paprika
2 eggs, beaten
1 1/2 c. milk
Butter

Mix first 9 ingredients. Spoon into buttered casserole. Dot with 2 tablespoons butter. Bake at 350 degrees for 1 hour. Yield: 6 servings.

Veda Kraich
Eta Psi, Akron, Colorado

DOREEN'S STUFFED EGGPLANT

1 lg. eggplant
1 tbsp. flour
1/2 c. sour cream
1 c. chopped ham
1/2 lg. onion, chopped
1/4 c. picante sauce
Several mushrooms, sliced
1/2 lg. green pepper, chopped
Miniature croutons
Parmesan cheese
American cheese, sliced into 2-in. strips
Paprika

Slice eggplant in half lengthwise. Cut around eggplant halves 1/4 inch from edge. Cut center pulp into cubes. Scoop out with spoon. Cook cubes in salted water for 5 minutes or until tender; drain. Saute for 1 minute until excess water evaporates. Remove from heat. Add flour blended with sour cream and next 5 ingredients. Spoon into shells. Sprinkle with croutons and Parmesan cheese. Arrange American cheese strips in V-patterns on top. Sprinkle with paprika. Bake in 9 x 9-inch pan at 350 degrees for 30 minutes. Yield: 2 servings.

Doreen Jones
Chi Zeta, Palestine, Texas

CHINESE GREEN PEAS

2 10-oz. packages frozen peas
3 sm. onions, chopped
1 1/2 c. chopped celery
1 8-oz. can water chestnuts, drained
1/4 c. each oil, olive oil
4 tsp. cornstarch
1 c. beef broth
1 tsp. soy sauce
Salt to taste

Saute peas, onions, celery and water chestnuts in hot oils until peas begin to pop. Cook over low heat for 10 to 15 minutes, stirring occasionally. Dissolve cornstarch in 1/4 cup beef broth; add remaining broth. Stir into vegetable mixture. Cook until slightly thickened, stirring constantly. Add soy sauce and salt. Cook for 1 minute longer. Yield: 10 servings.

Kathryn R. Young
Preceptor Iota, Shreveport, Louisiana

CREAM OF LEEK SOUP WITH STILTON

3 to 4 leeks, thinly sliced
3 tbsp. butter, melted
3 med. potatoes, sliced
4 c. chicken stock
2 c. heavy cream
Salt and pepper to taste
Pinch of nutmeg
1 tsp. lemon juice
4 to 6 oz. Stilton cheese, crumbled

Steam leeks in butter in saucepan. Add potatoes and stock; cook for 15 minutes or until potatoes are tender. Stir in cream. Simmer for 10 minutes. Puree in blender. Blend in seasonings and lemon juice. Heat to serving temperature. Sprinkle servings with cheese. Yield: 6-8 servings.

Donna Chapman
Xi Lambda, West Hill, Ontario, Canada

CHEDDAR-POTATO PUFF

6 med. potatoes, peeled, cubed
2 1/2 tbsp. butter
1/3 c. milk
1/2 tsp. salt
1/4 tsp. nutmeg
1 c. grated Cheddar cheese
1 egg, slightly beaten

Cook potatoes in salted water until tender; drain. Mash potatoes with butter, milk, salt and nutmeg. Fold in cheese and egg. Bake in greased 8 x 8-inch casserole at 350 degrees for 30 minutes or until puffed and golden. Yield: 6 servings.

Marjorie Svacina
Xi Beta Beta, Council Bluffs, Iowa

CHEESE AND SPINACH STRATA

1 10-oz. package shredded sharp Cheddar cheese
2 10-oz. packages frozen chopped spinach, thawed, squeezed dry
2/3 c. chopped onion
1/2 c. butter, softened
18 thinly sliced firm white bread slices
4 eggs
4 c. milk
1 tbsp. prepared mustard
2 tsp. salt
1/4 tsp. pepper

Combine 2 cups cheese, spinach and onion. Spread butter lightly on both sides of bread slices. Place 6 bread slices in bottom of greased 9 x 13-inch baking dish. Layer half the cheese mixture, 6 bread slices and remaining cheese mixture on top. Cut 6 bread slices into triangles. Arrange over casserole. Sprinkle with remaining cheese. Beat eggs, milk, mustard and seasonings; pour over casserole. Chill, covered, for 1 hour or longer. Bake at 350 degrees for 60 minutes or until knife inserted in center comes out clean. Let stand for 15 minutes before cutting into squares. Yield: 8-10 servings.

Photograph for this recipe on page 47.

CUP OF GOLD

3 c. cornflakes
1/4 c. shredded Cheddar cheese
1/4 c. margarine, melted
6 eggs
2 tbsp. Parmesan cheese

Mix cornflakes, Cheddar cheese and margarine. Press into 6 greased custard cups. Chill overnight. Break an egg into each cup. Sprinkle with Parmesan cheese. Bake on baking sheet at 350 degrees for 20 minutes. Yield: 6 servings.

Katherine Cone
Xi Gamma Epsilon, Midland, Georgia

DELMONICO POTATO CASSEROLE

1/4 c. butter, melted
3 tbsp. flour
1 1/2 c. milk, scalded
1 1/2 tsp. salt
1/4 tsp. pepper
1/2 tsp. garlic salt
Grated cheese
4 hard-boiled eggs, sliced
4 c. cooked potatoes, sliced
Paprika

Blend butter, flour and milk. Mix in seasonings. Cook until thick, stirring constantly. Simmer for 5 minutes. Stir in 1/2 cup cheese, eggs and potatoes. Spoon into greased 9 x 13-inch baking dish. Sprinkle with additional cheese and paprika. Bake at 350 degrees for 20 minutes. Broil for several minutes until lightly browned. Yield: 6 servings.

Lorretta Wolfcale
Preceptor Beta Psi, Miami, Florida

HASHED BROWN SCALLOPED POTATOES

2 lb. frozen hashed brown potatoes
3/4 c. butter, melted
1 tsp. salt
1/4 tsp. pepper
1/2 c. chopped celery
1 can cream of celery soup
1 pt. sour cream with chives
Chopped green pepper
2 c. grated Cheddar cheese
1 can pearl onions
2 c. crushed cornflakes

Place potatoes in 3-quart casserole. Mix 1/2 cup butter and next 8 ingredients. Spoon over potatoes. Sprinkle with cornflakes. Drizzle 1/4 cup melted butter over top. Bake at 350 degrees for 45 minutes. Yield: 12 servings.

Jeannette Brown
Xi Alpha Beta, Council Bluffs, Iowa

ROSIE'S DEVILED EGGS

18 hard-boiled eggs, cut in half
1 8-oz. package cream cheese, softened
1/2 c. salad dressing
1 tsp. prepared mustard
1/4 c. sweet pickle juice
1/4 tsp. each Tabasco sauce, Worcestershire sauce
2 tbsp. unflavored gelatin
18 stuffed olives, cut in half

Mash egg yolks in mixer bowl. Add next 6 ingredients. Beat until creamy. Beat in gelatin. Spoon into egg whites. Top with olives. Chill in tightly covered container. Yield: 3 dozen.

Rose Mary Coakes
Preceptor Alpha Omicron, Marshall, Michigan

PASTA PRIMAVERA

1 lb. thin asparagus
1 med. onion, finely chopped
1 lg. clove of garlic, crushed
1/2 c. unsalted butter
1/4 lb. mushrooms, thinly sliced
1 med. zucchini, sliced 1/4 in. thick
1 sm. carrot, sliced 1/8 in. thick
6 oz. cauliflowerets
1 c. whipping cream
1/2 c. chicken stock
2 tbsp. chopped basil
1 c. frozen tiny peas
2 oz. prosciutto, chopped
5 green onions, chopped
1 lb. fettucini, cooked
Salt and freshly ground pepper to taste
1 c. freshly grated Parmesan cheese

Trim asparagus tips; cut stalks diagonally into 1/4-inch pieces. Saute onion and garlic in butter. Add next 4 ingredients. Stir-fry for 2 minutes; reserve small amount of vegetables for garnish. Stir in cream, stock and basil. Bring to a boil. Simmer for 3 minutes. Mix in peas, ham and green onions. Cook for 1 minute. Stir in fettucini, seasonings and Parmesan cheese. Spoon into serving dish. Garnish with reserved vegetables. Yield: 4 servings.

Sharon Papastathis
Preceptor Kappa Psi, Sebastopol, California

BEET AND HORSERADISH RELISH

10 med. beets, cooked, peeled, coarsely grated
1/2 c. freshly grated horseradish
2 tsp. salt
2 c. vinegar
1/2 c. sugar
1 tbsp. mixed pickling spice

Mix beets with horseradish. Bring remaining ingredients to a boil. Strain into beet mixture; mix well. Pour into hot sterilized jars; seal.

Mary Reeves
Laureate Xi, Trail, British Columbia, Canada

BUTTER-PECAN COFFEE CAKE

3/4 c. butter, softened
1 1/4 c. sugar
1 tsp. vanilla extract
2 eggs
2 c. sifted flour
1 tsp. baking powder
1 tsp. soda
1/2 tsp. salt
1 c. sour cream
1/4 c. packed brown sugar
1/2 tsp. cinnamon
1/2 c. chopped pecans

Cream butter and 1 cup sugar. Beat in vanilla and eggs, 1 at a time. Mix sifted flour, baking powder, soda and salt into creamed mixture alternately with sour cream, beginning and ending with flour. Mix brown sugar, cinnamon, pecans and 1/4 cup sugar. Layer half the cake batter and brown sugar mixture in buttered 9 x 9-inch pan. Repeat layers. Bake at 350 degrees for 45 minutes. Yield: 12 servings.

Marian Clyatt
Xi Beta Mu, Fort Meade, Florida

STREUSEL COFFEE CAKE

Flour	1/2 c. milk
1 tbsp. baking powder	1 tsp. vanilla extract
1/4 tsp. salt	1/2 c. packed brown sugar
3/4 c. sugar	2 tsp. cinnamon
1/4 c. shortening	2 tbsp. melted butter
1 egg	1/2 c. finely chopped nuts

Sift 1 1/2 cups flour, baking powder, salt and sugar. Cut in shortening until crumbly. Beat in egg, milk and vanilla. Mix remaining ingredients with 2 tablespoons flour. Layer half the cake batter and brown sugar mixture in greased and floured 8 x 8-inch pan. Repeat layers. Bake at 375 degrees for 25 to 30 minutes.

Paula Dickerson
Xi Kappa Omicron, Crooksville, Ohio

EASTER EGG BRAIDS

15 eggs	2 pkg. dry yeast
Easter egg dye	1/2 c. shortening
4 1/2 c. sifted flour	1/2 c. milk
1/2 c. sugar	Grated rind of 2 lemons
1 tsp. salt	Candy sprinkles

Dye 12 uncooked eggs with Easter egg dye; set aside. Mix 1 1/2 cups flour, sugar, salt and yeast in mixer bowl. Heat shortening, milk and 1 cup water. Add to flour mixture. Beat at medium speed for 1 minute. Add 1/2 cup flour, lemon rind and 2 eggs. Beat at high speed for 2 minutes. Stir in enough flour to make medium-stiff dough. Knead on lightly floured surface until smooth and elastic. Place in greased bowl, turning to grease surface. Let rise, covered, in warm place for 1 hour or until doubled in bulk. Punch down; let rise for 30 minutes. Shape into four 36-inch ropes. Braid 2 ropes together loosely and shape into ring on greased baking sheet, leaving spaces for 6 eggs. Brush with 1 beaten egg. Insert tinted eggs in spaces. Decorate with sprinkles. Repeat with remaining dough. Bake at 375 degrees for 20 minutes. May shape dough into ring around each egg and bake for 15 minutes.

Donnis Helbourg
Preceptor Nu, Atlantic, Iowa

PINEAPPLE-CARROT BREAD

3 eggs	3 c. flour
1/2 c. oil	2 tsp. soda
1/2 c. butter, melted	1 1/2 tsp. cinnamon
1 1/2 c. sugar	1 tsp. salt
2 tsp. vanilla extract	3/4 tsp. nutmeg
2 c. shredded carrots	1 c. chopped nuts
1 8-oz. can crushed pineapple	1/2 c. raisins

Beat eggs, oil, butter, sugar and vanilla until foamy. Stir in carrots and pineapple. Add remaining ingredients, stirring until just moistened. Bake in 2 buttered and floured loaf pans at 325 degrees for 1 hour. Yield: 2 loaves.

Jane Nelson
Preceptor Tau, Tucson, Arizona

POPPY SEED BREAD

3 c. flour	2 tsp. each almond, vanilla extract
2 1/2 c. sugar	3/4 c. confectioners' sugar
3 eggs	1/4 c. orange juice
1 1/2 c. milk	1 1/2 tsp. melted margarine
1 1/2 tsp. baking powder	
1 1/2 tbsp. poppy seed	
1 1/2 tsp. salt	
Oil	

Combine first 7 ingredients with 1 1/8 cups oil and 1 1/2 teaspoons of each flavoring. Beat for 2 minutes. Bake in 2 prepared loaf pans at 350 degrees for 1 hour. Mix confectioners' sugar, orange juice, margarine and remaining 1/2 teaspoon flavorings. Pour over hot loaves. Yield: 2 loaves.

Peggy Conner
Eta Nu, Belton, Missouri

SWEDISH KRINGLA

2 c. flour	1 tsp. almond extract
Butter	1 c. confectioners' sugar
3 eggs	Milk

Mix 1 cup flour, 1/2 cup butter and 1 tablespoon water until smooth. Spread into two 3-inch strips on baking sheet. Bring 1/2 cup butter and 1 cup water to a boil; remove from heat. Mix in 1 cup flour. Beat in eggs 1 at a time. Stir in 1/2 teaspoon almond extract. Spread on dough strips. Bake at 350 degrees for 45 minutes. Mix confectioners' sugar, 1 tablespoon butter and 1/2 teaspoon almond extract with enough milk to make of spreading consistency. Spread on kringla. Cut into pieces. Yield: 2 dozen.

Karen Clayton
Gamma Chi, Overland Park, Kansas

RHUBARB BREAD

1 1/2 c. packed brown sugar
1 c. oil
1 egg, beaten
1 c. buttermilk
3 c. flour
1 tsp. each salt, soda
2 tsp. cinnamon
1 1/2 c. chopped rhubarb
1/2 c. sugar
1 tbsp. butter, melted

Mix brown sugar and oil. Beat in egg and buttermilk. Mix in flour, salt, soda and 1 teaspoon cinnamon. Fold in rhubarb. Spoon into 2 prepared small loaf pans. Mix sugar, butter and 1 teaspoon cinnamon. Sprinkle over loaves. Bake at 350 degrees for 1 hour.

Joyce Burke
Xi Eta Zeta, Emmetsburg, Iowa

BUTTERSCOTCH BREAKFAST ROLLS

1 c. chopped walnuts
25 frozen rolls
1 c. packed brown sugar
1 pkg. butterscotch pudding and pie filling mix
1/2 c. butter, melted

Sprinkle walnuts in greased bundt pan. Arrange rolls in pan. Sprinkle brown sugar and pudding mix over rolls. Drizzle with butter. Let rise, covered, in refrigerator overnight. Bake at 350 degrees for 30 minutes. Invert on serving plate. Yield: 10-20 servings.

Marlene Jensen
Xi Gamma, Blackfoot, Idaho

CINNAMON TWISTS

1 c. sour cream
2 tbsp. shortening
3 tbsp. sugar
1/8 tsp. soda
1 tsp. salt
1 egg, beaten
1 pkg. dry yeast
3 c. flour
1 tbsp. cinnamon
1/3 c. packed brown sugar
Confectioners' sugar frosting

Bring sour cream to a boil. Blend in shortening, sugar, soda and salt; cool to lukewarm. Stir in egg and yeast. Add flour; mix well. Knead on lightly floured surface until smooth and elastic. Let rest for 5 minutes. Roll out. Sprinkle cinnamon and brown sugar on half of the dough; fold dough in half. Cut into 1 x 6-inch strips. Twist and place on baking sheet. Let rise for 1 1/4 hours or until doubled in bulk. Bake at 350 degrees for 12 to 15 minutes. Frost lightly.

Linda Weigel
Nu Beta, WaKeeney, Kansas

HOT CROSS BUNS

6 tbsp. butter
2 c. flour
1/2 c. sugar
4 tsp. baking powder
1/2 tsp. each soda, salt, cinnamon
1/2 c. currants
1 1/4 c. cottage cheese
1 egg
3/4 tsp. vanilla extract
1 c. confectioners' sugar
1 1/2 to 2 tbsp. milk

Cut butter into first 6 dry ingredients until crumbly. Stir in currants. Process cottage cheese, egg and 1/2 teaspoon vanilla in blender until smooth. Stir into dough. Knead on lightly floured surface 10 times. Shape into balls. Bake on greased baking sheet at 425 degrees for 18 minutes; cool. Mix confectioners' sugar, 1/4 teaspoon vanilla and milk. Drizzle on buns in cross design. May substitute 1/2 cup whole wheat flour for 1/2 cup all-purpose flour. Yield: 1-1 1/2 dozen.

Eppie Gruling
Xi Alpha Nu, Merrill, Wisconsin

LEE'S HOT CROSS BUNS

2 pkg. dry yeast
2 c. sour cream
1/4 c. butter, softened
1/3 c. sugar
2 tsp. salt
2 eggs
6 c. flour
1 c. currants
3/4 c. chopped citron
2 1/2 tsp. cinnamon
1 tsp. nutmeg
1 egg yolk
Confectioners' sugar frosting

Dissolve yeast in 1/2 cup warm water. Heat sour cream to lukewarm over low heat. Combine with yeast, butter, sugar, salt, eggs and 2 cups flour; beat until smooth. Stir in currants, citron, cinnamon, nutmeg and remaining flour until dough forms ball. Knead on floured surface for 10 minutes. Place in greased bowl, turning to grease surface. Let rise, covered, in warm place for 1 hour or until doubled in bulk. Shape into 1 1/2-inch balls. Brush with egg yolk beaten with small amount of water. Bake on greased baking sheet at 375 degrees for 20 minutes; cool. Decorate with frosting cross. Yield: 3 dozen.

Lee McBarron
Preceptor Sigma, New Albany, Indiana

APPLE BAVARIAN TORTE

1/2 c. margarine, softened
1 c. flour
1/4 tsp. vanilla extract
Sugar
1 8-oz. package cream cheese, softened
1 can apple pie filling
1 tsp. cinnamon
1/4 c. sliced almonds

Mix margarine, flour, vanilla and 1/3 cup sugar. Spread in 8-inch springform pan. Cream 1/4 cup sugar with cream cheese. Spread over flour mixture. Mix pie filling, cinnamon and 2 tablespoons sugar. Spoon over cream cheese layer. Sprinkle with almonds. Bake at 425 degrees for 10 minutes; reduce temperature to 400 degrees. Bake for 20 minutes. Yield: 12 servings.

Anne Byard
Xi Alpha Xi, Brantford, Ontario, Canada

ALMOND SAUCE

5 egg yolks	1 c. light cream
1 1/4 c. sugar	1 2/3 tsp. almond extract
5 tbsp. flour	3 tbsp. butter

Beat first 4 ingredients until smooth. Bring to a boil in double boiler; remove from heat. Stir in almond flavoring and butter. Chill in refrigerator. Serve over angel food cake with whipped cream and slivered almonds. Yield: 6-8 servings.

Mary Goforth
Sigma Eta, Manchester, Missouri

BROKEN GLASS TORTE

1 3-oz. package each cherry, lime, orange gelatin	1 c. sugar
21 graham crackers, crushed	1 env. unflavored gelatin
	1 c. pineapple juice
	2 c. heavy cream, whipped
1/2 c. butter, softened	1 tsp. vanilla extract

Dissolve gelatins separately, using 1 1/2 cups boiling water for each. Pour into three 9 x 9-inch pans. Chill until firm; cut into small cubes. Mix graham cracker crumbs with butter and 1/2 cup sugar. Press 3/4 of the mixture into bottom of greased 9 x 13-inch baking dish. Soften unflavored gelatin in 1/4 cup cold water. Dissolve in boiling pineapple juice. Chill until partially set. Fold in whipped cream, 1/2 cup sugar, vanilla and gelatin cubes. Spoon over graham cracker layer. Top with remaining crumbs. Chill for 24 hours. Cut into squares to serve. Yield: 18 servings.

Marge Anderson
Preceptor Alpha Iota, Council Bluffs, Iowa

CHOCOLATE FROZEN DELIGHT

1 6-oz. package semisweet chocolate chips	1/2 c. butter
1 10 1/2-oz. package miniature marshmallows	2 c. graham cracker crumbs
1 c. evaporated milk	1 gal. vanilla ice cream, sliced
1 c. flaked coconut	1 c. chopped pecans

Melt chocolate chips and marshmallows with evaporated milk in double boiler; cool. Brown coconut lightly in butter. Mix in graham cracker crumbs. Press 3/4 of the mixture into 9 x 13-inch baking dish. Layer half the ice cream and chocolate sauce over crumbs. Repeat layers. Sprinkle with mixture of pecans and remaining crumbs. Freeze, covered with aluminum foil, for 24 hours. Yield: 12-16 servings.

Betty Seiler
Epsilon Chi, Apollo Beach, Florida

DOUBLE-CHOCOLATE ICE CREAM TORTE

1 15-oz. package M and M's plain chocolate candies	1/4 c. shortening
	3 pt. chocolate ice cream, softened

Melt candies and shortening over very low heat, stirring constantly. Spoon onto bottom of foil-lined springform pan, making ridge around edge. Chill for 15 minutes. Spread ridge 1 1/2 inches up side of pan to make shell. Freeze. Fill with ice cream. Freeze. Remove from pan; peel off foil. Place on flat serving plate. Garnish with toasted coconut and M and M's peanut chocolate candies.

Photograph for this recipe on page 47.

DAFFODIL DESSERT

1 pkg. yellow cake mix	1 20-oz. can crushed pineapple, drained
1 8-oz. package cream cheese, softened	5 bananas, sliced
2 c. milk	1 8-oz. carton whipped topping
1 3-oz. package vanilla instant pudding mix	1 c. finely chopped pecans

Prepare cake mix using package instructions. Bake in greased and floured 9 x 13-inch pan at 350 degrees for 20 minutes; cool. Beat cream cheese and 1/2 cup milk until smooth. Beat pudding mix with 1 1/2 cups milk until mixture begins to thicken. Mix with cream cheese mixture. Spread over cake. Chill for 30 minutes. Layer pineapple, bananas, whipped topping and pecans over cake. Chill in refrigerator.

Vicki Lange
Tau Phi, Portageville, Missouri

LEMON WHIP

3/4 c. margarine, softened	2 c. whipped topping
2/3 c. ground walnuts	2 sm. packages lemon instant pudding mix
1 1/2 c. flour	
1 8-oz. package cream cheese, softened	3 c. milk
1/2 c. confectioners' sugar	1 tbsp. lemon juice

Mix first 3 ingredients until crumbly. Press into 9 x 13-inch baking pan. Bake at 350 degrees for 20 minutes; cool. Beat cream cheese and confectioners' sugar until fluffy. Fold in 1 cup whipped topping. Spread over crust. Beat pudding mix, milk and lemon juice for 1 minute. Pour over cream cheese layer. Chill for 10 minutes. Top with 1 cup whipped topping. Chill for 3 to 4 hours. Garnish with additional walnuts. Yield: 12-16 servings.

Marjorie Parks
Xi Gamma Theta, Casa Grande, Arizona

LEMON BISQUE

1 3-oz. package lemon gelatin
1/3 c. honey
1/8 tsp. salt
Juice of 1 lemon
Grated rind of 1 lemon
1 13-oz. can evaporated milk, chilled
2 c. vanilla wafer crumbs

Dissolve gelatin in 1 1/2 cups boiling water. Stir in honey, salt, lemon juice and rind. Chill until partially set. Beat evaporated milk until stiff. Fold into gelatin mixture. Spread 1 cup crumbs in 9 x 13-inch pan. Pour filling over crumbs. Top with 1 cup crumbs. Chill, covered, overnight. Garnish with whipped cream. Yield: 12-16 servings.

Irene Fox
Laureate Beta, Council Bluffs, Iowa

NORTHERN LIGHTS

9 egg whites
3 tbsp. confectioners' sugar
9 tbsp. orange marmalade
Butter
Creme de Menthe

Beat egg whites until very stiff. Fold in confectioners' sugar and marmalade. Melt 1 1/8 cups butter in double boiler. Spoon in egg white mixture. Cook over moderate heat for 10 to 15 minutes or until poached. Spoon into parfait glasses. Top with melted butter and Creme de Menthe. Serve immediately. Yield: 8 servings.

Jeanne Throckmorton
Preceptor Alpha Rho, Arvada, Colorado

PARTY JELL-O

1 6-oz. package each lemon, grape, lime gelatin
3 pt. vanilla ice cream
Sour cream

Dissolve lemon gelatin in 2 cups boiling water. Stir in 1 pint ice cream. Pour into 10-cup mold. Chill until firm. Spread with thin layer sour cream. Repeat process with grape then lime gelatin, molding over lemon layer. Unmold on serving plate.

Adele Sabel
Xi Iota Omicron, Cary, Illinois

PUNCH BOWL TRIFLE

1 pkg. white cake mix
4 bananas, sliced
1 lg. can crushed pineapple
3 10-oz. packages frozen strawberries, thawed
1 16-oz. carton whipped topping
2 lg. packages vanilla pudding mix, prepared
Maraschino cherries, sliced (opt.)
Chopped pecans

Prepare and bake cake using package directions in 9 x 13-inch pan; cool. Cut in 1 1/2-inch pieces. Mix bananas with crushed pineapple. Place 1 package strawberries in large glass bowl. Layer with half the cake, half the whipped topping, 1 package strawberries, half the pineapple mixture and half the pudding. Layer remaining strawberries, pineapple mixture, cake, pudding and whipped topping on top. Arrange cherries and pecans on top. Yield: 15-20 servings.

Elaine Coxworth
Zeta Psi, Lawrenceville, Georgia

BASKET CAKE

Milk
Sugar
Flour
4 eggs, beaten
1 tsp. vanilla extract
1 c. whipping cream, whipped
1/4 c. butter, softened
1/2 tsp. almond extract
1 tsp. salt
1 9-in. sponge cake
Confectioners' sugar icing
Chopped nuts
Large red and green gumdrops

Scald 2 1/4 cups milk. Beat 3/4 cup sugar, 6 tablespoons flour and 3 eggs in double boiler until light. Add milk gradually. Bring to a boil, stirring constantly; remove from heat. Add vanilla; cool, stirring constantly. Fold in whipped cream. Cream butter, 1/3 cup sugar and 1 egg until light and fluffy. Add 1 tablespoon milk, almond extract and salt; beat well. Add 1 1/2 cups flour gradually. Shape into two 18-inch ropes. Shape and mark like handles. Bake at 350 degrees until lightly browned. Remove center of cake, leaving 2 inches on bottom and 1 1/2 to 2 inches around rim. Spread side and top with icing. Sprinkle with chopped nuts. Insert 1 cookie handle into side of cake. Fill center with custard cream. Roll gumdrops flat in sugar. Shape into roses and leaves. Arrange on cake.

Linda E. Austin
Preceptor Zeta, Decorah, Iowa

GOLDEN LAYER CAKE

1 1/4 c. sugar
1/2 c. shortening, softened
1/2 tsp. lemon extract
1 tsp. vanilla
2 eggs
2 c. sifted cake flour
1 tsp. baking powder
3/4 tsp. soda
1/2 tsp. salt
1 c. buttermilk
2 tbsp. cornstarch
2 tbsp. butter, melted
2 egg yolks, beaten
Frozen lemonade concentrate, thawed
Yellow food coloring
1 recipe seven-minute frosting
1 3 1/2-oz. can flaked coconut

Cream 1 cup sugar and shortening. Stir in flavorings. Beat in eggs, 1 at a time. Sift flour, baking powder, soda and 1/4 teaspoon salt. Beat into creamed mixture alternately with buttermilk, beginning and ending with flour. Bake in

Easter / 59

2 prepared 8-inch baking pans at 350 degrees for 30 minutes. Blend 1/4 cup sugar, cornstarch, 1/4 teaspoon salt and butter. Stir in 3/4 cup water gradually. Cook until thickened, stirring constantly. Mix egg yolks with 1/3 cup lemonade concentrate. Stir a small amount of hot mixture into egg yolks; stir egg yolks into hot mixture. Bring to a boil, stirring constantly. Tint with food coloring; cool. Spread between layers of cake. Frost cake with seven-minute frosting. Shake coconut in a jar with 1 tablespoon lemonade concentrate and several drops of food coloring. Spread on paper towel to dry. Sprinkle over cake.

Betty Christoff
Alpha Eta, Steamboat Springs, Colorado

GUMDROP CAKE

1/2 c. butter, softened
1 c. sugar
2 eggs, beaten
2 1/2 c. sifted flour
2 tsp. baking powder
1/4 tsp. salt
1 tsp. vanilla extract
3/4 c. milk
1 lb. small gumdrops
3/4 c. white raisins
1 recipe frosting

Cream butter and sugar. Add eggs; mix well. Sift 2 1/4 cups flour, baking powder and salt together twice. Add mixture of vanilla and milk to creamed mixture alternately with dry ingredients. Reserve 1/2 cup gumdrops. Toss remaining gumdrops with 1/4 cup flour to coat. Stir into batter with raisins. Bake in tube pan at 300 degrees for 1 1/4 hours. Frost and decorate with reserved gumdrops.

Terry Biadasz
Laureate Kappa, Palm Beach Gardens, Florida

STRAWBERRY CAKE

1 pkg. white cake mix
1 pkg. strawberry gelatin
3/4 c. oil
1 c. chopped nuts
4 eggs
2 tbsp. flour
1 10-oz. package frozen strawberries, thawed

Combine all ingredients; beat well. Bake in greased tube pan at 350 degrees for 45 minutes. Serve with whipped cream.

Trena Pierce
Nu, Huntsville, Alabama

EASTER EGG NANAIMO BARS

Butter, softened
1/4 c. sugar
1 egg
1 tbsp. cocoa
1 tsp. vanilla extract
2 c. graham cracker crumbs
1 c. shredded coconut
1/2 c. chopped walnuts
2 c. confectioners' sugar
3 tbsp. milk
2 tbsp. custard powder
8 oz. semisweet chocolate

Mix 1/2 cup butter and next 4 ingredients in double boiler. Cook until thick. Stir into crumbs, coconut and walnuts until well mixed. Shape into 8 eggs. Chill for 15 minutes. Blend 1/4 cup butter, confectioners' sugar, milk and custard powder. Spread over eggs. Chill for 15 minutes. Melt 2 tablespoons butter and chocolate in double boiler. Dip eggs in chocolate mixture; chill. Yield: 8 servings.

Jan Jarvie
Xi Alpha Zeta, Leduc, Alberta, Canada

BUTTER CREAM EASTER EGGS

Butter
1 8-oz. package cream cheese, softened
3 boxes confectioners' sugar
1 8-oz. package semisweet chocolate
1 2-in. square paraffin
1/4 tsp. vanilla extract

Cream 1/2 pound butter and cream cheese. Mix in sugar gradually. Shape into eggs. Melt remaining ingredients and 1 tablespoon butter in double boiler. Dip eggs in chocolate mixture; cool. Yield: 8 dozen.

Nancy S. Sykes
Zeta Psi, Grayson, Georgia

PEANUT BUTTER-MARSHMALLOW EASTER EGGS

3/4 lb. butter, softened
2 lb. confectioners' sugar
1 c. peanut butter
1 c. marshmallow creme
1 tbsp. vanilla extract
1/4 lb. paraffin
1 lb. sweet chocolate

Cream butter and 1/2 pound confectioners' sugar. Mix in next 3 ingredients. Mix in 1 1/2 pounds confectioners' sugar gradually. Shape into eggs. Chill overnight. Melt paraffin and chocolate in double boiler. Dip eggs in chocolate mixture; cool on waxed paper.

Jean Prince
Preceptor Theta, Selingsgrove, Pennsylvania

PEANUT BUTTER EGGS

1 stick margarine, melted
1 18-oz. jar peanut butter
1 16-oz. box confectioners' sugar
4 c. crisp rice cereal
1 6-oz. package chocolate chips
1 lg. chocolate bar
1/2 bar paraffin

Blend margarine and peanut butter. Mix in confectioners' sugar. Add cereal gradually. Shape into 1-inch eggs; chill. Melt remaining ingredients in double boiler. Dip eggs into chocolate mixture; chill until firm. Yield: 4 dozen.

Carole Appleby
Xi Xi, Altoona, Pennsylvania

60 / Easter

MAGIC EASTER EGGS

Butter, softened
2 tsp. vanilla extract
1 tsp. salt
1/2 can sweetened condensed milk
9 c. sifted confectioners' sugar
1/2 lb. semisweet chocolate
1/3 to 1/2 bar paraffin
1 egg white
Food coloring
2 tsp. heavy cream (opt.)

Cream 1/2 cup butter with 1 teaspoon vanilla and salt. Blend in milk until smooth. Mix in 6 cups confectioners' sugar gradually. Shape into eggs; chill. Melt chocolate and paraffin in double boiler. Dip eggs in chocolate mixture. Cool on waxed paper. Cream 1/3 cup butter, 1 teaspoon vanilla and 3 cups confectioners' sugar. Beat in egg white. Tint with food coloring. Blend in enough cream to make frosting which can be pressed through decorator tube. Decorate eggs with frosting. Chill for several hours to overnight.

Coconut Eggs
Add 3/4 cup flaked coconut.

Peanut Butter Eggs
Substitute 3/4 cup peanut butter for butter and use 1 can sweetened condensed milk and 4 cups confectioners' sugar.

Eileene King
Preceptor Iota Lambda, Hughson, California

COTTONTAILS

1/2 can sweetened condensed milk
1 14-oz. package caramels
1 1/2 sticks margarine
50 lg. marshmallows
Crisp rice cereal

Melt first 3 ingredients in double boiler. Dip marshmallows in mixture; roll in cereal. Yield: 50.

Harriett Laws
Xi Epsilon Mu, Cherokee, Iowa

EASTER STRAWBERRIES

1 c. ground nuts
1 7-oz. package shredded coconut
2 3-oz. boxes strawberry gelatin
1 can sweetened condensed milk
Green and red tinted sugar

Mix all ingredients except tinted sugar. Shape into strawberries. Dip top in green sugar; roll bottom in red sugar.

Pat Kleck
Mu Theta, Brownsberg, Indiana

COTTAGE CHEESE CHEESECAKES

4 1/2 c. flour
4 1/2 tsp. baking powder
1 1/2 tsp. soda
5 1/2 c. sugar
3/4 c. shortening
11 eggs
6 tbsp. milk
5 1/2 tsp. vanilla extract
4 24-oz. cartons small curd cottage cheese
1 lb. butter, softened
Juice of 2 lemons
6 2/3 tbsp. cornstarch
Cinnamon

Mix first 3 ingredients with 1 1/2 cups sugar; make well in center. Cream shortening with 3 eggs, milk and 1 1/2 teaspoons vanilla. Pour into dry ingredients; mix well. Roll out into 4 or 5 very thin circles on floured surface. Place in pie plates. Press cottage cheese through strainer. Beat in 8 eggs. Fold in butter, 4 cups sugar, lemon juice, cornstarch and 4 teaspoons vanilla. Pour into prepared shells. Sprinkle with cinnamon. Bake at 300 degrees for 45 minutes. Yield: 4-5 pies.

Jamie Bland
Beta Iota, Bozeman, Montana

BISCOTTI COOKIES

4 eggs, beaten
1/2 stick margarine
2 1/2 c. flour
2 1/2 tsp. each baking powder, cornstarch, salt
1 c. sugar
1 tbsp. anise extract
1 tsp. vanilla extract
1 1/2 c. slivered almonds

Beat eggs and margarine in bowl. Mix in sifted dry ingredients. Stir in flavorings and almonds. Shape in 2 long strips. Bake at 325 degrees until golden brown. Slice. Bake for 10 minutes on each cut side to brown. Yield: 3 dozen.

Shirley A. Scott
Xi Rho Eta, Santa Cruz, California

CARROT BARS

4 eggs, beaten
2 c. sugar
1 1/4 c. oil
2 7 1/2-oz. jars strained carrots
2 c. flour
2 tsp. soda
1 tsp. salt
1 1/4 tsp. cinnamon
2 3-oz. packages cream cheese, softened
2 1/2 c. confectioners' sugar
1 stick margarine, softened
2 tsp. vanilla extract

Mix eggs, sugar, oil and carrots. Stir in dry ingredients. Spoon batter into greased and floured baking pans. Bake at 350 degrees for 25 minutes. Blend remaining ingredients until smooth. Spread over cooled cakes. Garnish with jelly beans.

I. Marie Gilman
Xi Eta Zeta, Emmetsburg, Iowa

Recipes on pages 63 and 68.

Memorial Day

TWELVE O'CLOCK COCKTAILS

2 c. orange juice
2 bananas
1 c. blueberries
1/2 c. each strawberries, raspberries
2 tbsp. honey

Puree all ingredients. Serve with orange twist. May freeze in Popsicle molds.

Kathleen A. Lacey
Xi Theta, Chubbuck, Idaho

CONGEALED HAM SALAD

1 3-oz. package lemon gelatin
1 env. unflavored gelatin
1 tbsp. each vinegar, lemon juice
1/2 tsp. salt
1 c. chopped ham
1 c. each finely chopped cabbage, celery
6 sweet pickles, chopped
2 pimentos, chopped

Dissolve lemon gelatin in 1 1/2 cups boiling water. Soften unflavored gelatin in 1/2 cup cold water. Stir into hot mixture until dissolved. Stir in remaining ingredients. Pour into mold. Chill until firm. Unmold onto lettuce-lined plate. Yield: 6-8 servings.

Elizabeth Magee
Preceptor Iota, Shreveport, Louisiana

PINEAPPLE-CRAB SALAD

3/4 c. pineapple chunks
3/4 c. sliced celery
1/3 c. mayonnaise
1 tsp. minced onion
1 1/2 tsp. lemon juice
Tabasco sauce to taste
3 tbsp. almonds
1 tbsp. chopped pimentos
1 c. crab meat, drained, flaked
Sm. crepes

Mix first 8 ingredients. Fold in crab meat; toss to coat. Chill for 2 hours. Fit crepes into muffin cups; weight with dry beans. Bake at 350 degrees for 10 minutes or until crisp; cool. Add salad just before serving.

Tommye Barker
Rho Omega, Houston, Texas

BEEF STROGANOFF

2 lb. round steak, tenderized
Flour
Salt, pepper and cayenne pepper to taste
1/4 c. oil
1 med. onion, chopped
1 clove of garlic, chopped
1 6-oz. can tomato sauce
1 c. beef bouillon
1 can mushrooms
1 tbsp. Worcestershire sauce
1 bay leaf
1/2 c. white wine
1/2 pt. sour cream

Cut steak into 1 1/2-inch strips. Coat with mixture of flour, salt and peppers. Brown in oil; remove steak. Saute onion and garlic in pan drippings. Stir in steak, tomato sauce and next 5 ingredients. Simmer for 20 minutes. Stir in sour cream. Cook until heated through. Serve over rice or noodles. Yield: 6-8 servings.

Janet Bull
Xi Delta Mu, Connersville, Indiana

DILLY-BOBS

1 1/2 to 2 lb. round steak, partially frozen
12 oz. pineapple juice
1 c. lemon juice
1/2 c. oil
2 tbsp. Worcestershire sauce
1/2 c. packed brown sugar
1 tbsp. dillweed
2 tsp. salt
Green pepper pieces
Cherry tomatoes
Lg. mushrooms
Fresh pineapple chunks

Cut steak into thin strips. Bring next 7 ingredients to a simmer. Pour over steak. Marinate overnight. Drain, reserving marinade. Thread steak on skewers with vegetables and pineapple. Grill for 10 minutes, basting with marinade and turning frequently. Yield: 4-6 servings.

Susan Rada
Theta Lambda, Colorado Springs, Colorado

PEPPER STEAK

1 lb. lean round steak, tenderized
1 tbsp. paprika
2 tbsp. butter
2 cloves of garlic, chopped
1 1/2 c. beef broth
1/4 c. chopped onion
1 c. green pepper strips
2 lg. tomatoes, cut in 8 wedges
2 tbsp. cornstarch
1/4 c. soy sauce
3 c. cooked rice

Cut steak into 1/4-inch strips. Sprinkle with paprika. Let stand for several minutes. Brown steak in butter. Add garlic and broth. Simmer, covered, for 30 minutes. Stir in onion, green pepper and tomatoes. Cook, covered, for 5 minutes. Stir in cornstarch blended with soy sauce and 1/4 cup water. Cook until thickened, stirring constantly. Serve over rice. Yield: 6 servings.

Patricia Blount
Xi Upsilon Nu, Claremont, California

INDEPENDENCE BURGERS

2 lb. ground beef
1 c. grated sharp Cheddar cheese
1 1/2 tbsp. chopped green chilies
1 13 1/4-oz. can crushed pineapple
1/3 c. fine bread crumbs
2 tsp. garlic salt
1/2 tsp. oregano
2 1/2 tbsp. chopped parsley
Dash of pepper
8 sesame seed buns

Mix first 9 ingredients. Shape into 8 patties. Grill 4 inches from heat for 10 minutes; turn. Grill for 4 minutes. Serve on buns. Yield: 8 servings.

Betty Vetter
Eta Alpha, Quincy, California

HAM HAWAIIAN

2 lb. cooked ham chunks
1 20-oz. can pineapple chunks, drained
1 sm. tomato, peeled, seeded, finely chopped
1 sm. onion, finely chopped
1 can cream of celery soup
1 med. green pepper, chopped
4 c. cooked rice

Mix first 4 ingredients with soup in saucepan. Simmer until heated through, stirring occasionally. Stir in green pepper. Cook until tender-crisp. Do not overcook. Serve on rice. Yield: 6 servings.

Rhonda Westergard
Xi Eta Iota, Clarion, Iowa

PICNIC-PERFECT HAM

1 3-lb. canned ham
1/2 c. packed light brown sugar
2 tsp. cornstarch
1/4 c. orange marmalade
2 tbsp. butter
1 lb. fresh California apricots, pitted, sliced
1/4 c. dark seedless raisins

Bake ham in shallow pan at 350 degrees for 15 minutes. Blend brown sugar, cornstarch and 1/4 cup water in saucepan. Add marmalade and butter. Bring to a boil, stirring constantly. Brush over ham. Bake for 30 minutes longer. Add apricots and raisins to remaining sauce. Cook over low heat for 5 minutes. Wrap ham in foil. Pour apricot sauce into thermos for picnic. Yield: 6 servings.

Photograph for this recipe on page 61.

SHERYL'S SPRING BAKE

1 c. rice
2 1/2 c. milk
1 tsp. salt
2 c. chopped ham
1/2 c. grated American cheese
1 can cream of asparagus soup
1 tbsp. finely chopped onion
3/4 c. cornflake crumbs
3 tbsp. melted butter

Cook rice with 2 cups milk and salt in double boiler. Mix with ham, cheese, soup, onion and 1/2 cup milk. Pour into 1 1/2-quart casserole. Top with mixture of cornflake crumbs and butter. Bake at 375 degrees for 30 to 45 minutes. Yield: 6 servings.

Linda Beck
Beta Xi, Ft. Madison, Iowa

MAMA'S BARBECUED SPARERIBS

4 lb. spareribs
1 c. catsup
1/4 c. each vinegar, Worcestershire sauce
1 tsp. each salt, pepper
2 tsp. chili powder
1/4 tsp. cayenne pepper
1 to 2 onions, finely chopped
1 to 2 tbsp. brown sugar

Place ribs fat side up in 9 x 13-inch baking pan. Bake at 450 degrees for 30 minutes; drain. Combine remaining ingredients with 1 cup water; pour over ribs. Reduce heat to 350 degrees. Bake for 1 hour. Place ribs on grill. Grill until glazed, basting with sauce and turning frequently. Yield: 4-5 servings.

Linda Jeanne Conners
Xi Beta Beta, Keyser, West Virginia

CHEESY ONION RING CASSEROLE

8 chicken breasts, cooked, chopped
1 8-oz. bottle of Italian salad dressing
1 c. chopped celery
2 8-oz. cans mushrooms
2 c. mayonnaise
1 16-oz. jar Cheddar cheese spread
2 cans French-fried onion rings

Marinate chicken in salad dressing overnight. Mix with celery, mushrooms and mayonnaise. Place in greased 9 x 13-inch baking dish. Spread cheese on top. Bake at 350 degrees for 45 minutes. Top with onion rings. Bake for 15 minutes longer. Yield: 10-12 servings.

Paulette Womack
Xi Epsilon Iota, Bristol, Oklahoma

GOLDEN CRUSTY CHICKEN CASSEROLE

4 chicken breasts, cooked, cut up
6 slices bread, cubed
1 tbsp. finely chopped onion
1 can golden mushroom soup
2 cans chicken noodle soup
2 eggs, beaten
Salt and pepper to taste
1/4 c. dry bread crumbs
1/4 c. melted margarine

Mix first 6 ingredients, salt and pepper. Place in 2 1/2-quart casserole. Sprinkle with bread crumbs tossed with margarine. Bake at 375 degrees for 35 minutes. Yield: 6-8 servings.

Yvonne Sorge
Xi Kappa Theta, Lebanon, Ohio

LOW-CALORIE CHICKEN WITH WILD RICE

2/3 c. wild rice
1 lg. green pepper, coarsely chopped
4 stalks celery, coarsely chopped
1 1/2 c. chicken broth
4 chicken breasts
Soy sauce
2 green onions with tops, thinly sliced

Mix rice with pepper, celery and broth in buttered 2 1/2-quart casserole. Arrange chicken breasts brushed with soy sauce on top. Bake, covered, at 350 degrees for 1 1/2 hours. Sprinkle with green onions. Yield: 4 servings.

Lucille Burkett
Laureate Alpha Epsilon, Effingham, Illinois

SPECIAL CHICKEN SPAGHETTI

4 chicken breasts
Salt
1 16-oz. package spaghetti
1 onion, chopped
2 stalks celery, chopped
1/2 stick margarine, melted
1 can Ro-Tel, finely chopped
1 can cream of mushroom soup
1 can cream of chicken soup
1 sm. can mushrooms
1/2 lb. Velveeta cheese, cubed
1 tsp. garlic salt
1 tsp. Creole seasoning

Cook chicken in salted water until tender; reserve stock. Bone chicken; cut into bite-sized pieces. Cook spaghetti in reserved stock; drain. Saute onion and celery in margarine. Stir in Ro-Tel, soups, mushrooms and cheese. Cook until cheese is melted. Season with garlic salt and Creole seasoning. Stir in chicken and spaghetti. Bake in 6-quart casserole at 350 degrees for 30 minutes. Yield: 6 servings.

Blanche Bourge
Preceptor Delta, Sulphur, Louisiana

COUNTRY CAPTAIN

1 lg. chicken, cut up
1 tsp. each salt, pepper
1/2 c. flour
1 tsp. paprika
1/2 c. oil
1 c. chopped onion
1 c. chopped green pepper
2 cans tomatoes
1 tsp. curry powder
1 can mushrooms
1 c. currants
1/2 c. slivered almonds

Sprinkle chicken with salt and pepper. Coat with mixture of flour and paprika. Brown in oil; remove chicken to casserole. Saute onion and green pepper in pan drippings. Stir in next 3 ingredients. Simmer for 20 minutes. Pour sauce over chicken. Bake, covered, at 350 degrees for 1 1/4 hours. Sprinkle with currants and almonds. Serve over rice. Yield: 6-8 servings.

Elaine Myers
Xi Beta Iota, Chamblee, Georgia

OVEN-BARBECUED CHICKEN

2 2 1/2 to 3-lb. fryers, cut up
Salt and pepper
3 onions, sliced
1 1/2 c. tomato juice
4 1/2 tsp. Worcestershire sauce
3/4 c. cider vinegar
1 bay leaf
1 tsp. sugar
3 tbsp. butter
3 cloves of garlic
1/4 tsp. each cayenne pepper, dry mustard

Arrange chicken skin side up in single layer in roasting pan. Sprinkle with salt and pepper; add enough water to cover bottom of pan. Cover with onions. Bake at 350 degrees for 30 minutes; turn. Bake for 30 minutes. Drain, leaving 3/4 cup liquid. Simmer remaining ingredients and 2 teaspoons salt and 1/4 teaspoon pepper for 10 minutes. Pour over skin side up chicken. Bake for 1 hour, basting frequently. Yield: 6-8 servings.

Wyn Kish
Laureate Epsilon, Yorktown, Saskatchewan, Canada

PEACHIE CHICKEN BREASTS

6 chicken breasts
1/2 tsp. salt
1 16-oz. can sliced peaches
1 c. barbecue sauce
1 tbsp. soy sauce
1 clove of garlic, minced
2 tsp. cornstarch
1 16-oz. can small onions, drained

Sprinkle chicken breasts with salt. Bake in 9 x 13-inch pan at 375 degrees for 25 minutes. Drain peaches, reserving syrup. Bring syrup blended with barbecue sauce, soy sauce and garlic to a boil. Stir in cornstarch blended with 1 tablespoon water. Cook until thickened, stirring constantly. Process peaches in food processor until finely chopped. Stir into sauce. Pour over chicken. Arrange onions on top. Bake for 25 to 35 minutes, basting frequently. Yield: 6 servings.

Bobby A. Amini
Theta, Bethany, Oklahoma

CHICKEN AND SHRIMP GRILL

9 chicken breasts, boned
18 slices bacon, cut in half
36 lg. fresh shrimp, peeled
3/4 c. beer
1 1/2 tsp. dry mustard
1 1/2 tsp. chopped fresh ginger
1/3 c. soy sauce
3/4 tsp. pepper
1 clove of garlic, crushed
24 med. mushrooms, stemmed

Cut each chicken breast into 4 strips. Partially cook bacon. Wrap each shrimp with bacon, then chicken strip; secure with toothpick. Marinate for 1 to 2 hours in mixture of beer and next 5 ingredients. Alternate 3 shrimp with 2 mushrooms on each of 12 skewers. Grill for 15 to 25 minutes, basting frequently. Yield: 6 servings.

Katie H. Harper
Xi Alpha Zeta, Tucker, Georgia

CUCUMBER AND SALMON CASSEROLE

3 c. soft bread crumbs
1/2 c. margarine
Salt and pepper to taste
1/4 c. flour
1 1/4 c. milk
Juice of 1/2 lemon
1 egg yolk, beaten
1 med. can salmon, drained, flaked
1/2 cucumber, finely chopped
Chopped parsley

Brown bread crumbs in 6 tablespoons margarine. Season with salt and pepper. Blend flour with 2 tablespoons melted margarine. Stir in milk gradually. Cook until thickened, stirring constantly. Add lemon juice, egg yolk and salmon. Cook over low heat for 2 minutes. Do not boil. Stir in cucumber. Alternate layers of salmon mixture and crumbs in 2-quart casserole. Sprinkle with parsley. Bake at 375 degrees for 15 minutes. Yield: 6-8 servings.

Judy Jamieson
Zeta, Grand Falls, Newfoundland, Canada

GRILLED FISH

1/4 c. butter, melted
1/4 c. lemon juice
2 tbsp. soy sauce
1/2 tsp. each garlic salt, MSG, oregano
1 1/2 to 2 lb. whole fish

Mix first 6 ingredients with 2 tablespoons water in small saucepan. Warm on edge of grill. Grill fish on oiled foil 5 inches from heat source for 12 to 15 minutes per pound, turning once and basting frequently with sauce. Yield: 2-3 servings.

Bonnie Kemper
Xi Eta Phi, Altamont, Illinois

RALF'S FAVORITE FLOUNDER

1 6-oz. package chicken-flavored stuffing mix
2 tbsp. flour
1 c. milk
1/2 c. grated Cheddar cheese
1 tbsp. minced onion
1/2 tsp. seasoned salt
1 10-oz. package frozen chopped broccoli, thawed
1 1/4 lb. flounder fillets

Prepare stuffing mix using package instructions. Blend flour with 1 cup water. Cook over low heat until thickened, stirring constantly. Stir in milk, cheese, onion and seasoned salt. Cook until smooth, stirring frequently. Layer 1/2 cup sauce, stuffing, broccoli, flounder and remaining cheese sauce in greased 7 x 11-inch baking dish. Bake at 350 degrees for 35 to 40 minutes. Yield: 3 servings.

Ann E. Oster
Gamma Iota, Berlin, Maryland

SCALLOPS WITH VEGETABLES

1/2 lb. scallops, sliced
2 tbsp. oyster sauce
1 tsp. soy sauce
1/4 tsp. sugar
2 tsp. cornstarch
1 1/2 c. Chinese pea pods
2 green onions, chopped
2 tbsp. margarine

Mix first 5 ingredients. Saute pea pods and onions in margarine for 3 minutes or until tender-crisp. Add scallops mixture. Stir-fry over high heat for 3 minutes or until scallops are just tender and sauce is slightly thickened. Serve with rice. Yield: 4 servings.

Marilyn West
Xi Beta, Las Vegas, Nevada

GARLIC FRIED SHRIMP

4 eggs, beaten
1/2 c. evaporated milk
1 tbsp. lemon juice
1 tbsp. Worcestershire sauce
1 1/2 tbsp. garlic powder
1 lb. shrimp, cleaned
1 c. flour
Oil for deep frying

Mix first 5 ingredients. Marinate shrimp in mixture for 2 to 3 hours; drain. Coat with flour. Fry in 400-degree oil until brown. Yield: 4 servings.

Fay Burke
Sigma Iota, Lake Jackson, Texas

SHRIMP JAMBALAYA

1 stick butter, melted
1 can Ro-Tel, mashed
1 can cream of celery soup
1 can onion soup
2 c. rice
1 lb. shrimp, cleaned

Mix all ingredients. Bake in covered 9 x 13-inch pan at 350 degrees for 1 hour. Yield: 8-10 servings.

Patricia Frey
Xi Alpha Omega, Robertsdale, Alabama

PLEASURE ISLE CASSEROLE

1 lb. peeled shrimp
1 lb. crab meat
1/4 c. each chopped onion, green pepper, celery
2 tbsp. each Nature's seasoning, MSG
3 tbsp. mayonnaise
1/3 c. parsley flakes
2 eggs, beaten
1 c. cooked rice
1 10-oz. package frozen English peas
Salt and pepper to taste
Margarine
1 tbsp. flour
1 1/2 c. milk
1/4 c. sugar

Mix first 12 ingredients with salt and pepper to taste. Spoon into greased 10 x 12-inch baking dish. Blend 1 tablespoon margarine with flour in saucepan. Stir in milk gradually. Cook until thickened, stirring constantly. Stir in sugar, salt and pepper. Pour over seafood mixture. Dot with margarine. Bake at 375 degrees for 1 hour.

Karen Harrison
Delta Chi, Robertsdale, Alabama

BROCCOLI-HAM-EGG CASSEROLE

5 eggs, beaten
1 c. cottage cheese
1/4 c. flour
1/2 tsp. each salt, baking powder
1/4 c. melted butter
1/2 lb. Cheddar cheese, shredded
1 10-oz. package frozen chopped broccoli, thawed, drained
1 c. chopped ham

Mix all ingredients. Bake in 8 x 8-inch casserole at 350 degrees for 25 to 30 minutes or until set.

Martha Cleveland
Gamma Phi, Brookfield, Missouri

COMPANY CASSEROLE POTATOES

8 to 10 med. russet potatoes, peeled
1 8-oz. package cream cheese, softened
2/3 c. sour cream
1/2 c. minced green onions
8 slices crisp-fried bacon, crumbled
Salt and pepper to taste
2 tbsp. melted butter
2 tbsp. minced parsley

Cook potatoes in salted water until tender; drain. Dry in pan over low heat, shaking gently. Blend cream cheese and sour cream in mixer bowl. Beat until blended. Beat in potatoes 1 at a time. Mix in green onions, bacon, salt and pepper. Spoon into buttered casserole. Drizzle with butter. Bake at 375 degrees for 20 to 25 minutes. Sprinkle with parsley. Yield: 6-8 servings.

B. J. Russell
Xi Eta Lambda, Columbus, Ohio

HASHED BROWN POTATO CASSEROLE

2 lb. frozen hashed brown potatoes, thawed
3/4 c. butter, melted
1 tsp. salt
1/4 tsp. pepper
1/2 c. chopped onion
1 can cream of chicken soup
1 pt. sour cream (opt.)
2 c. shredded Cheddar cheese
2 c. bread crumbs (opt.)

Mix potatoes with 1/2 cup butter, salt and pepper. Mix in next 4 ingredients. Spoon into buttered 3-quart casserole. Top with mixture of 1/4 cup butter and crumbs. Bake at 350 degrees for 45 minutes. Yield: 6-8 servings.

Eleanor Jenkins
Laureate Alpha Epsilon, Altamont, Illinois

MICROWAVE ZESTY VEGETABLE MEDLEY

1 med. head cauliflower, broken into flowerets
1 bunch broccoli, cut into 1-in. pieces
1 lb. carrots, cut into 1/2-in. pieces
1 1/2 tsp. salt
1/4 c. chopped onion
1/4 c. horseradish, drained
1/4 tsp. pepper
1 c. mayonnaise
14 saltines, finely crumbled
2 tbsp. margarine, melted
1/8 tsp. paprika

Combine cauliflower, broccoli, carrots, 1/4 cup water and 1 teaspoon salt in glass baking dish. Microwave, covered, on High for 16 to 18 minutes, stirring after 8 minutes; drain. Mix onion, horseradish, 1/2 teaspoon salt, pepper and mayonnaise. Pour over vegetables; toss lightly to coat. Sprinkle mixture of crumbs, margarine and paprika over top. Microwave on High for 1 to 2 minutes. Yield: 5 servings.

Alice Cooper
Preceptor Theta, Beatrice, Nebraska

CRUSTLESS VEGETABLE PIE

1 med. eggplant, peeled, chopped
2 med. zucchini, chopped
1 lg. onion, chopped
1/4 c. oil
4 med. tomatoes, peeled, chopped
3 eggs
3/4 c. Parmesan cheese
1 tbsp. minced parsley
1/2 tsp. each basil, oregano
Salt and pepper to taste
1/4 lb. mozzarella cheese, thinly sliced

Saute eggplant, zucchini and onion in oil for 10 minutes. Add tomatoes. Simmer, covered, for 20 to 25 minutes; cool. Beat eggs with 1/4 cup Parmesan cheese, parsley, basil, oregano, salt and pepper. Add to vegetable mixture, mixing well. Spoon half into greased 10-inch pie plate. Sprinkle with 1/4 cup Parmesan cheese. Repeat layers. Top with mozzarella cheese. Bake at 350 degrees for 40 minutes or until set. Yield: 5-6 servings.

Mary Gamble
Xi Beta Alpha, Huntsville, Alabama

VEGETARIAN LASAGNA

2 lg. carrots, sliced
3/4 c. chopped onion
Garlic salt to taste
3 tbsp. oil
1 jar meatless spaghetti sauce
1 tsp. oregano
1/2 tsp. basil
2 c. fresh mushrooms, sliced
2 med. zucchini, sliced
1 pkg. lasagna noodles, cooked
1 pkg. frozen spinach, thawed, squeezed dry
1 can pitted black olives
1 carton cottage cheese
4 c. shredded mozzarella cheese

Saute carrots and onion with garlic salt in oil. Stir in spaghetti sauce, oregano and basil. Simmer, covered, until carrots are tender. Combine with mushrooms and zucchini in 9 x 13-inch pan. Top with layers of noodles, spinach, olives, cottage cheese and mozzarella cheese. Bake at 375 degrees for 35 minutes. Cool for 10 minutes. Yield: 12 servings.

Brenda Johnson
Alpha, Springfield, Missouri

EASY HERB BREAD

1/2 c. butter, softened
2 tsp. garlic powder
1/2 tsp. each savory, rosemary, thyme
1 tsp. each celery salt, sage
1/2 tsp. each chervil, basil, oregano
1 tbsp. parsley
1 loaf French bread, sliced

Blend butter and seasonings. Spread on bread slices. Bake, wrapped in foil, at 350 degrees for 30 minutes.

Kaye Lusk
Gamma Omicron, Sudbury, Ontario, Canada

Memorial Day / 67

EASY HOT ROLLS

2 pkg. dry yeast
1 pkg. white cake mix
1 tsp. salt
4 1/2 c. flour

Dissolve yeast in 2 1/2 cups warm water in mixer bowl. Mix in cake mix and salt using dough hook. Add flour gradually, beating constantly. Place dough in greased bowl, turning to grease surface. Let rise until doubled in bulk. Shape into rolls. Place in baking pan. Let rise until doubled. Bake at 350 degrees for 15 to 20 minutes. Yield: 4 dozen.

Mabel Foster
Xi Alpha Delta, Siloam Springs, Arkansas

SCRUMPTIOUS SOUR CREAM CORN BREAD

1 c. flour
1/2 tsp. each soda, salt
2 tsp. baking powder
1/4 c. sugar
3/4 c. yellow cornmeal
1/2 c. milk
1 egg, beaten
1 c. sour cream

Sift first 4 ingredients. Add sugar and cornmeal. Stir in mixture of milk, egg and sour cream. Bake in 8-inch square pan at 350 degrees for 35 minutes. Serve warm. Yield: 9 servings.

Dorothy Stampfel
Xi Alpha Kappa, Red Lodge, Montana

VEGETABLE BREAD

1 med. onion
1/2 green pepper
1 stick butter
1/2 lb. bacon, crisp-fried, crumbled
1/2 c. Parmesan cheese
3 cans refrigerator biscuits, quartered

Saute onion and pepper in butter. Stir in bacon and cheese. Mix with biscuits. Arrange in bundt pan. Bake at 350 degrees for 30 minutes.

Julia Gray
Alpha Gamma Pi, Stephenville, Texas

ICE CREAM CRUNCH

2 1/2 c. Rice Chex cereal, crushed
1 can flaked coconut
1 c. chopped pecans
3/4 c. packed brown sugar
1/2 c. melted margarine
1/2 gal. butter brickle ice cream
Caramel ice cream topping (opt.)

Mix first 5 ingredients. Press into bottom of 9 x 13-inch baking pan. Bake at 300 degrees for 30 minutes; stir after 10 minutes. Cool. Press 2/3 of cooled mixture over bottom of pan. Top with 1 to 1 1/4-inch thick ice cream slices. Sprinkle with remaining coconut mixture. Freeze. Top with caramel topping. Yield: 15-18 servings.

Ledah Prichard
Xi Delta Tau, Princeton, Missouri

DIAMOND HEAD CRUNCH

1 med. can crushed pineapple
1 can apple pie filling
1 pkg. lemonade mix
1 pkg. yellow cake mix
1 stick margarine, chopped
1/2 c. chopped nuts
1/2 c. coconut

Layer pineapple, pie filling, lemonade mix, dry cake mix, margarine, nuts and coconut in 9 x 13-inch baking pan. Bake at 350 degrees for 1 hour. Yield: 8-10 servings.

Karen McAndrew-Acker
Beta Omega, Allentown, Pennsylvania

COCO LOPEZ CAKE

1 pkg. yellow cake mix with pudding
1 lg. can cream of coconut
1 8-oz. carton whipped topping
1 sm. package flaked coconut

Prepare and bake cake in 9 x 13-inch pan using package directions. Prick cake with fork. Pour cream of coconut over cake gradually until absorbed. Chill overnight. Spread with whipped topping. Sprinkle with coconut. Chill until serving time.

Verna Wahl
Preceptor Alpha Chi, San Francisco, California

FROSTED ANGEL CAKE

1 8-oz. milk chocolate bar, melted
2 env. whipped topping mix, prepared
1 angel food cake

Fold cooled chocolate into whipped topping. Spread over cake. Chill.

Alberta L. Dixon
Preceptor Beta Xi, Joliet, Illinois

EASY GERMAN CHOCOLATE CAKE

1 pkg. white cake mix
1 sm. box chocolate instant pudding mix
3 egg whites
2 c. milk
1 c. sugar
1 c. evaporated milk
3 egg yolks, beaten
1/4 c. margarine
1 tsp. vanilla extract
1 c. chopped pecans
1 c. coconut

Mix cake mix, pudding, egg whites and milk. Bake in greased and floured 9 x 13-inch pan at 350 degrees for 35 to 40 minutes. Cook next 4 ingredients over medium heat for 3 to 5 minutes, stirring constantly. Stir in vanilla, pecans and coconut. Let stand until thickened. Spread over cooled cake. Yield: 15-20 servings.

Pat Symes
Iota Chi, Manchester, Missouri

LEMON SPONGE ROLL

1 c. sugar
1 tsp. grated lemon rind
3 eggs, well beaten
1 c. sifted cake flour
1 tsp. baking powder
1/4 tsp. salt
Confectioners' sugar
1/2 c. whipped cream
1 can lemon pie filling

Beat 1/4 cup water, 1 cup sugar and lemon rind into eggs gradually. Stir in next 3 sifted dry ingredients until just mixed. Pour into greased jelly roll pan lined with greased waxed paper. Bake at 350 degrees for 12 minutes. Invert onto towel sprinkled with confectioners' sugar. Roll as for jelly roll; cool. Unroll. Fold whipped cream into pie filling. Spread over cake; reroll. Sprinkle with confectioners' sugar. Chill until serving time. Yield: 10 servings.

Deb Miller
Delta Sigma, Janesville, Wisconsin

BLUEBERRY CHEESECAKE

1/2 c. melted butter
1 1/2 c. graham cracker crumbs
1/2 c. packed brown sugar
1 c. whipping cream, whipped
4 oz. cream cheese, softened
3/4 c. confectioners' sugar
4 c. blueberries
1 tbsp. lemon juice
Pinch of cinnamon
3/4 c. sugar
1 tbsp. cornstarch

Mix first 3 ingredients until crumbly. Press into 9-inch square pan. Blend whipped cream, cream cheese and confectioners' sugar. Spread in prepared pan. Chill for 2 hours. Mix remaining ingredients. Cook until thick, stirring constantly; cool. Pour over cheesecake.

Leslie Siska
Gamma Sigma, Fernie, British Columbia, Canada

CHOCOLATE SYRUP BROWNIES

Margarine
2 1/2 c. sugar
4 eggs
1 16-oz. can chocolate syrup
1 c. flour
6 tbsp. milk
1/2 c. chocolate chips
Chopped nuts

Cream 1 stick softened margarine and 1 cup sugar. Mix in eggs, chocolate syrup and flour. Bake in greased and floured 9 x 13-inch pan at 350 degrees for 30 minutes. Bring 6 tablespoons margarine, 1 1/2 cups sugar and milk to a boil. Cook for 30 seconds; remove from heat. Stir in chocolate chips until melted. Spread over brownies. Sprinkle with nuts. Yield: 2 dozen.

Nathalee Scheiwe
Epsilon Upsilon, Sierra Vista, Arizona

FRESH APRICOT PACKABLE PIES

2 10-oz. packages pie crust mix
1 lb. fresh California apricots, pitted, chopped
1/8 tsp. cinnamon
Dash of nutmeg
1/2 c. packed light brown sugar
Cream
Sugar

Prepare pie pastry using package directions. Roll into 1/8-inch thick circle. Cut into eleven 5-inch rounds. Combine apricots, spices and brown sugar. Spoon 3 tablespoons apricot filling on center of each round. Fold pastry in half and seal edges with fork; prick tops. Brush with cream; sprinkle with sugar. Bake on baking sheets at 425 degrees for 10 minutes.

Photograph for this recipe on page 61.

SOUTHERN CHOCOLATE-PECAN PIE

4 oz. German's sweet chocolate
3 tbsp. butter
1 tsp. instant coffee powder
1/3 c. sugar
1 c. light corn syrup
3 eggs, slightly beaten
1 tsp. vanilla extract
1 c. coarsely chopped pecans
1 unbaked 9-in. pie shell

Heat first 3 ingredients over low heat until chocolate is melted, stirring constantly. Bring sugar and corn syrup to a boil, stirring until sugar dissolves. Simmer for 2 minutes, stirring occasionally; remove from heat. Stir in chocolate mixture. Stir into eggs gradually. Stir in vanilla and pecans. Pour into pie shell. Bake at 375 degrees for 45 minutes or until completely puffed across top.

Sally Lyon
Delta Kappa, Ellisville, Mississippi

PEANUT BUTTER PIE

1 c. confectioners' sugar
1/2 c. peanut butter
1 baked 8-in. pie shell
2 c. milk
1/4 c. sifted cornstarch
2/3 c. sugar
1/4 tsp. salt
3 egg yolks, beaten
1/4 tsp. vanilla extract
2 tbsp. butter, softened

Mix confectioners' sugar and peanut butter until crumbly. Press into pie shell. Scald milk, stirring constantly. Stir mixture of cornstarch, sugar and salt into milk very gradually. Stir in egg yolks. Cook until thick, stirring constantly; remove from heat. Stir in vanilla and butter. Pour into pie shell. Chill for 4 hours. Garnish with 1/3 cup graham cracker crumbs. Yield: 8 servings.

Susan Harvey
Preceptor Delta Alpha, Ft. Myers, Florida

Recipes on pages 70, 72, 76 and 77.

Independence Day

APRICOT SLUSH

2 c. sugar
2 12-oz. cans frozen orange juice concentrate, thawed
2 c. apricot Brandy
2 12-oz. cans frozen lemonade concentrate, thawed
7-Up

Boil sugar until dissolved in 7 cups water; cool. Stir in orange juice, Brandy and lemonade. Freeze. Scoop slush into glasses. Add 1/2 cup 7-Up to each.

Caroline Carbone
Xi Delta Gamma, Salamanca, New York

PICNIC LEMONADE

1/2 c. light corn syrup
1/2 c. sugar
2 tbsp. grated lemon rind
1 1/4 c. lemon juice

Boil corn syrup, sugar, 2/3 cup water and lemon rind for 5 minutes; strain. Cool. Combine with lemon juice and 7 cups water in ice-filled pitcher; mix well. Garnish with maraschino cherries and lemon slices.

Photograph for this recipe on page 69.

PINA COLADA

1 46-oz. can pineapple juice
1 can cream of coconut
1 1/4 to 1 1/2 c. rum
7-Up

Blend first 3 ingredients. Freeze. Scoop into glasses; fill with 7-Up.

Jean Reedy
Xi Eta Zeta, Emmetsburg, Iowa

SUMMER SLUSH SURPRISE

3 c. sugar
4 tea bags
1 12-oz. can orange juice concentrate, thawed
1 12-oz. can lemon juice concentrate, thawed
1 fifth of Brandy
7-Up

Boil sugar until dissolved in 7 cups water. Steep tea bags in 1 1/2 cups boiling water. Combine all ingredients except 7-Up. Freeze. Spoon into glasses. Add 1/2 cup 7-Up to each. Yield: 1 gallon.

Linda Britschgi
Preceptor Tau, Holtville, California

WATERMELON WINE BOAT

Watermelon half
7-Up
Club soda
1 qt. orange juice
Sangria
Bourbon, light rum and Tequila

Hollow out watermelon to make boat. Mix 7-Up, club soda and orange juice to taste. Combine 1 part orange juice mixture with 2 parts wine. Add Bourbon, rum and Tequila to taste. Fill watermelon boat 2/3 full. Garnish with grapes, strawberries and honeydew and peach slices.

Deborah Goss
Sigma Delta, Kearney, Missouri

VODKA SLUSH

1 6-oz. can frozen orange juice concentrate, thawed
2 6-oz. cans frozen lemonade concentrate, thawed
1 c. sugar
2 6-oz. cans frozen limeade concentrate, thawed
2 c. vodka
2 28-oz. bottles of lemon-lime soda, chilled

Mix first 5 ingredients with 3 1/2 cups water. Freeze for 48 hours, stirring occasionally. Spoon 3/4 cup frozen mixture into each tall glass; fill with lemon-lime soda. Yield: 16 servings.

Terie Shull
Eta Lambda, Higginsville, Missouri

FIRECRACKER JEZEBEL SAUCE

1 20-oz. jar apple jelly
1 20-oz. jar pineapple preserves
3 tsp. dry mustard
1 4-oz. jar horseradish
Pinch of pepper
Cream cheese

Mix first 5 ingredients with wire whisk. Pour enough over block of cream cheese to cover. Serve with crackers. Store remaining sauce in refrigerator. Yield: 5 cups.

Ellen C. Crouthers
Beta, Rogers, Arkansas

CHINESE CHICKEN WINGS

2 lb. chicken wings, split, tips trimmed
2 eggs, beaten
1 c. flour
Garlic salt
1/4 c. pineapple juice
3/4 c. sugar
1/4 to 1/2 c. vinegar
3/4 c. catsup
1 tsp. MSG
1 tsp. soy sauce
1 1/2 tsp. salt
1 med. can pineapple chunks

Dip chicken wings in eggs, then in flour. Sprinkle with garlic salt. Let stand for several minutes. Brown in a small amount of oil. Heat pineapple juice and next 6 ingredients. Stir in pineapple. Pour over chicken wings in 9 x 13-inch baking dish. Bake at 350 degrees for 30 minutes. Yield: 4 servings.

Judi Eros
Gamma, Japan

Independence Day / 71

MIKE'S SALSA

4 lg. tomatoes, peeled, chopped
4 green onions, chopped
1/4 c. fresh parsley
1 clove of garlic
2 tbsp. green chilies
Dash of Tabasco sauce
1/4 tsp. each freshly ground pepper, oregano
1 tbsp. lemon juice

Process all ingredients in blender container until of desired consistency. Chill, covered, for 2 hours. Yield: 2 cups.

Diane Hudson
Nu Gamma, Crescent City, California

CHILI CON QUESO

3 slices bacon
2 lg. onions, chopped
2 lb. Velveeta cheese, melted
1 jar jalapeno salsa
2 sm. cans chopped green chilies
1/2 tsp. garlic powder
Tabasco sauce to taste

Fry bacon until crisp; remove and crumble. Saute onions in pan drippings; remove. Combine with bacon and remaining ingredients; mix well. Serve with corn chips or fresh vegetables.

Joan M. Allison
Nu, Lovelock, Nevada

SWEET HOT PICKLES

5 lb. sugar
6 cloves of garlic, chopped
1 gal. jar whole sour pickles, drained, sliced
1 sm. bottle of Tabasco sauce

Mix sugar and garlic. Alternate layers of pickles and garlic mixture in 1 gallon jar; press down. Pour Tabasco sauce over top; seal. Let stand for 6 days, inverting jar every other day. Yield: 1 gallon.

Ethlyn F. Held
Preceptor Gamma Phi, Houston, Texas

CREAMY TUNA GARDEN WEDGES

2 c. baking mix
1 8-oz. package cream cheese, softened
1/2 c. mayonnaise
1/2 c. sliced green onions
2 tsp. horseradish
1/8 tsp. red pepper sauce
1 6 1/2-oz. can tuna, drained
2 stalks celery, cut diagonally into 1/4-in. slices
Fresh vegetables
Shredded Cheddar cheese

Mix baking mix and 1/2 cup cold water until soft dough forms. Pat into ungreased 12-inch pizza pan, forming 1/2-inch rim. Bake at 450 degrees for 10 minutes; cool for 10 minutes. Mix next 6 ingredients. Spread over crust. Arrange celery over top spoke fashion to form 6 wedges. Top each wedge with vegetables. Sprinkle with cheese. Chill, covered, for 1 hour. Cut into bite-sized pieces to serve. Yield: 36 servings.

Pat Wullschleger
Preceptor, Home, Kansas

CHEDDAR RING MOLD

1 8 1/2-oz. can crushed pineapple
1 3-oz. package lemon gelatin
1 tbsp. lemon juice
1/4 lb. Cheddar cheese, shredded
1/2 pt. whipping cream, whipped

Drain pineapple, reserving juice. Dissolve gelatin in 1 cup boiling water. Mix reserved juice with enough cold water to measure 3/4 cup. Add to gelatin mixture. Stir in lemon juice; remove from heat and cool. Chill until partially set. Fold in pineapple, cheese and whipped cream. Pour into 1/2-quart ring mold. Chill until firm. Unmold. Garnish with lettuce and fruit. Yield: 8 servings.

Kathleen J. Shafer
Theta Epsilon, Julesburg, Colorado

RED-WHITE AND BLUE DELIGHT

1 3-oz. package raspberry gelatin
1 env. unflavored gelatin
1 c. half and half
1 c. sugar
1 tsp. vanilla extract
1 8-oz. package cream cheese, softened
1/2 c. chopped pecans
1 3-oz. package black raspberry gelatin
1 can blueberries

Dissolve raspberry gelatin in 2 cups boiling water. Pour into 9 x 13-inch pan. Chill until set. Soften unflavored gelatin in 1/2 cup cold water. Bring half and half and sugar to a boil. Mix with unflavored gelatin. Add vanilla and cream cheese. Pour over first layer. Sprinkle with pecans. Chill until set. Dissolve black raspberry gelatin with 1 cup boiling water. Add blueberries. Pour over layers. Chill until set. Yield: 12-20 servings.

Harriet Waite
Epsilon Nu, Blair, Nebraska

KIDNEY BEAN SALAD

2 c. kidney beans
2 c. corn
2 c. small peas
3 hard-boiled eggs, sliced
1 lg. tomato, sliced
1 c. (about) mayonnaise
1 tbsp. onion flakes
2 tsp. sugar
Pinch of salt

Combine first 5 ingredients. Stir in mayonnaise gradually until just moistened. Add onion flakes, sugar and salt.

Dianne Hoffmeyer
Preceptor Eta, Carrollton, Missouri

COPPER PENNIES SALAD

2 lb. carrots, sliced, cooked
1 lg. green pepper, thinly sliced
1 lg. onion, thinly sliced
1 can tomato soup
1 c. oil
1 tsp. salt
1 c. sugar
3/4 c. vinegar
1/2 tsp. celery seed

Mix carrots, green pepper and onion. Bring remaining ingredients to a boil. Pour over vegetables. Chill overnight.

Lila Warrell
Preceptor Upsilon, Muncie, Indiana

AUNT NELLIE'S EGG SALAD

1 15-oz. can pork and beans, mashed
1/2 c. salad dressing
1/2 lb. Cheddar cheese, grated
Sweet pickles, chopped
1 tbsp. prepared mustard
Salt and pepper to taste
24 hard-boiled eggs, chopped

Mix first 5 ingredients. Season with salt and pepper. Spoon over eggs; toss to mix. Chill in refrigerator.

Nellie P. Chance
Preceptor Alpha Beta, St. Joseph, Missouri

ITALIAN MARINADE

1 1/2 c. wine vinegar
1/2 c. each oil, olive oil
1 tsp. each sugar, salt
1 1/2 tsp. crushed oregano
1 12-oz. can button mushrooms
2 c. cauliflowerets
2 carrots, sliced
1 green pepper, cut into strips
12 pearl onions
1 bottle of stuffed olives

Heat vinegar, oils, sugar and seasonings; cool. Pour over vegetables and olives. Chill for 24 hours or longer.

Mona Burran
Xi Gamma Tau, Tifton, Georgia

OLD-FASHIONED POTATO SALAD

3/4 c. mayonnaise
1/2 c. vinegar
1 tsp. sugar
1 tsp. salt
1/3 c. chopped onion
1/4 tsp. tarragon
8 med. potatoes, cooked, peeled, sliced
3 hard-boiled eggs
1 c. chopped celery
1/4 c. chopped parsley

Blend mayonnaise, vinegar, 1/4 cup water, sugar and salt; stir in onion and tarragon. Pour over warm potatoes; cool. Chop 3 egg whites and 2 egg yolks. Add with celery and parsley to potato mixture. Chill in refrigerator. Mound salad on platter. Chop remaining egg yolk; sprinkle on top. Garnish with tomato slices. Yield: 4 servings.

Photograph for this recipe on page 69.

PATIO POTATO SALAD

1/2 c. milk
1/3 c. sugar
1/4 c. vinegar
1 egg
4 tbsp. butter, melted
1 tbsp. cornstarch
1 tsp. each salt, celery seed
1/4 c. chopped onion
1/2 c. mayonnaise
10 med. potatoes, cooked, chopped
3 hard-boiled eggs, chopped
1/2 c. chopped celery

Cook first 6 ingredients and seasonings over low heat until thickened, stirring constantly; remove from heat. Stir in onion and mayonnaise; cool. Pour over potatoes, eggs and celery; toss to coat. Garnish with additional chopped boiled egg and paprika. Yield: 10-12 servings.

Gretta Ludwig
Sigma, Rehoboth Beach, Delaware

RICE AND LENTIL SALAD

2 c. rice, cooked
1 c. lentils, cooked
1/2 c. each chopped tomatoes, green pepper, chives
1/2 c. each chopped celery, carrots, broccoli
1/2 c. each chopped cauliflower, mushrooms
1/2 c. each chopped radishes, avocado
1 bottle of Italian dressing

Mix cooled rice and lentils. Mix in remaining ingredients except dressing. Pour dressing over top. Chill for 1 to 2 hours. Yield: 4-6 servings.

Lana D. Livingston
Xi Eta, West Lebanon, New Hampshire

VERMICELLI SALAD

1 cucumber, chopped
1 tomato, chopped
1 jar Salad Supreme
1 lb. vermicelli, cooked, drained
1 8-oz. bottle of Italian dressing

Mix cucumber, tomato and Salad Supreme. Chill for 24 hours. Combine with cooled vermicelli and dressing; toss to coat. Chill in refrigerator.

Elizabeth Miller
Kappa, Tucson, Arizona

OVERNIGHT SPAGHETTI SALAD

1 lb. spaghetti, broken into 2 to 3-in. pieces, cooked
1 med. cucumber, seeded, chopped
1 med. green pepper, chopped
2 tomatoes, seeded, chopped
2 sm. onions, chopped
2 1/2 oz. Salad Supreme without cheese
1 8-oz. bottle of Italian dressing

Independence Day / 73

Mix spaghetti and vegetables. Add Salad Supreme and dressing; toss to coat. Chill, covered, overnight. Yield: 20-25 servings.

Miriam Watson
Preceptor Eta, Pikeville, Kentucky

SIMPLE SUMMER SALAD

- 1 pkg. ranch style salad dressing mix
- 3 stalks broccoli, cut into bite-sized pieces
- 1 lg. head cauliflower, cut into bite-sized pieces
- 1 med. onion, chopped
- 3 or 4 stalks celery, chopped
- 1 8-oz. carton sour cream
- 1/2 c. mayonnaise
- 1 10-oz. package frozen peas

Prepare salad dressing mix using package directions; chill. Mix broccoli, cauliflower, onion and celery. Add chilled dressing, sour cream and mayonnaise; mix well. Add peas; mix lightly. Chill for 1 hour or longer.

Margaret Ann Moyer
Preceptor Beta Alpha, Jeffersonville, Indiana

CHICKEN-RICE SALAD

- 2 c. rice
- 2 tsp. butter
- Salt
- 1 jar marinated artichoke hearts, chopped
- 1 sm. package frozen peas, thawed
- 1/2 c. chopped celery
- 1 sm. can sliced ripe olives, drained
- 1/4 c. chopped parsley
- 3 chicken breasts, cooked, chopped
- Mayonnaise
- Pepper to taste
- Pinch of curry powder

Cook rice with butter and 1 teaspoon salt in 4 cups boiling water for 20 minutes. Drain artichokes, reserving marinade. Mix peas, celery, olives, parsley, chicken, rice and artichokes. Add mixture of mayonnaise and reserved marinade; toss to coat. Season with salt to taste, pepper and curry powder.

Donna Crawford
Xi Zeta Zeta, Dunsmuir, California

FRUITED CHICKEN SALAD

- 4 c. chopped cooked chicken
- 1 15-oz. can pineapple chunks, drained
- 1 c. chopped celery
- 1 11-oz. can mandarin oranges, drained
- 1/2 c. sliced ripe olives
- 1/2 c. chopped green pepper
- 2 tbsp. grated onion
- 1 c. mayonnaise
- 1 tbsp. prepared mustard
- 1 5-oz. can chow mein noodles
- Lettuce leaves

Mix first 7 ingredients. Add mixture of mayonnaise and mustard; toss gently to coat. Chill, covered, for several hours. Stir in chow mein noodles just before serving. Serve in lettuce-lined bowl. Yield: 8 servings.

Judith K. Wagner
Preceptor Alpha, Peoria, Illinois

SHRIMP A LA LORRAINE

- 1 c. macaroni, cooked, drained
- 1 can shrimp
- 1/4 c. chopped green pepper
- 2 hard-boiled eggs, sliced (opt.)
- 1 c. chopped celery
- 1 sm. onion, chopped
- 1/2 tsp. salt
- 1/4 tsp. paprika
- 1 c. salad dressing
- 1/4 c. French dressing

Mix cooled macaroni with next 7 ingredients. Pour mixture of salad dressing and French dressing over top; toss to coat. Chill. Yield: 6 servings.

Lyeliene Ann Hoehne
Preceptor Alpha Omicron, Marshall, Michigan

HOT-COLD TUNA SALAD

- 2 c. cooked shell macaroni
- 1 1/2 c. shredded sharp Cheddar cheese
- 1 6 1/2-oz. can tuna, drained
- 2 med. tomatoes, chopped
- 2 med. cucumbers, peeled, chopped
- 1/2 med. green peppers, chopped
- 1 1/2 c. salad dressing

Mix hot macaroni, cheese and tuna. Add remaining ingredients; toss to coat. Chill for 2 hours. Yield: 4-6 servings.

Helen Rayetwine
Alpha Omicron, Suffolk, Virginia

CORN AND SIRLOIN KABOBS

- 1/2 c. red wine
- 1/3 c. oil
- 1 tbsp. chili powder
- 1 tsp. salt
- 1/2 tsp. dry mustard
- 1 clove of garlic, crushed
- 1 1/2 lb. sirloin, cut into 1-in. cubes
- 4 ears of corn, cut into 1-in. slices
- 2 each red, green peppers, cut into bite-sized pieces

Blend first 6 ingredients. Add sirloin and vegetables; toss to coat. Chill, covered, for 2 hours or longer, turning occasionally. Thread on skewers. Grill over hot coals to desired degree of doneness, basting occasionally with marinade.

Gale E. Vrtiak
Alpha Alpha, Worms, Germany

74 / Independence Day

HOLIDAY BARBECUED BEEF

1/4 c. vinegar
1/4 c. sugar
4 tsp. prepared mustard
1/4 tsp. each pepper, cayenne pepper
1 tbsp. salt
2 thick slices lemon
2 onions, sliced
1/2 c. butter
1 c. chili sauce
3 tbsp. Worcestershire sauce
4 c. chopped cooked beef

Simmer first 9 ingredients and 1 1/2 cups water for 20 minutes. Stir in chili sauce, Worcestershire sauce and beef; chill. Simmer for 45 minutes. Yield: 1 1/2 quarts.

Rosanna Fahl
Preceptor Alpha Epsilon, Oroville, California

BETA'S BEST BRISKET

1 8-oz. bottle of barbecue sauce
2 tbsp. brown sugar
1 tsp. each seasoned salt, garlic salt
1 tsp. minced onion
2 tsp. Worcestershire sauce
1/2 tsp. each pepper, dry mustard
1 5 to 6-lb. brisket

Mix first 8 ingredients. Marinate brisket in mixture for 3 hours or longer. Cook in Crock-Pot on Low heat for 8 to 9 hours. Yield: 10 servings.

Joan Menn
Xi Alpha Lambda, Sweetwater, Texas

STEAK-ON-A-STICK

1/4 c. Sherry
1 tbsp. soy sauce
1 1/2 tsp. wine vinegar
1 1/2 tsp. each catsup, honey
Dash of garlic salt
1 lb. boneless sirloin steak, cut into 1-in. pieces

Blend first 6 ingredients. Add steak. Marinate, covered, in refrigerator for 2 hours, turning occasionally. Thread steak on 7-inch skewers. Grill over medium-hot coals for 5 minutes on each side or to desired degree of doneness, basting frequently with marinade. Yield: 4 servings.

Connie Burgess
Xi Gamma Sigma, Concord, Tennessee

BAKED HAMBURGERS

1 c. soft bread crumbs
1/2 c. milk
1 lb. ground beef
1 tsp. salt
Pepper to taste
1/4 c. vinegar
1 1/2 tsp. Worcestershire sauce
1/2 c. catsup
1/2 c. chopped onion
3 tbsp. sugar

Mix bread crumbs and milk. Add ground beef, salt and pepper; mix well. Shape into 12 patties. Mix remaining ingredients and 1/2 cup water. Pour over patties in baking pan. Bake at 350 degrees for 50 minutes. Yield: 12 servings.

Lucille Dempster
Xi Beta Beta, Council Bluffs, Iowa

SWISS LOAF

2 lb. ground beef
1 1/2 c. chopped Swiss cheese
2 eggs, beaten
1/2 c. each chopped onion, green pepper
1 1/2 tsp. salt
1/2 tsp. each pepper, paprika
1 tsp. celery salt
3 c. milk
1 c. dry bread crumbs

Mix all ingredients in order given. Shape into loaf. Bake in 9 x 13-inch pan at 350 degrees for 1 1/2 hours. Yield: 8 servings.

Sharel Kelvington
Xi Pi Sigma, Highland, California

HAM-FILLED BUNS

1 can ham, finely chopped
2 to 3 green onions, finely chopped
3 to 4 hard-boiled eggs, finely chopped
1 pkg. Swiss cheese, cubed
15 olives, finely chopped (opt.)
Mayonnaise
1 doz. hot dog buns

Combine first 5 ingredients. Stir in enough mayonnaise to make of spreading consistency. Spread in buns. Bake, wrapped in foil, at 350 degrees for 20 to 25 minutes or until cheese melts. Yield: 12 servings.

Maurine Hassan
Alpha Tau, Oshawa, Ontario, Canada

HAM AND SWISS SANDWICHES

1/2 lb. butter, softened
1 tsp. Worcestershire sauce
3 tbsp. dry mustard
1 med. onion, grated
12 onion buns, split
1 1/2 lb. thinly sliced ham
12 slices Swiss cheese, cut in half

Mix first 4 ingredients until well blended. Spread over cut side of buns. Place ham slices on bottom halves. Crisscross cheese slices over ham. Replace top halves. Bake on baking sheet at 400 degrees for 10 minutes. May be frozen, wrapped in plastic wrap, before baking. Yield: 12 servings.

Betsy Shafer
Xi Beta Phi, Kalamazoo, Michigan

Independence Day / 75

DEM RIBS

3 lb. spareribs, cut in half
4 cloves of garlic
1 onion
Vinegar
1 12-oz. bottle of chili sauce
3/4 c. soy sauce
Cinnamon and cumin to taste (opt.)
Red pepper sauce and Worcestershire sauce to taste (opt.)
Grated onion (opt.)
Pepper to taste

Place spareribs in large stock pot. Add enough water to cover. Add 3 cloves of garlic, 1 whole onion and a dash of vinegar. Simmer, covered, for 30 minutes; remove spareribs. Mix 1 crushed clove of garlic, 2 tablespoons vinegar and remaining ingredients. Coat spareribs with sauce. Marinate in refrigerator for up to 2 days, turning occasionally. Grill over hot coals for 10 minutes on each side.

Beth Jackson
Alpha Kappa Upsilon, The Colony, Texas

SAUSAGE BREAD

1 lb. sausage
1 loaf frozen bread dough, thawed
1 c. each green olives, ripe olives
1 c. shredded mozzarella cheese
1 c. each chopped onions, green pepper
1 c. shredded Cheddar cheese
1 c. chopped celery
1 c. bacon bits
Margarine

Cook sausage until brown and crumbly; drain. Roll dough into 8 x 14-inch rectangle. Layer 1/4 of the sausage, olives, mozzarella cheese, onions, green pepper, Cheddar cheese, celery and bacon bits in center of dough in order given. Repeat layers until all ingredients are used. Fold dough over to enclose filling; tuck ends under. Bake on baking sheet at 350 degrees for 45 minutes. Spread margarine over top and slice. Yield: 4 servings.

Linda F. Saltzman
Epsilon Chi, Kaplan, Louisiana

EASTERN SHORE CRAB IMPERIAL

1 slice bread, trimmed, torn
1 c. milk
1 tsp. chopped parsley
1 tsp. prepared mustard
Dash of red pepper
1 tsp. salt
1 tsp. Worcestershire sauce
1 lb. crab meat
Paprika

Heat bread and milk until thick, stirring constantly. Mix next 6 ingredients. Stir in bread mixture. Spoon into greased 2-quart casserole. Sprinkle with paprika. Bake at 400 degrees for 20 minutes. Yield: 5 servings.

Rosemary C. Dodd
Xi Delta Beta, Fredericksburg, Virginia

ROXANE'S PRIZE BASS BAKE

Fish fillets or whole fish
1/2 c. Sherry
Butter, melted
1/4 c. cornmeal
1/2 tsp. salt
1/4 tsp. pepper
2 tbsp. chopped mushrooms
1 tsp. chopped green pepper
1/4 tsp. oregano
2 tbsp. lemon juice

Marinate fish in mixture of Sherry and 1 tablespoon butter for 2 hours; drain. Roll in cornmeal seasoned with salt and pepper. Saute in butter. Combine mushrooms, green pepper and oregano on foil. Arrange fish over vegetables; seal. Grill over hot coals for 20 minutes or until fish flakes easily. Pour melted butter and lemon juice over fish. Garnish with parsley and lemon wedges.

Roxane I. Fort
Zeta Sigma, Fairfield Bay, Arkansas

EASY SHRIMP CREOLE

1 med. onion, sliced
1 20-oz. can tomatoes
1 clove of garlic, minced
1 tsp. salt
1 8-oz. can tomato sauce
1/4 c. each chopped green pepper, celery
1/8 tsp. pepper
1 tsp. Italian seasoning
1 lb. shrimp, cleaned

Saute onion, tomatoes, garlic and salt in tomato sauce until onion is brown. Stir in green pepper, celery and remaining seasonings. Cook for 1 hour. Add shrimp. Cook until shrimp is heated through. Serve over rice. Yield: 6 servings.

Josephine Monty
Beta Epsilon, Greenville, Mississippi

SOUTHERN-FRIED CHICKEN WITH SQUASH

1 c. flour
1/4 tsp. each sage, thyme, marjoram
Salt and pepper to taste
2 eggs, beaten
1/4 c. milk
1 3-lb. chicken, cut up
2 3/4 c. cracker crumbs
Oil for frying
1 to 2 med. summer squash, cut into strips

Mix flour and seasonings. Beat eggs and milk. Dip chicken in flour mixture then in egg mixture. Roll in cracker crumbs; reserve mixtures for squash. Brown chicken in 1 inch hot oil; remove to 8 x 12-inch baking dish. Bake at 325 degrees for 30 minutes. Dip squash in flour mixture, eggs and crumbs. Fry in hot oil until brown. Serve with chicken.

Pamela S. Pigg
Epsilon Omicron, Cimarron, New Mexico

76 / Independence Day

OVEN-FRIED CHICKEN

1/2 c. fine dry bread
  crumbs
2 tsp. salt
1 tsp. paprika
1/4 tsp. pepper
1 chicken, cut up
1/4 c. oil

Combine bread crumbs, salt, paprika and pepper. Brush chicken with oil; roll in bread crumb mixture. Place skin side up in shallow baking pan. Bake at 425 degrees for 25 minutes or until chicken is tender.

Photograph for this recipe on page 69.

CHEESY BAKED CHICKEN

2 lb. boneless chicken
  breasts and thighs
1/4 lb. butter, melted
2 c. cornflake crumbs
1/2 tsp. each salt, onion
  salt, pepper
3 tbsp. parsley
1 can cream of celery
  soup
1 soup can chicken broth
1 c. grated mozzarella
  cheese

Dip chicken in butter. Roll in mixture of cornflake crumbs and seasonings. Blend soup and broth. Pour over chicken in 10 x 15-inch baking pan. Sprinkle with cheese. Bake at 375 degrees for 1 hour. Yield: 6 servings.

Naomi Morrow
Laureate, Schuylkill Haven, Pennsylvania

CROCK•POT BEANS

1/2 lb. small smoked
  sausage links, cooked,
  drained
1/2 lb. bacon, crisp-fried
  crumbled
1 lb. ground beef, cooked,
  drained
1 16-oz. can red beans
1 16-oz. can pork and
  beans
1 16-oz. can butter
  beans
2/3 c. packed brown
  sugar
1/2 c. sugar
2 tsp. vinegar
1/2 tsp. dry mustard
1/4 c. catsup
Salt to taste

Combine sausage, bacon, ground beef and beans in Crock·Pot. Mix remaining ingredients. Add to beans; mix well. Cook on Low for 8 hours or longer.

Kathy Hartmann
Xi Alpha Beta, Fremont, Nebraska

BARBECUED LIMA BEANS

1 lb. large lima beans
1 tsp. salt
4 to 6 slices bacon
1 c. chopped onion
1/2 c. chopped green
  pepper
1 c. barbecue sauce
1/2 tsp. sugar
1 8-oz. can tomato
  sauce with tomato
  bits

Soak beans, covered, in 5 cups water in refrigerator overnight. Do not drain. Add salt. Simmer, covered, for 1 to 1 1/2 hours or until tender, stirring occasionally. Fry bacon until crisp; remove and crumble. Saute onion and green pepper in pan drippings. Add barbecue sauce, sugar and tomato sauce. Bring to a boil. Combine with beans in 3-quart casserole. Bake at 325 degrees for 30 to 35 minutes. Top with crumbled bacon. Yield: 8 servings.

D. J. Murphy
Alpha, Overland Park, Kansas

FOUR-BEAN CASSEROLE

3/4 lb. bacon, crisp-fried,
  crumbled
4 lg. onions, chopped
1/3 c. vinegar
3/4 c. packed brown sugar
1 tbsp. dry mustard
1 can lima beans, drained
1 can pork and beans,
  drained
1 can kidney beans,
  drained
1 can butter beans,
  drained

Simmer first 5 ingredients for 20 minutes. Stir in beans. Bake in 3-quart casserole at 325 degrees for 2 hours. Yield: 10-12 servings.

Sheila Paulson
Lambda, Little Rock, Arkansas

CAULIFLOWER-TOMATO SCALLOP

1/2 c. finely chopped
  celery
1/4 c. each finely chopped
  onion, green pepper
5 tbsp. butter
3/4 tsp. salt
1/4 tsp. pepper
1/4 c. flour
2 c. milk
1 1/2 c. shredded sharp
  Cheddar cheese
1 lg. head cauliflower,
  broken into flowerets,
  cooked
3 lg. tomatoes, sliced
1/2 c. soft bread crumbs

Saute celery, onion and green pepper in butter. Blend in salt, pepper and flour. Stir in milk. Cook until thickened, stirring constantly. Blend in cheese; remove from heat. Arrange half the cauliflower in baking dish. Top with 1/3 of the cheese sauce and tomato slices. Layer 1/2 of the remaining cheese sauce, remaining cauliflower and remaining sauce over top. Sprinkle with bread crumbs. Bake at 400 degrees for 25 minutes.

Pam Berry
Lambda Psi, Marine City, Michigan

HERB-BAKED CORN ON THE COB

2 sticks butter, softened
2 cloves of garlic,
  crushed
2 tsp. each oregano, basil
1/2 tsp. salt
8 ears of corn
1 c. Parmesan cheese

Independence Day / 77

Mix butter and seasonings. Spread over corn. Wrap each ear tightly in foil. Bake at 350 degrees for 20 minutes or until tender; unwrap. Roll in cheese. Yield: 8 servings.

Carol Sassin
Xi Psi Beta, Beeville, Texas

CHEESY TEXAS POTATOES

- 1 2-lb. package frozen hashed brown potatoes, partially thawed
- 1/2 c. chopped green onions
- 1/4 tsp. pepper
- 1 tsp. salt
- 1 pt. sour cream
- 1 can cream of chicken soup
- 10 oz. grated sharp Cheddar cheese
- Bacon bits (opt.)
- 1/4 c. melted butter

Combine first 7 ingredients in 9 x 13-inch casserole. Sprinkle with bacon and additional cheese if desired. Drizzle with butter. Bake at 350 degrees for 1 hour. Yield: 6-8 servings.

Deborah J. Sanderson
Epsilon Omega, Sylva, North Carolina

BARBARA'S ZUCCHINI AND TOMATO CASSEROLE

- 2 lb. zucchini, sliced
- 2 lg. tomatoes, peeled, cut into wedges
- 1 1/2 tsp. salt (opt.)
- 1/2 tsp. each pepper, basil, oregano
- 1 onion, thinly sliced
- 3 tbsp. butter

Place zucchini in greased 2-quart casserole. Mix tomatoes and seasonings. Spoon over zucchini. Top with onion. Dot with butter. Bake at 350 degrees for 1 hour. Yield: 8 servings.

Barbara Phipps
Xi Beta Gamma, Florence, Alabama

MARGRIET'S CHILES RELLENOS CASSEROLE

- 2 sm. cans whole chilies, split
- 1 lb. Cheddar cheese, grated
- 1 lb. Monterey Jack cheese, grated
- 4 eggs, beaten
- 1 c. evaporated milk
- 2 tbsp. flour
- 1 c. salsa

Layer half the chilies, Cheddar cheese and Monterey Jack cheese in 8 x 8-inch baking pan. Repeat layers. Pour mixture of eggs, milk and flour over top. Bake at 350 degrees for 30 minutes. Pour salsa over top. Bake for 20 minutes longer. Yield: 6 servings.

Margriet Allen
Xi Rho Alpha, San Marcos, California

EASY DEVILED EGGS

- 6 hard-boiled eggs
- 2 tbsp. mayonnaise
- 1 tsp. mustard with horseradish
- 1/2 tsp. salt
- Dash of Worcestershire sauce (opt.)

Cut eggs in half lengthwise. Remove and mash yolks. Mix yolks with mayonnaise, mustard, salt and Worcestershire sauce. Spoon into egg whites. Chill in refrigerator.

Photograph for this recipe on page 69.

HOMINY-CHILI CASSEROLE

- 2 16-oz. cans white hominy, drained
- 2 tbsp. grated onion
- 1 1/2 c. white sauce
- 1 c. grated Monterey Jack cheese
- 1 4-oz. can chilies, chopped
- Salt to taste
- 1/4 c. dry bread crumbs
- 2 tbsp. butter

Mix first 6 ingredients. Spoon into 1 1/2-quart casserole. Sprinkle with bread crumbs. Dot with butter. Bake at 350 degrees for 30 minutes. Yield: 6-8 servings.

Marcie Marie Tipton
Delta Delta Alpha, North Fork, California

ONION-BUTTER SAUCE

- 1/4 c. chopped green onion
- 1/4 c. parsley flakes
- 1/4 c. butter
- 1/2 tsp. dry mustard
- 1/2 tsp. each salt, coarsely ground pepper
- 1 tsp. Worcestershire sauce

Mix all ingredients. Spread over broiled steaks. Yield: 4 servings.

Aloel Jacobs
Eta Rho, Bush, Louisiana

MEXICAN CORN BREAD

- 1 c. cornmeal
- 3/4 tsp. salt
- 1/2 tsp. soda
- 1 16-oz. can cream-style corn
- 2 eggs, beaten
- 1/4 c. bacon drippings
- 1 c. milk
- 1/2 lb. American cheese, grated
- 1 onion, chopped
- 2 canned chili peppers, seeded, chopped

Combine cornmeal, salt and soda. Mix in next 4 ingredients. Pour half the mixture into greased 10 x 10-inch baking pan. Top with mixture of cheese, onion and peppers. Pour remaining batter over top. Bake at 350 degrees for 45 minutes. Yield: 25 servings.

Virginia L. DeMarais
Xi Upsilon Delta, Borrego Springs, California

78 / Independence Day

FUNNEL CAKES

2 eggs
1 1/2 c. milk
2 c. flour
1/2 tsp. salt
2 tbsp. sugar
1 1/2 tsp. baking powder
1 1/2 tsp. baking powder
Oil for deep frying
2 c. confectioners' sugar
2 tbsp. cinnamon
1 tsp. nutmeg

Beat eggs with milk. Beat in mixture of next 4 dry ingredients. Pour a small amount of batter in spiral from funnel or pitcher into 375-degree oil. Deep-fry until brown, turning once. Sift mixture of confectioners' sugar, cinnamon and nutmeg over hot cakes. Yield: 6-8 cakes.

Pat Howell
Xi Pi Epsilon, Big Spring, Texas

AMONDRADO

2 env. unflavored gelatin
7 eggs, separated
Salt
1 3/4 c. sugar
Several drops each of red and green food coloring
2 c. milk
1/4 tsp. almond extract
1/4 c. finely chopped almonds

Soften gelatin in 1/4 cup cold water. Dissolve in 3/4 cup boiling water; cool. Beat egg whites with pinch of salt to soft peaks. Add 1 1/2 cups sugar gradually, beating until stiff. Beat in gelatin. Add several drops of red food coloring to 1/3 of the mixture and green food coloring to 1/3 of the mixture. Layer green, white and red mixtures in loaf pan. Chill until set. Mix milk, egg yolks, 1/4 cup sugar, 1/4 teaspoon salt and almond extract in saucepan. Cook until thick, stirring constantly. Invert chilled dessert on serving platter. Spoon cooled custard over top; sprinkle with almonds.

LaVerne Thomas
Preceptor Gamma Gamma, Long Beach, California

CAPIROTADA (MEXICAN BREAD PUDDING)

1 1/2 c. packed brown sugar
1 stick cinnamon
1/2 tsp. anise
1 loaf French bread, cut into 1/4-in. slices
Margarine
Raisins
Chopped pecans
Grated longhorn cheese

Mix brown sugar, cinnamon and anise with 1 quart water. Simmer for 15 to 20 minutes. Toast bread slices; spread with margarine. Place half the slices in greased 9 x 13-inch baking pan. Sprinkle with raisins, pecans and cheese. Pour half the brown sugar mixture over bread. Repeat with remaining ingredients. Bake at 350 degrees for 35 minutes. Yield: 6-8 servings.

Alicia Medina Long
Xi Rho, Brownwood, Texas

FLAMING BANANAS

1 tbsp. butter
3/4 c. packed brown sugar
1/8 tsp. cinnamon
1 oz. banana liqueur
6 bananas, cut in 1-in. pieces
2 to 3 oz. rum
6 scoops vanilla ice cream
Flaked coconut (opt.)

Melt butter in chafing dish. Stir in brown sugar, cinnamon and liqueur. Add bananas. Cook until lightly glazed. Add rum; ignite. Spoon sauce over banana until flames subside. Serve over ice cream lightly sprinkled with coconut. Yield: 6 servings.

Laura Dunn
Preceptor Theta, Reno, Nevada

FRUIT REFRESHER

7-Up
1 tsp. rum flavoring
1 med. can pineapple chunks, drained
1 c. blueberries
1 c. sliced strawberries
2 bananas, sliced
1 sm. cantaloupe, cut into bit-sized pieces

Stir 7-Up and flavoring gently into mixed fruits. Chill, covered, for several hours. Yield: 6 servings.

Becky Clayton
Xi Theta, Durham, North Carolina

PEACHES AND CREAM CHEESECAKE

3/4 c. flour
1 tsp. baking powder
1/2 tsp. salt
1 pkg. vanilla pudding and pie filling mix
3 tbsp. margarine, melted
1 lg. can sliced peaches, drained
Sugar
1 8-oz. package cream cheese, softened
3 tbsp. peach syrup
1 tsp. cinnamon

Mix first 5 ingredients until crumbly. Spread in 9-inch pie plate. Arrange peaches in pie plate. Cream 1/2 cup sugar, cream cheese and syrup. Spread over peaches to within 1 inch of edge. Sprinkle with mixture of cinnamon and 1 teaspoon sugar. Bake at 350 degrees for 25 minutes. Yield: 8 servings.

Marlene Ray
Xi Epsilon, Gulfport, Mississippi

RED-WHITE AND BLUE DESSERT PIZZA

1/2 c. margarine
1 c. flour
1/4 c. confectioners' sugar
1/2 c. chopped pecans
1/4 c. sugar
Lemon juice
1 8-oz. package cream cheese, softened
2 med. bananas, sliced
3 c. strawberry halves
2 c. blueberries

Independence Day / 79

Cut margarine into flour until crumbly. Mix in confectioners' sugar and pecans. Press into 14-inch pizza pan. Bake at 375 degrees for 15 minutes; cool. Cream sugar, 1 tablespoon lemon juice and cream cheese. Spread over crust. Dip bananas in lemon juice. Arrange on filling with strawberries and blueberries. Chill for 3 hours. Yield: 12 servings.

Bonnie Kelty
Alpha Nu, Stillwater, Oklahoma

TORONTO PIE DESSERT

2/3 c. sugar
1/2 tsp. vanilla extract
2 eggs, beaten
1/2 c. milk
2 tbsp. butter
1 c. cake flour
1 1/4 tsp. baking powder
Pinch of salt
2/3 c. raspberry jam
3 tbsp. confectioners' sugar

Beat sugar and vanilla gradually into eggs. Heat milk and butter until steaming. Fold sifted flour, baking powder and salt, then hot milk into egg mixture. Pour into greased and waxed paper-lined 9 x 9-inch pan. Bake at 350 degrees for 30 to 35 minutes; cool. Split into 2 layers. Spread jam between layers. Sift confectioners' sugar over top. Serve with ice cream. Yield: 24 servings.

Donna O'Neil
Laureate Alpha Zeta, Trenton, Ontario, Canada

FLAG CAKE

1 sm. package strawberry gelatin
1 pkg. white cake mix
1 8-oz. carton whipped topping
4 c. fresh strawberries
2 c. fresh blueberries

Dissolve gelatin in 3/4 cup boiling water. Add 1/2 cup cold water; cool. Prepare and bake cake mix in 9 x 13-inch pan using package directions. Prick deep holes 1 inch apart in cake using large fork. Pour cool gelatin over warm cake. Spread with whipped topping. Decorate with strawberries and blueberries to resemble flag. Store in refrigerator. Yield: 15 servings.

Sherri Ousley
Xi Gamma Sigma, Elwood, Indiana

FILLED CUPCAKES

1/4 c. cocoa
1 1/2 tsp. soda
2/3 c. shortening
Sugar
3 eggs
1 tsp. vanilla extract
Salt
2 1/2 c. flour
3/4 c. sour milk
1 8-oz. package cream cheese, softened
1 6-oz. package chocolate chips

Mix cocoa and soda with 1/2 cup water. Let stand for several minutes. Cream shortening and 1 3/4 cups sugar. Beat in 2 eggs, vanilla and 1/2 teaspoon salt. Add flour alternately with sour milk and cocoa mixture; mix well. Fill prepared muffin cups 2/3 full. Cream 1/3 cup sugar and cream cheese. Beat in 1 egg and pinch of salt. Stir in chocolate chips. Drop rounded teaspoonful into each cup. Bake at 350 degrees for 30 minutes. Yield: 2 1/2 dozen.

Cheryl Ferguson
Epsilon Nu, Moses Lake, Washington

FAVORITE APPLESAUCE BROWNIES

1/2 c. margarine, softened
Sugar
2 eggs, beaten
2 c. flour
2 tbsp. cocoa
1 tsp. soda
1/2 tsp. each salt, cinnamon
2 c. applesauce
1 c. milk chocolate chips
1/2 c. chopped nuts

Cream margarine and 1 1/2 cups sugar. Beat in eggs, dry ingredients and applesauce. Pour into greased 9 x 13-inch baking pan. Sprinkle with chocolate chips, nuts and 2 tablespoons sugar. Bake at 350 degrees for 40 minutes. Yield: 16 servings.

Sue Jedlicka
Preceptor Alpha Beta, Beatrice, Nebraska

PEANUT CRACKERS

1 lb. confectioners' sugar
4 egg whites, stiffly beaten
1 lb. peanuts, ground
Soda crackers

Sift confectioners' sugar. Beat confectioners' sugar into egg whites gradually. Fold in peanuts. Spread on crackers. Bake on ungreased baking sheet at 375 degrees for 10 minutes or until lightly browned; cool. May be stored in airtight container for several weeks. Yield: 5 dozen.

Grace H. Hart
Preceptor Alpha Omega, Evansville, Indiana

STRAWBERRY FANTASY ICE CREAM

1 3-oz. package strawberry gelatin
2 sm. packages frozen sweetened strawberries
2 pt. half and half
1/2 c. vanilla extract
4 bananas, mashed
2 cans sweetened condensed milk
Milk

Dissolve gelatin in 1 cup boiling water; cool. Add next 5 ingredients; mix well. Pour into freezer container. Add milk to fill line. Freeze using manufacturer's directions. Yield: 1 gallon.

Janeta Harrel
Xi Beta Iota, Elk City, Oklahoma

80 / Independence Day

FRESH PEACH ICE CREAM

5 eggs, beaten
2 1/2 c. sugar
1 tbsp. vanilla extract
1 13-oz. can evaporated milk
1 can sweetened condensed milk
Milk
2 c. mashed peaches

Beat eggs with 2 cups sugar. Beat in vanilla extract, evaporated milk and condensed milk. Pour into 1-gallon freezer container. Add milk to within 4 inches of top. Freeze for 5 minutes or until thickened; remove dasher. Stir in mixture of peaches and 1/2 cup sugar. Replace dasher. Freeze using manufacturer's directions. Yield: 1 gallon.

Jennie Burnham
Sigma Iota, Lake Jackson, Texas

CROWNING GLORY HOMEMADE ICE CREAM

3 tbsp. cornstarch
6 c. milk
2 2/3 c. sugar
4 eggs, beaten
3/4 tsp. salt
1 13-oz. can evaporated milk
1 pt. whipping cream
3 1/2 tbsp. vanilla extract

Mix cornstarch with 1/2 cup milk in double boiler. Cook until thickened, stirring constantly. Beat sugar, eggs, salt and evaporated milk in mixer bowl until smooth. Beat in cornstarch mixture. Stir in whipping cream, remaining milk and vanilla. Pour into freezer container. Freeze using manufacturer's directions. Yield: 20-25 servings.

Edna M. Coleman
Preceptor Alpha, Kansas City, Missouri

APPLE PRALINE PIE

3/4 c. shortening
2 1/4 c. flour
1 1/4 tsp. salt
6 c. thinly sliced peeled apples
3/4 c. sugar
1 tsp. cinnamon
6 tbsp. margarine
1/2 c. packed brown sugar
2 tbsp. half and half
1/2 c. chopped pecans

Cut shortening into 2 cups flour and 1 teaspoon salt until crumbly. Add 1/4 to 1/2 cup water gradually, stirring until dough leaves side of bowl. Mix apples with sugar, 1/4 cup flour, cinnamon and 1/4 teaspoon salt. Spoon into pastry lined 9-inch pie plate. Dot with 2 tablespoons margarine. Top with remaining pastry; seal edge and cut vents. Bake at 350 degrees for 50 to 55 minutes. Bring 1/4 cup margarine, brown sugar and half and half to a boil over low heat. Stir in pecans. Spread over pie. Bake for 5 minutes longer. Cool for 1 hour. Yield: 8 servings.

Sabrina Hall
Delta Tau, Petoskey, Michigan

APPLE CREAM PIE

1 unbaked pie shell
Sliced apples
3 tbsp. (heaping) flour
1 c. sugar
1 c. heavy cream
1 tsp. vanilla extract
1/8 tsp. lemon juice
Cinnamon

Fill pie shell with sliced apples. Sprinkle with mixture of flour and sugar. Mix cream, vanilla and lemon juice. Pour over apples. Sprinkle with cinnamon. Bake at 400 degrees for 5 minutes. Reduce temperature to 350 degrees. Bake until brown.

Joy Miller
Kappa Zeta, Lenox, Iowa

CANTALOUPE PIE

1 med. cantaloupe, cut up
Sugar
1/2 c. flour
1/4 tsp. salt
3 eggs, separated
1 tbsp. butter
1 tsp. vanilla extract
1 baked pie shell

Puree cantaloupe in blender. Bring to a simmer in saucepan. Stir in mixture of 1/2 to 3/4 cup sugar, flour and salt. Beat egg yolks with 2 tablespoons water. Stir a small amount of hot mixture into egg yolks; stir egg yolks into hot mixture. Cook until thick, stirring constantly; remove from heat. Stir in butter and vanilla. Pour into pie shell. Beat egg whites with 6 tablespoons sugar until stiff. Spread over pie, sealing to edge. Bake at 425 degrees until lightly browned. Serve warm or cold.

Ernie Horn
Beta Sigma Phi, Morenci, Arizona

FRESH STRAWBERRY PIE

Sugar
1 8-oz. package cream cheese, softened
2 tbsp. cream
1 tsp. vanilla extract
1 c. whipping cream, whipped
1 baked 9-in. pie shell
6 c. strawberries
2 tbsp. cornstarch
Pinch of salt
1 tbsp. lemon juice

Cream 1/3 cup sugar, cream cheese, cream and vanilla. Fold in half the whipped cream. Spread in pie shell. Chill. Mix 1 cup crushed strawberries with cornstarch, 3/4 cup sugar, salt and 1/3 cup water. Cook over low heat until thick, stirring constantly. Simmer, covered, for 5 minutes, stirring occasionally. Stir in lemon juice. Press through sieve; cool. Stir in remaining whole strawberries. Spoon over creamed mixture. Chill. Top with remaining whipped cream.

Kathryn Watt
Alpha, Regina, Saskatchewan, Canada

Recipes on page 85.

Labor Day

82 / Labor Day

SUPER DUPER TEA

1/4 c. white grape juice	2 tbsp. instant tea
2/3 c. sugar	1/4 c. lemon juice

Blend all ingredients with 1 quart water. Serve over ice. Yield: 4 servings.

Melanie Presser
Sigma Mu, Golconda, Illinois

DANISH PLUM SOUP

3/4 lb. plums, pitted, halved	1 stick cinnamon
1/4 c. sugar	2 1/2 tbsp. cornstarch
	3 tbsp. white wine

Cook plums, sugar and cinnamon in 1 quart water until softened. Strain through sieve. Bring to a boil. Stir in cornstarch mixed with small amount of cold water. Boil for 5 minutes. Stir in wine just before serving. Serve hot or cold with whipped cream. Yield: 8 servings.

Anna E. Chenin
Preceptor Beta Pi, Richmond Heights, Ohio

CRUNCHY GINGER-NUT DIP

1 8-oz. package cream cheese, softened	1 tbsp. crystallized ginger
1/4 c. Dr. Pepper	2 tbsp. coarsely chopped salted peanuts
1 tbsp. grated orange rind	

Process cream cheese and Dr. Pepper in blender container until light and fluffy. Stir in orange rind, ginger and peanuts. Serve with fruit. Yield: 1 1/2 cups.

Margaret H. Powell
Xi Iota, Danville, Virginia

TACO DIP

1 lg. avocado, mashed	2 or 3 jalapeno peppers, finely chopped
2 tbsp. lime juice	Dash of hot sauce
1 8-oz. package cream cheese, softened	

Mix all ingredients. Spread in shallow serving dish. Garnish with olives, lettuce, tomatoes and cheese. Serve with tortilla chips.

Candy Wagner
Gamma Epsilon, Burlington, Iowa

SLOW-BALL DIP

1 24-oz. round loaf bread	2 8-oz. packages cream cheese, softened
2 or 3 6 1/2-oz. cans clams	2 tbsp. grated onion
	2 tbsp. beer
2 tsp. each lemon juice, Worcestershire sauce	1/2 tsp. salt
1 tsp. hot pepper sauce	Vegetables for dipping (opt.)

Slice top from loaf; scoop out center reserving shell and top. Cut soft bread into cubes; reserve. Drain clams, reserving 1/4 cup liquid. Beat cream cheese until smooth. Add clams, reserved liquid, onion, beer, lemon juice and seasonings; mix well. Spoon into bread shell; replace top. Bake, wrapped in foil, at 250 degrees for 3 hours. Serve with fresh vegetables and reserved bread cubes. Yield: 8-12 servings.

Lou Ann Young
Xi Alpha Epsilon, Las Vegas, Nevada
Kathleen Whiteside
Preceptor Beta Mu, Palm Beach, Florida

CREAMY CHEESE AND CRACKERS

1 8-oz. package cream cheese	1/4 c. soy sauce
	1/4 c. sesame seed, toasted

Punch holes in cream cheese with toothpick. Pour soy sauce over top gradually, filling holes. Sprinkle with sesame seed. Serve with crackers.

Cindy Ravelli
Alpha Nu, Dawson Creek, British Columbia, Canada

SWEET PICKLE APPETIZER RING

3 8-oz. packages liver sausage	1 tsp. horseradish
1 8-oz. package cream cheese, softened	3/4 c. sweet pickle relish, well drained
1 tbsp. grated onion	1/4 c. chili sauce
	Pimento (opt.)

Blend first 4 ingredients. Stir in pickle relish and chili sauce. Spoon into ring mold. Chill until firm. Invert on serving plate. Garnish with pimento. Serve with crackers.

Elizabeth Griffith
Laureate Alpha Beta, Cambridge, Ohio

BARBECUED LITTLE SMOKIES

1 c. barbecue sauce	1 16-oz. package little smokies smoked cocktail weiners
1 c. catsup	
12 lg. marshmallows	
1/2 c. packed brown sugar	1/4 c. finely chopped onion (opt.)

Mix first 4 ingredients in fondue pot. Heat until marshmallows melt, stirring frequently. Add weiners and onion. Simmer for 30 minutes. Serve warm.

Maxine Quick
Alpha, Centralia, Illinois

Labor Day / 83

CINNAMON-RAISIN SNACK MIX

1/3 c. margarine, melted
2 tbsp. honey
1 tsp. cinnamon
6 c. popped popcorn
1 8-oz. jar roasted unsalted mixed nuts
1 c. raisins

Heat margarine, honey and cinnamon; stir to blend. Pour over mixture of popcorn, nuts and raisins; toss to coat. Bake in baking pan at 325 degrees for 20 minutes, stirring after 10 minutes; cool. Store in airtight container. Yield: 2 quarts.

Becky Whitener
Preceptor Epsilon, Florissant, Missouri

TIPSY HOT DOGS

1 8-oz. jar currant jelly
1/4 c. red wine
2 tsp. dry mustard
1 1/2 lb. hot dogs, cut into bite-sized pieces
2 tbsp. margarine

Heat jelly, wine and mustard until jelly is melted, stirring frequently. Brown hot dogs in margarine. Simmer in sauce for 30 minutes. Serve with toothpicks. Yield: 20 servings.

Louise H. Woodruff
Preceptor Tau, Memphis, Tennessee

GARDEN PIZZA

2 cans refrigerator crescent rolls
2 8-oz. packages cream cheese, softened
1 c. mayonnaise
1 env. ranch-style dressing mix
Finely chopped fresh vegetables

Spread crescent rolls on large baking sheet, pressing edges together. Bake at 400 degrees for 10 minutes or until lightly browned. Spread with mixture of cream cheese, mayonnaise and dressing mix. Top with vegetables; chill. Cut in squares to serve. Yield: 24 servings.

Janice Ragaisis
Delta Xi, Waukesha, Wisconsin

ROLLED TORTILLAS

3 8-oz. packages cream cheese, softened
1 16-oz. container sour cream
5 jalapeno peppers, finely chopped
1 sm. onion, grated
Juice of 1/2 lime
Hot sauce to taste
20 flour tortillas, softened
Picante sauce

Mix first 6 ingredients. Spread on softened tortillas. Roll as for jelly roll; chill. Slice and serve on toothpicks. Dip in picante sauce. Yield: 100.

Susan Jennings
Alpha Beta Chi, Lufkin, Texas

HAM-WRAPPED APPLES

4 tart green apples, cut into eighths
1 tbsp. lemon juice
2 3-oz. packages cream cheese, softened
2 tbsp. prepared mustard
2 tsp. horseradish
2 tbsp. cream
Dash of paprika
16 to 20 slices cooked ham

Dip apple wedges in 1 cup water mixed with lemon juice; pat dry. Blend cream cheese, mustard, horseradish, cream and paprika. Spread on ham slices. Cut into strips; wrap around apple wedges. Secure with toothpick. Garnish with parsley. May substitute salami for ham.

Norma Geirk
Preceptor Theta Delta, Vista, California

BROCCOLI-CHEDDAR CHEESE SALAD

3/4 lb. broccoli
2 tbsp. pine nuts
4 tbsp. olive oil
3 tbsp. lemon juice
2 tbsp. minced chives
1/8 tsp. white pepper
1/4 tsp. each garlic salt, dry mustard
4 oz. Cheddar cheese, slivered
1/4 lb. med. mushrooms, thinly sliced

Cut flowerets from broccoli and slice stalks crosswise. Steam for 5 minutes or until tender-crisp. Drain and rinse with cold water. Brown pine nuts in skillet over medium-low heat, stirring constantly. Mix oil, lemon juice, chives and seasonings. Pour over mixture of steamed broccoli, cheese and mushrooms; toss to coat. Sprinkle with pine nuts. Garnish with radishes.

Violet Soper
Preceptor Theta, Selinsgrove, Pennsylvania

SOUR CREAM POTATO SALAD

4 hard-boiled eggs
2/3 c. mayonnaise
3/4 c. sour cream
1 1/2 tsp. mustard with horseradish
1/2 lb. bacon, crisp-fried, crumbled
1/3 c. chopped green onion
7 c. chopped cooked potatoes
2/3 c. chopped pickles
1/3 c. Italian salad dressing
Salt and celery seed to taste

Cut eggs in half and remove yolks. Mash yolks with mayonnaise, sour cream and mustard. Chop egg whites. Mix with bacon, onion, potatoes, pickle and salad dressing. Fold in mayonnaise mixture. Season with salt and celery seed. Yield: 8-10 servings.

Geraldine Campbell
Preceptor Epsilon Upsilon, Denison, Texas

CANTALOUPE GELATIN SALAD

1 3-oz. package orange gelatin
Dash of salt
1 tsp. lemon juice
1 c. chopped cantaloupe
1/4 c. chopped celery
1/4 c. slivered almonds
1 3-oz. package cream cheese, softened
2 tbsp. mayonnaise

Dissolve gelatin and salt in 1 cup boiling water. Stir in 3/4 cup cold water and lemon juice. Chill half the gelatin mixture until thick. Fold in cantaloupe, celery and almonds. Pour into 1-quart mold; chill until set. Mix remaining half of gelatin mixture with cream cheese and mayonnaise. Spread over congealed layer. Chill until set. Unmold onto serving plate. Yield: 8-10 servings.

Joy Wilmarth
Preceptor Beta Kappa, Maryville, Missouri

CONFETTI SALAD

1 tsp. salt
1/2 tsp. pepper
1 c. sugar
3/4 c. white vinegar
1/2 c. oil
1 20-oz. can French-style green beans
1 20-oz. can green peas
1 20-oz. can Shoe Peg corn
1/2 c. chopped pimento
1 c. each chopped green pepper, celery, onion

Bring first 4 ingredients and 2 tablespoons water to a boil; cool. Stir in oil. Mix beans, peas, corn, pimento, green pepper, celery and onion. Pour dressing over vegetables; toss to coat. Chill in refrigerator. Yield: 15 servings.

Carolyn Ferry
Xi Alpha Pi, Greenwood, South Carolina

LABORSAVING SPAGHETTI SALAD

1/2 c. sweet pickle juice
1 c. Italian salad dressing
1 1/2 tsp. salt
1 tbsp. poppy seed
1 tsp. celery salt
1/2 tsp. caraway seed
1/4 tsp. garlic powder
2 tbsp. parsley flakes
1 bunch green onions, chopped
1 10-oz. package vermicelli, cooked

Combine all ingredients except vermicelli; mix well. Pour over vermicelli; mix well. Chill, covered, overnight.

Peggy Goss
Sigma Iota, Adrian, Missouri

SPECIAL MACARONI SALAD

1 lb. macaroni, cooked
1 lg. green pepper, chopped
1 med. onion, chopped
4 med. carrots, shredded
1 c. vinegar
1 can sweetened condensed milk
2 c. mayonnaise
1 tsp. salt
1/4 tsp. pepper

Mix cooled macaroni with vegetables. Blend vinegar, condensed milk, mayonnaise, salt and pepper. Stir into salad. Chill for 4 hours. Yield: 8-10 servings.

Janet Stovall
Preceptor Beta Eta, Richardson, Texas

ITALIAN DELI SALAD

1 1/4 c. sliced ripe olives
1 c. chopped green pepper
1/4 lb. hard salami, cut into strips
1 sm. red onion, sliced into rings
1/2 c. Parmesan cheese
1/4 c. chopped parsley
1 tbsp. capers (opt.)
1 c. Italian salad dressing
12 oz. spiral pasta, cooked

Mix first 8 ingredients. Add pasta; toss to coat well. Chill for 2 to 3 hours. Yield: 8 servings.

Donna M. Schiefer
Alpha Omega, Camp Springs, Maryland

GRANDMA WELLS' FAMOUS PEA SALAD

1 10-oz. package frozen peas, thawed
1 2-oz. jar chopped pimento
3/4 c. chopped celery
3 hard-boiled eggs, chopped
1/2 c. grated Cheddar cheese
4 or 5 green onions with tops, sliced
1/2 tsp. Salad Supreme
3/4 c. mayonnaise

Combine all ingredients; mix well. Let stand for 30 minutes before serving. Store in refrigerator. Yield: 8-10 servings.

Regena Goodwin
International Alpha, Kansas City, Missouri

TUNA SALAD VINAIGRETTE

1/2 c. olive oil
3 tbsp. lemon juice
2 cloves of garlic, crushed
Freshly ground black pepper to taste
1 tsp. basil
1 bunch scallions, minced
1 8-oz. package spiral pasta, cooked
2 7 1/2-oz. cans tuna, drained
1 16-oz. can green beans, drained
4 lg. tomatoes, sliced

Blend oil, lemon juice, garlic and seasonings. Mix scallions, pasta, tuna and beans. Pour dressing over top; toss to coat. Serve on individual salad plates topped with overlapping tomato slices. Sprinkle freshly ground pepper over top. Yield: 4 servings.

Irene E. Lozar
Xi Gamma Iota, Yuma, Arizona

SPECIAL RICE SALAD

1 can artichoke hearts
1 c. mayonnaise
Salt and pepper to taste
3 c. cooked rice
5 green onions, chopped
1/4 c. chopped celery
1/2 c. chopped green pepper
1/2 c. chopped ripe and Spanish olives

Drain and chop artichoke hearts, reserving liquid. Blend reserved liquid with mayonnaise and seasonings. Mix rice, vegetables and olives. Pour dressing over top; toss to coat. Garnish with parsley and cherry tomatoes.

Donna Fields
Gamma Gamma, Blackwell, Oklahoma

OVERNIGHT RICE SALAD

1 lg. jar marinated artichoke hearts, chopped
1 pkg. chicken-flavored rice, cooked
4 green onions, chopped
1 sm. jar chopped pimento, drained
1 can ripe olives, chopped
1/4 to 1/2 c. mayonnaise

Drain and chop artichoke hearts, reserving liquid. Mix cooled rice, reserved liquid, artichokes and remaining ingredients except mayonnaise. Stir in mayonnaise. Chill overnight. Yield: 4 servings.

Angela T. Galen
Gamma Phi, Herndon, Virginia

RUSSIAN VINAIGRETTE SALAD

2 c. cooked cubed peeled potatoes
1 16-oz. can red kidney beans, rinsed, drained
2 c. chopped dill pickle
2 med. onions, thinly sliced
1/2 c. olive oil
1/3 c. dill pickle liquid
2 tbsp. vinegar
1 3/4 tsp. salt
1/4 tsp. pepper
2 tsp. sugar
1 16-oz. can small whole beets, drained, sliced

Combine potatoes, beans, pickle and onions. Blend oil, pickle liquid, vinegar, seasonings and sugar. Pour 3/4 of the mixture over potatoes; toss lightly. Pour remaining dressing over beets. Chill, covered, for 3 hours or longer. Drain beets. Add to potatoes; toss lightly. Serve in lettuce-lined bowl.

Photograph for this recipe on page 81.

PICNIC POT ROAST

1 5-lb. boned rump roast
3 tbsp. oil
1 c. dill pickle liquid
1 c. chopped dill pickles
1 1/2 c. mayonnaise
1 1/2 tsp. lemon juice
1 tsp. prepared mustard

Brown roast in oil on all sides; drain. Add pickle liquid, 1 cup water and half the pickles. Simmer, covered, for 3 1/2 hours or until fork-tender. Remove roast, reserving drippings; cool. Chill, wrapped, overnight. Strain drippings. Boil until reduced to 1/2 cup. Chill overnight; skim. Blend remaining ingredients; add pickles and 2 tablespoons drippings. Chill for several hours. Serve with roast.

Photograph for this recipe on page 81.

TOP ROUND AROMATICA

1 2-lb. top round steak, 1-in. thick
1 tbsp. butter, softened
1 1/2 tbsp. crushed peppercorns
1/4 tsp. garlic powder
1 tbsp. oil
1/4 c. dry red wine
2 tbsp. Cognac
1/2 c. whipping cream
2 tbsp. chopped parsley
Salt to taste

Spread both sides of steak with mixture of butter, peppercorns and garlic powder. Brown steak in oil to desired degree of doneness; remove. Deglaze pan with wine and Cognac over high heat. Cook for 1 minute; reduce heat. Add cream and parsley. Cook for 1 to 2 minutes longer. Season with salt. Carve steak in thin slices diagonally across the grain. Pour sauce over steak. Garnish with sprigs of parsley. Yield: 4-6 servings.

Betty Van Blaricom
Beta Nu, Joseph, Oregon

SHISH KABOB MARINADE

1/3 c. soy sauce
1/4 c. honey
2 tbsp. oil
4 cloves of garlic, crushed
2 tbsp. lemon juice

Mix all ingredients. Use as marinade for beef, pork, vegetables or fruit. Marinate overnight.

Naomi L. Herren
Epsilon Chi, Ruskin, Florida

SPANISH ROLLS

1 lb. lean ground round
2 sm. onions, chopped
1 clove of garlic, chopped
1/2 can green chiles
1 c. chopped olives
1 can tomato sauce
2 tbsp. white vinegar
1 lb. Tillamook cheese, grated
12 French rolls

Brown ground round and onions, stirring frequently. Stir in next 6 ingredients. Heat until cheese is melted. Cut French rolls in half; scoop out centers. Spoon beef mixture into shells. Bake, wrapped in foil, on baking sheet at 300 degrees for 1 hour. Yield: 12 servings.

Hazel Halloran
Delta Delta Eta, Lake Isabella, California

CRAZY MARY'S CHILI

2 c. sliced mushrooms
1 c. each chopped celery, onion
Butter
2 tbsp. chili powder
1 tsp. salt
1/2 tsp. pepper
1 lb. lean ground beef
2 28-oz. cans tomatoes
1 tbsp. sugar
1 tsp. Worcestershire sauce
2 c. kidney beans, drained
Shredded Cheddar cheese
Sour cream

Saute mushrooms, celery and onion in butter for 10 minutes or until onion is tender. Mix chili powder, salt and pepper. Add ground beef and 1/4 of the seasonings to sauteed vegetables. Cook until beef is browned, stirring frequently. Stir in remaining chili powder mixture, tomatoes, sugar, Worcestershire sauce and 1/4 cup water. Simmer, covered, for 15 minutes. Add beans. Cook for 10 minutes longer. Sprinkle each serving with cheese. Top with dollop of sour cream. Yield: 6-8 servings.

Debbie L. Schlegel
Kappa, Bozeman, Montana

ZUCCHINI PIZZA

1/2 lb. ground beef
1 c. chopped onion
1 15-oz. can tomato sauce
1 tsp. basil
1/4 tsp. garlic salt
Zucchini
1/2 c. grated Cheddar cheese
2 eggs
1/2 tsp. each salt, pepper
1 c. sliced ripe olives
1 sm. can sliced mushrooms

Brown ground beef with onion, stirring frequently. Stir in tomato sauce, basil and garlic salt. Simmer for 30 minutes. Mix 2 cups grated zucchini, cheese, eggs and seasonings. Spread in greased pizza pan. Bake at 350 degrees for 30 minutes. Spread beef mixture over crust. Top with olives, mushrooms and thinly sliced zucchini.

Lib McKinley
Laureate Beta, Council Bluffs, Iowa

SAUCIJSJES (PIGS IN THE BLANKET)

3 c. flour
1 tbsp. sugar
2 tsp. baking powder
2 1/2 tsp. salt
1/2 c. margarine, softened
1/2 c. lard
3 eggs, beaten
7 c. milk
1 lb. ground beef
1 lb. lean pork sausage
3/4 c. rusk crumbs
1/2 tsp. pepper
1 tsp. allspice

Mix flour, sugar, baking powder and 1 teaspoon salt. Cut in margarine and lard until crumbly. Stir in 2 beaten eggs and milk until soft dough forms. Shape into ball; chill. Roll dough 1/8 inch thick on floured surface. Cut into 4-inch squares. Mix ground beef, sausage, crumbs, 1 1/2 teaspoons salt, pepper and allspice. Press into 9 x 9-inch square. Cut into 24 portions. Place 1 portion on pastry square; fold in corners to enclose filling. Brush with 1 beaten egg. Bake in shallow baking pan for 40 to 50 minutes. Yield: 24 servings.

Rose Lubach
Xi Zeta Xi, Pella, Iowa

BAKED HAM AND CHEDDAR CHEESE SANDWICHES

16 slices bread, trimmed
8 slices each ham, turkey
8 slices Cheddar cheese
6 eggs, beaten
3 c. milk
1/2 tsp. each onion salt, dry mustard
2 c. crushed cornflakes
1 stick margarine

Arrange 8 slices bread in greased 9 x 13-inch casserole. Top each with 1 slice ham, turkey, cheese and bread. Mix eggs, milk and seasonings. Pour over sandwiches. Chill overnight. Top with cornflakes; dot with margarine. Bake at 325 degrees for 1 1/4 hours. Yield: 8 servings.

Sue Ogle
Gamma Eta, Charleston, Tennessee

SAUSAGE ROLL

1 lb. pork sausage
1/2 c. bread crumbs
1 tsp. Worcestershire sauce
1 egg, slightly beaten
1 can sauerkraut, drained
1/4 c. finely chopped onions

Mix first 4 ingredients. Pat into 7 x 10-inch rectangle on waxed paper. Spread mixture of sauerkraut and onions over top. Roll up from narrow end. Bake in greased 9 x 13-inch glass baking dish at 350 degrees for 45 minutes. Yield: 8 servings.

Betty H. Alderton
Preceptor Iota, Quincy, Illinois

HONEY-GLAZED CHICKEN AND RIBS

1 lg. onion, chopped
2 cloves of garlic, minced
2 tbsp. olive oil
1 1/2 c. catsup
2/3 c. honey
1/2 c. soy sauce
2 tbsp. lemon juice
1 tsp. each salt, ginger
1/4 tsp. paprika
4 lb. spareribs, cut into serving portions, cooked
2 sm. chickens, cut up, cooked

Saute onion and garlic in oil until onion is tender. Stir in catsup, honey, soy sauce, lemon juice and seasonings. Simmer for 20 minutes or until thickened. Dip spareribs and chicken in sauce. Grill over hot coals for 20 minutes, basting and turning occasionally. Yield: 6-8 servings.

Florence Dawson
Zi Gamma, Medicine Hat, Alberta, Canada

Labor Day / 87

BUTTERMILK CHICKEN

1 c. buttermilk
1 egg, slightly beaten
1 c. flour
Pecans
1 tbsp. paprika
1/4 tsp. sesame seed
1 tbsp. salt
1/8 tsp. pepper
2 chickens, cut up
Melted margarine

Mix buttermilk with egg. Mix flour, 1 cup ground pecans, paprika, sesame seed, salt and pepper. Dip chicken in buttermilk mixture and in flour mixture. Place skin side down in 9 x 13-inch baking pan coated with melted margarine. Turn to coat with margarine. Top with 1/4 cup pecan halves. Bake at 350 degrees for 1 1/4 hours or until tender. Yield: 8 servings.

Eugenia W. Bell
Laureate Delta, Louisville, Kentucky

CURRIED CHICKEN

1 fryer, cut up
1 tsp. salt
1/2 tsp. freshly ground pepper
1/2 to 1 tsp. garlic salt
1/2 tsp. MSG
1 to 2 tsp. curry powder
3 tbsp. brown sugar
2 tbsp. oil
1 lg. onion, sliced

Sprinkle chicken with seasonings. Let stand for 1 hour. Melt brown sugar in 375-degree oil in electric skillet, stirring frequently. Brown chicken in oil and sugar. Add onion slices. Cook, covered, at 325 degrees for about 1 hour. Serve with rice. Yield: 4-6 servings.

Gwen Barclay
Kappa, Souris, Manitoba, Canada

SAVORY CRESCENT CHICKEN SQUARES

1 3-oz. package cream cheese, softened
3 tbsp. margarine
2 c. cooked chopped chicken
1/4 tsp. salt
1/8 tsp. pepper
1 tbsp. chopped chives
1 tbsp. chopped pimento (opt.)
1 8-oz. can refrigerator crescent dinner rolls
3/4 c. crushed seasoned croutons

Blend cream cheese and 2 tablespoons softened margarine until smooth. Mix in next 5 ingredients. Separate crescent dough into 4 rectangles; press perforations firmly to seal. Spoon 1/2 cup chicken mixture onto each rectangle. Pull 4 corners to top; twist slightly and seal edges. Brush with 1 tablespoon melted margarine. Sprinkle with crouton crumbs. Bake on baking sheet at 350 degrees for 20 to 25 minutes or until golden brown. Yield: 4 servings.

Cindy Horner
Kappa Sigma, Ackley, Iowa

BAKED TUNA RING

1 egg, beaten
2 7-oz. cans tuna, drained
1/2 c. chopped onion
1 10-oz. package frozen mixed vegetables
1/2 c. grated Cheddar cheese
1/4 c. chopped parsley
1/2 tsp. salt
1/4 tsp. pepper
1 tsp. celery salt
1 1/3 c. milk
4 c. biscuit mix

Reserve 2 tablespoons egg. Mix remaining egg with next 8 ingredients. Mix milk and biscuit mix until soft dough forms. Roll out on floured surface to 13 x 18-inch rectangle. Spread with tuna mixture. Roll up from wide end. Shape into ring on greased baking sheet. Cut 13 slits to but not through bottom. Brush top with reserved egg. Bake at 350 degrees for 35 to 40 minutes. Yield: 6 servings.

Melody Bellini
Chi, Tacoma, Washington

IMPOSSIBLE SEAFOOD PIE

1 c. flaked baked salmon
1 c. grated sharp cheese
1 3-oz. package cream cheese, cubed
1/4 c. thinly sliced green onions
2 c. milk
1 c. baking mix
4 eggs
3/4 tsp. salt
Dash of nutmeg

Combine salmon, cheeses and onions. Place in greased 10-inch pie plate. Combine remaining ingredients in blender container. Process on High for 15 seconds. Pour over salmon mixture. Bake at 375 degrees for 35 minutes or until pie tests done. Let stand for 5 minutes. Yield: 6-8 servings.

Frances Kucera
Laureate Omicron, Eugene, Oregon

SEAFOOD QUICHES

1 med. onion, chopped
1 green pepper, chopped
3/4 c. chopped celery
10 mushrooms, sliced
1 lb. shrimp, peeled
1 lb. crab meat
6 eggs
2 1/2 pt. whipping cream
Salt and pepper to taste
1 8-oz. package med. Cheddar cheese, grated
1 8-oz. package Monterey Jack cheese, grated
2 unbaked 9-in. pie shells

Saute onion, green pepper, celery and mushrooms. Saute shrimp and crab meat. Beat eggs and cream until thickened. Stir in seasonings. Combine cheeses; reserve enough cheese for topping. Spoon sauteed vegetables into pie shells. Alternate layers of cheese and seafood on top. Pour cream mixture over pies. Sprinkle with reserved cheese. Bake at 350 degrees for 45 to 50 minutes. Yield: 7-8 servings.

Jo Paula Lantier
Zeta Rho, Prairieville, Louisiana

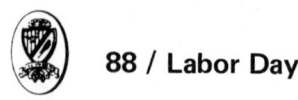

FAVORITE BAKED BEANS

2 c. dried beans
1 onion, chopped
1/4 lb. salt pork
1/2 c. molasses
1 tsp. each salt, dry
   mustard
Pinch of ginger

Boil beans in 2 quarts water for 2 minutes; remove. Let stand, covered, for 1 hour. Bring to a boil. Simmer, covered, for 1 hour or until tender; drain, reserving 2 cups liquid. Combine with onion and salt pork in 2 1/2-quart casserole. Mix reserved liquid with remaining ingredients. Pour over beans. Bake, covered, at 300 degrees for 5 to 6 hours, adding additional liquid if too dry. Yield: 8 servings.

Susan Carey
Beta Zeta, Lewiston, Maine

BEETS WITH SOUR SAUCE

2 tbsp. butter, melted
2 tbsp. flour
1/4 c. vinegar
1/4 c. cream
1/4 c. sugar
1/2 tsp. salt
1/4 tsp. pepper
6 med. beets, cooked,
   peeled, sliced

Blend butter and flour in saucepan. Cook until bubbly, stirring constantly. Stir in 1/2 cup water. Cook until thick, stirring constantly. Stir in vinegar, cream, sugar and seasonings. Cook for 4 minutes or until thick, stirring constantly. Pour over beets. Yield: 4 servings.

Lois M. Weber
Xi Beta Sigma, Denver, Colorado

FAVORITE EGGPLANT PARMIGIANA

1 sm. onion, chopped
1 tbsp. olive oil
2 8-oz. cans tomato
   sauce
2 tsp. salt
1 tsp. sugar
Dash each of pepper,
   garlic powder
1 bay leaf
1 tsp. oregano
1 med. eggplant, cut into
   1/8-in. slices
2 eggs
1 c. bread crumbs
1 c. Parmesan cheese
8 oz. mozzarella cheese,
   thinly sliced

Saute onion in olive oil. Mix in tomato sauce, 1 teaspoon salt, sugar, seasonings and 2 cups water. Simmer for 30 minutes, stirring occasionally. Dip eggplant in eggs beaten with 1 teaspoon salt. Dip in mixture of bread crumbs and Parmesan cheese. Fry in 1/8-inch deep oil until golden brown on both sides; drain on paper towels. Layer half the eggplant, mozzarella cheese and tomato sauce in 2-quart casserole. Repeat layers. Bake, covered, at 350 degrees for 30 to 35 minutes. Yield: 4-6 servings.

Brenda Owens
Upsilon Zeta, Edwardsville, Illinois

CORN FRITTERS

1 egg, beaten
1/2 c. milk
2 c. fresh corn
3/4 c. sifted flour
2 tsp. baking powder
1 tsp. sugar
1/2 tsp. salt
Oil for deep frying
Confectioners' sugar,
   sifted

Mix egg, milk and corn. Add sifted flour, baking powder, sugar and salt; mix well. Drop by teaspoonfuls into 375-degree oil. Fry for 3 to 4 minutes or until golden brown; drain on paper towels. Sprinkle with confectioners' sugar. Yield: 1 1/2 dozen.

Winnie Harlson
Xi Alpha Kappa, Mason City, Iowa

MILLIE'S HOT CORN

1 17-oz. can cream-style
   corn
1 10-oz. can
   Ro-Tel
1/2 to 3/4 c. grated
   cheese
1/2 to 3/4 c. coarsely
   crumbled crackers

Combine corn and Ro-Tel. Mix in cheese and enough crackers to absorb liquid. Bake at 350 degrees until cheese is melted. Yield: 4-6 servings.

Mildred Freeman
Xi Beta Upsilon, Logansport, Louisiana

SQUASH SOUFFLE

2 med. onions, chopped
8 yellow squash, sliced
8 butter crackers, crushed
Salt and pepper to taste
1/2 c. melted margarine
4 eggs, separated
2 c. grated American
   cheese

Steam onions and squash until tender; drain. Mix in cracker crumbs, salt, pepper, margarine, beaten egg yolks and cheese. Fold in stiffly beaten egg whites. Bake in greased 9 x 13-inch pan at 350 degrees for 45 minutes or until set. Yield: 10 servings.

Pat M. Henry
Xi Alpha Kappa, Clyde, North Carolina

MICROWAVE TOMATO CASSEROLE

1 lb. onions, thinly
   sliced
3 tbsp. butter, melted
1/2 c. bread crumbs
1/4 tsp. paprika
1/2 tsp. parsley flakes
1/2 tsp. basil
4 med. tomatoes, sliced
1 8-oz. package cheese
   slices
2 green peppers, sliced

Microwave onions in covered glass bowl on High for 4 minutes. Mix butter, bread crumbs and seasonings. Layer half the tomatoes, cheese, onions and green pepper in 1 1/2-quart glass casserole. Layer remaining cheese, onions and green peppers over top, ending with tomatoes. Top with seasoned bread crumbs. Microwave on High for 10 to 16 minutes.

Marie Hoyer
Alpha Mu, Sherwood Park, Alberta, Canada

PARTY ZUCCHINI BAKE

1 sm. onion, sliced into 1/2-in. strips
1/2 green pepper, sliced into 1/2-in. strips
2 tbsp. oil
1 med. zucchini, cut into 1-in. slices, quartered
1 4-oz. can mushrooms
1 lg. tomato, sliced
1/2 tsp. each parsley flakes, garlic powder
1 tsp. each salt, basil
Grated Romano cheese

Saute onion and green pepper in oil until just tender. Add zucchini and mushrooms. Cook for 5 minutes. Add tomato and seasonings. Simmer for 10 minutes. Spoon into 9 x 9-inch casserole. Sprinkle with cheese. Bake at 375 degrees for 30 to 40 minutes. Yield: 8-10 servings.

Diana L. Hudson
Gamma Sigma, Anderson, Indiana

SOMETHING SPECIAL ZUCCHINI

1 med. zucchini, sliced
1 med. onion, thinly sliced
1 sm. green pepper, sliced
2 med. tomatoes, sliced
2 tbsp. butter
Salt and pepper to taste
5 slices Velveeta cheese

Layer zucchini, onion, green pepper and tomatoes in 9 x 9-inch baking dish. Dot with butter. Season with salt and pepper. Bake, covered tightly with foil, at 350 degrees for 45 minutes. Top with cheese. Bake until cheese is melted.

Marjorie Laughner
Xi Phi, Lafayette, Indiana

POTLUCK RICE CUISINE

1 med. green pepper, coarsely chopped
1 med. red sweet pepper, coarsely chopped
1 med. onion, chopped
2 stalks celery, sliced diagonally
1 sm. can sliced mushrooms
1 clove of garlic, chopped
2 tbsp. butter
1 c. minute rice, cooked
1/8 tsp. salt
1 1/2 tsp. cornstarch
1/4 tsp. MSG
1 1/2 tsp. soy sauce
1 chicken bouillon cube
1/2 tsp. sugar
1 tbsp. Sherry

Saute vegetables and garlic in butter until tender. Stir in rice. Mix next 6 ingredients with 1/3 cup water. Stir into rice mixture. Add Sherry; mix well. Cook until heated through. Yield: 4 servings.

Louise Davis
Laureate Alpha Chi, Silsbee, Texas

CHEESE-RICE CASSEROLE

2/3 lb. mozzarella cheese, cubed
3 c. cooked rice
2/3 lb. Cheddar cheese, shredded
2 c. sour cream
1 4-oz. can chopped green chilies
1/2 c. chopped ripe olives
Dash of salt, pepper and paprika

Combine all ingredients in 7 x 11-inch casserole. Sprinkle with additional paprika. Bake at 350 degrees for 30 minutes. Yield: 15 servings.

Zell-Rae Schuttie
Preceptor Pi, Raymond, Washington

RICE POLYNESIAN

1/2 onion, chopped
1/4 green pepper, finely chopped
2 tbsp. bacon drippings
1 can water chestnuts, sliced
3 med. mushrooms, sliced
1 1/2 c. bean sprouts (opt.)
6 slices crisp-fried bacon, crumbled
2 c. cooked rice
3 to 4 tbsp. soy sauce
2 tbsp. Sake

Saute onion and green pepper in bacon drippings. Stir in water chestnuts, mushrooms, bean sprouts and bacon. Cook for 2 to 3 minutes. Stir in rice, soy sauce and Sake. Simmer until hot. Yield: 6 servings.

Billie Porter
Preceptor Iota Beta, Camarillo, California

FREEZER CUCUMBER SLICES

2 qt. pickling cucumbers, peeled, sliced
2 tbsp. non-iodized salt
1 onion, chopped
1 1/2 c. sugar
1/2 c. cider vinegar

Combine cucumbers and salt. Let stand for 2 hours. Add onion. Stir in sugar dissolved in vinegar. Freeze in freezer containers. Yield: 2 quarts.

Alberta C. Schultz
Xi Eta Phi, Teutopolis, Illinois

TARTAR SAUCE

1 qt. salad dressing
1 bunch parsley, chopped
1 1/2 lb. onions, chopped
1 pt. dill pickles, sliced
1/2 head cabbage, chopped
1 green pepper, chopped
1/8 bottle of horseradish
1/2 bunch celery, chopped
1/2 oz. celery salt

Process all ingredients, a small amount at a time, in blender container until smooth. Chill in refrigerator. Yield: 2 quarts.

Carol Rash
Mu Nu, Union, Iowa

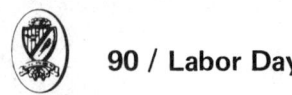

SAVORY DANISH RING

6 tbsp. margarine
1 3/4 c. flour
Salt
1 tbsp. sugar
1 1/2-oz. yeast cake
1/2 c. lukewarm milk
3 eggs
1 onion, chopped
Pepper
3 tbsp. bread crumbs
2 tbsp. ground almonds
1 c. grated Cheddar cheese
1 tbsp. Parmesan cheese
1 tbsp. poppy seed

Cut 1 tablespoon margarine into sifted flour and 1/2 teaspoon salt until crumbly. Make a well in center. Cream sugar and yeast. Add to flour mixture with milk and 1 beaten egg; mix until soft dough forms. Knead on lightly floured surface until smooth and elastic. Let rise until doubled in bulk. Punch dough down. Roll out on floured surface. Spread 1/4 cup margarine over top. Fold and roll as for puff pastry. Saute onion in 1 tablespoon margarine until tender. Mix with salt and pepper to taste, bread crumbs, almonds, Cheddar cheese and 1 beaten egg. Roll dough into rectangle. Spread onion mixture over dough. Roll as for jelly roll; seal edges. Shape into ring on baking sheet. Cut ring 2/3 through at 1-inch intervals. Let rise for 15 to 20 minutes. Glaze with half the beaten egg. Sprinkle with Parmesan cheese and poppy seed. Bake at 400 degrees for 45 to 50 minutes.

Ruth Shippen
Upsilon, Quebec, Canada

GINGERBREAD MUFFINS

1 c. sugar
1 c. shortening
4 eggs
1 c. molasses
4 c. flour
1 tsp. salt
1 c. buttermilk
2 tsp. soda
1 tsp. cinnamon
1/2 tsp. each cloves, allspice
2 tsp. ginger
1 c. chopped pecans
1 c. raisins

Cream sugar and shortening. Beat in eggs 1 at a time. Stir in molasses. Add sifted flour and salt alternately with buttermilk and soda mixture, beating well. Stir in spices, pecans and raisins. Fill greased muffin cups 3/4 full. Bake at 350 degrees for 25 minutes. Batter may be stored in refrigerator for 2 weeks. Yield: 4 dozen.

Jimmye Watson
Member at Large, Waxahachie, Texas

ZUCCHINI-NUT BREAD

1 c. oil
3 eggs
3 c. sugar
3 c. flour
3 tsp. cinnamon
1 tsp. each salt, soda, baking powder
1 c. chopped nuts
2 c. grated zucchini
1 c. raisins (opt.)

Mix oil, eggs and sugar. Stir in remaining ingredients. Bake in 2 greased and floured loaf pans at 350 degrees for 50 to 60 minutes. Yield: 2 loaves.

Linda Rogers
Epsilon Omega, Cullowhee, North Carolina

APPLE DUMPLINGS

3/4 c. shortening
2 c. flour
1 tsp. salt
2 tsp. baking powder
1/2 c. milk
6 apples, peeled, cored
Cinnamon
Sugar
Butter
1/4 tsp. nutmeg

Cut shortening into mixture of flour, salt and baking powder until crumbly. Mix in milk. Roll dough on floured surface to 1/4 inch thick. Cut into six 5-inch squares. Place 1 apple on each square. Sprinkle with cinnamon and sugar. Dot with butter. Fold corners to enclose apple. Place 2 inches apart in greased baking pan. Cook mixture of 2 cups sugar, 2 cups water, 1/4 teaspoon cinnamon, nutmeg and 1/4 cup butter for 5 minutes. Pour over apples. Bake at 350 degrees for 35 minutes. Serve warm with vanilla ice cream. Yield: 6 servings.

Glenda Blackburn
Upsilon Nu, Versailles, Missouri

BERRY SLUMP

1/4 c. shortening
1 1/4 c. sugar
1/2 c. milk
1 1/2 c. sifted flour
1/4 tsp. salt
1 1/2 tsp. baking powder
1/4 tsp. cinnamon
1/4 c. cornstarch
3 c. raspberries

Cream shortening and 1/4 cup sugar. Add milk; mix well. Stir in mixture of flour, salt and baking powder. Blend 1 cup sugar, cinnamon and cornstarch in saucepan. Stir in 1 cup boiling water gradually. Simmer until thick, stirring constantly. Fold in raspberries. Drop batter by spoonfuls over raspberry mixture. Simmer, covered, for 10 minutes or until dumplings are cooked through. Serve hot with cream or vanilla ice cream. Yield: 6-8 servings.

Cheri Brown
Preceptor Sigma, Fort Washington, Maryland

PEACH DELIGHT

1 stick margarine, softened
Flour
1 c. chopped pecans
1/4 c. packed brown sugar
1 3-oz. package cream cheese, softened
1 3/4 c. sugar
1 tsp. vanilla extract
2 eggs, beaten
1 qt. peaches, sliced

Mix margarine, 1 1/4 cups flour, pecans and brown sugar until crumbly. Press into 9 x 13-inch baking pan. Bake at 325 degrees for 10 to 15 minutes; cool. Beat cream cheese, 3/4 cup sugar, vanilla and eggs. Pour into cooled crust. Bake at 325 degrees for 20 minutes; cool. Cook peaches, 1 cup sugar, 1/2 cup water and 1/3 cup flour over medium heat until thickened, stirring constantly; cool. Pour over top. Chill overnight. Serve with whipped topping. Yield: 20 servings.

Brenda Goggans
Alpha Gamma, Temple, Texas

RHUBERRY KUCHEN

1 1/2 c. sifted flour
1 tsp. baking powder
1/4 tsp. salt
Sugar
Butter
1 tbsp. milk
1 egg, slightly beaten
3 c. cut rhubarb
1 3-oz. package strawberry gelatin
1/2 tsp. cinnamon

Sift 1 cup flour, baking powder, salt and 2 tablespoons sugar into bowl. Cut in 1/4 cup butter until crumbly. Stir in mixture of milk and egg. Press into 9-inch square pan. Cover with rhubarb. Sprinkle with gelatin. Top with mixture of 1/2 cup flour, cinnamon, 1 cup sugar and 1/3 cup butter. Bake at 375 degrees for 45 minutes.

Madeline Long
Preceptor Zeta Omega, Bakersfield, California

MASTER'S TRIFLE

1/4 c. Sherry
Sponge cake, crumbled
1 jar strawberry jam
1 lg. package strawberry gelatin
2 c. strawberries
2 pkg. vanilla pudding mix
1 can blueberry pie filling
1/2 pt. whipping cream, whipped

Sprinkle Sherry over sponge cake in large glass bowl. Spread jam over top to seal. Let stand for 1 hour. Prepare gelatin using package directions. Chill until partially set. Fold in strawberries. Spoon over jam. Chill until firm. Prepare pudding mix using package directions; cool. Spread over congealed layer. Top with pie filling and whipped cream. Garnish with cherries.

Diane Kerins
Lambda Xi, Dayton, Ohio

NEIGHBOR CAKE

2 c. packed brown sugar
1 c. oats
1/4 c. each shortening, butter
1 c. flour
1 tsp. soda
1/2 tsp. salt
1 tsp. cinnamon
1/2 tsp. each nutmeg, cloves
2 eggs, well beaten
1/2 c. chopped dates
1/2 c. chopped walnuts

Mix brown sugar, oats, 1 cup boiling water, shortening and butter in mixer bowl. Let stand for 20 minutes. Mix in sifted flour, soda, salt and spices gradually. Beat for 2 minutes. Stir in eggs, dates and 1/4 cup walnuts. Pour into greased 8-inch square baking pan. Sprinkle 1/4 cup walnuts over top. Bake at 350 degrees for 45 minutes.

Marie Holms
Preceptor Gamma, Souris, Manitoba, Canada

FRESH APPLE CAKE

2 c. sugar
1 1/2 c. oil
2 eggs
2 1/2 c. plus 1 tbsp. flour
1 tsp. each soda, salt
2 tsp. vanilla extract
3 c. finely chopped apples
1 c. chopped pecans
1 c. packed brown sugar
1/4 c. milk
1 stick margarine, melted

Mix sugar and oil. Beat in eggs 1 at a time. Mix in sifted flour, soda and salt. Stir in vanilla, apples and pecans. Bake in greased and floured 9 x 13-inch pan at 350 degrees for 1 hour. Cook brown sugar, milk and margarine over medium heat for 3 minutes, stirring frequently. Pour over cake. Let stand for 2 hours.

Sally Fulton
Beta Tau, Pelham, Alabama

HAWAIIAN PINEAPPLE CAKE

1 20-oz. can crushed pineapple
1 3/4 c. sugar
3/4 c. sour cream
3/4 c. margarine, softened
2 tsp. vanilla extract
2 eggs
2 c. baking mix
1 c. flour
1 tsp. soda
8 tsp. rum

Drain pineapple, reserving syrup. Beat 1 cup sugar, sour cream, 1/2 cup margarine and vanilla in mixer bowl for 2 minutes. Add eggs. Beat for 1 minute. Add mixture of baking mix, flour and soda. Beat for 1 minute. Stir in pineapple and 2 teaspoons rum. Bake in well-greased bundt pan at 350 degrees for 30 minutes. Heat 3/4 cup sugar, 1/4 cup margarine and 1/4 cup reserved pineapple syrup until sugar is dissolved, stirring constantly; remove from heat. Stir in 2 tablespoons rum. Spoon half the glaze over cake. Let stand for 10 minutes. Invert onto serving plate. Pour remaining glaze over top; cool.

Sharon Maranich
Beta Tau, Birmingham, Alabama

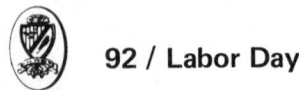

FRESH PEACH CAKE

1/4 c. shortening
1/2 c. sugar
1 egg
1 1/2 c. flour
1 tbsp. baking powder
1/4 tsp. salt
1/2 c. milk
1/2 tsp. vanilla extract
Sliced fresh peaches
Cinnamon-sugar
Butter

Cream shortening and sugar. Stir in egg. Sift flour, baking powder and salt. Add to creamed mixture alternately with mixture of milk and vanilla, beating well after each addition. Pour into greased 8 x 8-inch baking pan. Arrange peaches over top. Sprinkle with cinnamon-sugar; dot with butter. Bake at 350 degrees for about 30 minutes.

Anne Marie Mullis
Pi, Baltimore, Maryland

QUICK RHUBARB CAKE

5 c. chopped rhubarb
1 3-oz. package cherry gelatin
1/2 c. sugar
1 pkg. yellow cake mix
Whipped topping

Arrange rhubarb in 9 x 12-inch baking pan. Sprinkle gelatin, sugar and cake mix over rhubarb in order given. Pour 2 cups water over top. Bake at 350 degrees for 1 hour. Serve warm with whipped cream or vanilla ice cream. Yield: 8-10 servings.

Suzanne L. Davie
Beta Zeta, Lewiston, Maine

SIX-THREE ICE CREAM

3 c. each half and half, milk
3 c. sugar
Juice and pulp of 3 oranges, 3 lemons
3 bananas, mashed

Mix half and half, milk and sugar in ice cream freezer container until sugar is dissolved. Freeze using manufacturer's instructions for 10 to 12 minutes or until mushy. Stir in remaining ingredients. Freeze using manufacturer's directions.

Margaret Beaver
Lambda Sigma, Centralia, Missouri

GRANDMA SEVEDGE'S HOMEMADE ICE CREAM

4 eggs, well beaten
10 c. milk
2 c. cream
3 c. sugar
1 tsp. (heaping) flour
1 tsp. each vanilla, lemon extract

Beat eggs with 6 cups combined milk and cream. Beat in mixture of sugar and flour. Bring to a boil over medium heat, stirring constantly; remove from heat. Stir in remaining milk, cream and flavorings; cool. Pour into ice cream freezer container. Freeze according to manufacturer's instructions. May stir one 12-ounce package chocolate chips into hot mixture until melted; omit lemon extract. Yield: 1 gallon.

Vicki Smith
Xi Beta Rho, Bellevue, Washington

FRESH PEACH SHERBET

4 med. peaches, peeled, sliced
3/4 c. sugar
1 tsp. lemon juice
1/4 tsp. almond extract
1 c. sour cream

Puree all ingredients on High in blender. Freeze until nearly firm. Beat until smooth. Freeze until firm. Let stand at room temperature for 15 minutes before spooning into dessert glasses. Yield: 3 1/2 cups.

Laura Lee Casagrande
Preceptor Alpha Epsilon, Oroville, California

BLUEBERRY FUNNY CAKE PIE

2 c. blueberries
3/4 c. sugar
2 tbsp. lemon juice
1/4 c. butter
1 tsp. vanilla extract
1 egg
1 1/4 c. flour
1 tsp. baking powder
Pinch of salt
1/2 c. milk
1 unbaked 9-in. pie shell

Bring blueberries, 1/2 cup sugar and lemon juice to a simmer, stirring constantly; cool to lukewarm. Cream butter with 1/4 cup sugar and vanilla. Beat in egg. Add combined dry ingredients alternately with milk, beating until just mixed. Fold in blueberry mixture, stirring just to marbleize. Pour into pie shell. Bake at 375 degrees for 25 minutes or until pie tests done. Serve warm.

Edyth M. Schuyler
Preceptor Rho, Lakewood, Colorado

VERY BERRY PIE

3/4 c. sugar
2 tbsp. cornstarch
1/4 tsp. salt
1/2 pkg. berry-flavored gelatin
1 qt. berries
1 baked 9-in. pie shell

Cook sugar, cornstarch, salt and 1 cup water until thick and clear, stirring constantly; remove from heat. Stir in gelatin; cool. Pour over berries in pie shell. Chill. Serve with whipped topping.

Julia A. Jackson
Alpha Psi, Shreveport, Louisiana

Recipes on pages 94, 100 and 103.

Halloween

CINNAMON PUNCH

12 tart apples, chopped
1 12-in. cinnamon stick
2 c. cinnamon candies
4 c. pineapple juice
1 c. lemon juice
1 qt. ginger ale

Simmer apples in 1 gallon water with cinnamon stick until tender. Remove cinnamon stick. Drain through colander; press lightly to obtain some pulp. Chill. Simmer cinnamon candies in pineapple juice until dissolved; chill. Add apple and lemon juices; pour into punch bowl. Stir in ginger ale just before serving; add ice. Yield: 20-25 servings.

Rita Lowery
Eta Epsilon, Altamont, Illinois

OPEN HOUSE PUNCH

1 6-oz. can frozen lemon juice
1 6-oz. can frozen lemonade concentrate
1 6-oz. can frozen orange concentrate
1 fifth of Southern Comfort
3 qt. 7-Up

Chill all ingredients. Blend first four ingredients in punch bowl. Add ice and 7-Up. Yield: 35 servings.

Carol Ridlen
Xi Kappa Iota, Round Lake Beach, Illinois

SPICED CHERRY-APPLE PUNCH

1 8-oz. jar maraschino cherries
1 qt. apple juice
2 tbsp. lemon juice
1/4 tsp. ginger
1/8 tsp. ground cloves
4 sm. cinnamon sticks
2 to 5 tbsp. light brown sugar

Drain cherry syrup into medium saucepan; set cherries aside. Add apple and lemon juices, spices and sugar. Cook over medium heat until sugar dissolves, stirring constantly. Simmer for 10 minutes. Add cherries. Simmer for 1 minute. Pour into warmed punch bowl. Garnish with lemon slices studded with whole cloves. Yield: 1 quart.

Photograph for this recipe on page 93.

EASY HOT CIDER

1/2 c. packed brown sugar
1/2 tsp. salt
4 cinnamon sticks
1 1/2 tsp. whole cloves
1 1/2 qt. cranberry juice
2 qt. apple cider

Place mixture of brown sugar, salt, cinnamon and cloves in basket of 30-cup percolator. Pour cranberry juice and cider into percolator. Percolate; remove basket. Yield: 12 servings.

Elaine Olson
Xi Rho, Glendive, Montana

PARTY HOT CIDER PUNCH

2 qt. apple cider
8 cloves
2 cinnamon sticks
4 ginger crystals
1 qt. orange juice

Mix all ingredients. Heat to serving temperature. Serve hot from Crock·Pot.

Marsha Small
Xi Beta Upsilon, North Brunswick, New Jersey

HOT SPICED CIDER

2 qt. apple cider
1/2 c. packed brown sugar
1/4 tsp. salt
1 whole cinnamon stick
1 tsp. each whole allspice, cloves

Mix cider, brown sugar and salt. Add spices tied in cheesecloth. Simmer, covered, for 20 minutes. Remove spices. Yield: 2 quarts.

Evelyn Martin
Preceptor Chi, Pineville, West Virginia

GAMMA THETA HOT SPICED TEA

4 tea bags
4 cinnamon sticks
12 whole cloves
6 strips orange rind
3 strips lemon rind
3/4 c. sugar
3/4 c. orange juice
1/4 c. lemon juice

Simmer tea, spices, orange and lemon rinds in 5 cups water for 20 minutes. Remove tea bags. Add sugar, orange and lemon juices. Heat to serving temperature. Yield: 1 1/2 quarts.

Rosemary Lowell
Gamma Theta, Baltimore, Maryland

HOT SPICED TEA MIX

1 c. orange powdered breakfast drink
1 c. instant tea
1/4 c. Sugartwin
2 tbsp. each cloves, cinnamon

Combine all ingredients. Store in airtight container. Dissolve 1 to 2 teaspoonfuls in 1 cup hot water. Yield: 50 servings.

Deidre Broadus
Preceptor Gamma, New Albany, Indiana

CHEESE AND BACON STRIPS

1/2 lb. grated sharp Cheddar cheese
12 slices crisp-fried bacon, crumbled
1 sm. onion, chopped
1 sm. package slivered almonds, finely chopped
1 c. mayonnaise
2 tsp. Worcestershire sauce
Salt and pepper to taste
1 1-lb. loaf thin-sliced bread

Halloween / 95

Mix first 6 ingredients and salt and pepper. Spread on bread. Trim crusts. Cut each slice into 4 strips. Freeze on baking sheets. Store in bags in refrigerator. Bake at 400 degrees for 10 minutes or until cheese melts. Yield: 2-3 dozen.

Cheryl Blue
Omega, London, Ontario, Canada

HOT SPICY CHEESE DIP

1 lb. ground chuck
1 lb. pork sausage
1 onion, minced
1/2 lb. package Velveeta cheese, cubed
1 7 1/2-oz. can jalapeno relish
1 can mushroom soup
1 tsp. garlic powder

Brown ground chuck, sausage and onion, stirring frequently; drain. Add cheese. Stir over low heat until melted. Stir in remaining ingredients. Serve hot with corn chips or nachos.

Helen Gamet
Xi Delta Tau, Princeton, Missouri

PARTY CHEESE SANDWICHES

2 sticks butter, softened
2 3-oz. jars Old English cheese spread
1 tbsp. celery seed
1 tbsp. dillweed
1/2 tsp. Tabasco sauce
1/2 tsp. onion powder
1 tsp. Worcestershire sauce
1/2 tsp. cayenne
2 loaves very thin-sliced bread

Mix first 8 ingredients. Spread on slices of bread to make triple decker sandwiches. Cut into thirds. Repeat with remaining ingredients. Freeze on waxed paper-lined cookie sheet. Store in plastic bag in freezer. Bake on greased baking sheet at 350 degrees for 15 minutes. Yield: 36 servings.

Kitty Harding
Preceptor Epsilon Epsilon, El Paso, Texas

CURRIED CHEESE AND OLIVE SANDWICHES

1 c. chopped ripe olives
1 c. thinly sliced green onions
1 1/2 c. shredded American cheese
1/2 c. mayonnaise
1/2 tsp. salt
1/2 tsp. curry powder
English muffin halves

Mix first 6 ingredients. Spread on English muffins. Use additional sliced olives to make Halloween faces. Broil until cheese melts. Serve open-faced. Yield: 16 servings.

Joan Miller
Xi Delta Pi, Mason City, Iowa

CURRY-FILLED PASTRY SHELLS

1/2 sm. onion, finely chopped
1/2 sm. green pepper, finely chopped
3 tbsp. oil
1 lb. ground round
2 tbsp. curry powder
1/2 sm. jar pimentos, finely chopped
1 8-oz. can tomato sauce
Miniature pastry shells, baked

Saute onion and green pepper in oil. Add ground beef. Cook until ground beef is brown, stirring frequently; drain. Stir in curry powder, pimentos and tomato sauce. Simmer for 25 minutes. Spoon into warm pastry shells. Yield: 3 dozen.

Lora Lee Davis
Xi Iota, Texarkana, Texas

FRIED ZUCCHINI ROUNDS

1/3 c. baking mix
1/4 c. Parmesan cheese
1/8 tsp. pepper
2 eggs, slightly beaten
2 c. shredded zucchini
2 tbsp. melted butter

Mix first 5 ingredients in order listed. Drop by spoonfuls into butter in skillet. Fry until golden brown.

Lindy Grindel
Preceptor Gamma Upsilon, Gladstone, Missouri

LAYERED APRICOT SALAD

1 can apricots
2 3-oz. packages apricot gelatin
1 can apricot nectar
1 c. sour cream

Drain apricots, reserving liquid. Dissolve gelatin in hot apricot nectar and enough reserved liquid to measure 4 cups; cool. Pour half the gelatin over apricots in 8 x 8-inch dish. Chill until set. Spread sour cream over congealed layer. Pour remaining gelatin mixture over top. Chill until set. Garnish with tinted whipped cream. Yield: 6-8 servings.

Nancy A. Edwards
Laureate Alpha, Agawam, Massachusetts

APPLE CIDER SALAD

1/2 c. white raisins
6 c. apple cider
3 pkg. orange gelatin
1/2 c. walnuts
2 med. apples

Let raisins stand in 1/2 cup cider for 30 minutes. Dissolve gelatin in 2 cups boiling cider. Let stand for 1 minute. Add 3 1/2 cups cold cider. Drain raisins, reserving liquid. Stir reserved liquid into gelatin mixture. Chill until partially set. Add walnuts, apples and raisins. Yield: 12 servings.

Ann M. Pearce
Xi Beta Iota, Ellenwood, Georgia

96 / Halloween

MANDARIN ORANGE-ALMOND SALAD

1/2 c. sliced almonds
5 tbsp. sugar
1/2 head each iceberg, romaine lettuce
1 c. chopped celery
2 green onions, chopped
1/4 c. oil
2 tbsp. vinegar
Dash of Tabasco sauce
1/2 tsp. salt
Dash of pepper
1 tbsp. chopped parsley
1 11-oz. can mandarin oranges, drained

Cook almonds in 3 tablespoons sugar over medium heat until sugar is dissolved and almonds coated, stirring constantly; cool. Store in airtight container. Mix iceberg and romaine lettuce, celery and onions. Blend oil, vinegar, Tabasco sauce, remaining 2 tablespoons sugar, seasonings and parsley. Pour over vegetables; toss to coat. Add almonds and oranges just before serving. Yield: 10 servings.

Vickie Collier
Gamma Gamma, Blackwell, Oklahoma

TRICK OR TREAT SALAD

2 3-oz. packages orange gelatin
1 6-oz. can orange juice concentrate
1 lg. can crushed pineapple, drained
1 lg. can mandarin oranges, drained
1 3-oz. package French vanilla instant pudding mix
1 1/2 c. cold milk
1 c. whipped topping
1 c. grated sharp Cheddar cheese

Dissolve gelatin in orange juice and 2 cups boiling water. Add pineapple and mandarin oranges. Pour into 9 x 13-inch pan. Chill until set. Mix pudding and milk; stir until thick. Fold in whipped topping. Spread pudding over gelatin. Sprinkle with cheese.

Marlene K. Coffman
Xi Xi, North Pole, Alaska

HOT BACON SALAD

2 heads Boston lettuce
1 bunch spinach
6 slices bacon, chopped
1 med. onion, minced
1/3 c. cider vinegar
3 tbsp. sugar
1 1/2 tsp. salt
1/4 tsp. pepper
Mustard to taste
2 eggs, slightly beaten

Tear lettuce and spinach into bite-sized pieces. Fry and drain bacon, reserving drippings. Saute onion in drippings. Add vinegar, sugar, salt, pepper and mustard. Cook until sugar dissolves. Stir a small amount of hot mixture into eggs; stir eggs into hot mixture. Simmer until thick, stirring constantly. Pour over salad greens; toss lightly. Serve immediately. Yield: 8-10 servings.

Brenda Kohler
Preceptor Alpha Delta, Annandale, Virginia

BREAD SALAD

1/2 c. butter, softened
1 loaf white sandwich bread, trimmed
6 hard-boiled eggs, chopped
3 green onions, chopped
2 cans shrimp, drained
1 can crab meat, drained
3 c. mayonnaise

Butter bread lightly on both sides; cut into cubes. Mix with eggs and green onions. Chill, covered, overnight. Add shrimp, crab meat and mayonnaise. Let stand for 3 to 4 hours.

Janice L. Hall
Lambda, Walla Walla, Washington

BEEF AND NOODLES

1 lb. beef tenderloin, cubed
1/4 c. instant minced onion
1 1/2 tsp. garlic salt
Salt and pepper
1/4 c. butter
1 can beefy mushroom soup
1 can beef broth
1/3 c. flour
1 8-oz. package extra wide noodles, cooked

Brown tenderloin with onion, garlic salt, salt and pepper in butter. Add soup and broth, reserving 2/3 cup broth. Bring to a simmer. Blend flour with reserved broth. Stir into skillet. Simmer until thick, stirring constantly. Stir in noodles. Simmer for 15 to 20 minutes. Yield: 6 servings.

Shirley L. Strunk
Epsilon Mu, Carbondale, Kansas

HALLOWEEN OVEN-BAKED BEEF STEW

3 lb. beef cubes
1 tsp. basil
6 carrots, quartered
6 sm. potatoes
4 stalks celery, sliced in half
3 onions, chopped
1/2 tsp. pepper
Salt to taste
1/4 tsp. oregano
4 or 5 tomatoes, crushed
1/4 c. oil

Combine first 10 ingredients in large baking pan. Sprinkle with oil; toss lightly. Bake, covered, at 350 degrees for 1 hour, basting frequently. Bake, uncovered, for 1 1/4 hours or until beef is tender.

Claire Cortopassi
Preceptor Iota Lambda, Turlock, California

SHERRIED BEEF AND RICE

3 lb. beef cubes
2 cans cream of mushroom soup
3/4 c. Sherry
1 env. dry onion soup mix
1 lg. onion, chopped
1 stick butter
1 3/4 c. rice
2 cans consomme
1 c. mushrooms
1 1/2 c. grated Cheddar cheese
1/2 c. chopped almonds

Halloween / 97

Mix first 4 ingredients in 3-quart casserole. Bake, covered, at 325 degrees for 3 hours. Saute onion in butter. Mix in remaining ingredients. Bake, covered, in 3-quart casserole at 325 degrees for 1 1/2 hours. Serve beef over rice. Yield: 8 servings.

Pauline Di Pasquale
Preceptor Beta, Portland, Oregon

ROUND STEAK WITH DRESSING

2 lb. tenderized round steak
Salt and pepper to taste
1 box stuffing mix, prepared
1/2 lb. bacon
1 can cream of mushroom soup

Sprinkle steak with salt and pepper. Spread stuffing over steak. Roll as for jelly roll. Wrap with bacon; secure with toothpicks. Place in baking dish. Add 1/2 cup water. Bake, covered, at 350 degrees for 2 hours. Pour soup over steak. Bake for 20 minutes longer. Yield: 6-8 servings.

Dawn Lorenzen
Sigma, Cedar Rapids, Iowa

MARVELOUS MEXICAN CASSEROLE

1/2 c. chopped onion
1/4 c. chopped green pepper
3 to 4 tbsp. oil
1 can cream of chicken soup
1 can hominy
1 can beef tamales
1/2 c. chopped ripe olives
1 jar chopped pimentos
1 c. grated Cheddar cheese

Saute onion and green pepper in oil. Stir in soup. Add drained hominy and enough reserved liquid to make of desired consistency. Remove wrappers from tamales; cut into 1/2-inch pieces. Stir into hominy mixture. Mix in olives and pimentos. Spoon into 1 1/2-quart casserole. Sprinkle with cheese. Bake at 350 degrees for 15 to 20 minutes. Yield: 5-6 servings.

Dorothy A. Kramer
Laureate Theta, Omaha, Nebraska

QUICK CHILI

1 lb. ground beef
1 onion, chopped
1 can hot chili beans
1 can tomatoes
1 pkg. chili seasoning mix
Chili powder to taste
1 tsp. sugar

Brown ground beef with onion, stirring frequently; drain. Add remaining ingredients and 1 cup water. Simmer for 1 hour.

Renee Lupton Russell
Xi, Durham, North Carolina

HALLOWEEN MEATZA PIE

1 lb. ground beef
1 c. fine bread crumbs
1 egg
Salt and pepper to taste
1 can tomato paste
1 med. onion, finely chopped
1/2 c. chopped green pepper
1/2 c. chopped mushrooms
1/2 c. sliced olives
Dash of garlic powder
Mozzarella cheese, grated
American cheese slices

Mix ground beef, bread crumbs, egg, salt and pepper. Press over bottom and side of pie pan. Spread with tomato paste. Add next 5 ingredients. Sprinkle with mozzarella cheese. Top with American cheese slices. Bake at 350 degrees for 20 minutes.

Jeanne Perisho
Gamma Psi, Paris, Illinois

DINNER-IN-A-PUMPKIN

1 med. pumpkin, seeded
1 onion, chopped
2 tbsp. oil
1 1/2 to 2 lb. ground beef
2 tbsp. soy sauce
2 tbsp. brown sugar
1 4-oz. can sliced mushrooms, drained
1 can cream of chicken soup
1 1/2 c. cooked rice

Decorate pumpkin as jack-o-lantern using permanent marker. Saute onion in oil. Add ground beef. Cook until brown, stirring frequently; drain. Mix in soy sauce, brown sugar, mushrooms and soup. Simmer for 10 minutes, stirring occasionally. Stir in rice. Spoon into pumpkin shell; replace top. Bake at 350 degrees for 1 hour or until pumpkin is tender. Use pumpkin as centerpiece. Serve from pumpkin, using cooked pumpkin as vegetable. Yield: 6 servings.

Karen Fitch
Xi Theta Phi, Chesterfield, Missouri

HOLIDAY PUMPKIN DINNER

2 lb. ground beef
1 green pepper, chopped
1 onion, chopped
2 cloves of garlic, chopped
1/2 c. raisins
1/2 tsp. vinegar
3 eggs, beaten
2 1/2 tsp. oregano
1 15-oz. can tomato sauce
1 tsp. pepper
1 10-in. pumpkin, seeded

Brown ground beef with green pepper, onion and garlic, stirring frequently. Stir in remaining ingredients except pumpkin. Spoon into pumpkin shell. Bake, covered, at 350 degrees until pumpkin is tender. Yield: 10 servings.

Cherllyn McAndrew
Lambda, Boise, Idaho

98 / Halloween

RUNZAS

1 pkg. dry yeast
1/2 c. sugar
Salt
7 c. sifted flour
2 eggs
Shortening
2 lb. ground beef
2 c. finely chopped onions
4 c. shredded cabbage
1 tbsp. Worcestershire sauce
1/4 tsp. each oregano, savory, pepper
1/2 tsp. each MSG, seasoned salt
1 egg yolk

Dissolve yeast in 2 cups warm water in mixer bowl. Let stand for 5 minutes. Mix with sugar, 1 teaspoon salt and 2 cups flour. Beat in 2 eggs and 2 tablespoons melted shortening until smooth. Stir in 5 cups flour. Beat for 5 minutes. Let rise, covered, in warm place until doubled in bulk. Knead on lightly floured surface for several seconds. Roll into twelve 6 x 8-inch rectangles. Cook ground beef, stirring frequently; drain. Steam onions and cabbage with 1 tablespoon shortening and 2 tablespoons water for 10 to 15 minutes; drain. Add to ground beef mixture with 1 tablespoon salt, Worcestershire sauce and seasonings; cool. Spoon 2/3 cup ground beef mixture lengthwise down center of each rectangle; seal sides and ends together. Place seam side down on greased baking sheet. Bake at 400 degrees for 15 minutes. Brush with egg yolk beaten with 2 tablespoons water. Bake for 5 to 10 minutes longer. Yield: 12 servings.

Wanda Gish
Preceptor Alpha Omicron, Marshall, Michigan

MICROWAVE SWEET AND SOUR PORK

1 1/2 lb. fresh pork, cubed
1 med. onion, chopped
1 8-oz. can pineapple chunks
1/4 c. packed brown sugar
2 tbsp. cornstarch
2 tbsp. lemon juice
1 tbsp. soy sauce
1/2 tsp. salt
1/8 tsp. each pepper, ginger
1 sm. green pepper, sliced
1 6-oz. package frozen pea pods

Mix first 7 ingredients and seasonings in 2-quart glass baking dish. Microwave, covered, on High for 13 to 15 minutes, stirring after 5 minutes. Stir in green pepper and pea pods. Microwave, covered, on High for 5 to 6 minutes or until vegetables are tender-crisp, stirring after 2 1/2 minutes. Serve over rice. Yield: 4 servings.

Marcia Smith
Lambda Psi, Marine City, Michigan

ITALIAN SAUSAGE SOUP

1 lb. Italian sausage, sliced
1/2 c. chopped onion
2 16-oz. cans tomatoes
2 tbsp. chopped celery leaves
1 tbsp. salt
2 beef bouillon cubes
1/4 c. chopped parsley
1 c. diagonally sliced celery
1 bay leaf
1/2 tsp. pepper
1 tbsp. lemon juice

Brown sausage in saucepan over medium heat. Add onion. Cook for 5 minutes. Add remaining ingredients and 1 1/2 cups water. Simmer for 40 minutes or until potatoes are tender.

M. Goldie Woolen
Preceptor Gamma Chi, Liberty

CHEESE-TOPPED CHICKEN CACCIATORE

1 3-lb. fryer, cut up
1/4 c. olive oil
2 onions, sliced
2 cloves of garlic, crushed
1 16-oz. can Italian-style tomatoes
1 8-oz. can tomato sauce
1 tsp. salt
1/4 tsp. pepper
1 tsp. oregano
2 bay leaves
Italian-style grated cheese

Brown chicken in olive oil; remove chicken. Saute onions and garlic in pan drippings. Add next 6 ingredients. Simmer for 5 minutes. Add chicken. Cook, covered, for 45 minutes. Place chicken on hot platter. Skim sauce; remove bay leaves. Pour over chicken. Sprinkle with cheese. Yield: 4 servings.

Susan Jackson
Kappa, Kansas City, Missouri

CHICKEN-CHEESE ROLLS

3 whole chicken breasts, split, boned
1 8-oz. container whipped cream cheese with chives
1 tbsp. butter
6 slices bacon

Pound each chicken breast to 1/2-inch thickness between waxed paper. Spread 3 tablespoons cream cheese on each; dot with 1/2 teaspoon butter. Fold ends to enclose filling. Wrap with 1 slice bacon. Place seam side down in 9 x 12-inch baking pan. Bake on top oven rack at 400 degrees for 40 minutes. Broil for 5 minutes or until bacon is crisp. May be prepared ahead and refrigerated until ready to use. Yield: 6 servings.

Sandi Kenny
Xi Kappa Omicron, Thornville, Ohio

CHICKEN BREASTS PARMESAN

Chicken breasts, boned
1 egg, beaten
Bread crumbs
Parmesan cheese
Spaghetti sauce
Mozzarella cheese, thinly sliced
Oregano

Dip chicken in egg, then in mixture of bread crumbs and Parmesan cheese. Brown in a small amount of oil. Pour spaghetti sauce over chicken in baking dish. Bake at 350 degrees for 30 to 35 minutes. Top with mozzarella slices. Sprinkle with oregano. Bake until cheese melts.

Joy Loesche
Upsilon Omega, Princeton, Florida

MAPLE CHICKEN

1 c. maple syrup	Salt and pepper
1 tbsp. oil	1 4 1/2-lb. chicken,
1/4 c. white wine vinegar	cut up
1 14-oz. can tomato	1 med. onion, chopped
paste	1/4 lb. mushrooms, sliced
1/2 c. dry Sherry	2 tbsp. sultana raisins
1 tbsp. soy sauce	2 oz. blanched almonds
2 tsp. hot curry powder	1 green pepper, sliced
1 tsp. marjoram	2 stalks celery, chopped
2 cloves of garlic	

Pour mixture of first 11 ingredients over chicken in casserole. Marinate at room temperature for 4 hours. Bake at 300 degrees for 2 hours. Add remaining ingredients. Bake, covered, for 30 minutes. Serve with wild rice. Yield: 6 servings.

Carol Firmin
Gamma Sigma, Fernie, British Columbia, Canada

BAKED CARROTS

3 c. sliced cooked carrots	1/2 stick margarine,
2 tbsp. chopped onion	melted
1/2 c. cubed Velveeta	Salt to taste
cheese	Crushed potato chips

Mix carrots, onions, cheese and margarine. Season with salt. Spoon into 1-quart baking dish. Sprinkle with potato chips. Bake at 350 degrees for 30 minutes. Yield: 6 servings.

Lynnette Groepper
Mu Nu, Eldora, Iowa

CARROT BISQUE

3 to 5 slices bacon,	1 c. coarsely chopped
chopped	celery with leaves
4 c. coarsely chopped	5 1/2 c. chicken broth
carrots	1/4 tsp. thyme
1 c. coarsely chopped	1 sm. bay leaf
mushrooms	1 1/4 c. half and half
1/2 c. coarsely chopped	Salt and pepper to taste
scallions with tops	

Fry bacon over medium heat until crisp. Add vegetables. Saute for 5 minutes. Simmer, covered, for 10 minutes. Stir in broth, thyme and bay leaf. Bring to a boil. Simmer, covered, for 50 minutes. Cool; remove bay leaf. Puree a small amount at a time in blender. Heat to serving temperature. Stir in half and half and salt and pepper to taste. Serve in warm bowls. Yield: 8 servings.

Linda Boyle
Beta Theta, Columbia, Maryland

QUICK AND EASY CORN PUDDING

1 15-oz. can whole	2 eggs
kernel corn, drained	1 stick margarine, melted
1 15-oz. can cream-style	1 8-oz. package corn
corn	bread mix
1 8-oz. carton sour	3 to 4 green onions with
cream	tops, finely chopped

Mix all ingredients until just moistened. Bake in greased 9 x 13-inch casserole at 325 degrees for 45 minutes or until set. Yield: 12 servings.

Martha Kniseley
Preceptor Alpha Gamma, Ames, Iowa

BEVERLY'S SWEET POTATO SURPRISE

6 med. sweet potatoes	1 c. apricot juice
1 1/2 c. packed brown sugar	1 c. apricots, drained
1 1/2 tbsp. cornstarch	2 tbsp. butter
1 tsp. grated orange rind	1/2 c. chopped pecans
1/8 tsp. cinnamon	

Cook sweet potatoes in a small amount of water for 20 minutes; peel. Mix brown sugar, cornstarch, orange rind and cinnamon in saucepan. Stir in apricot juice. Cook until thickened, stirring constantly. Stir in apricots. Pour over sweet potatoes in 8 x 8-inch baking dish. Dot with butter. Sprinkle with pecans. Bake at 375 degrees for 25 minutes. Yield: 6 servings.

Beverly Oldaker
Preceptor Delta, Pueblo, Colorado

VESTA'S MUSHROOM PILAF

1 1/2 c. rice	1 8-oz. can mushrooms
1/2 c. melted butter	1 1/2 c. shredded Cheddar
1 can onion soup	cheese
1 can beef consomme	

Mix rice and butter in 2-quart casserole. Stir in soup, consomme and mushrooms. Bake, covered, at 325 degrees for 55 minutes or until rice is tender and liquid is absorbed. Top with cheese. Bake for 5 minutes longer or until cheese melts. Yield: 6-8 servings.

Nancy Galliher
Xi Gamma Omega, Beavertown, Pennsylvania

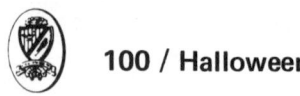

100 / Halloween

ORANGE COFFEE RING

2 10-count pkg. refrigerator biscuits
1/4 c. melted butter
3/4 c. sugar
1 tsp. grated orange rind
1 oz. cream cheese
1 tsp. orange juice
3/4 c. confectioner's sugar
1/4 tsp. vanilla extract
Shredded coconut
Chopped pecans

Dip biscuits in melted butter, then in mixture of sugar and orange rind. Arrange in overlapping circle in greased 9-inch pan. Bake at 425 degrees for 15 to 20 minutes. Invert onto serving plate. Blend cream cheese, orange juice, confectioners' sugar and vanilla. Spread over coffee ring. Sprinkle with coconut and pecans. Yield: 16 servings.

Gladys Kelly
Alpha Rho Theta, Friendswood, Texas

VEGETABLE SPOON BREAD

2 eggs, slightly beaten
1 10-oz. package frozen chopped spinach, thawed
1 8 3/4-oz. can cream-style corn
1 c. sour cream
1/2 c. melted butter
1 c. chopped ham (opt.)
1 8 1/2-oz. package corn muffin mix
1/2 c. shredded process cheese

Mix eggs, spinach, corn, sour cream, butter and ham. Stir in corn muffin mix. Bake in greased 9-inch pan at 350 degrees for 35 to 40 minutes. Sprinkle with cheese. Bake for 2 minutes longer or until cheese melts. May substitute broccoli or cauliflower. Yield: 8 servings.

Barbara Parmer
Alpha Rho Alpha, Joshua, Texas

SPUDNUTS

1 3/4 c. milk, scalded
1/2 c. shortening
1/2 c. sugar
1/2 c. mashed potatoes
1 pkg. dry yeast
2 eggs, beaten
1/2 tsp. vanilla extract
6 1/2 to 7 c. sifted flour
1 tsp. baking powder
2 tsp. salt
Oil for deep frying
Cinnamon-sugar

Mix milk, shortening, sugar and mashed potatoes; cool to lukewarm. Add yeast dissolved in 1/2 cup warm water. Stir in eggs and vanilla. Mix in sifted dry ingredients gradually. Place in greased bowl, turning to grease surface. Let rise until doubled in bulk. Roll on floured surface to 1/2-inch thickness. Cut with doughnut cutter. Let rise on waxed paper until doubled in bulk. Deep-fry until brown; drain. Coat with cinnamon-sugar. Yield: 3 1/2-4 dozen.

Esther M. Steil
Iota Phi, West Bend, Iowa

BUTTERMILK DOUGHNUTS

2 eggs, beaten
1 c. sugar
1/4 c. oil
1 tsp. vanilla extract
4 c. flour
4 tsp. baking powder
3/4 tsp. salt
1/4 tsp. soda
1/2 to 1 tsp. nutmeg (opt.)
1 c. buttermilk
Shortening for deep frying
Confectioners' sugar

Beat eggs and sugar until smooth. Stir in oil and vanilla. Mix in combined dry ingredients alternately with buttermilk. Roll 1/2 inch thick on floured surface. Cut with floured doughnut cutter. Deep-fry at 375 degrees for 3 minutes or until golden. Drain on paper towels. Sprinkle with confectioners' sugar. Yield: 1 1/2 dozen.

Martha Carrier
Alpha Beta, Exeter, New Hampshire

CHERRY DOUGHNUTS

1 pkg. hot roll mix
1 4-oz. jar maraschino cherries, drained, chopped
1/2 tsp. nutmeg
Oil for deep frying
Sugar

Prepare hot roll mix using package directions, adding cherries and nutmeg to yeast mixture before adding flour. Let rise until doubled in bulk. Roll into 9 x 22-inch rectangle. Cut into 1/2 x 4-inch strips. Twist strips; shape into doughnut shape. Let rise until doubled in bulk. Deep-fry 2 or 3 doughnuts at a time in 365-degree oil for 2 minutes or until browned on both sides. Drain on paper towels. Roll in sugar. Yield: 15 servings.

Photograph for this recipe on page 93.

HOCUS-POCUS BUNS

1 pkg. dry yeast
3/4 c. lukewarm milk
1 1/4 c. sugar
1 tsp. salt
1 egg
1/4 c. shortening
3 1/2 c. flour
24 lg. marshmallows
1 c. melted butter
1 tbsp. cinnamon

Dissolve yeast in 1/4 cup warm water. Mix yeast, milk, 1/4 cup sugar, salt, egg, shortening and half the flour until smooth. Stir in remaining flour. Knead on lightly floured surface for 5 minutes. Place in greased bowl, turning to grease surface. Let rise, covered, for 1 1/2 hours or until doubled in bulk. Punch dough down. Let rise for 30 minutes or until doubled. Roll 1/4 inch thick. Cut into twenty-four 3 1/2-inch circles. Dip marshmallows in melted butter, then into mixture of cinnamon and 1 cup sugar. Wrap 1 pastry circle around each marshmallow. Pinch edges to seal. Dip in butter, then in cinnamon-sugar mixture. Place in greased muffin cups. Let rise for 20 minutes. Bake at 375 degrees for 30 minutes. Yield: 2 dozen.

Judy Surgnier
Xi Alpha Gamma, Ada, Oklahoma

Halloween / 101

ORANGE STREUSEL MUFFINS

1 egg, beaten	1 tbsp. baking powder
1/2 c. orange juice	1 tsp. salt
1/2 c. orange marmalade	Sugar
1/4 c. milk	1/2 tsp. cinnamon
1/4 c. oil	1/4 tsp. nutmeg
2 c. flour	

Mix egg with next 4 ingredients. Stir in flour, baking powder, salt and 1/3 cup sugar until just moistened. Fill greased muffin cups 2/3 full. Mix 1/4 cup sugar, cinnamon and nutmeg. Sprinkle over top. Bake at 400 degrees for 20 to 25 minutes. Yield: 1 dozen.

Janet Burke
Sigma Iota, W. Columbia, Texas

HOLIDAY CARAMEL CORN

2 c. packed brown sugar	1/2 tsp. soda
1 c. margarine	1 tsp. vanilla extract
1/2 c. light corn syrup	8 qt. popped popcorn

Boil first 3 ingredients for 5 minutes; remove from heat. Stir in soda and vanilla. Pour over popcorn; stir to coat. Bake on baking sheet at 250 degrees for 1 1/2 to 2 hours, stirring occasionally. Yield: 8 quarts.

Karin Krauter
Xi Gamma Phi, Littleton, Colorado

CARAMEL FONDUE

1 14-oz. package caramels	1 c. miniature marshmallows
2/3 c. evaporated milk	

Melt caramels over low heat. Add remaining ingredients and 1 tablespoon water. Heat until marshmallows are melted, stirring constantly. Serve in fondue pot with apple slices for dipping. Yield: 2 1/2 cups.

Rita Wolfinger
Preceptor Theta, Southport, Indiana

FANCY POPCORN BALLS

3/4 c. light corn syrup	1 c. miniature marshmallows
1/4 c. butter	1 c. Spanish peanuts
1 16-oz. package confectioners' sugar	5 qt. popped popcorn

Bring first 4 ingredients and 2 tablespoons water to a boil. Stir in peanuts. Pour over popcorn; toss to coat. Spoon onto waxed paper. Shape into balls with buttered hands. Yield: 25 servings.

Georgia Schaefer
Beta Nu, Joseph, Oregon

BEET CAKE WITH CREAM CHEESE FROSTING

1 1/4 c. oil	1 tsp. each soda, salt
2 c. sugar	1 c. raisins
2 cans beets, drained, finely chopped	1 c. chopped nuts
4 eggs	1/4 c. margarine, softened
3 c. flour	1 8-oz. package cream cheese, softened
2 tsp. baking powder	1 16-oz. box confectioners' sugar
1 tsp. cinnamon	

Mix oil, sugar, beets and eggs. Mix in sifted dry ingredients. Stir in raisins and nuts. Bake in greased and floured tube pan at 350 degrees for 1 hour; cool. Cream margarine, cream cheese and confectioners' sugar. Spread over cake. Yield: 12-14 servings.

Barbara Haley
Xi Beta Tau, Cape May Point, New Jersey

CHOCOLATE CUSTARD DEVIL'S FOOD CAKE

3 1-oz. squares unsweetened chocolate, melted	1/2 c. shortening
	2 egg yolks, beaten
	2 c. cake flour
1 1/2 c. milk	1/4 tsp. salt
1 egg, beaten	1 tsp. soda
1 2/3 c. sugar	1 tsp. vanilla extract

Combine chocolate, 1/2 cup milk, egg and 2/3 cup sugar. Cook over low heat until thick, stirring constantly; cool. Cream shortening and 1 cup sugar. Beat in egg yolks. Mix in sifted dry ingredients alternately with 1 cup milk and vanilla. Stir in chocolate mixture. Bake in 2 waxed paper-lined 8-inch cake pans at 350 degrees for 25 to 30 minutes. Yield: 8-12 servings.

Shelley Chapman
Preceptor Beta Omega, San Diego, California

PUMPKIN CAKE DESSERT

1 lg. package vanilla pudding and pie filling mix	5 c. milk
	1 angel food cake
	Orange food coloring
1 lg. package chocolate pudding and pie filling mix	1/2 pt. whipping cream, whipped

Cook each pudding according to package directions, using 2 1/2 cups milk; cool slightly. Slice cake horizontally. Alternate layers of puddings and cake in large round mold. Cover and weight to press into mold. Chill for 3 hours or until set; unmold onto serving plate. Spread with orange-tinted whipped cream. Cut banana top for stem of pumpkin, if desired. Yield: 12 servings.

Rose Pearson
Alpha Alpha, Rockford, Illinois

102 / Halloween

PUMPKIN CAKE ROLL

3 eggs
1 c. sugar
3/4 c. cooked mashed pumpkin
1 tsp. lemon juice
3/4 c. flour
1 tsp. baking powder
2 tsp. cinnamon
1/2 tsp. nutmeg
1 tsp. ginger
1/2 tsp. salt
1 c. chopped nuts
1 6-oz. package cream cheese
1/4 c. butter, softened
Confectioners' sugar
1/2 tsp. vanilla extract

Beat eggs at high speed for 5 minutes. Beat in sugar gradually. Fold in pumpkin and lemon juice. Fold in next 6 combined dry ingredients. Spread in greased and floured jelly roll pan. Sprinkle with nuts. Bake at 375 degrees for 15 minutes. Invert on towel sprinkled with confectioners' sugar. Roll cake and towel as for jelly roll; cool. Beat cream cheese, butter, 1 cup confectioners' sugar and vanilla until smooth. Unroll cake, removing towel. Spread with filling. Reroll. Chill.

Debee Nicklett
Alpha Iota, Lewiston, Idaho

STRAWBERRY JAM CAKE

3 sticks margarine, softened
2 c. sugar
5 eggs, beaten
3 c. flour
1 1/2 tsp. each cinnamon, cloves, allspice
1 tsp. soda
1 c. buttermilk
2 c. strawberry jam
1 c. chopped nuts
1 8-oz. package cream cheese, softened
1 16-oz. box confectioners' sugar
1 tsp. vanilla extract

Cream 2 sticks margarine. Beat in sugar gradually, until fluffy. Beat in eggs. Beat in combined flour and spices alternately with soda dissolved in buttermilk. Stir in jam and nuts. Pour into greased and waxed paper-lined 11 x 13-inch baking pan. Bake at 325 degrees for 30 to 40 minutes. Cream 1 stick margarine and cream cheese. Beat in confectioners' sugar until fluffy. Stir in vanilla. Spread over cooled cake. Decorate cake slices with Halloween candy. Yield: 24 servings.

Alice Macomber
Preceptor Delta Alpha, Cape Coral, Florida

GOBLIN'S DELIGHT CUPCAKES

1 1/2 c. flour
1 1/3 c. sugar
1/3 c. cocoa
1 tsp. soda
Salt
1/3 c. oil
1 tbsp. vinegar
1 tsp. vanilla extract
1 8-oz. package cream cheese, softened
1 egg
2 tsp. grated orange rind
2 drops each of red and yellow food coloring
1 c. chocolate chips

Mix flour, 1 cup sugar, cocoa, soda and 1/2 teaspoon salt in mixer bowl. Beat in oil, 1 cup water, vinegar and vanilla at low speed. Fill paper-lined muffin cups 2/3 full. Beat cream cheese, 1/3 cup sugar, egg, orange rind, 1/8 teaspoon salt and food colorings until creamy. Stir in chocolate chips. Place 1 tablespoonful on each cupcake. Bake at 350 degrees for 20 minutes. Yield: 2 dozen.

Mary McCarthy
Mu Theta, Brownsburg, Indiana

APPLE BONBONS

1 12-oz. package peanut butter chips
3 tbsp. shortening
3 c. 3/4-inch apple chunks
Chopped peanuts

Melt peanut butter chips and shortening in double boiler; stir until smooth. Dip apples in mixture; drain. Place on waxed paper. Sprinkle with peanuts. Store in refrigerator for 2 days or less. Yield: 50 servings.

Chris Modaff
Lambda Sigma, Columbia, Missouri

HAYSTACKS

1 3-oz. package cream cheese, softened
1/4 c. milk
4 c. confectioners' sugar
4 oz. unsweetened chocolate, melted
1/2 tsp. vanilla extract
Dash of salt
6 c. miniature marshmallows
7 oz. flaked coconut

Blend cream cheese and milk. Mix in confectioners' sugar gradually. Stir in chocolate, vanilla and salt. Fold in marshmallows. Drop by heaping spoonfuls into coconut; toss to coat. Chill for 1 hour or until firm. Yield: 35 servings.

Drenda Bland
Xi Beta Tau, North Cape May, New Jersey

ROCKY ROAD HALLOWEEN SQUARES

1 12-oz. package chocolate chips
1 can sweetened condensed milk
2 tbsp. butter
2 c. dry-roasted peanuts
1 10 1/2-oz. package miniature marshmallows

Melt chocolate chips in condensed milk and butter in double boiler; remove from heat. Mix peanuts and marshmallows; fold into chocolate mixture. Spread in waxed paper-lined 9 x 13-inch pan. Chill for 2 hours or until firm; remove from pan. Peel off waxed paper; cut into squares. Store, covered, at room temperature. Yield: 40 servings.

Micki McCorkle
Omicron, Missoula, Montana

Halloween / 103

CHERRY CANDY APPLES

2 c. sugar
2/3 c. red maraschino cherry syrup
3/4 tsp. red food coloring
8 med. red apples on wooden skewers

Dissolve sugar in syrup and 3/4 cup water; add food coloring. Cook over medium heat to 300 degrees on candy thermometer. Remove from heat. Twirl apples in hot syrup until completely covered; drain over saucepan. Cool on foil.

Photograph for this recipe on page 93.

SPIDERS

1 6-oz. package chocolate chips
1 6-oz. package butterscotch chips
1 pkg. salted peanuts
1 can chow mein noodles
Silver candy shot

Melt chocolate and butterscotch chips over low heat, stirring constantly. Stir in peanuts and noodles. Drop by spoonfuls onto waxed paper. Add silver candy shot for eyes. Yield: 2-3 dozen.

Paula Heck
Mu Lambda, Fairfax, Missouri

CARROT BARS

4 eggs, beaten
2 c. sugar
1 1/2 c. oil
2 c. flour
3 sm. jars strained carrots
1 tsp. each salt, cinnamon, soda
1 c. chopped nuts
1 8-oz. package cream cheese, softened
1/4 c. melted margarine
3 1/2 c. confectioners' sugar
1 tsp. vanilla extract

Mix eggs, sugar, oil and flour. Beat in carrots, salt, cinnamon and soda. Stir in nuts. Bake in 2 greased and floured 9 x 13-inch baking pans at 350 degrees for 35 minutes; cool. Beat cream cheese, margarine, confectioners' sugar and vanilla until creamy. Spread over top. Cut into bars. Yield: 24 servings.

Betty Wilken
Preceptor Upsilon, Derby, Kansas

DATE AND ORANGE SLICE BARS

1/2 lb. dates, chopped
Sugar
Flour
3/4 c. shortening
1 c. packed brown sugar
2 eggs
1 tsp. vanilla extract
1 tsp. soda
1/2 tsp. salt
1/2 c. chopped nuts (opt.)
1 15-oz. package candy orange slices

Mix dates, 1/2 cup sugar, 2 tablespoons flour and 1 cup water. Cook until thick, stirring constantly; cool. Cream shortening and brown sugar. Beat in eggs. Add vanilla and soda dissolved in 2 tablespoons hot water. Stir in 1 3/4 cups flour, salt and nuts. Cut orange slices into thirds lengthwise. Layer half the batter, orange slices, date mixture and remaining batter in 9 x 13-inch baking pan. Sprinkle with mixture of sugar and nuts if desired. Bake at 350 degrees for 35 to 40 minutes. Cut into bars. Yield: 2 dozen.

Cindi Sweedler
Mu Iota, Williams, Iowa

MEAL-IN-ONE ZOWIE BARS

1/2 c. butter, melted
1/3 c. packed dark brown sugar
1 egg
3/4 c. packed grated carrots
3 oz. Cheddar cheese, shredded
1 c. oats
1/2 c. whole wheat flour
1/4 c. wheat germ
1/2 c. nonfat dry milk powder
1/2 c. chopped dates
1/2 c. raisins
1/2 c. unsalted sunflower seed
1 tsp. vanilla extract
1 tsp. cinnamon
1/2 tsp. allspice
1/2 tsp. baking powder
1/4 tsp. soda

Mix first 3 ingredients. Combine remaining ingredients; mix well. Stir into butter mixture. Spread in greased 9 x 13-inch baking pan. Bake at 350 degrees for 20 minutes. Cool for 30 minutes before cutting into bars.

Janice Stoffel
Alpha Beta, Las Vegas, Nevada

PUMPKIN BARS WITH CREAM CHEESE FROSTING

4 eggs
2 c. sugar
1 c. oil
2 c. mashed cooked pumpkin
2 c. flour
1 tsp. salt
2 tsp. soda
1 tsp. cinnamon
1 3-oz. package cream cheese, softened
4 tbsp. margarine, softened
1 1/2 c. confectioners' sugar
1 tsp. vanilla extract

Beat eggs, sugar and oil until lemon colored. Blend in pumpkin. Beat in sifted flour, salt, soda and cinnamon gradually. Bake in greased and floured 10 x 15-inch baking pan at 350 degrees for 20 to 25 minutes; cool. Blend cream cheese, margarine, confectioners' sugar and vanilla until smooth. Spread over top. Cut into bars. Yield: 20 servings.

Lori-Dolores A. McCausland
Preceptor Alpha Xi, Goleta, California

104 / Halloween

GOLDEN CARROT COOKIES

3/4 c. sugar	3 tsp. baking powder
3/4 c. shortening	1/2 tsp. salt
1 egg	1 c. confectioners' sugar
1 c. hot mashed carrots	Grated rind of 1 orange
2 c. flour	Orange juice

Cream sugar and shortening. Mix in egg and carrots. Stir in mixture of flour, baking powder and salt gradually. Drop by spoonfuls onto cookie sheet. Bake at 375 degrees for 10 to 12 minutes. Blend confectioners' sugar, orange rind and enough orange juice to make of spreading consistency. Frost hot cookies.

Velma Price
Preceptor Beta Epsilon, Florence, Colorado

CRACKERJACK COOKIES

1 c. butter	1 tsp. baking powder
1 c. sugar	1 tsp. soda
1 c. packed brown sugar	2 c. oats
2 eggs	1 c. flaked coconut
2 tsp. vanilla extract	2 c. Rice Krispies
1 1/2 c. flour	

Cream butter and sugars. Beat in eggs; add vanilla. Stir in sifted dry ingredients. Mix in oats, coconut and Rice Krispies. Drop by teaspoonfuls onto greased cookie sheet. Bake at 350 degrees for 10 minutes.

Beverley Towler
Souris Manitoba, Canada

GINGERBREAD BOYS

1 c. margarine, softened	2 tsp. soda
1 c. sugar	1 tsp. cloves
1 egg	1/4 tsp. salt
1 tbsp. vinegar	1 c. molasses
4 1/2 to 5 c. flour	Raisins

Cream margarine and sugar. Mix in egg and vinegar. Mix in sifted flour, soda, cloves and salt alternately with molasses. Chill overnight. Roll 1/4 inch thick on floured surface. Cut with gingerbread boy cutter. Add raisin eyes, mouth and buttons. Bake on cookie sheet at 375 degrees for 8 minutes. Yield: 2 dozen.

Kathy Pugh
Delta Zeta, Troy, Alabama

FAVORITE GINGERSNAPS

1 1/2 c. shortening	4 c. sifted flour
Sugar	2 tsp. soda
2 eggs	2 tsp. each cinnamon,
1/2 c. molasses	cloves, ginger

Cream shortening and 2 cups sugar. Beat in eggs. Add molasses and sifted dry ingredients. Shape into 1-inch balls. Roll in sugar. Bake at 375 degrees for 15 minutes.

Evelyn L. Fisher
Laureate Beta, Lancaster, Pennsylvania

JACK O'-LANTERN TEA CAKES

1 recipe sugar cookie dough	1/2 tsp. orange extract
1 1/2 c. confectioners' sugar	Green, red and yellow food coloring
1 to 2 tbsp. milk	Candy corn
	Shoestring licorice

Shape cookie dough into pumpkins with stems. Bake using recipe directions. Blend confectioners' sugar, milk and orange flavoring to spreading consistency. Tint 1 tablespoonful with green food coloring for stems. Tint remaining frosting with red and yellow food coloring blended to make orange. Frost cookies. Decorate with candy corn for eyes and nose and licorice for mouth. Yield: 2 dozen.

Edris Christians
Beta Beta, Holiday Island, Arkansas

MOLASSES CRINKLES

3/4 c. shortening	1/4 tsp. salt
1 c. packed brown sugar	1/2 tsp. cloves
1 egg	1 tsp. each cinnamon, ginger
1/4 c. molasses	Sugar
2 1/4 c. sifted flour	
2 tsp. soda	

Cream shortening, brown sugar, egg and molasses. Stir in sifted dry ingredients except sugar. Chill. Shape into balls; dip tops in sugar. Place sugared side up 3 inches apart on greased cookie sheet. Sprinkle with water to produce a crackled surface. Bake at 375 degrees for 10 minutes or until set. Yield: 4 1/2 dozen.

Anna Mae Cruise
Eta Epsilon, Effingham, Illinois

HOLIDAY PUMPKIN COOKIES

1 1/2 c. margarine, softened	4 c. flour
2 c. packed brown sugar	2 c. oats
1 c. sugar	2 tsp. each soda, cinnamon
1 egg	1 tsp. salt
1 tsp. vanilla extract	1 16-oz. can pumpkin
	1 c. chocolate chips

Beat margarine and sugars until fluffy. Stir in egg and vanilla. Add mixture of next 5 dry ingredients alternately with pumpkin. Stir in chocolate chips. Drop by 1/4 cupfuls onto greased cookie sheet. Shape into pumpkins with stems. Bake at 350 degrees for 20 to 25 minutes. Decorate with icing, raisins, nuts and candies. Yield: 2 1/2-3 dozen.

Sandra Hackenschmidt
Kappa, Souris, Manitoba, Canada

MONSTER COOKIES

6 eggs
1 lb. brown sugar
2 c. sugar
1 1/2 tsp. vanilla extract
1 1/2 tsp. corn syrup
4 tsp. soda
1/2 lb. margarine, softened
1 24-oz. jar peanut butter
9 c. oats
1 6-oz. package chocolate chips
1 8-oz. package M and M's

Mix first 8 ingredients until smooth. Stir in oats, chocolate chips and M and M's. Drop by ice cream scoopfuls onto greased cookie sheet. Bake at 350 degrees for 12 minutes. Yield: 9 dozen.

Debbie Winkler
Kappa Zeta, Mt. Carmel, Illinois

ANIMAL COOKIES

2 c. margarine
2 1/2 c. sugar
1 c. milk
3 eggs
7 1/2 c. flour
7 1/2 tsp. baking powder
1 tsp. vanilla extract

Combine all ingredients; mix well. Roll dough out onto floured surface. Cut into desired shapes. Place on lightly greased cookie sheet. Bake at 350 degrees for 8 to 10 minutes. Yield: 12 dozen.

Mary Lou Mack
Preceptor Tau, Collins, Ohio

SURPRISE BONBONS

1/2 c. mayonnaise
3/4 c. confectioners' sugar
1 tbsp. vanilla extract
1/8 tsp. salt
1 1/2 c. flour
2/3 tbsp. milk
1 sm. jar maraschino cherries
Candy kisses
1/4 c. nut halves

Blend mayonnaise, confectioners' sugar and vanilla. Stir in salt, flour and milk. Shape tablespoonfuls of dough around cherries, kisses and nuts. Bake on ungreased cookie sheet at 350 degrees for 12 to 15 minutes. Yield: 4 dozen.

Jolene Broussard
Preceptor Delta, Sulphur, Louisiana

EASY ORANGE BALLS

1 7 1/4-oz. package vanilla wafers, crushed
3/4 c. grated coconut
1/2 c. frozen orange juice concentrate
Confectioners' sugar

Combine crumbs with coconut and orange juice concentrate. Shape into 1-inch balls. Place on cookie sheet. Chill for 3 hours. Roll in confectioners' sugar before serving. Yield: 36 servings.

Hazel M. Gerber, Pres.
Laureate Alpha Eta, Moses Lake, Washington

STREUSEL-FILLED BAKED APPLES

4 apples
Brown sugar
2 tbsp. butter or margarine, softened
1 tbsp. flour
3 tbsp. each raisins, chopped nuts
1 tbsp. lemon juice
1 1/2 tsp. ground cinnamon

Core apples, leaving bottom intact; pare 1/3 of way down from top. Combine 2 tablespoons packed brown sugar, butter, flour, raisins and nuts. Fill apples with mixture. Place in baking dish. Combine 3/4 cup water, 1/2 cup packed brown sugar, lemon juice and cinnamon in saucepan. Bring to a boil. Cook for 5 minutes; stir occasionally. Pour sauce over apples. Bake, uncovered, at 325 degrees for 45 minutes, basting occasionally. Serve warm. Yield: 4 servings.

Betty F. Veach
Xi Lambda Xi, Clarendon, Texas

GRANDMA BODIN'S APPLE TARTS

1/2 c. butter
1 c. sugar
2 eggs, beaten
1 tsp. baking powder
1/2 tsp. salt
3 c. flour
1/2 c. cream
1 tsp. vanilla extract
Freshly grated apples
Cinnamon and nutmeg to taste

Cream butter and sugar; add eggs. Sift baking powder, salt and flour together; add to creamed mixture. Add cream and vanilla. Roll dough out on floured surface to 1/4-inch thickness. Add small amount flour if needed for handling ease. Cut into 30 circles; fit into greased muffin cups. Combine apples with additional sugar to taste and cinnamon and nutmeg. Pour into pastry-lined muffin cups. Cover with lattice top. Bake at 350 degrees for 35 to 40 minutes. Cool before removing from tins. Yield: 30 tarts.

Susan Woods
Omicron Gamma, Liberty, Missouri

BLACK BOTTOM PIE

2 c. milk, scalded
4 eggs, separated
1 c. sugar
1 tbsp. cornstarch
1 tsp. vanilla extract
1 6-oz. package semisweet chocolate chips
1 baked 9-in. pie shell
1 tbsp. unflavored gelatin

Stir milk into beaten egg yolks. Stir in mixture of 1/2 cup sugar and cornstarch. Cook in double boiler over hot water until custard coats spoon, stirring constantly; remove from heat. Add vanilla. Stir chocolate chips into 1 cup custard until melted. Pour into pie shell; chill. Soften gelatin in 1/4 cup cold water. Stir into remaining hot custard until dissolved. Chill until slightly thickened. Beat egg whites until soft peaks form; add 1/2 cup sugar gradually, beating until stiff. Fold into gelatin mixture. Pour over chocolate layer. Chill until firm. Garnish with chocolate shavings and diagonally sliced bananas.

Elsie MacInnis
Sigma, Newfoundland, Canada

GERMAN CHOCOLATE PIE

1 4-oz. package sweet chocolate
1/4 c. margarine
1 2/3 c. evaporated milk
1 1/2 c. sugar
3 tbsp. cornstarch
1/8 tsp. salt (opt.)
2 eggs, beaten
1 tsp. vanilla extract
1 10-in. unbaked pie shell
1 1/3 c. shredded coconut
1/2 c. chopped pecans

Melt chocolate and margarine over low heat, stirring until blended. Remove from heat; blend in milk gradually. Mix sugar, cornstarch and salt in large mixing bowl. Beat in eggs and vanilla. Blend in chocolate mixture gradually. Pour into pie shell. Mix coconut and pecans; sprinkle over filling. Bake at 375 degrees for 45 minutes. Cool for 4 hours.

Karin Swelling
Xi Beta Delta, Albuquerque, New Mexico

TWO-TONE HOLIDAY PIE

1 1/2 c. mincemeat
1 unbaked 9-in. pie shell
1 19-oz. can pumpkin pie filling
1/4 c. orange juice
1 c. evaporated milk
1/2 tsp. grated orange rind

Spread mincemeat in pie shell. Prepare pumpkin pie filling according to package directions substituting orange juice and evaporated milk for liquid. Stir in orange rind. Pour over mincemeat. Bake at 400 degrees for 45 minutes; cool. Garnish with whipped cream rosettes. Yield: 6 servings.

Charlotte R. Fulton
Xi Eta, Truro, Nova Scotia, Canada

COFFEE PIE

1 c. vanilla wafer crumbs
1/3 c. chopped pecans
1/3 c. melted margarine
Pinch of salt
1 1/2 pt. coffee ice cream, softened

Combine first 4 ingredients. Pat into 9-inch pie plate. Bake at 325 degrees for 15 minutes. Cool. Fill with ice cream. Freeze. Let stand at room temperature for 10 minutes before serving. Yield: 8-10 servings.

Diane Church
Preceptor Alpha Beta, Beatrice, Nebraska

PEG'S CHIFFON PIE

6 tbsp. butter
2 c. graham cracker crumbs
Sugar
4 eggs, separated
1 3-oz. package cherry Jell-O
1 21-oz. can cherry pie filling
1/2 tsp. cream of tartar

Combine butter, crumbs and 2 tablespoons sugar. Pat into 2 nine-inch pie plates. Chill. Combine egg yolks, 3/4 cup water and Jell-O in saucepan. Cook for 5 to 8 minutes. Add pie filling. Beat egg whites and cream of tartar until soft peaks form. Add 1/4 cup sugar slowly, beating until stiff peaks form. Fold cherry mixture into egg whites. Pour into pie crust. Chill until serving time.

Peg Baldwin
Gamma Tau, Kenton, Ohio

SOUR CREAM PUMPKIN PIE

1 env. unflavored gelatin
3 eggs, separated
Sugar
1 1/4 c. pumpkin, canned or homemade
1/2 c. sour cream
1/2 tsp. salt
1 tsp. cinnamon
1/4 tsp. each cloves, nutmeg
1 c. sifted confectioners' sugar
1/2 tsp. each vanilla, rum extract
1 c. whipped heavy cream
1 9-in. baked pie shell
1/2 c. chopped pecans

Soften gelatin in 1/4 cup water. Beat egg yolks with 1/3 cup sugar until thick. Add pumpkin, sour cream, salt and spices. Cook over medium heat, stirring constantly, until mixture comes to a boil. Reduce heat; cook for 2 minutes, stirring constantly. Remove from heat; stir in softened gelatin. Stir until gelatin is dissolved. Cool. Beat egg whites until frothy. Add 1/4 cup sugar gradually, beating until stiff peaks form. Fold into pumpkin mixture. Add confectioners' sugar, vanilla and rum extract to whipped cream, mixing well. Spoon half the pumpkin mixture into cool pie shell; spread half the whipped cream mixture on top. Repeat. Sprinkle with pecans. Chill for 2 hours or longer before serving. Yield: 8 servings.

Carolyn Saldi
Xi Theta, Durham, North Carolina

Recipes on pages 109, 110, 117 and 121.

Thanksgiving

108 / Thanksgiving

CHAMPAGNE PUNCH

Cranberry juice, chilled
2 6-oz. cans frozen orange juice concentrate
1 6-oz. can frozen pineapple juice concentrate
2 tbsp. lemon juice
1 qt. 7-Up, chilled
2 bottles of Champagne, chilled

Make ice ring with cranberry juice. Mix concentrates and lemon juice. Add 1 quart cranberry juice and remaining ingredients just before serving. Pour over ice ring in punch bowl.

Janis Roden
Laureate Alpha Zeta, Odessa, Texas

ANCHOVY STUFFING FOR CELERY

2 3-oz. packages cream cheese, softened
1 lg. clove of garlic, crushed
2 tbsp. Worcestershire sauce
1 tbsp. horseradish
1 tbsp. (about) anchovy paste
Celery, cut into 3-in. pieces

Mix cream cheese with garlic, Worcestershire sauce and horseradish. Stir in anchovy paste to taste. Spread on celery.

Nancy Blake
Zeta Xi, Brush, Colorado

SCRAMBLES

1 sm. box Wheat Chex
1 sm. box Rice Chex
1 10-oz. box Cheerios
1 box pretzel sticks
1 pkg. small pretzel twists
1 16-oz. can mixed salted nuts
3 c. oil
3 tbsp. Worcestershire sauce
1 1/2 tsp. each garlic salt, celery salt, onion salt
1 1/2 tsp. seasoned salt

Mix cereals, pretzels and nuts in large baking pan. Mix oil, Worcestershire sauce and seasonings. Pour over cereal mixture, tossing to coat. Bake at 250 degrees for 2 hours, stirring every 15 minutes.

Joyce A. Lockwood
Preceptor Kappa Kappa, Fairfield, California

CRUNCHY CRANBERRY SALAD

4 c. cranberries
2 c. sugar
15 marshmallows
1 c. chopped celery
1 c. chopped apples
1 c. chopped nuts
2 env. unflavored gelatin

Cook cranberries, sugar and 1 cup water until cranberries pop. Add marshmallows; stir until melted. Add celery, apples and nuts. Dissolve gelatin in 1 cup cold water. Stir in cranberry mixture. Spoon into serving dish. Chill until set. Yield: 8 servings.

Lois Ruth Petitt
Xi Alpha Iota, Paqosa Springs, Colorado

CRANBERRY-CREAM CHEESE SALAD

1 3-oz. package cherry gelatin
1 can whole cranberry sauce
1/2 c. chopped celery
1/4 c. chopped nuts
1 c. sour cream

Dissolve gelatin in 1 cup boiling water. Let stand until partially set. Stir in cranberry sauce, celery and nuts. Blend in sour cream. Pour into mold. Chill until set. Yield: 6 servings.

Judy Johnson
Preceptor Beta Iota, Columbus, Indiana

CRANBERRY-APPLE RELISH

2 c. sugar
2 3-oz. packages raspberry gelatin
1 lb. cranberries
4 or 5 med. apples, cored
1/2 c. ground pecans

Dissolve sugar in 2 cups boiling water. Add gelatin; stir until dissolved. Stir in 1 cup cold water. Chill until partially set. Chop cranberries and apples in food processor container. Add to gelatin with pecans; mix well. Chill until firm.

Jenny Luchsinger
Xi Epsilon Zeta, Cincinnati, Ohio

CREAMY CRANBERRY MOLD

3/4 c. sugar
2 8-oz. packages cream cheese, softened
1 2/3 c. evaporated milk
2 3-oz. packages lemon gelatin
1 tsp. grated lemon rind
5 tbsp. lemon juice
2 tsp. cornstarch
1 8-oz. can whole cranberry sauce

Mix 1/2 cup sugar and cream cheese together. Blend in evaporated milk gradually. Dissolve gelatin in 2 cups boiling water. Mix into cream cheese mixture with lemon rind and 3 tablespoons lemon juice. Chill in 6 or 7-cup mold until firm. Mix cornstarch and 1/4 cup sugar in saucepan. Stir in cranberry sauce. Cook over low heat until thickened, stirring constantly. Stir in 2 tablespoons lemon juice; chill. Spoon over salad. Yield: 8-12 servings.

Linda Christl
Beta Upsilon, Modesto, California

CRANBERRY RELISH MOLD

1 3-oz. package lemon gelatin
1 3-oz. package cherry gelatin
1/2 c. sugar
1 8 3/4-oz. can crushed pineapple
1 tbsp. lemon juice
2 c. cranberries, rinsed, drained
1 sm. orange, quartered
1 c. diced celery
1/2 c. chopped walnuts

Dissolve gelatins and sugar in 3 cups boiling water. Add pineapple and lemon juice. Chill until partially set. Put cranberries and orange through grinder. Fold into gelatin mixture with celery and walnuts. Pour into 8 1/2-cup mold. Chill until firm. Unmold on lettuce leaves. Yield: 10-12 servings.

Photograph for this recipe on page 108.

FRESH CRANBERRY SALAD

2 3-oz. packages cherry gelatin
1 c. sugar
1 c. pineapple juice
1 lb. cranberries, ground
2/3 c. crushed pineapple
1 c. chopped walnuts

Dissolve gelatin and sugar in 2 cups boiling water. Stir in remaining ingredients. Pour into mold. Chill until set.

Roberta M. Matt
Preceptor Xi, Seal Beach, California

MAKE-AHEAD CRANBERRY SALAD

1 pkg. cranberries, ground
1 c. sugar
1 to 2 c. crushed pineapple, drained
1 to 3 c. miniature marshmallows
1/2 pt. whipping cream, whipped

Mix cranberries and sugar together. Combine pineapple and marshmallows. Chill both mixtures for 24 hours or longer. Combine cranberry mixture and pineapple mixture. Chill for 24 hours longer. Fold in whipped cream. Chill for about 8 hours. Yield: 8-10 servings.

Cherie Hippler
Xi Pi Upsilon, Cypress, California

FRUIT SALAD WITH SOUR CREAM-FRUIT DRESSING

1 can fruit cocktail, drained
1 can apricot halves, drained
1 can pineapple chunks, drained
1/2 c. maraschino cherry halves
1 c. boysenberries
1 can mandarin oranges, drained
2 or 3 bananas, sliced
1/2 c. sugar
2 tbsp. flour
1 egg yolk, beaten
2 tbsp. lemon juice
1/2 c. pineapple juice
1 c. sour cream
1 10-oz. package frozen strawberries, thawed, drained

Mix first 7 ingredients. Chill in refrigerator. Mix sugar and flour in saucepan. Stir in egg yolk, lemon and pineapple juices. Cook until thick, stirring constantly. Chill. Stir cream cheese and strawberries into chilled sauce. Pour over fruit just before serving; toss lightly. May add marshmallows and nuts.

Jane Mercer
Xi Alpha Gamma, Ada, Oklahoma

RICH MANDARIN ORANGE SALAD

1 3-oz. package orange tapioca pudding mix
1 3-oz. package vanilla pudding mix
1 3-oz. package orange gelatin
1 env. whipped topping mix, prepared
2 sm. cans mandarin oranges, drained

Cook first 3 ingredients in 3 cups water until thickened, stirring frequently; cool slightly. Beat well; chill. Fold in whipped topping and mandarin oranges. Chill in refrigerator. Yield: 8 servings.

Barbara Helfrich
Preceptor Upsilon, Greeley, Colorado

PICKLED PEACH SALAD

1 sm. package lemon gelatin
1/2 c. pickled peach juice
1 jar pickled peaches, chopped
1 c. finely chopped celery
1/2 c. chopped pecans

Dissolve gelatin in boiling peach juice and 1 cup water. Chill until partially set. Mix in remaining ingredients. Pour into mold. Chill until firm. Garnish with mayonnaise. Yield: 6-8 servings.

Patty Kight
Xi Alpha Eta, Lyons, Georgia

RASPBERRY-APPLESAUCE SALAD

1 6-oz. package raspberry gelatin
2 pkg. frozen raspberries, thawed
2 c. applesauce
1 c. sour cream
Miniature marshmallows

Dissolve gelatin in 2 cups boiling water. Mix raspberries and applesauce. Stir into gelatin. Pour into 9 x 13-inch pan. Chill until set. Mix sour cream with as many marshmallows as possible. Chill overnight. Beat well. Spread over congealed layer. Yield: 15 servings.

Joyce Rath
Xi Eta Zeta, Emmetsburg, Iowa

110 / Thanksgiving

TOMATO ASPIC

1 3-oz. package lemon gelatin
1 2/3 c. tomato juice, strained
1/4 c. fresh lemon juice
3/4 tsp. onion juice
2/3 tsp. pepper
1/8 tsp. cloves
1/4 tsp. paprika
1 tsp. salt
1/2 c. finely chopped celery
1/4 c. sweet pickle relish
3/4 lb. crab meat

Dissolve gelatin in boiling tomato juice. Add lemon juice, onion juice and seasonings. Stir in celery and relish. Pour into 8 individual ring molds. Chill until set. Unmold on lettuce-lined plates. Fill center with crab meat.

Susan Holliday
Omega, Whitefish, Montana

FRUIT-STUFFED RIB ROAST

1 4-lb. pork loin center rib roast, backbone loosened
Salt and pepper
1 20-oz. can sliced apples
1 lb. ground pork
9 slices dry raisin bread, cubed
1 tsp. cinnamon
1/2 tsp. ground cardamom
1/4 tsp. allspice

Place roast rib side down in roasting pan. Cut pockets between ribs. Season with salt and pepper. Drain apples, reserving juice. Chop apples finely. Add water to reserved juice to measure 1 cup. Brown ground pork; drain. Stir in bread cubes, spices, 3/4 teaspoon salt and dash of pepper. Fold in apples. Stir in juice. Spoon 1/2 cup stuffing into each pocket. Place remaining stuffing in 1-quart casserole. Chill in refrigerator. Bake roast at 325 degrees for 1 1/2 hours. Bake, covered loosely with foil, for 1 to 1 1/2 hours longer or to 170 degrees on meat thermometer. Bake stuffing casserole during last 40 minutes of baking time. Yield: 8 servings.

Sandra Collins
Gamma Iota, Rome, New York

ITALIAN-STUFFED SWEET PEPPERS

2 1/2 lb. ground beef-Italian sausage mixture
2 c. Italian-style bread crumbs
Salt and pepper to taste
10 green peppers
1 c. tomato sauce
1/2 c. olive oil

Mix beef-sausage mixture, bread crumbs and seasonings. Spoon into green pepper shells. Place in deep baking pan in enough water to almost cover peppers. Pour mixture of tomato sauce and olive oil over peppers. Sprinkle with additional bread crumbs. Bake, covered with foil, at 350 degrees for 1 1/2 hours. Yield: 10 servings.

Betty Comstock
Laureate Delta, Biloxi, Mississippi

CRANBERRY-GLAZED HAM

1 10 to 12-lb. smoked precooked whole ham
Whole cloves
2 c. sugar
4 tsp. dry mustard
4 c. cranberries, rinsed, drained
1 c. Burgundy

Score ham into diamonds; press clove into each diamond. Roast in shallow pan at 350 degrees for 1 hour. Combine sugar, mustard and 1 cup water; stir until smooth. Add remaining ingredients. Boil until cranberries are tender. Remove ham from oven; spread with glaze. Bake for 30 minutes. Place on platter. Spoon warmed glaze over ham. Yield: 12-14 servings.

Photograph for this recipe on page 107.

SPECIAL CHICKEN PARMESAN

6 chicken breasts, boned
2 eggs
Salt to taste
1/8 tsp. pepper
1/2 c. flour
3/4 c. fine bread crumbs
1/2 c. oil
2 c. tomato sauce
Pinch of basil
1/4 tsp. oregano
1/8 tsp. garlic powder
1/2 c. Parmesan cheese
8 oz. sliced mozzarella cheese

Pound chicken with meat mallet to 1/4-inch thickness. Beat eggs with salt and pepper. Dip chicken in flour, egg mixture and bread crumbs in order listed. Brown chicken in oil; remove to baking dish. Remove excess drippings from skillet. Add tomato sauce, basil, oregano and garlic powder. Simmer for 10 minutes. Pour sauce around chicken. Sprinkle with Parmesan cheese. Bake, covered, at 350 degrees for 30 minutes. Top with mozzarella cheese. Bake, uncovered, for 10 minutes longer. Yield: 6 servings.

Patricia Andersen
Xi Gamma Lambda, Cobourg, Ontario, Canada

GOODBYE TURKEY CASSEROLE

5 tbsp. flour
1 tsp. salt
1/4 tsp. onion salt
1/4 c. melted butter
2 1/2 c. milk
1 1/2 c. turkey broth
1 1/3 c. minute rice
1/2 c. grated American cheese
1 1/2 c. cooked asparagus
6 slices turkey
2 tbsp. slivered almonds

Mix flour, 1/2 teaspoon salt, onion salt and butter in double boiler. Stir in milk. Cook until thickened, stirring occasionally. Pour mixture of broth and 1/2 teaspoon salt over rice in 2-quart baking dish. Layer half the cheese, all the asparagus and all the turkey over top. Pour sauce over all. Sprinkle with remaining cheese. Top with almonds. Bake at 375 degrees for 20 minutes.

Dorothy Franks
Xi Alpha Kappa, Lafayette, Georgia

Thanksgiving / 111

OVERNIGHT TURKEY

1 14 to 20-lb. turkey
Salt and pepper to taste
1 recipe stuffing
1 lg. onion

Season turkey cavity with salt and pepper. Fill with stuffing. Pour 8 cups water into roasting pan. Add onion. Place turkey on rack in pan. Bake, tightly covered, at 500 degrees for 1 hour; turn oven off. Let turkey stand in closed oven for 8 hours. Bake, uncovered, at 350 degrees until top is browned.

Sandra St. Clair Gray
Xi Omega, Waukesha, Wisconsin

CHINESE TURKEY CASSEROLE

3 1/2 c. chopped cooked turkey
1 pkg. long grain and wild rice, cooked
1 c. chopped celery
2 cans cream of chicken soup
3/4 c. mayonnaise
2 tbsp. chopped onion
1 can sliced water chestnuts, drained
2 c. cornflakes
1/2 stick butter, melted

Mix turkey, rice and next 5 ingredients. Spoon into casserole. Top with cornflakes and butter. Bake at 350 degrees for 40 to 50 minutes. Chow mein noodles may be substituted for cornflakes. Yield: 8-10 servings.

Dawn Lorenzen
Sigma, Cedar Rapids, Iowa

CRUSTY TURKEY PIE

2 c. gravy
1 can whole kernel corn
1 can green beans
2 c. chopped cooked turkey
2 c. baking mix
2 tsp. parsley flakes
Pinch each of basil, salt, pepper
1 sm. onion, finely chopped
3/4 c. grated cheese
1/2 c. milk

Heat gravy. Combine with corn, green beans and turkey in deep-dish pie plate. Mix remaining ingredients. Roll 3/4-inch thick on floured surface to fit pie plate. Place over pie; seal edge. Cut vents. Bake at 400 degrees for 10 minutes or until brown. Yield: 6 servings.

Lorraine Arbuckle
Kappa, Souris, Manitoba, Canada

TURKEY-WILD RICE CASSEROLE

1 c. wild rice, cooked
1/4 lb. bacon, chopped
1 c. each chopped celery, onion
1/2 c. chopped green pepper
1 can mushrooms
1/2 c. white rice
2 to 3 c. chopped cooked turkey
Salt and pepper to taste
1 can chicken with rice soup

Rinse cooked wild rice in cold water for 5 minutes; drain. Cook bacon until crisp. Add celery, onion, green pepper, mushrooms and white rice. Saute for several minutes. Add turkey. Combine with wild rice in 1 1/2-quart casserole. Add seasonings and soup; toss to mix. Bake, covered, at 350 degrees for 1 hour, stirring occasionally. May add chicken bouillon if mixture becomes too dry. Yield: 6 servings.

Dorothy Joseph
Laureate Alpha, Williston, North Dakota

LAYERED TURKEY CASSEROLE

9 slices bread
5 c. chopped cooked turkey
1 4-oz. can sliced mushrooms, drained
2 cans sliced water chestnuts, drained
9 slices Cheddar cheese
1/2 tsp. salt
2 c. milk
4 eggs
1 can cream of celery soup
1 can cream of chicken soup
1/2 c. toasted almonds
Butter

Trim and cube bread; reserve crusts. Layer bread, turkey, mushrooms, water chestnuts and cheese in 9 x 13-inch casserole. Mix salt, milk and eggs. Pour over turkey mixture. Spread soups over top. Bake at 350 degrees for 1 hour. Mix reserved bread crust crumbs and almonds in melted butter. Sprinkle over casserole. Bake for 15 minutes longer.

Lucy Lockhart
Alpha Lambda, Carroll, Iowa

TURKEY CHOW MEIN

4 c. chopped cooked turkey
2 c. finely chopped onions
1 c. shortening
7 c. chopped celery
2 tsp. salt
1/4 c. cornstarch
1 tbsp. Brown Sauce
1/4 c. soy sauce
1/4 tsp. pepper
1 can bean sprouts
1 sm. can chopped pimento
1 can sliced water chestnuts
1 sm. can mushrooms
1 can chow mein noodles

Saute turkey and onions in shortening. Stir in celery, salt and 2 cups water. Simmer for 10 minutes. Mix cornstarch, Brown Sauce, soy sauce, pepper and 2 tablespoons water until smooth. Add bean sprouts, pimento, water chestnuts and mushrooms to turkey mixture. Stir in cornstarch mixture. Cook until thick, stirring constantly. Serve over chow mein noodles. Yield: 18 servings.

Willie Belle Shotts
Laureate Zeta, Birmingham, Alabama

TURKEY DIVINE

1 10-oz. package frozen broccoli, partially cooked
1 c. chopped cooked turkey
1 sm. can mushrooms
1 can cream of chicken soup
1 1/2 tsp. instant minced onion
1/2 c. mayonnaise
1/2 tsp. lemon juice
1/2 tsp. parsley flakes
1/4 tsp. curry powder
1/2 c. grated Cheddar cheese
1/2 c. crushed potato chips

Layer first 3 ingredients in 9 x 12-inch baking dish. Mix soup, onion, mayonnaise, lemon juice and seasonings. Pour over casserole. Top with cheese and potato chips. Bake at 350 degrees for 30 to 45 minutes.

Ginny Richards
Omega, Whitefish, Montana

STUFFED QUAIL

12 quail
1 lb. pork sausage
12 thin slices bacon
2 c. flour
Salt and pepper to taste
2 sticks margarine
2 c. red wine
3 tbsp. grape jelly

Stuff quail with sausage. Wrap 1 slice bacon around each quail breast. Roll quail in flour seasoned with salt and pepper; reserve flour mixture. Brown quail in margarine; remove. Stir enough reserved flour into pan drippings to make gravy. Stir in wine and jelly. Pour over quail in 3-quart baking dish. Bake, covered with foil, at 250 degrees for 1 1/2 to 2 hours or until tender. Yield: 12 servings.

Frances McKenzie
Epsilon Mu, Mansfield, Louisiana

ROAST PHEASANT

1 pheasant
Salt
Pepper
2 slices onion
2 slices lemon
1/8 tsp. basil
1 bay leaf
1/4 tsp. minced garlic
2 whole cloves
1/2 tsp. each parsley, dried celery leaves
Bacon
1/4 c. white wine
1/2 c. chicken stock

Season outside of pheasant with salt and pepper. Place 1/4 teaspoon salt, 1/8 teaspoon pepper, onion, lemon and remaining seasonings in cavity. Place strips of bacon over breast and around each leg. Place in baking pan. Baste with mixture of wine and chicken stock. Bake, loosely covered with foil, at 300 degrees for 2 hours or until tender, basting frequently with wine mixture. Make gravy from pan drippings.

Beverly Phillips
Theta Tau, Meeker, Colorado

DELICIOUS PHEASANT

1 pheasant, cut up
2 c. flour
Salt and pepper to taste
3 tbsp. butter
1 c. cream
1/4 c. chopped onion (opt.)

Dip pheasant in flour seasoned with salt and pepper. Brown in butter in Dutch oven. Pour cream over pheasant. Add onion. Bake, covered, at 325 degrees for 1 hour and 30 minutes or until pheasant is tender. Yield: 4-6 servings.

Rita Higgins
Xi Eta Phi, Effingham, Illinois

CORNISH HENS WITH RICE

1/2 c. chopped celery
1 4-oz. can mushrooms, drained
4 tbsp. margarine, melted
3/4 c. rice
3/4 c. wild rice
2 env. dry onion soup mix
4 Cornish game hens, split
Salt

Saute celery and mushrooms in 2 tablespoons margarine. Add white rice. Saute for several minutes. Stir in wild rice. Spread over bottom of roasting pan. Combine soup mix and 3 1/2 cups boiling water. Pour over rice mixture. Rub hens with salt and 2 tablespoons margarine. Arrange hens over rice mixture. Bake at 400 degrees for 50 to 60 minutes, basting occasionally. Yield: 8 servings.

Suzan Kaminski
Xi Delta Delta, Olathe, Kansas

CORNISH HENS WITH MUSHROOM STUFFING

4 Cornish game hens
4 c. bread crumbs
1/4 c. chopped onion
1/2 tsp. each salt, pepper, garlic salt
1 8-oz. can sliced mushrooms
1 can cream of mushroom soup

Wash hens; pat dry inside and out. Stuff with mixture of bread crumbs, onion, seasonings, mushrooms and 1/4 cup soup. Place hens in 9 x 12-inch baking dish. Top with remaining soup. Bake at 375 degrees for 1 1/2 hours. Yield: 4 servings.

Tina Marie Biggers
Sigma Tau, Carmichael, California

ARTICHOKE-RICE CASSEROLE

2 jars marinated artichokes
1 pkg. chicken-flavored Rice-A-Roni
1 pkg. almond-flavored Rice-A-Roni
1/2 c. mayonnaise
2 tsp. curry powder
1 bunch green onions, chopped
1 can water chestnuts, sliced

1 green pepper, chopped
Chopped chicken (opt.)
Flaked tuna (opt.)

Drain artichokes, reserving marinade. Prepare Rice-A-Roni using package directions. Blend mayonnaise, curry powder and reserved marinade. Combine with remaining ingredients. Stir in Rice-A-Roni and artichokes. Serve at room temperature. Yield: 20 servings.

Lila Lampkin
Preceptor Rho, Little Rock, Arkansas

HOLIDAY GREEN BEANS

1 med. onion, chopped
2 tbsp. butter
2 cans mushroom soup
1/4 lb. Cheddar cheese, cubed
2 drops of Tabasco sauce
2 tsp. soy sauce
1 tsp. each salt, MSG
1 can water chestnuts, sliced
3 cans French-style green beans
1 sm. package slivered almonds

Saute onion in butter. Stir in soup and cheese. Cook until cheese is almost melted, stirring frequently. Stir in seasonings. Add water chestnuts and green beans. Spoon into 9 x 13-inch baking pan. Sprinkle with almonds. Bake at 375 degrees for 20 to 30 minutes. Yield: 8-10 servings.

Becky Huntin
Gamma Gamma, Blackwell, Oklahoma

HOLIDAY CELERY CASSEROLE

6 c. 1/2-inch celery pieces
2 cans cream of chicken soup
1 c. slivered almonds
3 c. buttered bread crumbs
Parmesan cheese

Cook celery in 1 1/2 cups boiling water for 16 minutes; drain. Place in 9 x 13-inch casserole. Top with mixture of soup and almonds. Sprinkle with bread crumbs and cheese. Bake at 350 degrees for 30 minutes. Yield: 6-8 servings.

Joyce Barrett
Xi Xi, Phoenix, Arizona

CHEESE-SCALLOPED CARROTS

1 sm. onion, minced
1 to 2 tsp. chopped green pepper (opt.)
1/4 c. butter
1/4 c. flour
1 tsp. salt
1/4 tsp. dry mustard
2 c. milk
1/8 tsp. pepper
1/4 tsp. celery salt
12 med. carrots, sliced, cooked
1 8-oz. package cheese slices
3 c. bread crumbs

Saute onion and green pepper in butter for 2 to 3 minutes. Stir in flour, salt, mustard and milk. Cook until smooth, stirring constantly. Add pepper and celery salt. Layer carrots and cheese alternately in 2-quart casserole until all ingredients are used, ending with carrots. Cover with sauce. Sprinkle with bread crumbs. Bake at 350 degrees for 25 minutes. Yield: 8 servings.

Gloria Dyck
Phi, Swift Current, Saskatchewan, Canada

ZUCCHINI-CARROT CASSEROLE

1 pkg. stuffing mix with rye bread
1 stick margarine, melted
6 c. sliced zucchini
1 med. onion, chopped
1 can cream of chicken soup
1 8-oz. carton sour cream
2 c. shredded carrots

Mix stuffing mix and margarine. Bring zucchini and onion to a boil. Let stand, covered, for several minutes. Mix soup and sour cream. Spread half the stuffing mixture in 3-quart baking dish. Layer zucchini mixture, carrots, soup mixture and remaining stuffing mixture over top. Bake at 350 degrees for 45 minutes. Yield: 8 servings.

Barbara Van Heuvel
Preceptor Gamma Iota, Largo, Florida

BAKED CORN PUDDING

2 eggs, slightly beaten
1 8 1/2-oz. package corn muffin mix
1/2 c. margarine, melted
1 8-oz. can cream-style corn
1 8-oz. can whole kernel corn, drained
1 8-oz. carton sour cream
1 c. shredded Swiss cheese

Mix eggs, muffin mix, margarine, corn and sour cream. Spread in 7 x 11-inch baking dish. Bake at 350 degrees for 30 minutes. Sprinkle with cheese. Bake for 5 to 10 minutes longer. Yield: 8 servings.

Elizabeth Funk
Xi Eta Iota, Hagerstown, Maryland

SWEET POTATO CRUNCH

3 c. mashed cooked sweet potatoes
1 c. sugar
2 eggs, beaten
1 c. milk
2 tsp. Sherry
1 tsp. vanilla extract
2 sticks margarine
1 c. packed brown sugar
1/3 c. flour
1 c. chopped nuts

Mix first 6 ingredients and 1 stick melted margarine. Spoon into buttered 2-quart casserole. Mix brown sugar, 1 stick melted margarine, flour and nuts. Spread over casserole. Bake at 325 degrees for 30 to 40 minutes.

Maurine Bradford
Epsilon Nu, Statesboro, Georgia

SWEET POTATO-BACON BOATS

6 med. sweet potatoes, baked
1 c. shredded Cheddar cheese
1/4 c. butter
1 tsp. salt
Dash of pepper
6 slices crisp-fried bacon, crumbled

Slice top off each potato. Scoop out pulp carefully; reserve shells. Beat potato pulp, cheese, butter, salt and pepper in mixer bowl until fluffy. Stir in bacon. Spoon into potato shells. Bake at 350 degrees for 25 to 30 minutes. Garnish with additional cheese and bacon. Yield: 6 servings.

Ginger E. Harrington
Alpha Phi, Watertown, South Dakota

ORANGE YAMBOREE BAKE

2 tbsp. cornstarch
2/3 c. packed brown sugar
2/3 c. sugar
1/2 tsp. salt
4 tsp. grated orange rind
6 tbsp. butter, melted
2 c. orange juice
8 yams, cooked, peeled, sliced 1/4-in. thick
5 navel oranges, sliced into 1/4-in. rounds
1/2 c. chopped peanuts

Mix first 5 ingredients. Stir in butter and orange juice. Cook over low heat until thick, stirring constantly. Layer yams, oranges and peanuts in greased 1 1/2-quart baking dish. Pour sauce over top. Bake at 350 degrees for 1 hour. Yield: 8-10 servings.

Elizabeth R. Cocks
Alpha Iota, Walden, New York

CAULIFLOWER-CHEESE CASSEROLE

1 tbsp. chopped onion
1/4 c. butter
1/4 c. flour
1 1/2 c. milk
3 eggs, separated
1 c. grated cheese
Dash each of salt, white pepper
1 head cauliflower, cooked, chopped
Paprika

Saute onion in butter. Blend in flour. Stir in milk. Cook over low heat until thickened, stirring constantly; remove from heat. Stir a small amount of hot mixture into beaten egg yolks; stir egg yolks into hot mixture. Stir in cheese, salt and pepper. Fold in stiffly beaten egg whites. Place cauliflower in buttered 2-quart casserole. Pour sauce over top; mix lightly. Sprinkle with paprika. Place casserole in pan of water. Bake at 325 degrees for 1 1/4 hours. Yield: 6-8 servings.

Marion Grandin
Preceptor Beta, Montreal, Quebec, Canada

LAYERED EGGPLANT PARMESAN

1 lg. eggplant, peeled, cut into 1/4-in. slices
3 eggs, beaten
1 c. bread crumbs
3/4 c. oil
2 tsp. oregano
1/2 c. grated Parmesan cheese
1/2 lb. shredded mozzarella cheese
3 8-oz. cans tomato sauce

Dip eggplant in eggs and bread crumbs. Saute in hot oil until browned on both sides. Layer half the eggplant, oregano, Parmesan cheese, 1/3 of the mozzarella cheese and half the tomato sauce in 2-quart casserole. Repeat layers, ending with mozzarella cheese. Bake at 350 degrees for 30 minutes or until bubbly. Yield: 6 servings.

Gail B. Cummins
Xi Alpha Eta, Cleveland, Mississippi

MARTELLO'S SPINACH CASSEROLE

4 pkg. chopped spinach, thawed
1 can cream of asparagus soup
1 can cream of mushroom soup
1 4-oz. jar mushrooms (opt.)
1 8-oz. package shredded Cheddar cheese
1 sm. onion, chopped
1 stick butter, melted
1 16-oz. package herb-seasoned stuffing mix

Mix first 6 ingredients. Spoon into 9 x 13-inch casserole. Stir butter into stuffing mix to moisten. Spoon over spinach mixture; press slightly. Bake at 350 degrees for 30 minutes. Yield: 10-15 servings.

Toni Martello
Xi Alpha Xi, Memphis, Tennessee

CRUMB-TOPPED ZUCCHINI CASSEROLE

3 lb. zucchini, thinly sliced
3/4 c. each chopped celery, green pepper, onion
1/2 c. bacon drippings
1 tsp. salt
1/8 tsp. pepper
1 tsp. MSG
1/4 to 1/2 tsp. garlic powder
3 eggs, beaten
8 oz. Cheddar cheese, grated
1 1/2 c. bread crumbs
2 tbsp. melted butter
1/4 c. Parmesan cheese

Cook zucchini for 5 minutes in a small amount of water; drain. Saute celery, green pepper and onion in bacon drippings. Add seasonings. Mix in eggs, cheese and zucchini. Spoon into greased 9 x 12-inch casserole. Mix remaining 3 ingredients. Sprinkle over top. Bake at 325 degrees for 35 to 45 minutes.

Carol Leimkuehler
Mu Theta, Brownsburg, Indiana

Thanksgiving / 115

SCALLOPED ONIONS

6 med. onions, sliced
1 c. chopped celery
1/2 c. butter
3 tbsp. flour
1 tsp. salt
1/8 tsp. pepper
1 1/2 c. milk
1/2 c. chopped pecans
1/3 c. Parmesan cheese

Saute onions and celery in 3 tablespoons butter for 5 minutes or until tender; remove. Add remaining butter. Blend in flour, salt and pepper. Stir in milk gradually. Cook over low heat until thick, stirring constantly. Pour over onions and celery in 2-quart baking dish. Sprinkle with pecans and cheese. Bake at 350 degrees for 30 minutes. Yield: 6-8 servings.

Evelyn Tallyn
Iota Chi, St. Louis, Missouri

CREAMY GARDEN VEGETABLE SOUP

1 10-oz. package frozen
  cauliflower
1 10-oz. package frozen
  broccoli
1 10-oz. package frozen
  sliced carrots
1/4 c. flour
1/4 c. margarine, melted
3 c. milk
1 med. onion, chopped
1 tsp. chopped parsley
1/8 tsp. pepper
1/4 tsp. salt
Dash of curry powder

Steam frozen vegetables for 7 minutes. Blend flour and margarine. Cook until bubbly, stirring constantly. Stir in 1 cup milk gradually. Cook until thick, stirring constantly. Stir in onion and steamed vegetables. Add enough remaining milk to make desired consistency. Stir in parsley and seasonings. Simmer for several minutes. Yield: 6 servings.

Claudia Miller
Zeta Phi, Bryan, Ohio

VEGETABLES EN CASSEROLE

1 c. chopped onion
1/2 tbsp. corn syrup
2 tbsp. oil
1 c. chopped celery
1 c. chopped French-style
  green beans
2 c. thinly sliced potatoes
Dash of pepper
1 tbsp. cornstarch
2 c. tomatoes
1/2 c. fine bread crumbs
1/4 c. grated Cheddar
  cheese

Saute onion in corn syrup and oil. Add celery, beans and potatoes. Stir in pepper and cornstarch. Layer onion mixture and tomatoes in 3-quart casserole. Add enough water to cover. Sprinkle with crumbs mixed with cheese. Bake, covered, at 350 degrees for 1 hour. Bake, uncovered, for 30 minutes longer. Yield: 6 servings.

Susan Hershey
Beta Theta, Grissom, Indiana

GARDEN MEDLEY

2 cans white Shoe Peg
  corn, drained
1/2 c. each chopped onion,
  green pepper, celery
2 cans French-style green
  beans, drained
1/2 c. grated sharp
  Cheddar cheese
1 can celery soup
1 8-oz. carton sour
  cream
1 stick butter, melted
1 c. butter cracker
  crumbs
1/2 c. sliced almonds

Mix vegetables, cheese, soup and sour cream. Spoon into 9 x 13-inch pan. Mix butter, cracker crumbs and almonds. Sprinkle on top. Bake at 350 degrees for 45 minutes. Yield: 15 servings.

Ramona Ketron
Xi Beta Upsilon, Kingsport, Tennessee

SPECIAL MIXED VEGETABLE CASSEROLE

1 can asparagus,
  drained
1 can English peas,
  drained
1 can cream of celery
  soup
1 can chopped pimento,
  drained
1 can sliced water
  chestnuts, drained
1 1/4 c. grated Cheddar
  cheese

Layer asparagus, peas, soup, pimento and water chestnuts in large casserole. Sprinkle with cheese. Bake at 350 degrees for 30 minutes. Yield: 6 servings.

Marilynn Smith
Alpha Rho Beta, Deer Park, Texas

CONNOISSEUR'S CASSEROLE

2 12-oz. cans Shoe Peg
  corn, drained
1 16-oz. cans
  French-style green
  beans, drained
1 7-oz. jar chopped
  pimento, drained
1 c. each chopped celery,
  onion
1 c. sour cream
1 c. grated sharp Cheddar
  cheese
2 cans cream of celery
  soup
1 tsp. salt
1/2 tsp. pepper
2 c. crushed butter
  crackers
1 stick butter, melted
1 c. slivered almonds

Mix vegetables, sour cream, cheese, soup and seasonings. Spoon into 3-quart casserole. Mix cracker crumbs and butter. Stir in almonds. Sprinkle over top. Bake at 350 degrees for 50 minutes. Yield: 14 servings.

Hannah Tipper
Preceptor Eta, Ladson South Carolina

BARLEY CASSEROLE WITH MUSHROOMS

1 lg. onion, finely chopped
4 to 5 tbsp. butter
1 c. pearl barley
1 sm. can chopped mushrooms
Salt and pepper to taste
3 c. chicken broth

Saute onions in butter. Add barley. Cook for 5 to 10 minutes or until lightly browned. Add mushrooms and seasonings. Spoon into 2-quart casserole. Pour broth over top. Bake, covered, at 375 degrees for 35 minutes, adding additional broth if necessary. Bake, uncovered, for 10 minutes longer. Yield: 4-8 servings.

Beverley F. Marks
Gamma Gamma, Virginia Beach, Virginia

SOUTHERN CORN BREAD DRESSING

6 c. crumbled corn bread
4 c. crumbled biscuits
1 c. each chopped celery, onion
1/2 c. melted margarine
3 eggs, beaten
1 tbsp. each poultry seasoning, sage
1 tsp. each salt, pepper
4 c. chicken broth

Combine corn bread, biscuits, celery and onion. Stir in margarine, eggs and seasonings. Mix in broth. Spoon into greased 9 x 13-inch baking pan. Bake at 350 degrees for 30 minutes. Cut into squares to serve.

Betty A. Ramey
Xi Pi, Seneca, South Carolina

FAVORITE CORN BREAD DRESSING

1 recipe corn bread, crumbled
4 slices bread, crumbled
3 eggs
3 hard-boiled eggs, chopped
1 c. chopped celery
1 onion, chopped
Salt and pepper to taste
2 tsp. thyme
Turkey broth

Combine first 6 ingredients and seasonings. Mix in enough broth to moisten. Bake in pan at 350 degrees for 1 hour.

Kathy Welborn
Epsilon Epsilon, Rogers, Arkansas

OYSTER-OLIVE STUFFING

Herb-seasoned stuffing mix
1 lg. onion, chopped
2 c. chopped celery
1 sm. jar green olives
1 8-oz. can oysters

Mix all ingredients. Stir in enough water to moisten. Stuff and roast poultry as desired.

Carole Lowder
Xi Alpha Rho, Lakewood, Colorado

CORN BREAD-PECAN STUFFING FOR POULTRY

1/2 c. chopped onion
1 c. chopped pecans
1 tsp. sage
3 tsp. salt
1 c. chopped celery
1/2 tsp. pepper
1 tsp. poultry seasoning
6 c. crumbled corn bread
1 c. melted butter
4 c. bread cubes
Consomme

Combine all ingredients except consomme. Add enough consomme to moisten. Stuff and roast poultry as desired.

Naomi E. Golden
Beta Rho, Van Buren, Ohio

WILD RICE DRESSING

2 4-oz. cans button mushrooms
2 cans water chestnuts, chopped
1 pkg. slivered almonds, lightly toasted
1/4 c. chopped onion
1 stick butter, melted
4 tbsp. flour
Salt, pepper and poultry seasoning to taste
1 tsp. Worcestershire sauce
4 c. cooked wild rice

Drain mushrooms and water chestnuts, reserving liquid. Saute mushrooms, water chestnuts, almonds and onion in butter. Stir in flour and enough reserved liquid to make medium-thick gravy. Stir in seasonings and Worcestershire sauce. Layer half the rice and half the gravy mixture in 2-quart casserole. Repeat layers. Bake at 350 degrees for 30 minutes or until heated through. Yield: 6-8 servings.

Bonnie J. Britton
Epsilon Pi, Silver City, New Mexico

SAUSAGE-RICE RING

1 lb. hot sausage
1 lg. onion, chopped
8 oz. mushrooms, sliced
2 pkg. long grain and wild rice, cooked
1 can cream of mushroom soup

Brown sausage with onion, stirring frequently. Add mushrooms. Cook for 5 minutes. Combine rice, sausage mixture and soup. Pack into 8-cup bundt pan. Chill, covered with foil, overnight. Bake at 350 degrees for 30 to 45 minutes. Unmold onto serving platter. Garnish with lemon twists and sprigs of parsley. Yield: 12-14 servings.

Kim Medley
Beta Upsilon, Hattiesburg, Mississippi

WILD RICE HOT DISH

2 lb. ground beef
1 1/2 c. chopped onion
2 c. chopped celery
1 can cream of mushroom soup
1 sm. can sliced

1 c. wild rice
1 can chicken with rice soup
mushrooms
Slivered almonds (opt.)
Seasonings to taste

Brown ground beef. Stir in onion and celery. Combine with remaining ingredients in casserole. Bake at 300 degrees for 2 hours, stirring once. Yield: 6 servings.

Kathy M. Johnson
Zeta Zeta, Junction City, Kansas

FRESH CRANBERRY MUFFINS

1 c. cranberries, rinsed, chopped
3/4 c. sugar
1 tsp. grated orange rind
1 egg, beaten
1/2 c. orange juice
2 tbsp. oil
2 c. biscuit mix

Mix cranberries, 1/2 cup sugar and orange rind. Combine egg, remaining 1/4 cup sugar, orange juice and oil; add to biscuit mix. Stir until just moistened. Fold in cranberry mixture. Fill greased muffin cups 2/3 full. Bake at 400 degrees for 20 minutes. Yield: 1 1/2 dozen.

Photograph for this recipe on page 107.

THANKSGIVING PUMPKIN MUFFINS

1/2 c. sugar
1 c. flour
2 tsp. baking powder
1/4 tsp. salt
1/2 tsp. each cinnamon, nutmeg
1/4 c. butter
1 egg, beaten
1/2 c. pumpkin
1/2 c. evaporated milk
1/2 c. raisins
Brown sugar (opt.)

Combine first 4 ingredients and spices in bowl. Cut in butter until crumbly. Stir in egg, pumpkin, milk and raisins until just moistened. Fill greased muffin cups 2/3 full. Sprinkle with brown sugar. Bake at 400 degrees for 20 minutes. Yield: 1 1/3 dozen.

Debra Clark
Beta Beta, Eureka Springs, Arkansas

CARROT AND PINEAPPLE MUFFINS

2/3 c. oil
1 c. sugar
1 tsp. vanilla extract
2 eggs
1 1/2 c. flour
1 tsp. baking powder
1 tsp. soda
1/2 tsp. salt
1 tsp. cinnamon
1 c. grated carrots
1/2 c. crushed pineapple
1/2 c. raisins

Mix oil, sugar and vanilla. Beat in eggs. Mix in sifted dry ingredients. Stir in carrots, pineapple and raisins. Fill muffin cups 2/3 full. Bake at 325 degrees for 25 to 30 minutes. Yield: 1 1/2 dozen.

Gerry Peppler
Laureate Epsilon, Yorkton, Saskatchewan, Canada

ATLANTIC COMMUNITY'S WALNUT BREAD

1 c. flour
1/2 c. whole wheat flour
1/2 tsp. each soda, salt
1/4 c. molasses
1/4 c. honey
3/4 c. buttermilk
3/4 c. coarsely chopped walnuts

Combine flours, soda and salt. Stir in molasses, honey and buttermilk until just moistened. Stir in walnuts. Spoon into greased 4 x 8-inch loaf pan. Bake at 350 degrees for 40 to 45 minutes. Cool on rack. Yield: 10-12 servings.

Marian Taylor
Preceptor Nu, Atlantic, Iowa

CRANBERRY-LEMON-WALNUT BREAD

1/4 c. butter, softened
Sugar
2 eggs
2 tsp. grated lemon rind
2 c. sifted flour
2 1/2 tsp. baking powder
1 tsp. salt
3/4 c. milk
1 c. chopped cranberries, rinsed, drained
1/2 c. chopped mixed candied fruit
1/2 c. chopped walnuts
2 tsp. lemon juice

Cream butter and 3/4 cup sugar. Add eggs and lemon rind; beat well. Sift flour, baking powder and salt. Beat into creamed mixture alternately with milk. Stir in fruits and walnuts. Bake in greased loaf pan at 350 degrees for 55 minutes. Cool in pan for 10 minutes. Combine lemon juice and 2 tablespoons sugar; spoon over top. Let stand, wrapped, overnight.

Photograph for this recipe on page 107.

HARVEST LOAF

1/2 c. margarine, softened
1 c. sugar
2 eggs
1 1/2 c. flour
1 tsp. soda
1/2 tsp. salt
1/4 tsp. each ginger, cloves
Cinnamon
Nutmeg
3/4 c. canned pumpkin
1 c. chopped walnuts
1 6-oz. package chocolate chips
1/2 c. confectioners' sugar
2 tbsp. milk

Cream margarine and sugar. Beat in eggs. Mix flour, soda, salt, ginger, cloves, 1 teaspoon cinnamon and 1/2 teaspoon nutmeg. Add to creamed mixture alternately with pumpkin, beating well after each addition. Stir in 3/4 cup walnuts and chocolate chips. Spoon into greased 5 x 9-inch loaf pan. Sprinkle remaining walnuts over top. Bake at 350 degrees for 65 minutes; cool. Blend confectioners' sugar, milk and dash each of nutmeg and cinnamon. Drizzle over loaf.

Deborah Fletcher
Delta Psi, Lake, Michigan

CASSEROLE DILL BREAD

2 c. flour
2 tbsp. sugar
1 tsp. salt
1 tbsp. instant minced onion
2 tsp. dillweed
1/4 tsp. soda
1 pkg. dry yeast
1 tbsp. margarine, softened
1 c. creamed cottage cheese, at room temperature
1 egg

Combine 1/4 cup flour and next 6 ingredients in mixer bowl. Add margarine. Stir in 1/4 cup hot water. Beat for 2 minutes at medium speed, scraping bowl occasionally. Add cottage cheese, egg and 1/2 cup flour. Beat at high speed for 2 minutes. Stir in enough flour to make stiff dough. Let rise, covered, for 1 1/2 hours or until doubled in bulk. Turn into greased 1 1/2-quart casserole. Let rise, covered, for 50 minutes or until doubled in bulk. Bake at 350 degrees for 30 minutes. Cool on rack.

Ronda McLean
Beta Kappa, Meeteetse, Wyoming

NEVER-FAIL EGG BREAD

1/2 c. sugar
1 1/2 tsp. salt
2 pkg. dry yeast
4 eggs, beaten
10 c. flour
1/2 c. oil
Melted margarine

Mix sugar, salt, yeast and 3 cups lukewarm water. Allow yeast to proof. Mix in eggs and 2 cups flour. Add oil. Stir in 8 cups flour gradually. Knead on floured surface until smooth and elastic. Place in greased bowl, turning to grease surface. Let rise for 2 hours or until doubled in bulk. Punch dough down. Let rise until doubled in bulk. Place in 3 loaf pans. Let rise for 1 hour. Bake at 375 degrees for 20 to 30 minutes. Brush warm bread with melted margarine. Yield: 3 loaves.

Janielle Ann Riley
Xi Zeta Epsilon, Westfield, Indiana

BRANDIED PERSIMMON BREAD

1/2 c. raisins
1/4 c. Brandy
1 c. packed dark brown sugar
1 c. persimmon pulp
1/2 c. oil
2 eggs
2 c. flour
2 tsp. soda
1/4 tsp. salt
1/4 tsp. ginger
1/2 tsp. each cinnamon, nutmeg
1/2 c. chopped walnuts

Soak raisins in Brandy until plump; set aside. Mix brown sugar, persimmon pulp and oil. Beat in eggs 1 at a time. Mix in sifted dry ingredients. Stir in walnuts and raisins. Bake in 2 greased and floured loaf pans at 350 degrees for 1 hour. Cool on rack.

Sherleen McKinney
Lambda Omega, Columbus, Indiana

ALMOND PUFF

1 c. margarine
2 c. flour
2 tsp. almond extract
3 eggs
1 1/2 c. confectioners' sugar
2 tbsp. butter, melted
1/2 c. sliced almonds

Cut 1/2 cup margarine into 1 cup flour. Sprinkle with 2 tablespoons water; mix with fork. Shape into ball; divide in half. Pat into two 3 x 12-inch strips. Place 3 inches apart on baking sheet. Bring 1/2 cup margarine and 1 cup water to a boil; remove from heat. Stir in 1 teaspoon almond extract and 1 cup flour. Cook over low heat for 1 minute, stirring constantly; remove from heat. Beat in eggs until smooth. Divide in half. Spread over dough, covering completely. Bake at 350 degrees for 1 hour or until crisp; cool. Mix confectioners' sugar, butter, 1 teaspoon almond extract and 1 to 1 1/2 tablespoons warm water. Drizzle over puffs. Garnish with almonds.

Mildred Chrissley
Preceptor Theta, Watertown, New York

INDIA HOUSE SWANS

6 tbsp. butter
1 c. flour
4 eggs
1 pt. whipping cream
1/4 c. confectioners' sugar
1/4 c. cranberry liqueur
1 8-oz. can jellied cranberry sauce, cut into 1/2-in. cubes

Melt butter in 1 cup water. Stir in flour. Cook until mixture forms ball, stirring constantly. Cool for 5 minutes. Beat in eggs, 1 at a time. Spoon 1/3 of the dough into pastry tube with 1/2-inch round tip. Pipe into eight 4-inch high S shapes on cookie sheet. Bake at 400 degrees for 15 to 20 minutes. Spoon remaining dough into 8 mounds on cookie sheet. Bake for 35 minutes. Pierce puffs. Bake for 5 minutes longer; cool. Slice off top third; cut in half. Whip cream with confectioners' sugar and liqueur until stiff. Fold in cranberry sauce. Spoon into puffs, mounding on top. Insert S shapes and wings into cream to complete swans. Yield: 8 servings.

Barbara Buroker
Epsilon Sigma, Ville Platte, Louisiana

ORANGE-CRANBERRY TORTE

1 c. chopped nuts
1 c. chopped dates
1 c. cranberries
Grated rind of 2 oranges
2 1/4 c. sifted flour
2 c. sugar
1/4 tsp. salt
1 tsp. soda
1/4 tsp. baking powder
2 eggs
1 c. buttermilk
3/4 c. oil
1 c. orange juice

Thanksgiving / 119

Combine nuts, dates cranberries and orange rind. Sift in flour, 1 cup sugar, salt, soda and baking powder; mix well. Stir in mixture of eggs, buttermilk and oil. Bake in greased 10-inch tube pan at 350 degrees for 1 hour. Cool in pan before removing to wire rack placed over a pan. Mix orange juice and remaining 1 cup sugar. Pour over cake; repeat process until all is absorbed. Chill, wrapped in foil, for 24 hours or longer.

Nadine M. Smith
Kappa Iota, Vallejo, California

CRANBERRY ICE

1 lb. cranberries	1 tsp. grated orange rind
2 c. sugar	Ginger ale (opt.)
1/4 c. lemon juice	

Cook cranberries in 2 cups water until skins pop. Press through sieve into saucepan. Add sugar. Bring to a boil, stirring constantly; remove from heat. Stir in lemon juice, orange rind and 2 cups cold water. Freeze until partially set; beat well. Freeze until firm. Spoon into serving dishes. Pour ginger ale over each. Yield: 2 quarts.

Jacqueline S. Uber
Preceptor Alpha Pi, Gettysburg, Pennsylvania

MOM'S MINCEMEAT

2 lb. beef	1 1/2 tsp. cinnamon
4 lb. apples	1 1/4 tsp. allspice
2 1/2 lb. raisins	Salt to taste
Sugar to taste	Rum (opt.)
1/2 tsp. cloves	Cider

Grind beef and apples together. Stir in remaining ingredients. Cook to desired consistency. Pour into sterilized jars; seal.

Hazel Pecht
Xi Beta Sigma, Mt. Pleasant Mills, Pennsylvania

FROZEN PUMPKIN MOUSSE

2 c. whipping cream	3 tbsp. finely chopped
1 1/2 c. mashed cooked	candied ginger
pumpkin	1 tsp. vanilla extract
1 c. packed brown sugar	1 tsp. cinnamon
1 c. milk	1/8 tsp. cloves
1/4 c. Brandy	1/4 tsp. salt

Mix all ingredients. Pour into a 9 x 13-inch pan. Freeze until firm. Break up frozen mixture. Spoon into chilled 6 1/2-cup mold. Freeze, covered, until firm. Yield: 8-10 servings.

Marlene D. Gill
Theta Epsilon, Wapato, Washington

OLD-FASHIONED BREAD PUDDING WITH EVERYDAY SAUCE

8 c. soft bread crumbs	3/4 tsp. salt
4 c. milk, scalded	3 1/2 tsp. cinnamon
4 eggs, beaten	3 tbsp. cornstarch
Butter, melted	4 tsp. vanilla extract
2 c. sugar	3/4 tsp. nutmeg

Mix first 3 ingredients. Stir in 1/2 cup melted butter, 1 cup sugar, 1/2 teaspoon salt and 2 teaspoons cinnamon. Bake in greased 9 x 13-inch pan placed in pan filled with 1-inch water at 350 degrees for 30 to 40 minutes. Mix 1 cup sugar, 1/4 teaspoon salt and cornstarch in saucepan. Stir in 6 tablespoons butter and 3 cups water. Cook until slightly thickened, stirring constantly. Stir in vanilla, 1 1/2 teaspoons cinnamon and nutmeg. Pour warm sauce over pudding.

Pam Kelly
Lambda Nu, Galva, Illinois

PUMPKIN CRUNCH

1 1/2 c. sifted flour	1/4 tsp. salt
1 1/2 c. oats	3/4 c. butter
1 1/4 c. packed brown sugar	1 29-oz. can pumpkin pie filling
1/2 tsp. soda	

Mix first 5 ingredients. Cut in butter until crumbly. Pat into greased 9 x 13-inch baking pan. Prepare pumpkin filling using directions on can. Pour in prepared pan. Bake at 425 degrees for 15 minutes. Reduce temperature to 350 degrees. Bake for 45 minutes. Garnish with whipped cream. Yield: 12-15 servings.

Betty L. Gotte
Preceptor Beta Beta, Canon City, Colorado

PUMPKIN SQUARES

1 16-oz. can pumpkin	3 eggs
1 can evaporated milk	1 pkg. white cake mix
1 c. sugar	1 1/2 sticks butter, sliced
1/2 tsp. salt	1 c. chopped nuts
2 tsp. pumpkin pie spice	

Mix first 6 ingredients. Pour into 9 x 13-inch baking dish. Sprinkle cake mix over top. Dot with butter. Sprinkle with nuts. Bake at 350 degrees for 50 to 60 minutes. Serve with whipped cream or ice cream. Yield: 10-12 servings.

Kathleen J. Toews
Laureate Xi, Santa Barbara, California

BUTTERNUT SQUASH-ALMOND TORTE

1 1 1/4-lb. butternut squash
4 eggs, separated
1/3 c. oil
1/4 tsp. cream of tartar
3/4 c. sugar
1 1/2 c. flour
2 tsp. baking powder
1/2 tsp. salt
1/2 tsp. almond extract
1/2 c. sliced almonds
1 12-oz. jar apricot preserves
1 c. whipping cream
1/2 tsp. vanilla extract

Cut squash in half lengthwise; remove seeds. Steam until tender; drain and cool. Scoop out pulp; mash. Mix with egg yolks, oil and 1/3 cup water. Beat egg whites with cream of tartar in mixer bowl on high speed until soft peaks form. Beat in sugar, 2 tablespoons at a time until stiff. Combine flour, baking powder, salt, 1 cup beaten egg whites and almond extract with squash mixture in mixer bowl. Beat at low speed until blended. Fold in remaining egg whites. Spoon into 9-inch springform pan. Bake at 325 degrees for 1 hour and 10 minutes. Invert on wire rack to cool. Bake almonds on foil-lined baking pan at 350 degrees for 10 minutes; cool. Slice cake horizontally into 4 layers. Spread apricot preserves between layers, beginning with cake layer cut side up and ending with cake layer cut side down. Beat whipping cream with vanilla until soft peaks form. Frost top and side of torte. Decorate top with half the almond slices. Mince remaining almonds; press into side. Chill.

Therese Caron
Alpha Beta, Exeter, New Hampshire

CRANBERRY PUDDING CAKE

1 c. confectioners' sugar
Softened butter
2 eggs, separated
2/3 c. sugar
1/3 c. milk
1 c. (heaping) flour
1 tsp. (rounded) baking powder
1 c. cranberries

Mix confectioners' sugar, 1/3 cup butter and egg whites. Let stand while cake bakes. Cream 1 tablespoon butter and sugar. Stir in egg yolks, milk, flour and baking powder. Mix in cranberries. Bake in 8-inch square pan at 350 degrees for 20 minutes or until light brown. Serve sauce over warm cake.

Rae Thieme
Preceptor Beta Mu, Sioux City, Iowa

AUTUMN SHORTCAKE

2 c. chopped cranberries
2 c. chopped tart apples
1 c. pineapple tidbits
2 c. sugar
1/4 tsp. salt
3 c. baking mix
1 egg yolk, slightly beaten
Butter
1 c. whipping cream, whipped

Mix cranberries, apples, pineapple, sugar and salt. Chill for 2 hours. Prepare baking mix shortcake using package directions. Spread in greased 8-inch cake pan. Brush with egg yolk; sprinkle with additional sugar. Bake at 450 degrees for 18 to 20 minutes; remove from pan. Slice in half horizontally; butter cut surfaces. Spread cranberry mixture between layers and over top. Serve with whipped cream. Yield: 8 servings.

Kathy Woodard
Xi Gamma Omicron, Wichita, Kansas

COVER MOUNTAIN CARROT CAKE

1 1/2 c. oil
1 1/2 c. sugar
4 eggs, beaten
3 c. grated carrots
2 c. unbleached flour
1/2 tsp. salt
2 tsp. soda
2 tsp. each cinnamon, allspice
1 c. chopped pecans
1 c. raisins
2 tsp. vanilla extract
1/2 c. margarine, melted
1 8-oz. package cream cheese, softened
2 c. sifted confectioners' sugar

Cream oil and sugar. Mix in eggs and carrots. Mix flour, salt, soda and spices. Beat into carrot mixture a small amount at a time. Stir in pecans, raisins and 1 teaspoon vanilla. Bake in greased and sugared 10 x 14-inch pan at 325 degrees for 1 hour. Beat margarine, cream cheese and confectioners' sugar until well blended. Stir in 1 teaspoon vanilla. Spread over cooled cake. Yield: 12-20 servings.

Carolyn R. Cobb
Preceptor Beta Epsilon, Penrose, Colorado

PERSIMMON CAKE

Butter
2 1/2 c. sugar
2 eggs, beaten
2 tsp. vanilla extract
2 c. persimmon pulp
2 c. flour
2 tsp. cinnamon
2 tsp. baking powder
2 tsp. soda
1 1/8 tsp. salt
1/2 c. milk
2 c. raisins
2 c. chopped nuts
1 tbsp. cornstarch
1 tbsp. grated lemon rind

Cream 1/2 cup butter and 2 cups sugar. Stir in eggs, vanilla and persimmon pulp. Sift flour, cinnamon, baking powder, soda and 1 teaspoon salt. Add to creamed mixture alternately with milk, blending well. Stir in raisins and nuts. Bake in greased 9 x 13-inch pan at 350 degrees for 40 to 45 minutes. Dissolve 1/2 cup sugar and cornstarch in 1 cup boiling water. Cook over low heat until thickened and clear, stirring constantly; remove from heat. Add 2 tablespoons butter, lemon rind and 1/8 teaspoon salt. Serve over warm cake.

Louise Marino
Preceptor Alpha Chi, Daly City, California

PISTACHIO CAKE

1 pkg. white cake mix
2 pkg. pistachio instant pudding mix
1 c. 7-Up
3 eggs
3/4 c. oil
1 1/2 c. milk
1 pkg. whipped topping mix
1/2 c. coconut
1/2 c. chopped pecans

Combine cake mix and 1 package pudding mix. Add next three ingredients; beat well. Bake in greased and floured 9 x 13-inch pan at 325 degrees for 45 minutes. Mix milk and remaining pudding mix. Stir in topping mix. Beat until stiff. Spread on cooled cake. Top with coconut and pecans.

Vanna Lou Wortham
Laureate Alpha Zeta, Odessa, Texas

PUMPKIN POUND CAKE

1 pkg. yellow cake mix
1 sm. package butterscotch instant pudding mix
4 eggs
1/4 c. oil
1 c. pumpkin
2 tsp. pumpkin pie spice
Confectioners' sugar

Blend first 6 ingredients with 1/4 cup water in mixer bowl. Beat at medium speed for 4 minutes. Bake in greased and floured 10-inch tube pan at 350 degrees for 50 to 55 minutes. Cool in pan for 15 minutes before inverting on wire rack. Sprinkle confectioners' sugar over cooled cake.

Darlene M. Kuebler
Xi Epsilon Iota, Manchester, Michigan

PUMPKIN-WALNUT-RUM CAKE

1 c. walnuts
3/4 c. butter, softened
1 1/2 c. sugar
1/2 c. packed brown sugar
3 eggs
2 1/4 c. flour
1 1/2 tsp. pumpkin pie spice
1 1/2 tsp. baking powder
1 tsp. soda
1/2 tsp. salt
1 c. pumpkin
2 tbsp. rum
3 tbsp. cornstarch
1 1/2 c. orange juice
Dark rum to taste

Sprinkle greased 9-inch bundt pan with 1/4 cup finely chopped walnuts. Cream 1/2 cup butter, 1 cup sugar and brown sugar. Beat in eggs 1 at a time. Mix next 5 sifted dry ingredients alternately with pumpkin, 1/2 cup water and rum. Stir in 3/4 cup coarsely chopped walnuts. Bake in prepared pan at 350 degrees for 1 hour and 20 minutes. Cool in pan for 15 minutes before inverting on wire rack. Mix cornstarch and 1/2 cup sugar; stir in heated orange juice. Cook until thickened, stirring constantly. Stir in 1/4 cup butter; remove from heat. Add dark rum to taste. Serve sauce with cake.

Viola Baker
Alpha Tau, Page, Arizona

FRESH RHUBARB CAKE

1/2 c. shortening
1 1/4 c. packed brown sugar
3/4 c. honey
2 eggs
1 tsp. vanilla extract
2 c. flour
1/2 tsp. salt
1 tsp. soda
1 c. buttermilk
2 c. finely chopped rhubarb
1 c. raisins (opt.)
1 tsp. cinnamon
1 recipe lemon icing

Cream shortening. Beat in 3/4 cup brown sugar, honey, eggs and vanilla. Add sifted flour, salt and soda alternately with buttermilk, blending well. Fold in rhubarb and raisins. Pour into greased 9 x 13-inch baking pan. Sprinkle with mixture of 1/2 cup brown sugar and cinnamon; press into batter. Bake at 350 degrees for 40 to 45 minutes. Frost with lemon icing.

Isobel Saville
Laureate Delta, Saskatoon, Saskatchewan, Canada

SPECIAL GINGERSNAP COOKIES

3/4 c. shortening
1 c. packed brown sugar
1 egg
1/4 c. molasses
2 1/4 c. flour
2 tsp. soda
1/2 tsp. each ginger, cloves
1 tsp. cinnamon
Sugar

Combine shortening, brown sugar, egg and molasses. Stir in sifted flour, soda and spices. Shape into small balls; roll in sugar. Place 2 inches apart on greased cookie sheet. Bake at 375 degrees for 10 minutes; cool slightly before removing from pan. Yield: 5 dozen.

Theresa Jones
Preceptor Alpha Chi, San Francisco, California

CRANBERRY CHEESECAKE

1 1/2 c. graham cracker crumbs
1 3/4 c. sugar
1/2 tsp. cinnamon
1/3 c. melted butter
3 8-oz. packages cream cheese, softened
5 eggs
1/4 tsp. salt
1 tsp. vanilla extract
1 tbsp. cornstarch
1 1/2 c. cranberries, rinsed, drained

Mix graham cracker crumbs, 3/4 cup sugar and cinnamon. Stir in butter. Press over bottom of springform pan. Beat cream cheese until fluffy. Beat in 1 cup sugar. Add eggs; beat until smooth. Beat in salt and vanilla. Pour into prepared pan. Bake at 350 degrees for 45 minutes or until firm. Cool in oven. Chill. Mix cornstarch, 1 cup sugar and 1/2 cup water until smooth; add cranberries. Cook over low heat until thick, stirring constantly. Simmer for 2 minutes. Cool. Spread on top of cheesecake. Chill until serving time.

Photograph for this recipe on page 107.

HOLIDAY PUMPKIN CHEESECAKE

- 1 recipe graham cracker crust mixture
- 1 20-oz. can crushed pineapple
- 1 16-oz. can pumpkin
- 1 c. packed brown sugar
- 3 eggs, beaten
- 1 tsp. cinnamon
- 1/2 tsp. ginger
- 1 env. unflavored gelatin
- 2 8-oz. packages cream cheese, softened
- 1 tbsp. vanilla extract
- 1/2 c. miniature marshmallows
- 1/2 c. whipping cream, whipped

Press crust mixture over bottom and 1 1/2 inches up side of springform pan. Bake at 350 degrees for 10 minutes. Drain pineapple, reserving 3/4 cup juice. Chill pineapple, covered, in refrigerator. Simmer pineapple juice, pumpkin, sugar, eggs, spices and gelatin, covered, for 30 minutes, stirring occasionally. Beat cream cheese and vanilla until fluffy. Blend in warm pumpkin mixture. Pour in prepared pan. Chill, covered, overnight. Remove side from pan. Fold pineapple and marshmallows into whipped cream. Spoon over cheesecake.

Janie Brown
Kappa Zeta, Lenox, Iowa

FUDGE CUPCAKES

- 1 stick margarine, melted
- 1 tbsp. oil
- 3 tbsp. cocoa
- 2 eggs, beaten
- 1 c. sugar
- 3/4 c. flour
- 1 tsp. vanilla extract
- 1/4 c. chopped nuts (opt.)

Combine margarine, oil and cocoa; set aside. Beat eggs, sugar and flour together. Add cocoa mixture; blend well. Add vanilla and nuts. Pour into paper-lined muffin tins. Bake at 350 degrees for 25 minutes. Yield: 12 servings.

Debby Roberts
Xi Epsilon Mu, Hooker, Oklahoma

OPAL'S RAISIN PIE

- 2 tbsp. butter
- 1 c. sugar
- 4 eggs, separated
- 3 tbsp. vinegar
- 1/2 tsp. each cinnamon, allspice and cloves
- 1 c. chopped raisins
- 1 8-in. unbaked pie shell

Cream butter and sugar. Add beaten egg yolks, vinegar, spices and raisins; mix well. Fold in stiffly beaten egg whites. Pour into pie shell. Bake in 350-degree oven for 30 minutes or until firm.

Opal Fillmore
Preceptor Mu, Cushing, Oklahoma

FRENCH SILK PIE

- 1 1/4 c. butter
- 1 1/2 c. vanilla wafers
- 1/3 c. filberts or almonds, finely ground
- 1 1/4 lb. semisweet dark chocolate
- 1/2 c. sugar
- 8 eggs, beaten
- 2 tbsp. vanilla extract
- 1/4 c. half and half

Melt 1/4 cup butter; add crushed vanilla wafers and nuts. Pat mixture into bottom and sides of 9-inch springform pan, reserving 1 tablespoon mixture for topping. Bake at 300 degrees until lightly brown. Melt chocolate in top of double boiler. Cream 1 cup butter and sugar until smooth. Add eggs and vanilla; mix until very smooth. Add small amount of chocolate mixture to eggs, mixing well. Add chocolate mixture slowly, stirring constantly; mix well. Add half and half. Pour into pie crust. Sprinkle reserved crumb mixture over top. Refrigerate or freeze until set. Serve with whipped cream. Yield: 8-10 servings.

Emily Cooper
Delta Xi, Aloha, Oregon

KENTUCKY PECAN PIE

- 1 c. light corn syrup
- 1 c. packed dark brown sugar
- 1/3 tsp. salt
- 1/3 c. melted butter
- 1 tsp. vanilla extract
- 3 eggs, slightly beaten
- 1 9-in. unbaked pie shell
- 1 c. whole pecans

Combine corn syrup, brown sugar, salt, butter and vanilla; mix well. Add eggs. Pour into pie shell. Sprinkle pecans over all. Bake at 350 degrees for 45 minutes.

Ann Caine
Eta Iota, Moore, Oklahoma

PUMPKIN-CHEESE PIE

- 1 8-oz. package cream cheese, softened
- 3/4 c. sugar
- 1/2 tsp. vanilla extract
- 3 eggs
- 1 unbaked 9-in. pie shell
- 1 1/4 c. pumpkin
- 1 tsp. cinnamon
- 1/4 tsp. each ginger, nutmeg
- 1 c. evaporated milk

Beat cream cheese, 1/4 cup sugar and vanilla. Stir in 1 egg. Spread in pie shell. Mix pumpkin, 1/2 cup sugar and spices. Blend in 2 slightly beaten eggs and evaporated milk. Pour over cream cheese layer. Bake at 350 degrees for 65 to 70 minutes.

Julie Byrd
Xi Zeta Nu, Lauderhill, Florida

123

Recipes on pages 138, 141 and 142.

Christmas

BUBBLING HOLIDAY PUNCH

1 10-oz. package frozen strawberries, thawed
2 limes, thinly sliced
2 c. light rum
2 6-oz. cans frozen daiquiri mix
3 bottles of Cold Duck

Freeze 1 inch water in ring mold. Arrange strawberries and lime slices over ice. Add 1/4 inch water. Freeze. Fill mold with water. Freeze. Blend rum and daiquiri mix in punch bowl. Add ice ring. Pour in Cold Duck. Yield: 20 servings.

Sherie Bargar
Eta Xi, Casselberry, Florida

CRANBERRY CRUSH

1 pt. apricot Brandy
1 12-oz. can frozen lemonade concentrate, thawed
1 48-oz. bottle of cranberry juice
1 32-oz. bottle of 7-Up

Mix first 3 ingredients. Freeze. Fill wine glasses with equal amounts of Brandy mixture and 7-Up. Garnish with sprig of holly and maraschino cherry.

Diane Korle
Omicron, Ottawa, Kansas

CRANBERRY BANGER PUNCH

1 12-oz. can frozen orange juice concentrate, thawed
1/2 c. orange liqueur
1 fifth of vodka
8 c. cranberry juice, chilled
2 16-oz. bottles of lemon-lime soda, chilled

Mix orange juice concentrate, 3 cups water and orange liqueur. Freeze in ice cube trays. Mix vodka and cranberry juice in punch bowl. Pour lemon-lime soda in slowly; stir. Float orange juice ice cubes on top. Yield: 32 servings.

Cindy Scruggs
Pi Sigma, Elgin Air Force Base, Florida

WINE PUNCH

1 6-oz. can frozen lemonade concentrate, thawed
1 6-oz. can frozen limeade concentrate, thawed
1 gal. Burgundy
1 12-oz. can apricot nectar
2 32-oz. bottles of lemon-lime soda
1 sm. package frozen strawberries

Mix concentrates. Stir in Burgundy and apricot nectar. Pour in soda. Fold in strawberries.

M. Janie Tiller
Xi Epsilon, Lake Charles, Louisiana

EASY EGGNOG

2 eggs, beaten
1 can sweetened condensed milk
1 tbsp. vanilla extract
1/2 tsp. salt
1 qt. milk
1/2 pt. whipping cream, whipped
Nutmeg

Beat first 4 ingredients until smooth. Beat in milk. Fold in whipped cream. Sprinkle with nutmeg.

Linda H. Howard
Preceptor Zeta, Glencoe, Alabama

EGGNOG PARTY PUNCH

6 eggs, beaten
1/2 c. light corn syrup
1/4 tsp. each ginger, cloves, nutmeg, cinnamon
2 qt. orange juice, chilled
1/2 c. lemon juice, chilled
1 qt. ginger ale, chilled
1 qt. vanilla ice cream
Rum to taste (opt.)

Mix eggs, corn syrup and spices. Stir in juices. Pour ginger ale over scoops of ice cream in punch bowl. Stir in egg mixture and rum. Garnish with additional nutmeg. Yield: 1 1/2 gallons.

Jewel Naufel
Xi Beta Theta, Hastings, Nebraska

MOCHA EGGNOG

6 eggs
4 c. half and half
1/2 c. sugar
1/3 c. instant coffee
1 1/4 c. Amaretto liqueur
1 c. chocolate syrup
2 c. whipping cream
Nutmeg

Beat eggs until fluffy. Beat in half and half and sugar gradually. Stir in instant coffee dissolved in 1 cup Amaretto and chocolate syrup; chill. Whip cream with remaining 1/4 cup Amaretto. Spoon over eggnog. Sprinkle with nutmeg. Yield: 12 servings.

Beverly Neugebauer
Preceptor Alpha Nu, El Paso, Texas

HOT RUM PUNCH

1 qt. apple juice
1 qt. pineapple juice
1 3-in. stick cinnamon
1 tbsp. whole allspice
1 tsp. whole cloves
1 c. rum
2 tbsp. butter

Simmer juices and spices for 20 minutes. Stir in rum and butter; strain. Yield: 6 servings.

Pat DeVaux
Laureate Mu, Roanoke, Virginia

PERKY CRANBERRY PUNCH

2 32-oz. bottles of cranberry juice
1 46-oz. can unsweetened pineapple juice
1 1/3 c. packed brown sugar
2 tbsp. each whole cloves, whole allspice
12 2-in. sticks cinnamon

Mix juices, 2 cups water and brown sugar in 20-cup percolator. Stir until brown sugar is dissolved. Place remaining ingredients in percolator basket. Percolate according to manufacturer's directions.

Frances Warren
Xi Theta Beta, Ocala, Florida

ENGLISH WASSAIL

3/4 c. sugar
2 qt. apple juice
1 pt. cranberry juice
1 tsp. aromatic bitters
1 c. rum
2 sticks cinnamon
1 tsp. whole allspice
1 sm. whole orange, studded with cloves

Dissolve sugar in juices in Crock·Pot. Add remaining ingredients. Cook on High for 1 hour. Simmer on Low for 4 to 8 hours. Yield: 16-18 servings.

Dawn Wilson
Pi Beta, Chino, California

MICROWAVE ARTICHOKE DIP

1 8-oz. can artichoke hearts, drained, mashed
1 c. mayonnaise
1 c. grated Romano cheese
1 tsp. lemon juice
1/2 tsp. garlic powder
Dash of pepper

Mix all ingredients. Microwave, covered, on medium for 5 minutes. Stir until cheese melts. Spoon into chafing dish. Serve warm with assorted crackers for dipping. Yield: 8-10 servings.

Darlene Rhodes
Preceptor Rho, Rockport, Indiana

KOLDTBORD APPETIZER

1 can crab
1 env. Knorr's vegetable soup mix
1 sm. can water chestnuts, sliced
1 c. sour cream
1 pkg. frozen chopped spinach, thawed
1 round loaf sourdough bread

Combine first 5 ingredients; mix well. Chill. Scoop out bread to make shell. Serve dip in bread shell with crackers.

Nina K. Bunnell
Laureate Pi, Phoenix, Oregon

SALMON DIP

1 16-oz. can red sockeye salmon
1 8-oz. package cream cheese, softened
1 tbsp. lemon juice
2 tsp. grated onion
1 tbsp. horseradish
1/4 tsp. salt
1/2 tsp. liquid smoke
1/2 c. walnuts
2 sprigs of fresh parsley

Mix first 7 ingredients. Sprinkle with walnuts. Garnish with parsley. May substitute almonds for walnuts.

Barbara J. Wind
Theta Lambda, Monument, Colorado

SPECIAL SPINACH DIP

1 10-oz. package frozen chopped spinach, thawed, drained well
1 c. mayonnaise
1 c. sour cream
1 8-oz. can water chestnuts, chopped
1 pkg. dry vegetable soup mix
1 green onion, chopped

Mix spinach, mayonnaise, sour cream, water chestnuts, soup mix and onion. Chill, covered, for several hours. Serve with chips or vegetables for dipping.

Frances Dillman
Laureate Alpha Beta, Buena Park, California

OVERNIGHT CRAB SPREAD

1 can mushroom soup
2 3-oz. packages cream cheese, softened
1 env. unflavored gelatin
2/3 c. mayonnaise
1 6-oz. package frozen crab meat, thawed
1 c. chopped celery
1/3 c. chopped green onions

Heat soup with cream cheese, stirring until smooth. Soften gelatin in 3 tablespoons cold water. Blend into soup. Stir in mayonnaise, crab meat, celery and onions. Pour into greased mold. Chill overnight. Serve with assorted crackers. Yield: 3-4 cups.

Jeannette Dybdal
Xi Nu Eta, Covina, California

BEER-CHEESE BITES

2 c. baking mix
1/2 c. shredded Cheddar cheese
1/2 c. beer
2 tbsp. margarine, melted
Sesame seed

Mix first 3 ingredients to form soft dough. Beat for 20 strokes. Knead 5 times on floured cloth-covered surface. Roll into 10 x 16-inch rectangle. Cut into 2-inch squares; cut squares into triangles. Brush with margarine. Sprinkle with sesame seed. Bake on baking sheet at 450 degrees for 8 minutes or until brown. Yield: 80 servings.

Shirley A. Gibbins
Mu Theta, Brownsburg, Indiana

WEBB'S ANTIPASTO

3 carrots, sliced
3 stalks celery, sliced
1 head cauliflower, broken into flowerets
White vinegar
5 cloves of garlic, sliced
1 can hot enchilada sauce
2/3 c. tomato juice
2/3 c. oil
1 6-oz. can tomato paste
2 tsp. Worcestershire sauce
3/4 tsp. chili powder
1 12-oz. jar hot peppers, drained
1 sm. jar pickled onions, drained
1 sm. jar sliced sour pickles, drained
1 can pitted med. black olives, drained
1 8-oz. can button mushrooms, drained
1 8-oz. jar stuffed green olives, drained
2 cans artichoke hearts, drained, cut into halves

Cook carrots, celery and cauliflower in salted vinegar water until tender; drain. Boil 1/2 cup vinegar and next 7 ingredients for 7 minutes; cool completely. Pour over mixture of cooked vegetables and remaining ingredients. Chill overnight. Serve at room temperature. May store in refrigerator for several weeks.

Marjorie C. Webb
Xi Beta Nu, North Canton, Ohio

HOLIDAY SANDWICH WREATH

1 4 1/2-oz. can deviled ham
1/4 c. finely chopped celery
1/2 tsp. Worcestershire sauce
1 4 3/4-oz. can chicken spread
1/4 c. finely chopped apples
1 tbsp. sour cream
1 4 3/4-oz. can liverwurst spread
1/4 c. finely chopped green pepper
1 tbsp. mayonnaise
Butter, softened
2 8-oz. loaves party rye bread
1 8-oz. loaf party pumpernickel bread

Mix deviled ham, celery and Worcestershire sauce. Combine chicken spread, apples and sour cream. Mix liverwurst, green pepper and mayonnaise. Make 10 sandwiches with each filling using buttered bread slices. Arrange in circle on serving plate. Decorate with satin bow or ornaments for wreath. Yield: 30 servings.

Evalyn B. McCarty
Preceptor Iota Beta, Ventura, California

SWEET AND SOUR MEATBALLS

2 lb. ground beef
1/2 c. milk
1 slice bread, crumbled
1 egg
2 tsp. salt
Dash each of pepper, garlic salt
2 tbsp. cornstarch
2 tbsp. soy sauce
1 can beef bouillon
1 20-oz. can pineapple chunks, drained
1/4 c. vinegar
2 green peppers, cut into bite-sized peices
1 1/4 c. sugar

Mix first 3 ingredients. Add egg and seasonings. Shape into small balls. Broil until brown. Blend cornstarch with soy sauce. Cook with remaining ingredients until thick, stirring constantly. Add meatballs. Serve hot.

Shirley M. Thillen
Preceptor Sigma, Rockford, Illinois

TANGY TURKEY MEATBALLS

2 eggs, slightly beaten
1/4 c. milk
1/3 c. chopped onion
1 tbsp. finely chopped parsley
1 1/4 c. bread crumbs
1 tsp. thyme
1 1/2 lb. ground fresh turkey
1/4 tsp. each salt, pepper
1 8-oz. can jellied cranberry sauce
2 tbsp. horseradish

Combine eggs and milk. Add next 5 ingredients and salt and pepper; mix well. Shape into 1-inch balls. Bake at 350 degrees for 10 to 15 minutes; turn. Bake for 10 minutes longer. Melt cranberry sauce in 1/4 cup water. Stir in horseradish. Pour over hot meatballs. Yield: 5 dozen.

Juanita Mattice
Laureate Alpha Delta, Amarillo, Texas

BAKED STUFFED MUSHROOMS

1 lb. mushrooms
3 tbsp. oil
6 2 1/2 x 4-in. butter crackers, finely crushed
3 tbsp. Parmesan cheese
3 tbsp. white wine
1 tsp. each salt, pepper
1/4 tsp. garlic powder
1/2 tsp. paprika
1 tbsp. parsley flakes

Remove mushroom stems; chop. Set aside caps. Mix stems with half the oil and remaining ingredients. Stuff mushroom caps with mixture. Arrange in remaining oil in 9 x 13-inch baking pan. Bake at 375 degrees for 20 to 30 minutes.

Peggy C. Amato
Preceptor Pi, Brewer, Maine

MICROWAVE STUFFED MUSHROOMS

6 slices bacon, chopped
2 tbsp. minced green pepper
1/4 c. minced onion
1 lb. fresh mushrooms
1/2 tsp. salt
1/2 tsp. Worcestershire sauce
1 3-oz. package cream cheese, softened
1 c. soft bread crumbs
2 tbsp. butter

Mix bacon, green pepper and onion in glass baking dish. Microwave, covered, on High for 4 minutes, stirring once; drain. Remove stems from mushrooms. Mix chopped stems and next 3 ingredients with bacon mixture. Fill mushroom caps. Microwave bread crumbs and butter on High for 1 minute; mix well. Press over tops of stuffed mushrooms. Microwave on High for 1 to 2 minutes. Yield: 40-50 servings.

Linda Whithead
Xi Beta Rho, Manassas, Virginia

MARINATED MUSHROOMS

1 tsp. each dillweed,
 pepper, garlic powder
1 tbsp. MSG
4 lb. fresh mushrooms
1 lb. butter
1 qt. Burgundy
1 1/2 tbsp. Worcestershire
 sauce
4 beef bouillon cubes
4 chicken bouillon cubes

Combine spices, 2 cups boiling water and remaining ingredients. Bring to a boil. Simmer, covered, for 5 to 6 hours. Simmer, uncovered, in Crock·Pot for 3 to 5 hours; cool. May be frozen. Yield: 1-2 quarts.

Julie Buell
Eta Nu, Raymore, Missouri

MINI QUICHE APPETIZERS

1 8-oz. can refrigerator
 butter flake rolls
1/2 lb. Italian sausage
2 eggs, beaten
1 c. cottage cheese
1 tbsp. minced chives
1/4 tsp. pepper
1/4 c. grated Parmesan
 cheese

Separate each roll into 8 sections. Press into miniature muffin cups to form crust. Brown sausage, stirring frequently; drain. Spoon into muffin cups. Pour mixture of remaining ingredients over sausage. Bake at 350 degrees for 15 minutes or until lightly browned.

Janette Volz
Xi Epsilon Chi, Carroll, Iowa

SHRIMP COCKTAILS

2 6-oz. cans shrimp,
 drained, rinsed
1/2 c. oil
2 tbsp. prepared mustard
1/4 c. lemon juice
4 green onions, thinly
 sliced
1/2 stalk celery, thinly
 sliced
Salt and pepper to taste

Mix all ingredients. Chill overnight. Serve in chilled cocktail glasses lined with chopped lettuce. Yield: 6 servings.

Darlene Turner
Beta Nu, Joseph, Oregon

SHRIMP PATTIES

1 1/2 c. flour
1/2 tsp. baking powder
1/4 tsp. each salt, pepper
3 eggs
3 stalks celery, chopped
1 med. onion, chopped
1 1/2 lb. fresh shrimp,
 cleaned, cut in half
2 tbsp. oil

Mix dry ingredients with eggs and enough water to make thick batter. Stir in celery and onion. Let stand for several minutes. Boil shrimp for 1 minute or until pink. Stir into batter. Drop by tablespoonfuls into hot oil. Cook until browned on both sides. Yield: 25-30 servings.

Gerry Rainey
Pi Xi, Boca Raton, Florida

SAUSAGE-APPLE ROLLS

1 10-count can
 refrigerator biscuits
1/2 lb. pork sausage
1 c. shredded Colby cheese
1 c. finely chopped apples
1/4 c. packed brown sugar
1/2 tsp. cinnamon
1/4 tsp. nutmeg

Roll biscuit dough into two 7 x 10-inch rectangles on floured surface. Brown sausage, stirring frequently; drain. Combine with remaining ingredients. Sprinkle half the mixture over each rectangle. Roll as for jelly roll from wide end. Cut into slices. Bake in lightly greased foil pie plates at 400 degrees for 20 minutes. Yield: 20 servings.

Lou Ann Shoue
Xi Alpha Beta, La Porte, Indiana

FRESH CAULIFLOWER SOUP

1/2 c. chopped onion
6 tbsp. butter
1 c. chopped celery
1 carrot, thinly sliced
1 head fresh cauliflower,
 cut into flowerets
1 tbsp. chopped parsley
8 c. chicke broth
1 tsp. dried leaf tarragon
1/2 tsp. whole
 peppercorns
1/2 bay leaf
2/3 c. flour
2 c. milk
1 c. light cream
2 tsp. salt
1/2 c. Goldfish Cheddar
 cheese crackers

Saute onion in 2 tablespoons butter in saucepan over medium heat. Add celery and carrot. Cook for 2 minutes. Add cauliflowerets and parsley; cover. Cook over low heat for 15 minutes. Add chicken broth. Tie tarragon, peppercorns and bay leaf in cheesecloth. Add to soup. Bring to a boil. Simmer for 5 minutes. Melt remaining 4 tablespoons butter in 2-quart saucepan. Stir in flour. Cook for 1 minute. Stir in milk gradually. Cook until mixture thickens, stirring constantly. Stir in cream. Add milk mixture and salt to soup. Simmer for 20 minutes. Remove herbs. Pour into blender container; process to puree soup. Top with Goldfish Cheddar cheese crackers. Yield: 8 servings.

Photograph for this recipe on page 2.

128 / Christmas

RED AND GREEN HOLIDAY SALAD

2 c. torn lettuce leaves
2 c. broccoli flowerets
1 c. cherry tomatoes
1/3 c. olive oil
2 tbsp. lemon juice
1/4 tsp. prepared mustard
1/4 tsp. salt
Pinch of pepper
1/2 c. herb and cheese-
  seasoned croutons

Line salad bowl with lettuce. Arrange broccoli and tomatoes on top. Combine olive oil, lemon juice, mustard, salt and pepper in small bowl; mix well. Pour over salad. Sprinkle with croutons. Yield: 4 servings.

Photograph for this recipe on page 2.

PEARS WITH FRESH CRANBERRY SAUCE

1 3/4 c. orange juice
1 4-in. cinnamon stick
4 firm pears, stems
  attached, peeled
1 c. sugar
1 tsp. freshly grated
  orange rind
2 c. fresh cranberries

Combine 1 1/4 cups orange juice and cinnamon stick in large saucepan. Add pears. Bring orange juice to a boil. Simmer, covered, for 20 to 25 minutes or until pears are just tender, basting often. Remove pears from saucepan. Chill thoroughly. Discard cinnamon stick. Add remaining orange juice, sugar and orange rind to orange juice in saucepan. Bring to a boil. Stir in cranberries. Simmer for 10 minutes. Cool. Pour into blender container; puree until smooth. Force sauce through sieve to remove seeds. Serve sauce over poached pears. Yield: 4 servings.

Photograph for this recipe on page 2.

CHRISTMAS RIBBON SALAD

1 3-oz. package
  strawberry gelatin
1 16-oz. can whole
  cranberry sauce
1 3-oz. package lemon
  gelatin
1 8-oz. package cream
  cheese, softened
1 c. crushed pineapple
1/4 c. chopped pecans
1 3-oz. package lime
  gelatin
1 16-oz. can grapefruit
  sections
2 tbsp. sugar

Dissolve strawberry gelatin in 1 1/4 cups boiling water. Mix in cranberry sauce. Chill until partially set. Pour into 8-cup ring mold. Chill until set. Dissolve lemon gelatin in 1 1/4 cups boiling water in mixer bowl. Beat in cream cheese on medium speed. Stir in pineapple. Chill until partially set. Fold in pecans. Spoon over cranberry layer. Chill until nearly set. Dissolve lime gelatin in 1 cup boiling water. Stir in grapefruit and sugar. Chill until partially set. Spoon over cream cheese layer. Chill overnight. Yield: 10-12 servings.

Emilie Warren
Laureate Beta Chi, Palm Springs, California

STUFFED CINNAMON APPLES

2/3 c. cinnamon candies
6 apples, peeled, cored
1 3-oz. package cream
  cheese, softened
2 tbsp. milk
1 tsp. lemon juice
1/3 c. chopped dates
1 9-oz. can pineapple
  tidbits, drained
2 tbsp. chopped walnuts
Lettuce

Dissolve candies in 2 cups water over low heat; add apples. Simmer for 15 minutes or until tender. Chill in syrup for several hours; drain. Mix next 6 ingredients. Arrange apples on lettuce; stuff centers with creamed cheese mixture. Yield: 6 servings.

Mary Jo Bent
Laureate Lambda, Kansas City, Missouri

CHARTREUSE SALAD

2 pkg. lime gelatin
1 8-oz. package cream
  cheese, softened
1/2 pt. cream
1 c. chopped celery
1 sm. can crushed
  pineapple
1/2 c. chopped black
  walnuts

Dissolve gelatin in 1 1/2 cups boiling water; cool. Beat cream cheese and cream until smooth. Add to gelatin with remaining ingredients. Chill in mold until firm.

Madolyn Warrington
Nu, Lincoln, Delaware

FROZEN CRANBERRY SALAD

2 3-oz. packages cream
  cheese, softened
2 tbsp. sugar
2 tbsp. mayonnaise
1 can whole cranberry
  sauce
1 15-oz. can crushed
  pineapple, drained
1 carton whipped
  topping
1/2 c. chopped pecans

Beat cream cheese, sugar and mayonnaise until smooth. Add cranberry sauce and pineapple. Stir in whipped topping and pecans. Freeze in mold until firm. Yield: 12 servings.

Lori Unruh
Mu Gamma, McPherson, Kansas

EGGNOG CHRISTMAS SALAD

1 env. unflavored gelatin
1 8-oz. can crushed
  pineapple
3 tbsp. lime juice
1 1/2 c. eggnog
1/2 c. chopped celery
1 3-oz. package
  raspberry gelatin
1 1/2 c. cranberry juice
1 14-oz. jar cranberry-
  orange relish

Soften gelatin in mixture of pineapple and lime juice for 5 minutes. Cook until gelatin dissolves, stirring constantly;

cool. Stir in eggnog and celery. Spoon into 7 x 12-inch pan. Chill until almost set. Dissolve raspberry gelatin in boiling cranberry juice. Fold in cranberry-orange relish. Pour over eggnog layer. Chill until firm. Cut into squares. Serve on lettuce leaves; garnish with frosted cranberries. Yield: 12 servings.

Marge Ward
Preceptor Beta Omega, La Mesa, California

MYSTERY SALAD

1 can cherry pie filling
1 can mandarin oranges, drained
1 14-oz. can sweetened condensed milk
1 c. nuts
1 8-oz. carton whipped topping
1 c. miniature marshmallows
1 tsp. red food coloring (opt.)

Mix all ingredients. Chill overnight. Yield: 24 servings.

Julie Holkenbrink
Eta Mu, Merced, California

RASPBERRY RED SALAD

2 3-oz. packages raspberry gelatin
1 pkg. frozen raspberries
1 20-oz. can applesauce
48 miniature marshmallows
1 pt. sour cream

Dissolve gelatin in 2 cups boiling water. Add raspberries and applesauce; stir until raspberries thaw. Chill until firm. Soften marshmallows in sour cream in refrigerator for 8 hours or longer. Serve over salad. Yield: 8 servings.

Kay L. Bruning
Preceptor Alpha Beta, Sun City, Arizona

TWENTY-FOUR HOUR SALAD

2 c. grapes, seeded, cut in half
2 c. drained pineapple tidbits
2 c. orange sections, chopped
2 c. miniature marshmallows
1 c. blanched almonds chopped
2 eggs, beaten
2 tbsp. sugar
1/4 c. cream
Juice of 1 lemon
1 c. whipping cream, whipped

Mix fruits, marshmallows and almonds. Combine eggs, sugar, cream and lemon juice. Cook in double boiler until thick, stirring constantly; cool. Fold in whipped cream. Pour over fruit mixture; mix lightly. Let stand for 24 hours. Cherries may be substituted for grapes and pecans for almonds. Yield: 12 servings.

Lucille Wanee
Laureate Beta Upsilon, Chico, California

RED VELVET SALAD

3 3-oz. packages raspberry gelatin
1 3-oz. package lemon gelatin
3/4 c. miniature marshmallows
1 8-oz. can crushed pineapple
1 8-oz. package cream cheese, softened
1/2 c. salad dressing
1/2 pt. whipping cream, whipped

Dissolve 2 packages raspberry gelatin in 3 1/2 cups boiling water. Pour into 9 x 13-inch pan. Chill until firm. Dissolve lemon gelatin in 1 cup boiling water. Stir in marshmallows dissolved in 1/2 cup boiling water. Chill until partially set. Drain pineapple, reserving juice. Blend reserved juice and cream cheese. Stir in salad dressing and pineapple. Fold in whipped cream and gelatin mixture. Spoon over congealed layer. Dissolve remaining package raspberry gelatin in 1 3/4 cups boiling water; cool. Pour over cheese mixture. Chill until firm. Yield: 12 servings.

Carolyn Hollick
Xi Xi Mu, Bakersfield, California

SINFUL SALAD

1 6-oz. package strawberry gelatin
3 med. bananas, mashed
2 10-oz. packages frozen strawberries, drained
1 20-oz. can crushed pineapple, drained
1 c. chopped pecans
1 16-oz. carton sour cream

Dissolve gelatin in 1 cup boiling water. Stir in bananas, strawberries, pineapple and pecans. Chill half the mixture in 8 x 12-inch pan for 1 hour or until set. Spread sour cream over congealed layer. Spoon remaining gelatin over top. Chill, covered, until firm. Yield: 12-16 servings.

Mary Anne Young
Xi Delta Theta, Reidsville, Georgia

PARTY SHRIMP SALAD MOLD

1 3-oz. package lemon gelatin
1 1/3 c. tomato juice
2/3 c. salad dressing
1 c. cottage cheese
1/2 c. chopped celery
2 tbsp. chopped green pepper
3 tbsp. grated onion
1 4 1/2-oz. can shrimp, drained, rinsed

Dissolve gelatin in boiling tomato juice. Chill until partially set. Beat in salad dressing and cottage cheese. Stir in celery, green pepper, onion and shrimp. Chill in 1-quart mold until set. Unmold on lettuce-lined plate. Yield: 6-8 servings.

Carolyn Qualey
Xi Pi, Moscow, Indiana

HOLIDAY FRUIT BUTTER

8 lg. cooking apples, cored, quartered
5 lg. pears, cored, quartered
2 bananas, sliced
4 c. sugar
1 tsp. grated orange rind
1/3 c. fresh orange juice

Combine 1/2 cup water, apples and pears in 5-quart saucepan. Cook over medium heat until tender, stirring occasionally. Stir in bananas. Put fruit through sieve; return to saucepan. Stir in remaining ingredients. Cook over medium heat for about 1 hour or until thick; stir frequently. Cool. Pour into 1-pint jars. Store in refrigerator. Yield: 6 pints.

Photograph for this recipe on cover.

SUE'S APPLE CIDER STEW

2 lb. beef, cubed
3 tbsp. flour
2 tsp. salt
1/4 tsp. each thyme, pepper
3 tbsp. oil
2 c. apple cider
2 tbsp. vinegar
2 onions, chopped
10 mushrooms, sliced
1 stalk celery, chopped
1 green pepper, chopped
4 carrots, sliced
3 potatoes, quartered
1 apple, sliced

Coat beef with mixed dry ingredients. Brown in oil. Stir in cider, vinegar and 1/2 cup water. Bring to a boil, stirring constantly. Simmer, covered, for 1 1/2 hours or until beef is tender. Add vegetables and apple slices. Cook for 35 minutes longer or until vegetables are tender. Yield: 6-8 servings.

Lou Marriott
Preceptor Mu, Franklin, Tennessee

TENDERLOIN OF PORK WITH CHERRY SAUCE

1 5-lb. pork tenderloin, rolled, tied
1/2 tsp. salt
Dash of pepper
1 12-oz. jar whole cherry preserves
2 tbsp. light corn syrup
1/4 c. wine vinegar
1/2 tsp. cinnamon
1/4 tsp. each nutmeg, cloves
1/4 c. slivered almonds

Rub pork with 1/4 teaspoon salt and pepper. Place on foil. Add 2 tablespoon water. Seal, leaving vent at top. Bake on rack in roasting pan at 325 degrees for 3 hours. Bring cherry preserves, corn syrup, vinegar, 1/4 teaspoon salt and spices to a boil, stirring frequently. Simmer for 5 minutes. Add almonds. Spoon glaze over roast. Bake for 30 minutes longer, basting frequently. Serve remaining sauce over roast. Yield: 4-6 servings.

Cheryl K. Blue
Omega, London, Ontario, Canada

CRANBERRY MEAT LOAF

1/4 c. packed brown sugar
1/2 c. cranberry sauce, mashed
1 1/2 lb. ground beef
1/2 lb. ground smoked ham
3/4 c. milk
3/4 c. cracker crumbs
2 eggs
1 1/2 tsp. salt
1/8 tsp. pepper
2 tbsp. diced onion
3 bay leaves

Sprinkle brown sugar over bottom of greased loaf pan. Spread cranberry sauce over sugar. Combine next 8 ingredients; shape into loaf. Place in prepared pan; top with bay leaves. Bake at 350 degrees for 1 hour. Remove bay leaves.

Beatrice Webber
Preceptor Kappa Psi, Sebastopol, California

CHRISTMAS MORNING SAUSAGE RING

2 lb. sausage
1 1/2 c. cracker crumbs
2 eggs, slightly beaten
1/2 c. milk
1/4 c. minced onion
1 c. finely chopped apples

Mix all ingredients. Pack lightly into greased 6-cup ring mold. Chill for several hours; unmold onto jelly roll pan. Bake at 325 degrees for 1 hour. Serve with scrambled eggs in center of sausage ring. Yield: 12 servings.

Mrs. Arnold W. Johnson
Preceptor Alpha Psi, Topeka, Kansas

QUICHE NOEL

1 recipe 1-crust pie pastry
3/4 c. chopped cooked chicken
1 c. shredded Cheddar cheese
2 tbsp. chopped pimento
1/4 c. chopped green pepper
6 eggs, beaten
1 c. half and half
1 tbsp. minced onion
1/2 tsp. seasoned salt
1/4 tsp. white pepper

Line 9-inch quiche dish with pastry; trim. Prick bottom and side. Bake at 400 degrees for 3 minutes; remove from oven. Prick. Bake for 5 minutes longer; cool. Sprinkle chicken, cheese, pimento and green pepper in pie shell. Mix remaining ingredients; pour over layers. Bake at 425 degrees for 30 minutes or until set. Let stand for 10 minutes before serving. Yield: 6-8 servings.

Eileen Ueckermann
Xi Alpha Iota, Pleasantville, New Jersey

RUBY CHICKEN

1 sm. onion, chopped
1 tsp. salt
1 broiler-fryer, cut up
1/4 c. margarine, melted
1/4 tsp. each cinnamon, ginger
3/4 c. orange juice
1/8 tsp. Tabasco sauce
1 1/2 c. cranberries
1/3 to 1/2 c. sugar
2 tbsp. molasses
3 tbsp. cornstarch

Brown onion and salted chicken in margarine. Add spices, orange juice and Tabasco sauce. Simmer, covered, for 30 to 35 minutes. Stir in cranberries, sugar and molasses. Cook, uncovered, for 5 minutes. Blend cornstarch and 2 tablespoons water. Stir into chicken mixture gradually. Cook for 1 minute longer, stirring constantly. Serve over rice. Yield: 4 servings.

Heidi Malowany
Pi, Nepean, Ontario, Canada

CHICKEN NO-PEEKIE

1 1/2 c. minute rice	Butter
1 can cream of celery soup	2 to 3 lb. chicken, cut up
1 can cream of mushroom soup	1 env. dry onion soup mix

Mix rice, canned soups and 1/2 soup can of water. Spread in buttered 11 x 13-inch casserole. Arrange chicken over rice. Sprinkle with onion soup mix. Bake, tightly covered, at 325 degrees for 2 hours. Yield: 4-5 servings.

Sidnee McKinney
Xi Rho Mu, San Jose, California

CHICKEN WELLINGTON

1 1-oz. package chicken marinade mix	2 tbsp. chives
1/2 c. dry white wine	Salt, pepper and nutmeg to taste
2 chicken breasts, skinned, boned, split	4 thin slices boiled ham
1 tbsp. minced onion	1/2 c. grated Cheddar cheese
2 tbsp. butter	1 sheet frozen puff pastry
1/2 lb. fresh mushrooms, finely minced	1 egg
2 tbsp. chopped parsley	

Combine marinade mix with wine and 1/2 cup water in shallow baking dish. Prick chicken breasts deeply with fork. Add to marinade; turn to coat. Marinate for 15 minutes; turn twice. Place chicken on ungreased baking sheet. Bake at 425 degrees for 15 minutes. Cool. Saute onion in butter in skillet. Add mushrooms. Cook for 15 to 20 minutes longer, stirring frequently. Add parsley, chives and seasonings. Cut each chicken breast in half horizontally. Spread cut sides of half the chicken with mushroom mixture. Top with ham slices and grated cheese. Cover with remaining chicken pieces, cut side down. Set aside. Thaw pastry for 20 minutes. Unfold. Roll pastry into 12 x 16-inch rectangle; trim edges. Cut into 4 rectangles. Place one filled chicken breast in center of each rectangle. Beat egg with 1 tablespoon water. Moisten edges of pastry with egg mixture; fold pastry to enclose chicken. Seal edges. Brush with egg mixture. Decorate top with pastry trimmings. Brush with egg mixture. Prick pastry 3 or 4 times. Place on ungreased baking sheet. Bake at 425 degrees for 25 to 30 minutes or until golden brown and puffed. Yield: 4 servings.

Photograph for this recipe on page 2.

GLAZED ENGLISH ROAST GOOSE WITH WILD RICE CASSEROLE

1 10 to 12-lb. goose	1 c. chopped dried apricots
Salt and pepper	2 tbsp. sugar
1 8-oz. package herb-seasoned stuffing mix	1 c. chicken broth
1 c. chopped prunes	1/2 c. currant jelly
1 c. cranberries	Juice of 1/2 lemon

Rub goose with salt and pepper inside and out. Mix next 6 ingredients. Stuff goose with dressing; truss. Bake in foil-lined roasting pan at 350 degrees for 3 1/2 hours. Melt jelly in lemon juice. Spoon over goose; roast for 15 minutes longer. Repeat process. Roast until goose is tender. Spoon remaining glaze over goose before serving. Serve with Wild Rice Casserole.

Wild Rice Casserole

1 c. cubed Cheddar cheese	1/2 c. chopped mushrooms
1 c. cubed Velveeta cheese	1/4 c. olive oil
1/2 c. each minced onion, green pepper	1 16-oz. can tomatoes
1 c. chopped ripe olives	Butter

Layer all ingredients except butter in 3-quart casserole in order listed. Dot with butter. Pour 1 cup boiling water over layers. Bake, covered, at 350 degrees for 1 1/2 hours. Bake, uncovered, at 325 degrees for 30 minutes. Cool for 15 minutes before serving. Yield: 10-12 servings.

Marcia M. Zerbst
Preceptor Delta Xi, Fort Lauderdale, Florida

SAUCY TURKEY FLORENTINE

2 tbsp. flour	1/8 tsp. pepper
1 c. sour cream	1 tsp. seasoned salt
3 c. 1/2-inch turkey cubes	1 can cream of chicken soup
2 tbsp. chopped ripe olives	2 c. cooked noodles
1 4-oz. can mushroom pieces, drained	Paprika
1 tbsp. instant onion	Pimento (opt.)
1/8 tsp. thyme	

Stir flour into sour cream; simmer, stirring constantly. Mix next 7 ingredients. Stir in sour cream mixture and soup. Add noodles; mix well. Bake, covered, in 2-quart casserole at 375 degrees for 30 to 35 minutes. Garnish with paprika; and pimento poinsettia. Yield: 4 servings.

Linda L. Hamilton
Delta Epsilon, Toledo, Ohio

OYSTER PUDDING

6 slices bread
Butter, softened
1 pt. oysters
Milk
2 eggs, beaten
1 tsp. salt
1/4 tsp. pepper
6 slices sharp American cheese

Spread 1 side of bread lightly with butter; cut into cubes. Drain oysters, reserving liquid. Add enough milk to liquid to measure 2 1/2 cups. Mix in eggs and seasonings. Layer bread cubes, cheese and oysters in baking pan, ending with bread cubes. Pour milk mixture over layers. Bake at 325 degrees for 1 hour or until set. Yield: 4-6 servings.

Ruth Foltz
Laureate, Hagerstown, Maryland

DIAMOND HEAD SANDWICHES

2 c. cooked shrimp
1 tbsp. lemon juice
1/2 c. chopped celery
2 hard-boiled eggs, chopped
1 tbsp. chopped parsley
1 tsp. finely chopped onion
1/2 c. sour cream
1/2 loaf Vienna bread
Butter, softened
2 4 1/2-oz. cans deviled ham
8 slices pineapple, drained, cut in half
12 slices tomato
1 c. shredded Cheddar cheese
Chopped parsley

Sprinkle shrimp with lemon juice. Mix with celery, eggs, parsley and onion. Stir in sour cream. Slice bread in half horizontally; spread with butter. Toast in broiler. Cut each half partially through vertically into 3 pieces. Spread buttered sides with deviled ham. Layer pineapple, tomato and shrimp mixture over ham; top with cheese. Broil until cheese melts. Cut into portions. Garnish with parsley. Yield: 6 servings.

Millie LaRoque
Gamma Upsilon, Bagley, Minnesota

BETTY'S SHRIMP SCAMPI

1/4 c. chopped scallions
2 tbsp. minced garlic
1 c. butter
1/4 c. olive oil
2 lb. shrimp, peeled, cleaned
1 tbsp. lemon juice
1 tbsp. white wine
1/2 tsp. salt
Coarsely ground pepper
1 tsp. whole dillweed
2 tbsp. parsley
2 tbsp. sesame seed

Saute scallions and garlic in butter and olive oil. Stir in shrimp, lemon juice, wine, salt and pepper. Cook for 4 minutes, stirring occasionally. Add dillweed, parsley and sesame seed. Serve over rice. Yield: 6-8 servings.

Betty L. Whittinghill
Laureate Theta, New Albany, Indiana

CHRISTMAS CABBAGE

1 med. head red cabbage, coarsely sliced
2 tbsp. red wine vinegar
1 tsp. sugar
2 tsp. salt
6 tbsp. oil
1 10-oz. package frozen peas
1 med. coarsely sliced head green cabbage
1 med. onion, chopped
1/2 tsp. caraway seed
Sprigs of watercress

Cook red cabbage in mixture of vinegar, sugar, 1 teaspoon salt and 3 tablespoons oil for 25 minutes or until cabbage is tender, stirring occasionally. Add peas. Cook until heated through. Cook green cabbage with onion, caraway seed and 1 teaspoon salt in 3 tablespoons oil for 20 minutes or until cabbage and onion are tender, stirring occasionally. Serve red and green cabbage on platter separated by watercress sprigs. Yield: 10 servings.

Mary Muller
Beta Beta, Eureka Springs, Arkansas

CARROTS LYONNAISE

1 lb. carrots, cut in julienne strips
1 chicken bouillon cube
3 med. onions, chopped
1/4 c. margarine
1 tbsp. flour
1/4 tsp. salt
Pepper to taste
Sugar to taste

Cook carrots in bouillon dissolved in 1/2 cup boiling water for 10 minutes. Cook onions in margarine in covered saucepan for 15 minutes. Stir in flour, salt, pepper and 3/4 cup water. Bring to a boil. Mix in carrots and bouillon. Simmer, uncovered, for 10 minutes. Stir in sugar. Yield: 6 servings.

Linda L. Barnes
Delta Upsilon, Newman Grove, Nebraska

BUTTERMILK CORN CHOWDER

2 slices bacon
1 sm. onion, chopped
2 med. potatoes, peeled, chopped
2 c. corn
1 stalk celery, chopped
1/2 tsp. salt
1/4 tsp. pepper
2 c. chicken broth
2 tbsp. flour
2 c. buttermilk

Cook bacon until crisp; remove. Saute onion in bacon drippings. Add next 5 ingredients and 1 1/2 cups chicken broth. Simmer for 15 to 20 minutes. Blend flour and 1/2 cup broth; stir into mixture. Cook until thick and bubbly, stirring constantly; reduce heat. Stir in buttermilk. Simmer until heated through. Sprinkle with crumbled bacon. Yield: 6 servings.

C. L. Lovell
Preceptor Iota Theta, Clayton, California

CORN CUSTARD FIESTA

1 16-oz. can cream-style corn	1/4 c. chopped green pepper
2 eggs, beaten	1 tbsp. chopped pimento
1/2 c. crushed crackers	6 drops of Tabasco sauce
1/4 c. melted butter	1/2 tsp. salt
1/4 c. evaporated milk	1 1/2 tsp. sugar
1/4 c. shredded carrots	1/2 c. shredded cheese
1 tbsp. chopped celery	Paprika

Mix all ingredients except cheese and paprika in 1-quart casserole. Top with cheese. Sprinkle with paprika; garnish with olive halves. Bake at 350 degrees for 30 minutes. Yield: 4 servings.

Shirley Wilson
Gamma Alpha, Clinton, Illinois

SHOPPER'S LIFESAVER POTATO SOUP

6 potatoes, peeled, chopped	2 tsp. salt
2 onions, chopped	Pepper to taste
2 carrots, chopped	1/3 c. butter
2 stalks celery, sliced	1/2 tsp. dillweed
4 chicken bouillon cubes	1 13-oz. can evaporated milk
1 tbsp. parsley flakes	

Mix all ingredients except evaporated milk with 5 cups water in 4-quart saucepan. Cover and bring to a hard boil. Reduce heat. Simmer for 45 minutes. Add evaporated milk. Simmer for 2 to 3 minutes. Mash potatoes if desired before serving. Yield: 6 servings.

Gertrude Mickler
Xi Zeta Alpha, St. Augustine, Florida

FAVORITE NEW ENGLAND CASSEROLE

1 20-oz. package frozen cauliflower	3 c. milk
1 20-oz. package frozen broccoli	1 1/2 c. grated Cheddar cheese
3 c. chopped ham	1 c. grated Parmesan cheese
3 tbsp. flour	1/2 tsp. salt
1/2 c. butter, melted	3 c. fresh bread crumbs

Cook vegetables using package directions until tender-crisp; drain. Place in 4-quart casserole. Top with ham. Stir flour into 1/4 cup butter. Add milk gradually; cook until thickened, stirring constantly. Blend in cheeses and salt. Cook until cheese is melted, stirring constantly. Pour over layers. Sprinkle mixture of bread crumbs and 1/4 cup butter around edge. Bake at 350 degrees for 25 minutes. Yield: 10 servings.

Pauline Hall
Preceptor Mu, Glen Burnie, Maryland

HOLIDAY VEGETABLE CASSEROLE

1 10-oz. package frozen broccoli spears	Dash of Worcestershire sauce (opt.)
1 10-oz. package frozen cauliflower	1 c. grated cheese
1 10-0z. package frozen green beans	2 cans cream of mushroom soup
1 sm. onion, finely chopped	French-fried onion rings (opt.)
Salt and pepper to taste	Chopped pimento (opt.)

Arrange slightly thawed vegetables and onion in 9-inch square pan. Sprinkle with seasonings and Worcestershire sauce. Melt cheese in soup. Pour over vegetables. Top with onion rings and pimento. Bake at 350 degrees for 45 to 50 minutes. Yield: 6-8 servings.

Judy Schies
Xi Kappa Tau, Dallas, Texas

FRESH VEGETABLE JARDINIERE

3 tbsp. mixed whole pickling spices	3 turnips, peeled, thinly sliced
2 1/4 c. white vinegar	2 bunches radishes, trimmed
1 1/2 c. sugar	1 red onion, thinly sliced
1 1/2 tsp. salt	1 head cauliflower, separated into flowerets
1 bay leaf	
1 clove of garlic, split	1 bunch broccoli, trimmed, separated into flowerets
2 carrots, peeled, sliced diagonally	
3 stalks celery, sliced diagonally	

Tie pickling spices in cheesecloth bag. Place in large saucepan. Add 3 cups water, vinegar, sugar, salt, bay leaf and garlic. Simmer, covered, for 10 minutes. Add vegetables. Simmer, covered, for 3 minutes. Drain, reserving liquid. Discard pickling spices, bay leaf and garlic. Cool vegetables and liquid. Layer vegetables in two 1-quart jars; add liquid to cover. Store in refrigerator.

Photograph for this recipe on cover.

ORANGE-GLAZED CARROTS AND PARSNIPS

3 carrots, sliced 1 in. thick	2 tbsp. honey
3 med. parsnips, sliced 1 in. thick	1 tbsp. butter
	1/4 tsp. grated orange rind
2 tbsp. orange juice	

Cook carrots and parsnips in 1 inch boiling salted water in medium saucepan until tender-crisp; drain. Add orange juice, honey, butter and orange rind. Cook over medium heat until vegetables are tender and evenly glazed, tossing occasionally. Yield: 4 servings.

Photograph for this recipe on page 2.

CHEESE ENCHILADAS

2 c. flour
Oil
1/4 to 1/2 c. chili powder
1/8 tsp. salt
1/2 tsp. each oregano, garlic salt
12 corn tortillas
1 to 2 lb. longhorn cheese, grated
1 c. chopped onion
1 6-oz. can chopped green chilies
1 c. sour cream

Brown flour in 2 tablespoons oil. Stir in 2 cups cold water and chili powder. Bring to a boil; add seasonings. Fry tortillas in 2 to 6 tablespoons oil for 1 second on each side. Spoon 2 tablespoons sauce on each tortilla; sprinkle with cheese, onion and green chilies; roll up. Arrange in 9 x 13-inch baking pan; spoon remaining sauce over rolls, topping with cheese. Bake at 350 degrees for 30 minutes. Serve with sour cream, guacamole or fried eggs. Yield: 12 servings.

Paula Miller
Alpha Beta, Rocky Ford, Colorado

CRANBERRY CASSEROLE

3 c. chopped apples
2 c. cranberries
1 1/4 c. sugar
1 1/2 c. quick-cooking oats
1/3 c. pecans, chopped
1/2 c. packed brown sugar
1/2 c. margarine, melted

Mix apples, cranberries and sugar in 2-quart casserole. Top with mixture of remaining ingredients. Bake at 350 degrees for 1 hour. Good with turkey or chicken. Yield: 10-12 servings.

Wynelle G. Graves
Xi Psi, Cullman, Alabama

PIEROGIS

3 eggs
2 c. flour
1/2 c. sour cream
1 tsp. salt
1 tsp. sugar
1 10 to 12-oz. container cottage cheese, drained

Mix 2 eggs, flour and sour cream. Roll to 1/4-inch thickness on floured surface. Cut out 3-inch circles. Blend remaining egg and remaining ingredients until smooth. Place 1 teaspoon filling in each circle. Fold to enclose filling; seal edges. Place Pierogis in boiling salted water. Cook until Pierogis rise to top, stirring frequently. Cook for 10 minutes longer; drain. Brown lightly in butter if desired. Yield: 30-40 servings.

Barbara Wittenberg
Alpha Alpha, St. Catharines, Ontario, Canada

BLACK WALNUT BREAD

3 c. sifted flour
4 1/2 tsp. baking powder
1/2 c. sugar
1 tsp. salt
1 c. chopped black walnuts
2 eggs
1 c. milk
1/4 c. butter, melted

Sift dry ingredients together. Stir in black walnuts. Add mixture of eggs, milk and butter. Bake in greased loaf pan at 350 degrees for 1 hour.

Phyllis B. Painter
Preceptor Omega, Staunton, Virginia

BREAKFAST BREAD

1/3 c. margarine
1/3 c. sugar
2 eggs
1 c. orange juice
2 tsp. grated orange rind
2 c. flour
1 1/2 c. cornflakes, crushed
1 tbsp. baking powder
1/2 tsp. salt
1/2 c. chopped nuts
1/2 c. raisins

Cream margarine and sugar. Mix in eggs, orange juice and rind. Add mixture of next 4 ingredients. Stir in nuts and raisins. Bake in loaf pan at 350 degrees for 50 minutes or until bread tests done.

Vera G. Hansen
Xi Beta Alpha, Davenport, Iowa

CASSIE'S EGGNOG BREAD

1 egg, beaten
1 1/2 c. eggnog
1/4 c. melted butter
3 c. sifted flour
1 c. sugar
1 tbsp. baking powder
1 tsp. salt
1/2 tsp. each nutmeg, cinnamon
1 c. chopped pecans
3/4 c. chopped candied fruit

Mix egg, eggnog and butter into sifted dry ingredients. Stir in pecans and fruit. Bake in greased loaf pan at 350 degrees for 1 hour.

Cassandra A. Lathe
Xi Tau Phi, Canyon Lake, Texas

GRANDMA LUNSFORD'S NUT BREAD

2 eggs
Dash of salt
2 c. packed brown sugar
4 c. flour, sifted
1 tsp. soda
3 tsp. baking powder
2 c. buttermilk
1 c. chopped nuts

Beat eggs and salt. Mix in brown sugar until smooth. Beat in sifted dry ingredients and buttermilk alternately, beginning and ending with flour. Mix until smooth. Stir in nuts. Bake in greased loaf pan at 350 degrees for 50 minutes. Yield: 3 loaves.

Debra Angel
Xi Nu Pi, Apple Valley, California

COTTAGE CHEESE-FRUIT BREAD

6 tbsp. butter, softened
1/2 c. packed brown sugar
2 eggs
1 tbsp. each grated orange, lemon rind
1 1/2 c. cottage cheese
2 c. flour
2 tsp. baking powder
3/4 tsp. each soda, salt
1 c. finely chopped mixed dried fruit with raisins
1/2 c. chopped pecans

Cream butter and sugar. Beat in eggs 1 at a time. Stir in orange and lemon rind and cottage cheese. Blend in combined dry ingredients. Fold in fruit and pecans. Bake in buttered loaf pan at 350 degrees for 45 to 50 minutes; cool on wire rack.

Donna Lou Keller
Preceptor Pi, Scottsbluff, Nebraska

SWEET POTATO-CRANBERRY BREAD

3/4 c. mashed cooked fresh sweet potato
3/4 c. packed brown sugar
1/4 c. butter, melted
3 eggs, slightly beaten
1 tsp. grated orange rind
1/3 c. fresh orange juice
2 1/2 c. sifted flour
1 1/2 tsp. baking powder
1/2 tsp. each soda, salt
1/4 tsp. cinnamon
1/8 tsp. mace
1 c. coarsely chopped fresh cranberries
1/2 c. chopped nuts

Combine sweet potato, brown sugar, butter, eggs, orange rind and orange juice in bowl; mix well. Sift in flour, baking powder, soda, salt, cinnamon and mace. Stir in cranberries and nuts. Pour into greased and floured loaf pan. Bake at 350 degrees for 50 to 60 minutes or until bread tests done. Remove from pan to cool. Let stand, tightly wrapped, overnight before slicing.

Photograph for this recipe on cover.

CINNAMON YEAST ROLLS

2 pkg. yeast
1/2 c. sugar
1/2 c. butter-flavored oil
2 tsp. salt
1 egg
7 1/2 to 8 c. flour
1 stick butter, melted
Cinnamon
Brown sugar

Dissolve yeast in 3 cups warm water. Mix in sugar, oil, salt, egg and flour. Knead 8 to 10 times on floured surface. Place in greased bowl, turning to grease surface. Let rise, covered, for 45 minutes or until doubled in bulk. Roll into three 1/2-inch thick rectangles. Coat with butter. Sprinkle with cinnamon and brown sugar. Roll up; cut into 1-inch slices. Let rise in greased pan, covered, for 45 to 55 minutes or until doubled in bulk. Bake at 350 degrees for 25 to 30 minutes. Yield: 2 1/2-3 dozen.

Judith A. Stewart
Xi Gamma Alpha, Fort Smith, Arkansas

QUICK BRAN MUFFINS

3 tbsp. margarine, melted
1/3 c. milk
1/2 c. All-Bran
1 1/2 tbsp. dark brown sugar
1 egg, slightly beaten
1 c. baking mix
1/2 c. chocolate-covered raisins

Melt margarine in milk. Pour over cereal. Stir in brown sugar. Mix in egg and baking mix. Stir in raisins. Bake in greased miniature muffin cups at 400 degrees for 15 minutes. Yield: 36 servings.

Annie L. Knowles
Laureate Alpha Zeta, Jacksonville, Illinois

BRANDY ALEXANDER SOUFFLE

Butter
Sugar
Chocolate shavings
1 1/2 env. unflavored gelatin
6 eggs, separated
2 3-oz. packages cream cheese, softened
1/3 c. Brandy
1/3 c. Creme de Cacao
1/4 tsp. cream of tartar
2 c. whipping cream, whipped

Butter and sugar bottom and side of 1 1/2-quart souffle dish. Butter 4-inch foil collar; sprinkle with shaved chocolate. Fasten to prepared dish leaving 2-inch rim. Combine 1/4 cup sugar, gelatin and 1/2 cup water in saucepan. Let stand for 1 minute. Cook over low heat until gelatin melts; remove from heat. Beat egg yolks for 5 minutes. Stir a small amount of gelatin mixture into egg yolks; stir egg yolks into gelatin mixture. Cook over low heat for 2 minutes, stirring constantly. Blend in cream cheese, Brandy and Creme de Cacao. Chill for 45 minutes. Beat egg whites and cream of tartar until foamy. Add 1/4 cup sugar gradually, beating until stiff. Fold chilled mixture and 3/4 of the whipped cream into egg whites. Pour into prepared dish. Chill until firm. Remove collar. Garnish with shaved chocolate. Serve with remaining whipped cream.

Kathy Hanson
Xi Alpha Zeta, Orofino, Idaho

FROZEN MOCHA TAFFY DESSERT

1 1/2 pkg. ladyfingers
2 tbsp. instant coffee
1 1/2 qt. vanilla ice cream, softened
7 Heath candy bars
1 lg. carton whipped topping
3 tbsp. Creme de Cacao

Line bottom and side of springform pan with ladyfingers. Dissolve coffee in 1 tablespoon water. Stir into ice cream with 6 crushed candy bars. Spoon over ladyfingers. Freeze covered. Cut into wedges. Top with whipped topping mixed with Creme de Cacao. Sprinkle with remaining crushed candy bar. Yield: 12 servings.

Phyllis C. Harrington
Preceptor Pi, Bangor, Maine

CHOCOLATE MOUSSE

1 c. milk
1 env. unflavored gelatin
6 tbsp. coffee-flavored Brandy
1 egg
1/4 c. sugar
1/8 tsp. salt
1 6-oz. package semisweet chocolate chips
1 c. heavy cream

Process 1/4 cup cold milk and gelatin in blender container until gelatin is softened. Add 3/4 cup scalded milk. Blend until gelatin is dissolved. Add next 5 ingredients. Process until smooth. Add cream and 2 ice cubes. Process until liquified. Pour into 1 1/2-quart mold. Chill overnight. Yield: 8 servings.

Cecelia Barnes
Delta Theta, Columbus, Mississippi

CHOCOLATE-PEPPERMINT ICE CREAM DESSERT

2 c. crushed vanilla wafers
3/4 c. melted butter
4 1-oz. squares unsweetened chocolate, melted
1 1/2 c. sugar
1 sm. can evaporated milk
1 tsp. vanilla extract
1 qt. peppermint ice cream, softened

Press mixture of vanilla wafer crumbs and 1/4 cup melted butter into 9 x 13-inch baking pan. Bake at 350 degrees for 10 minutes; cool. Combine chocolate, 1/2 cup butter, sugar and evaporated milk. Bring to a boil; cool. Stir in vanilla. Pour into cookie crust. Freeze. Spread ice cream over top. Freeze. Garnish with small candy canes.

Terry Siebold
Xi Kappa, Menomonie, Wisconsin

FUDGE MINT TORTE

1 1/2 c. packed light brown sugar
1 12-oz. package semisweet chocolate chips, melted
1 c. butter, melted
4 eggs
1 1/2 c. sifted flour
2 c. whipping cream
1/3 c. Creme de Menthe
2 tbsp. confectioners' sugar

Beat brown sugar into melted chocolate and butter. Beat in eggs 1 at a time. Mix in flour. Pour into 3 greased and waxed paper-lined 9-inch cake pans. Bake at 375 degrees for 15 to 20 minutes. Cool in pan for 10 minutes before removing to wire rack to cool completely. Beat remaining ingredients until stiff. Spread between layers and over top of torte. Garnish with chocolate shavings.

Carol Coleman
Xi Delta Nu, Colorado Springs, Colorado

CHERRIES IN THE SNOW

2 env. unflavored gelatin
1/2 c. sugar
2 tsp. salt
1 tsp. lemon juice
1 20-oz. can crushed pineapple
1 c. chopped nuts
1 9-in. angel food cake
Whipped topping
1 can coconut
1 jar maraschino cherries

Soften gelatin in 2 tablespoons cold water. Mix in 1 cup hot water, sugar, salt, lemon juice, pineapple and nuts. Chill for 30 minutes. Tear cake into bite-sized pieces. Add cake and 1 medium carton whipped topping to gelatin mixture. Chill for several hours. Top with 1 small carton whipped topping. Sprinkle with coconut. Top with cherries. Yield: 12 servings.

Bernice P. Cogburn
Xi Eta Delta, Jacksonville, Florida

EGGNOG CUP

2 env. unflavored gelatin
1/4 c. sugar
1 qt. eggnog
4 tsp. rum flavoring
1 c. whipping cream, whipped

Combine gelatin, sugar and 1 cup eggnog in double boiler. Heat until gelatin and sugar are dissolved; remove. Stir in remaining eggnog and flavoring. Chill until thick. Beat until fluffy. Fold in whipped cream. Garnish with additional whipped cream, nutmeg and holly sprigs. Yield: 12 servings.

Nancy A. Tosetti
Omicron Delta, Nokomis, Illinois

EGGNOG RING

1 3-oz. package lemon gelatin
1/4 tsp. rum extract (opt.)
3/4 c. eggnog
1 11-oz. can pear halves
1 can mandarin oranges
1 3-oz. package cherry gelatin
1 1/2 c. pecans (opt.)

Dissolve lemon gelatin in 1 cup boiling water. Stir in 1/4 cup cold water and flavoring. Add eggnog to 3/4 cup gelatin; reserve remaining mixture. Pour eggnog mixture into 6-cup ring mold. Chill for 25 minutes or until partially set. Drain fruit, reserving liquid. Add enough water to reserved liquid to measure 3/4 cup. Dissolve cherry gelatin in 1 cup boiling water. Stir in liquid and reserved lemon gelatin. Chill until thickened. Add chopped pears. Spoon over eggnog mixture. Arrange oranges in gelatin around edge of mold; press down slightly. Chill until firm. Unmold onto serving platter. Garnish with maraschino cherries. Fill center with pecans. Yield: 10 servings.

Corinne Rivest
Alpha Mu, Sherwood Park, Alberta, Canada

Christmas / 137

DELICIOUS CHRISTMAS DATE CUPS

1 pkg. dates
1 c. chopped pecans
1 1/2 tsp. soda
3/4 c. butter
2 c. sugar
1 egg
1 1/2 c. flour
1/4 tsp. salt
1 c. whipping cream
1 tsp. vanilla extract

Mix dates, pecans, 1 cup boiling water and 1 teaspoon soda. Let stand for 10 to 15 minutes. Cream 1/4 cup butter and 1 cup sugar. Mix in egg. Sift in flour, salt and 1/2 teaspoon soda; mix well. Stir in date mixture. Fill 18 muffin cups 2/3 full. Bake at 350 degrees for 35 minutes. Combine 1/2 cup butter, 1 cup sugar, cream and vanilla in saucepan. Boil for 10 minutes, stirring constantly. Serve over warm muffins.

Margie Wills
Preceptor Delta Pi, Orange Park, Florida

HEAVENLY HASH

1 lb. walnuts, chopped
1 lb. dates, chopped
12 soda crackers, crushed
2 tsp. baking powder
6 eggs
2 c. sugar
1/2 pt. whipping cream, whipped
12 maraschino cherries, cut in half

Combine walnuts and dates. Mix in crackers dredged in baking powder. Beat eggs and sugar until light; mix into walnut mixture. Bake in greased and waxed paper-lined 9 x 13-inch pan at 350 degrees for 40 minutes. Remove waxed paper while pan is hot; cool. Break into small pieces in serving dish. Fold in whipped cream. Top with cherries. Yield: 12 servings.

Wanda Stipp
Laureate Gamma, Anchorage, Alaska

HOLIDAY BOMBE WITH MINCEMEAT

2 pt. strawberry ice cream, slightly softened
2 pt. vanilla ice cream, slightly softened
1 1/2 pt. pistachio ice cream, slightly softened
1 9-oz. package condensed mincemeat, crumbled
1/4 c. dark corn syrup
1/4 c. dark rum

Spread strawberry ice cream over side and bottom of 10-cup mold. Press vanilla ice cream firmly over strawberry. Pack in pistachio ice cream. Freeze, covered. Unmold on chilled serving plate. Bring mincemeat, corn syrup and 1 1/2 cups water to a boil. Cook for 1 minute; cool. Stir in rum. Serve hot or cold over ice cream bombe. Yield: 12 servings.

Judy K. Engibous
Omega, Whitefish, Montana

MANDARIN TIPSY TRIFLE

1 sm. pound cake, cut into 1/2-in. slices
4 to 6 tbsp. orange liqueur
1 pkg. French vanilla pudding, prepared, chilled
2 10-oz. cans mandarin orange sections, drained
2 c. whipping cream, whipped, sweetened
Toasted almonds

Arrange half the cake slices in bottom of glass bowl. Sprinkle with 2 to 3 tablespoons liqueur. Layer with half the pudding, half the mandarin sections and half the whipped cream. Layer remaining cake, liqueur, pudding and whipped cream over top. Top with remaining orange sections and almonds. Chill for several hours.

F. Jewell Patton
Xi Theta Eta, W. Melbourne, Florida

SNOWBALLS

2 1/2 c. crushed pineapple, drained
1 1/2 c. finely chopped nuts
1 stick butter, softened
1 tsp. vanilla extract
Confectioners' sugar
6 doz. vanilla wafers
1/2 pt. whipping cream, whipped
Flaked coconut (opt.)
Maraschino cherry halves
1 recipe confectioners' sugar frosting, tinted green

Mix first 4 ingredients with 2 cups confectioners' sugar. Spread between 3 vanilla wafers. Repeat with remaining vanilla wafers. Frost with whipped cream sweetened with confectioners' sugar. Sprinkle with coconut. Top with cherry half. Decorate with green frosting holly. Freeze; thaw before serving. Yield: 24 servings.

Jo Ann Smith
Preceptor Theta Upsilon, Fortuna, California

APPLESAUCE-NUT CAKE

1 c. margarine, softened
2 c. sugar
2 c. unsweetened applesauce
2 tsp. soda
2 tsp. cinnamon
1 tsp. cloves
4 c. flour
3 tbsp. Ghirardelli cocoa
1 tsp. salt
2 c. raisins
2 c. chopped nuts

Cream margarine. Beat in sugar gradually. Mix in combined applesauce and soda. Mix in dry ingredients. Stir in raisins and nuts. Bake in greased and floured loaf pan at 350 degrees for 1 hour.

Cecilia Getz
Delta Gamma Omicron, Fairfield, California

CROCK•POT APPLE CAKE

2 c. sugar
1 c. oil
2 eggs
3 or 4 apples, cut up
1 c. raisins
2 tsp. vanilla extract
2 c. flour
1 tsp. each salt, soda
1 tsp. cinnamon

Beat sugar, oil and eggs. Stir in apples and raisins; beat well. Mix in remaining ingredients. Pour into greased Crock•Pot cake pan; cover with foil. Bake in 3 1/2-quart Crock•Pot on High for 3 1/2 hours.

Bonnie J. Farber
Eta Beta, Longwood, Florida

BUCHE DE NOEL

5 eggs
1 c. sugar
1 tsp. vanilla extract
1 c. cake flour
1/4 c. cocoa
1 tsp. baking powder
1/4 tsp. salt
Sifted confectioners'
    sugar
1/4 c. milk
2 tbsp. Creme de Menthe
6 sq. unsweetened
    chocolate
2 tbsp. butter, softened

Beat 3 eggs until stiff and lemon-colored. Beat in sugar 1 tablespoon at a time. Stir in 1/3 cup water and vanilla. Fold in next 4 sifted ingredients. Spread in greased jelly roll pan lined with greased waxed paper. Bake at 350 degrees for 15 to 20 minutes. Invert on towel sprinkled with confectioners' sugar; remove paper and trim crusts. Roll as for jelly roll; cool. Combine 2 cups confectioners' sugar, remaining 2 eggs, milk, Creme de Menthe, 4 squares of melted chocolate and butter in mixer bowl. Beat at high speed until well blended. Place bowl in pan of ice water. Beat for 3 minutes longer or until of spreading consistency. Unroll cake. Spread with 2/3 of the mixture; reroll. Place seam side down on serving plate. Frost with remaining mixture. Soften remaining 2 squares chocolate on foil in warm oven. Spread in thin layer; chill. Crumble into small pieces; chill. Sprinkle over ends and side of log. Sprinkle with confectioners' sugar. Yield: 8-10 servings.

Cheryl Hug
Preceptor Alpha, Sarasota, Florida

FRESH COCONUT WREATH CAKE

1 coconut
Milk
1 1/4 c. butter, softened
Sugar
5 eggs
1 tbsp. grated fresh
    lemon rind
3 3/4 c. sifted cake flour
2 1/2 tsp. baking powder
1 tsp. salt
Dry bread crumbs
1/3 c. fresh lemon juice
Grape clusters
Lemon slices

Pierce eyes of coconut; drain coconut milk into measuring cup. Add enough milk to measure 1 1/4 cups. Bake coconut at 350 degrees for 15 minutes. Crack shell with hammer; remove meat. Peel with vegetable peeler. Grate coconut meat; set aside. Combine butter, 2 1/2 cups sugar, eggs, 2 tablespoons grated coconut and lemon rind in mixer bowl. Beat at high speed for 3 minutes. Sift flour, baking powder and salt. Beat into creamed mixture alternately with milk, at low speed, beginning and ending with flour. Dust buttered tube pan with crumbs. Pour in batter. Bake at 325 degrees for 1 hour and 45 minutes or until cake tests done. Cool in pan on rack for 15 minutes. Turn out onto serving plate. Combine 2/3 cup sugar and lemon juice in small saucepan. Cook over low heat until sugar dissolves, stirring constantly. Brush cake with 3/4 of the lemon glaze. Sprinkle 1 cup grated coconut over top. Dip grape clusters in remaining glaze; coat with additional sugar. Place on cake. Arrange twisted lemon slices between grape clusters. Brush sides of cake with remaining glaze.

Photograph for this recipe on cover.

CRANBERRY HOLIDAY CAKE

2 tsp. baking powder
2 c. sifted flour
1/2 tsp. salt
2 c. sugar
2 1/2 c. whole cranberries
1 c. milk
Butter
3/4 c. whipping cream

Sift first 3 ingredients and 1 cup sugar. Stir in cranberries. Combine milk and 3 tablespoons melted butter. Mix into dry ingredients. Bake in greased bundt pan at 375 degrees for 40 to 50 minutes. Pierce surface with toothpick. Bring 1/2 cup butter, 1 cup sugar and cream to a boil. Cook for 3 minutes or until slightly thickened, stirring constantly. Pour over hot cake. Serve warm. Yield: 10-12 servings.

Susan Street
Beta Xi, Carbondale, Illinois

SPIRITED FRUITCAKE

2 1/2 c. golden raisins
1 3/4 c. chopped dried
    apricots
1 3/4 c. chopped candied
    pineapple
Brandy
1 1/2 c. butter, softened
2 c. sugar
1 tsp. vanilla extract
6 eggs
4 c. flour
1/2 tsp. salt
3/4 c. milk
3 c. coarsely chopped
    blanched almonds,
    lightly toasted
1 c. sifted confectioners'
    sugar

Combine raisins, apricots, pineapple and 1/4 cup Brandy. Let stand for 30 minutes. Cream butter, sugar and vanilla. Beat in eggs 1 at a time. Beat in combined flour and salt alternately with milk. Stir in almonds and fruit mixture. Bake in greased 10-inch tube pan at 275 degrees for 3

Christmas / 139

hours. Cool on wire rack. Remove from pan. Combine confectioners' sugar, 4 to 6 teaspoons water and 2 teaspoons Brandy; mix well. Drizzle over cake. May store unglazed cake, wrapped in double layer cheese cloth moistened with 3 tablespoons Brandy, in refrigerator for 3 weeks or less. Moisten cheesecloth with 2 to 3 tablespoons Brandy once each week.

Photograph for this recipe on page 123.

MIXED FRUIT CAKES

3/4 c. shortening	4 c. flour
2 c. sugar	4 tsp. soda
3 c. applesauce	1/2 tsp. salt
1 lb. mixed dried fruit	1 tsp. each cinnamon, nutmeg
8 oz. chopped dates	
1 1/2 c. raisins	1/2 tsp. each allspice, cloves
1 c. chopped nuts	

Cream shortening and sugar. Stir in applesauce, dried fruit, dates, raisins and nuts. Mix in sifted dry ingredients. Bake in 3 greased and floured loaf pans at 350 degrees for 50 minutes.

Della L. Amen
Preceptor Pi, Burley, Idaho

GUMDROP CAKE

2 c. raisins	2 eggs
1 lb. gumdrops, chopped	1 tsp. vanilla extract
2 c. flour	1 c. milk
1/2 c. margarine	1/2 tsp. cinnamon
1 c. sugar	1 tsp. baking powder
1 tsp. salt	

Coat raisins and gumdrops with a small amount of flour. Cream margarine, sugar and salt. Beat in eggs. Stir in vanilla and milk. Add cinnamon, remaining flour and baking powder. Mix in raisins and gumdrops. Bake in tube pan at 350 degrees for 1 hour.

Marie Neville
Alpha, Happy Valley, Labrador, Newfoundland

LANE CAKE

1 1/2 c. raisins	1 1/2 c. quartered candied cherries
1/2 c. Bourbon	
12 egg yolks	1 tsp. vanilla extract
3 3/4 c. sugar	3 c. flour
3/4 tsp. salt	1 tbsp. baking powder
1 3/4 c. butter, softened	1 c. milk
1 1/2 c. chopped pecans	8 egg whites
1 1/2 c. shredded coconut	

Soak raisins in Bourbon for 2 hours or longer. Cook egg yolks, 1 3/4 cups sugar, 1/2 teaspoon salt and 3/4 cup butter in double boiler for 15 minutes or until thick, stirring constantly. Add pecans, coconut, cherries and undrained raisins. Chill overnight. Cream 1 cup butter, 1 1/2 cups sugar and vanilla. Stir in combined flour and baking powder alternately with milk. Beat egg whites and 1/4 teaspoon salt until soft peaks form. Beat in 1/2 cup sugar gradually until stiff. Fold into creamed mixture. Bake in 3 greased and floured 9-inch cake pans at 350 degrees for 20 to 25 minutes. Cool in pans for 5 minutes; cool completely on wire racks. Spread chilled frosting between layers and over top and side of cake.

Maggie Jordan
Laureate Alpha, Lynchburg, Virginia

ITALIAN RUM CAKE

1 white cake mix	1/4 c. sweet rum
6 egg yolks, beaten	1 pt. whipping cream, whipped
1 qt. milk	
1/2 c. sugar	3 oz. toasted almonds, finely chopped
1/2 c. flour	
Grated rind of 1 lemon	

Prepare and bake cake mix according to package directions using 3 round cake pans. Beat egg yolks with milk. Blend in sugar, flour and lemon rind. Cook over low heat until thick, stirring constantly. Do not boil. Cool. Beat 2 tablespoons rum into custard; drizzle remaining rum over layers. Spread custard between layers and over top of cake. Frost with whipped cream; sprinkle almonds over top and side.

Barbara Andreozzi
Omega, Whitefish, Montana

YULE CAKES

1 1/2 c. whole Brazil nuts	1/2 c. seedless raisins
1 1/2 c. walnut halves	3/4 c. sifted flour
1 7 1/4-oz. package pitted dates	3/4 c. sugar
	1/2 tsp. each baking powder, salt
2/3 c. candied pineapple	
1/2 c. each red, green maraschino cherries, drained	1 tsp. vanilla extract
	3 eggs, beaten

Combine first 7 ingredients. Add sifted dry ingredients; toss to coat. Stir in mixture of vanilla and eggs. Mixture will be stiff. Bake in 2 greased loaf pans at 300 degrees for 1 1/2 hours. These cakes freeze well. Yield: 20 servings.

Helen V. Still
Mu Alpha, Smithville, Missouri

POPPY SEED LOAVES

1 pkg. yellow cake mix
2 pkg. vanilla instant pudding mix
2 oz. poppy seed
4 eggs
1/2 c. oil

Beat all ingredients and 1 cup water until smooth. Bake in 3 prepared loaf pans at 350 degrees for 40 minutes or until golden brown.

Berta Schumacher
Eta Mu, Merced, California

AUSTRALIAN PAVLOVA

4 egg whites
Pinch of salt
1 1/4 c. extra fine sugar
1 tbsp. cornstarch
2 tsp. vinegar
Butter
1 sm. carton whipping cream, whipped
Strawberries, sliced
Kiwi fruit and passion fruit

Beat egg whites and salt until stiff. Beat in sugar gradually until very stiff. Fold in cornstarch and vinegar with metal spoon. Butter 9-inch circle on waxed paper on greased baking sheet; dust with additional cornstarch. Spread meringue on circle. Place in 400-degree oven. Reduce temperature to 150 degrees. Bake for 1 hour and 20 minutes. Let cool in closed oven. Peel off paper; place on serving dish. Top with whipped cream and fruit.

Janice Brennand
Alpha Zeta, Victoria, British Columbia, Canada

COMPANY CHRISTMAS COOKIES

2 c. shortening
2 c. sugar
1 tsp. soda
1 tbsp. corn syrup
3 eggs
1 c. chopped nuts
1 c. chopped dates
1 c. chopped maraschino cherries
5 c. flour
2 tsp. vanilla extract

Cream shortening and sugar. Mix in remaining ingredients. Shape into 3 or 4 long rolls. Wrap in waxed paper. Chill; slice. Bake on greased cookie sheet at 325 degrees for 15 minutes. Yield: 8-10 dozen.

Karilyn Tevebaugh
Xi Epsilon Rho, Perry, Oklahoma

CHRISTMAS BALL COOKIES

Flour
2/3 c. butter, softened
1 c. sugar
2 eggs
2 tsp. vanilla extract
1/4 tsp. salt
1/2 c. finely chopped walnuts
Cherry and mint jelly

Sift flour 4 times; measure 2 cups. Cream butter and 1/2 cup sugar. Beat in 1 egg white and 2 egg yolks. Stir in vanilla, salt and flour. Shape into 1/2 to 3/4-inch balls. Dip into beaten egg white. Roll in mixture of walnuts and 1/2 cup sugar. Make small depression in center using handle of wooden spoon. Fill with jelly. Bake at 300 degrees for 12 to 15 minutes. Yield: 5-7 dozen.

Diane Elder
Xi Xi Delta, Long Beach, California

COCONUT CHEWS

1/2 c. butter, softened
1 1/4 c. flour
3 tbsp. sugar
2 eggs, slightly beaten
3/4 c. sugar
1/2 tsp. baking powder
1/2 tsp. salt
1 tsp. vanilla extract
1 1/3 c. flaked coconut
1/2 c. chopped maraschino cherries
1/4 c. chopped walnuts

Mix butter, 1 cup flour and sugar. Press into 9-inch square pan. Bake at 350 degrees for 25 minutes. Mix 1/4 cup flour and remaining ingredients. Spoon over baked layer. Bake at 350 degrees for 35 minutes. Cut into bars while warm. Yield: 2 dozen.

Margaret Burton
Laureate Beta Phi, Modesto, California

WAFFLE COOKIES

1 c. butter
4 sq. unsweetened chocolate, melted
4 eggs
1 1/2 c. sugar
2 c. flour
2 tsp. vanilla extract
1 recipe chocolate frosting

Combine butter and chocolate; stir until butter melts. Beat in eggs and sugar. Stir in flour and vanilla. Drop by teaspoonfuls onto hot waffle iron. Bake for 1 minute. Top with chocolate frosting. Garnish with colored sugar or chopped nuts. Yield: 5-6 dozen.

Peg Kilkus
Mu, Winona, Minnesota

PASQUATAS

2 c. shortening
8 eggs
2 c. sugar
2 1/2 tsp. salt
2 c. milk
4 tsp. vanilla extract
1 tbsp. aniseed
8 c. sifted flour
2 tbsp. baking powder

Mix ingredients in order listed. Shape into holiday shapes. Bake at 350 degrees for 10 minutes or until lightly browned. Brush with tinted frosting made of confectioners' sugar and milk. Yield: 6-7 dozen.

Colleen Lord
Kappa Omicron, E. Stroudsburg, Pennsylvania

MERRY CHERRY BARS

1 c. butter, softened
1 c. sugar
1 egg
1/2 tsp. almond extract
2 c. flour
1/4 tsp. salt
3/4 c. coarsely chopped red candied cherries
1/3 c. coarsely chopped green M and M's plain chocolate candies
1 c. sifted confectioners' sugar

Cream butter and sugar. Blend in egg and flavoring. Add combined flour and salt; mix well. Stir in 1/2 cup cherries. Spread in greased jelly roll pan. Sprinkle with 1/4 cup cherries and candies. Bake at 300 degrees for 30 to 35 minutes. Cool. Mix confectioners' sugar and 5 teaspoons warm water until smooth. Drizzle over cookies. Cut into bars.

Photograph for this recipe on page 123.

NUTTY BUTTERY GEMS

1 c. flour
1/2 c. butter, softened
1/4 c. sugar
1/4 tsp. salt
1 egg, separated
2 tbsp. rum
2/3 c. coarsely chopped pecans
24 whole candied cherries

Combine flour, butter, sugar, salt, egg yolk and 1 tablespoon rum; mix well. Chill, covered, until firm. Beat egg white with remaining 1 tablespoon rum until foamy. Shape dough into 3/4-inch balls. Dip into egg white mixture; roll in pecans. Place 2 inches apart on cookie sheet. Press cherry into each cookie. Bake at 350 degrees for 13 to 15 minutes. Cool on wire rack. Yield: 2 dozen.

Photograph for this recipe on page 123.

SUGAR PLUM COOKIE TREE

1 1/2 c. butter
3 c. sugar
3 eggs, beaten
5 tsp. vanilla extract
6 c. flour
4 1/2 tsp. baking powder
1 1/2 tsp. salt
3 tbsp. milk
4 egg whites
9 c. sifted confectioners' sugar
Green food coloring
1/2 c. green M and M's plain chocolate candies, cut in half
Silver dragees

Cream butter and sugar. Blend in 3 eggs and 1 tablespoon vanilla. Beat in next 3 combined dry ingredients alternately with milk. Divide dough into 6 portions. Chill, wrapped, until firm. Roll each 1/8 inch thick on cookie sheet. Cut out 2 cookies from each of 9 graduated star patterns. Remove excess dough. Chill. Roll to 1/4-inch thickness. Cut out three 3-inch circles, eight 2-inch circles and five 1 1/2-inch circles. Bake at 350 degrees for 10 to 12 minutes. Cut 3/4 to 1-inch hole in center of each star and circle except in 1 small star and circle. Cool on wire rack. Beat egg whites until foamy. Add confectioners' sugar gradually. Add 2 teaspoons vanilla and 1 tablespoon water at a time, beating until of spreading consistency. Reserve 1 1/2 cups glaze; cover with damp cloth. Add green food coloring to remaining glaze; mix well. Frost each star and circle with green glaze; let dry. Drizzle white glaze over edges of each star; decorate star with candies and silver dragees, securing with additional glaze. Secure 12-inch long 1/2-inch wooden dowel in center of 1/2 inch thick 10-inch wooden circle. Frost top and side of base with white glaze; let dry. Slip largest star over dowel followed by largest circle. Alternate stars and circles in order of decreasing size, ending with smallest star. Top with solid star or circle.

Photograph for this recipe on page 123.

MARVEL BARS

1/2 c. butter
1 c. packed light brown sugar
1 egg
2 tbsp. orange juice
1 1/2 c. flour
1 tsp. baking powder
1/2 tsp. salt
1/4 tsp. soda
1 c. quick-cooking oats
1/2 c. chopped nuts
2/3 c. chopped M and M's plain chocolate candies
1/2 c. orange marmalade
1/4 c. flaked coconut

Cream butter and brown sugar. Blend in egg and orange juice. Add mixture of flour, baking powder, salt and soda; mix well. Stir in oats, 1/4 cup nuts and 1/3 cup candies. Spread half the dough over bottom of greased 9 x 13-inch baking pan. Spread mixture of marmalade, 1/4 cup nuts and coconut over top. Drop remaining dough by rounded teaspoonfuls over marmalade mixture. Sprinkle with 1/3 cup candies. Bake at 350 degrees for 25 minutes or until golden brown. Cut into bars when cool.

Photograph for this recipe on page 123.

TASSIE COOKIES

1 c. melted butter
1 8-oz. package cream cheese, softened
2 c. flour
2 tbsp. sugar
Chopped nuts
3 c. packed brown sugar
4 eggs
2 tsp. vanilla extract

Mix 3/4 cup butter, cream cheese, flour and sugar. Chill for 1 hour. Shape into balls. Press over bottom and sides of miniature muffin cups. Sprinkle 1/2 teaspoon nuts into each. Mix brown sugar, 1/4 cup melted butter, eggs and vanilla. Fill muffin cups 2/3 full. Sprinkle with nuts. Bake at 350 degrees for 30 minutes.

Lynda Bohn
Epsilon Nu, Centreville, Virginia

RUSSIAN TEA CAKES

1 c. butter, softened
Confectioners' sugar
1 tsp. vanilla extract
2 1/4 c. flour
1/4 tsp. salt
3/4 c. finely chopped pecans

Cream butter and 1/2 cup sifted confectioners' sugar. Stir in vanilla. Mix in sifted dry ingredients. Stir in pecans. Chill. Shape into 1-inch balls. Bake on cookie sheet at 350 degrees until set. Do not brown. Roll warm cookies in confectioners' sugar; cool. Roll in confectioners' sugar.

Carol Lang
Xi Gamma Pi, Colorado Springs, Colorado

SUGAR AND SPICE SNAPS

3/4 c. butter, softened
1 c. sugar
1 egg
1/4 c. molasses
2 c. flour
2 tsp. soda
1 tsp. cinnamon
1/2 tsp. nutmeg
1/4 tsp. salt
Sifted confectioners' sugar

Cream butter and sugar. Blend in egg and molasses. Add mixture of flour, soda, cinnamon, nutmeg and salt; mix well. Chill, covered, until firm. Shape into 3/4-inch balls; place 2 inches apart on greased cookie sheet. Bake at 350 degrees for 8 minutes. Sprinkle warm cookies heavily with confectioners' sugar. Yield: 6 dozen.

Photograph for this recipe on page 123.

SOUR CREAM-APPLE PIE

Sugar
Flour
2 c. finely chopped apples
1/2 tsp. salt
1 c. sour cream
1 egg, beaten
1/2 tsp. vanilla extract
1 9-in. unbaked pie shell
1/4 c. butter
1/4 tsp. cinnamon

Combine 3/4 cup sugar and 2 tablespoons flour; add apples. Add salt, sour cream, egg and vanilla; mix well. Pour into pie shell. Bake at 400 degrees for 15 minutes. Reduce temperature to 325 degrees. Bake for 45 minutes longer. Remove from oven. Combine 1/3 cup sugar, 1/3 cup flour and cinnamon; add butter. Sprinkle over pie. Bake for about 10 minutes longer. Yield: 6-8 servings.

Cheryl Ulrickson
Xi Alpha, West Fargo, North Dakota

FRESH CRANBERRY-WHIPPED CREAM PIE

2 c. cranberries
1/2 orange
1 1/4 c. sugar
1 env. unflavored gelatin
2 egg whites
1/4 tsp. salt
1/2 c. whipping cream, whipped
1 tsp. vanilla extract
1 baked pie shell

Put cranberries and orange through food chopper. Add 1 cup sugar. Soften gelatin in 1/4 cup cold water; dissolve over hot water. Mix into cranberry mixture. Chill until thickened. Beat egg whites and salt until soft peaks form. Add remaining 1/4 cup sugar gradually, beating until stiff. Fold into cranberry mixture with whipped cream and vanilla. Spoon into pie shell. Chill until firm. Garnish with additional whipped cream.

Linda Kelso
Alpha Pi, Maple Grove, Minnesota

WHITE CHRISTMAS PIE

1 c. sugar
1/4 c. flour
1 env. unflavored gelatin
1/2 tsp. salt
1 3/4 c. milk
3/4 tsp. vanilla extract
1/4 tsp. almond flavoring
3 egg whites
1/4 tsp. cream of tartar
1/2 c. whipping cream, whipped
1 c. shredded coconut
1 baked 9-in. pie shell

Combine 1/2 cup sugar, flour, gelatin and salt in saucepan. Stir in milk gradually. Boil for 1 minute, stirring constantly. Cool in pan of cold water until thickened. Stir in flavorings. Beat egg whites and cream of tartar until soft peaks form. Add remaining 1/2 cup sugar gradually, beating until stiff. Fold cooked mixture into meringue. Fold in whipped cream and coconut. Spoon into pie shell.

Kay Spikes
Xi Eta Alpha, Hugoton, Kansas

FRENCH RAISIN PIES

1 1/2 c. sugar
2 tbsp. cornmeal
1/2 tbsp. cinnamon
1/2 c. margarine, melted
1/2 tsp. allspice
3 eggs, beaten
1/2 c. raisins
1/2 c. chopped pecans
1 tbsp. vanilla extract
1 tbsp. vinegar
2 unbaked pie shells

Mix first 10 ingredients. Pour into pie shells. Bake at 300 degrees for 30 minutes.

Janis Young
Xi Alpha Omicron, Conway, Arkansas

PERFECT LEMON PIE

1 1/2 c. sugar
7 tbsp. cornstarch
3 egg yolks, slightly beaten
4 tbsp. lemon juice
1 1/2 tbsp. grated lemon rind
3 tbsp. butter
1 9-in. baked pie shell
1 recipe meringue

Combine sugar and cornstarch in top of double boiler. Add 1 1/2 cups boiling water; cook over low heat until thick, stirring constantly. Place over hot water in double boiler. Cook for 10 minutes longer, stirring constantly. Add small amount of hot mixture to beaten eggs; add egg mixture to hot mixture, stirring constantly. Add lemon juice, rind and butter, stirring until blended. Remove from heat. Cool. Pour into pie shell. Top with meringue, sealing to edges. Bake at 350 degrees for 15 to 20 minutes or until brown.

Otha Neckels
Preceptor Gamma Xi, Santa Cruz, California

DANISH ALMOND-RICE PUDDING

1 c. long grain rice
1 qt. milk
1/2 tsp. salt
1 env. unflavored gelatin
1 to 1 1/2 oz. almond flavoring
1 tsp. vanilla extract
1 c. sugar
1/2 to 3/4 c. chopped blanched almonds
2 c. whipping cream, whipped

Combine rice, milk and salt in double boiler; do not stir. Cook until rice is tender and milk is absorbed. Dissolve gelatin in 1/2 cup cold water. Mix with rice, flavorings, sugar and almonds; cool slightly. Fold in whipped cream. Serve with raspberries thickened with cornstarch.

Joan de Coninck Smith
Xi Alpha Alpha, D'Arcy, Saskatchewan, Canada

SUET PUDDING

1 tsp. soda
1 c. raisins
1 c. chopped suet
1/2 c. flour
1 c. molasses
1/3 c. sugar
2 tbsp. flour
1 egg, beaten
1 tsp. vanilla extract

Cook first 5 ingredients and 1/2 cup water in double boiler for 2 1/2 to 3 hours; stir occasionally. Mix sugar and flour into egg. Stir in 3 cups boiling water gradually. Cook until thick, stirring constantly; remove from heat. Stir in vanilla. Top suet pudding with vanilla sauce. Yield: 6-8 servings.

Ada E. Martin
Xi Delta Kappa, Champaign, Illinois

CHRISTMAS CRANBERRY STEAMED PUDDING

Butter
3 c. sugar
1/4 tsp. salt
1 c. milk
1 egg
2 c. flour
1 tbsp. baking powder
3 c. whole cranberries
1 c. cream

Cream 3 tablespoons butter, 1 cup sugar and egg together. Beat in sifted flour, baking powder and salt alternately with milk. Fold in cranberries. Pour into greased bundt pan. Bake at 350 degrees for 45 minutes. Cool for 10 minutes; remove from pan. Heat 1 cup butter, cream and 2 cups sugar until sugar is dissolved. Serve warm sauce with pudding.

Char Butler
Iota Tau, Rock Rapids, Iowa

STEAMED CRANBERRY PUDDING AND EGGNOG SAUCE

Butter
2 1/4 c. sugar
2 eggs
2 1/4 c. flour
2 1/2 tsp. baking powder
1/4 tsp. salt
1/2 c. milk
2 c. whole cranberries
1/2 c. chopped pecans
1 c. eggnog
2 tsp. rum extract

Cream 6 tablespoons butter and 3/4 cup sugar. Beat in eggs. Add sifted dry ingredients alternately with milk. Stir in cranberries and pecans. Pour into greased bundt pan; cover tightly with foil. Place in large pot. Add enough water to cover half the bundt pan. Steam for 2 to 2 1/2 hours. Heat 1 cup butter, 1 1/2 cups sugar, eggnog and flavoring until butter is melted; mix well. Serve over pudding.

Ellen Wilkinson
Xi Alpha Sigma, Chesapeake, Virginia

PRIZE PLUM PUDDING

1 1/4 c. flour
1 tsp. each cinnamon, nutmeg
1/2 tsp. each mace, cloves
1/2 tsp. salt
1 1/2 c. stale bread crumbs
1 1/2 c. shredded suet
1 c. packed brown sugar
1 c. sultana raisins
1 c. Muscatel
3/4 c. seedless raisins
1 c. currants
1 c. chopped figs (opt.)
1 1/2 c. chopped candied orange rind
3/4 c. sliced almonds
1 c. glace cherry halves
1/2 c. honey
4 eggs, beaten
1/2 c. fruit juice
1/2 to 2/3 c. milk
1/2 tsp. soda

Mix first 19 ingredients in order listed. Add soda dissolved in 1 tablespoon warm water. Fill greased molds 2/3 full. Cover tightly with foil. Steam for 4 to 5 hours. Yield: 8-10 servings.

Sherryl Nebocat
Tau, Butte, Montana

NOODLE KUGLE

1 8-oz. carton sour cream
4 eggs
4 oz. cream cheese, softened
6 tbsp. sugar
1 lb. broad noodles, cooked
Raisins (opt.)
1 jar apricot jam
1 1/2 c. crushed cornflakes
Dash of cinnamon
1/2 stick butter, melted

Process first 3 ingredients and 1/3 cup sugar in blender. Fold into noodles and raisins. Spread in greased 10 x 12-inch baking dish. Spread jam over top. Sprinkle mixture of remaining ingredients and 2 teaspoons sugar over top. Bake at 325 degrees for 1 hour.

Margery Schopp
Preceptor Laureate Gamma, Kenmore, New York

MANDARIN ORANGE CHEESECAKE

1/2 c. melted butter
1 3/4 c. graham cracker crumbs
1/2 tsp. cinnamon
Sugar
2 8-oz. packages cream cheese, softened
2 eggs
1 tsp. vanilla extract
1 pt. sour cream
3 or 4 mandarin oranges
1 tbsp. cornstarch
1/3 c. orange juice

Combine butter, crumbs, cinnamon and 1 tablespoon sugar. Press into bottom and side of 8-inch baking pan. Bake at 350 degrees for 5 minutes. Mix cream cheese, eggs, vanilla and 1/2 cup sugar. Spoon into crust. Bake at 350 degrees for 30 minutes. Spread with mixture of sour cream and 1/4 cup sugar. Bake at 350 degrees for 15 to 20 minutes; cool. Arrange oranges over top. Mix cornstarch and 1/4 cup sugar. Stir in orange juice. Cook over medium heat until thick and clear, stirring constantly. Cool. Spoon over cheesecake.

Dereth Haag
Eta, Saskatoon, Saskatchewan, Canada

FESTIVE RUM-RAISIN CREAM

2/3 c. dark raisins
6 tbsp. dark rum
2 egg whites
2/3 c. fine sugar
1 500-ml container whipping cream
1/2 c. sweetened flaked coconut
1/2 c. chopped pecans
Red and green cherries (opt.)

Cover raisins with boiling water for a few minutes; drain. Combine raisins and rum; let stand for 1 hour. Beat egg whites until frothy. Beat in 4 tablespoons sugar gradually; continue beating until stiff peaks form. Whip cream until thick; beat in remaining sugar slowly. Combine coconut, pecans and raisin-rum mixture. Fold mixture and meringue into whipped cream. Spoon into serving bowl. Freeze until firm. Remove from freezer a few minutes before serving. Decorate with red and green cherries and additional whipped cream if desired. This recipe may be halved or doubled. Yield: 12 servings.

Joan MacDonald
Laureate Gamma, Vancouver, British Columbia, Canada

COFFEE WALNUTS

1 c. packed brown sugar
1/2 c. sugar
1/2 c. sour cream
1 tbsp. instant coffee
1 tsp. vanilla extract
3 c. walnuts

Cook first 4 ingredients to soft-ball stage; remove from heat. Stir in vanilla and walnuts. Spread on buttered baking sheet to cool. Separate walnuts. Yield: 1 quart.

Betty Gene Johnson
Preceptor Alpha Mu, San Jose, California

HOLIDAY WREATH

30 lg. marshmallows
1/2 c. butter or margarine
1 tsp. vanilla extract
2 tsp. green food coloring
3 1/2 c. cornflakes

Combine marshmallows, butter, vanilla and food coloring in top of double boiler. Heat over boiling water until marshmallows and butter melt, stirring frequently. Stir in cornflakes gradually. Drop from teaspoon onto waxed paper. Shape into 9-inch wreath with hands. Decorate with red candied cherries or red hots.

Diane Reyher
Lamar Gamma Mu, Wiley, Colorado

WONDERFUL CHRISTMAS SCENT

1 qt. pineapple juice
1 qt. apple cider
4 slices gingerroot
3 3-in. cinnamon sticks
16 whole cloves
1 tsp. allspice
1 to 2 tsp. pickling spice

Mix all ingredients with 1 quart water. Bring to a boil; simmer to fill room with Christmas scent. Add more water, if necessary. Can be reused. Do not drink.

Martha Hallman
Mu, Jackson, Tennessee

HOLIDAY SCENT RECIPE

Rind of 1/2 orange
Rind of 1/2 lemon
1 lg. stick cinnamon
6 whole cloves
2 bay leaves

Mix all ingredients with 2 cups water. Simmer for holiday scent, adding more water, if necessary. Do not drink.

Pat Moore
Xi Iota Kappa, St. Peters, Missouri

Recipes on pages 150, 151 and 152.

Gourmet Food Gifts

CRANBERRY CORDIAL

1 16-oz. package fresh cranberries, coarsely chopped	3 c. sugar
	2 c. gin

Combine all ingredients in 2-quart jar; seal. Let stand in cool place for 3 weeks, inverting daily. Strain through cheesecloth before serving. Chill in refrigerator.

Phyllis T. Zimmer
Laureate Theta, Boise, Idaho

KAHLUA

3 c. sugar	1 tbsp. vanilla extract
6 tbsp. instant coffee	3 c. vodka

Dissolve sugar in 3 cups boiling water, stirring frequently. Simmer for 45 minutes. Stir in coffee. Simmer for 15 minutes; cool. Stir in vanilla and vodka. Store in airtight container. Serve in coffee or over ice cream. Yield: 2 quarts.

Paula Wille
Alpha Zeta, Moberly, Missouri

HOT BUTTERED RUM

1 lb. butter, softened	1/2 gal. French vanilla ice cream, melted
1 16-oz. box confectioners' sugar	Rum
1 16-oz. box brown sugar	

Blend all ingredients except rum in bowl. Place 2 tablespoons sugar mixture and 1 jigger of rum in cup. Fill with boiling water. Yield: 50 servings.

Linda Schwartzberg
Xi Iota Kappa, St. Peters, Missouri

FRIENDSHIP TEA

1 18-oz. jar orange-flavored breakfast drink	1/2 c. instant tea
	1 3-oz. package apricot gelatin
1 c. sugar	2 1/2 tsp. cinnamon
1/2 c. sweetened lemonade mix	1 tsp. ground cloves

Combine all ingredients; mix well. Store in airtight container. Mix 1 1/2 tablespoons with boiling water in cup.

Sharon Johnson
Preceptor Alpha Beta, Mena, Arkansas

PEPPERMINT SCHNAPPS

2 1/2 c. sugar	1 tsp. wintergreen flavoring
1 pt. grain alcohol	
1 oz. peppermint flavoring	

Boil sugar and 11 cups water for 10 minutes; cool to room temperature. Stir in remaining ingredients. Yield: 6 1/2 pints.

Gwen Cumberland
Xi Epsilon Eta, Millersburg, Iowa

MA'S CHEESE APPLE

8 oz. American cheese, shredded, softened	2 tbsp. Worcestershire sauce
8 oz. sharp Cheddar cheese, shredded, softened	1 tbsp. Tabasco sauce
	1 clove of garlic, crushed
1 8-oz. package cream cheese, softened	1 tsp. each chili powder, paprika

Combine first 6 ingredients; mix well. Shape into apple. Roll in mixture of chili powder and paprika. Chill for several days. Garnish with parsley for stem. Yield: 20 servings.

Sue Casey
Xi Gamma Psi, Okmulgee, Oklahoma

PARTY CHEESE BALL

1 10-oz. package sharp Cheddar cheese, grated, softened	1 tbsp. each chopped green onion, green pepper
	1 tsp. lemon juice
1 8-oz. package cream cheese, softened	2 tsp. Worcestershire sauce
1 tbsp. chopped pimento	1/2 c. chopped pecans

Combine all ingredients except pecans; mix well. Chill for 30 minutes. Shape into ball. Roll in pecans. Serve with crackers.

Shirley M. John
Gamma Theta, Jacksonville, North Carolina

CEREAL PARTY MIX

1 1/2 lb. almond bark, melted	2 c. Rice Chex
	2 c. Cheerios
3 tbsp. oil	1 12-oz. can mixed nuts
1 13-oz. box Trix cereal	1 8-oz. package pretzels

Mix melted almond bark and oil. Pour over cereal, nuts and pretzels in 9 x 13-inch pan; mix well.

T. Ann Kerschner
Preceptor Beta Mu, McPherson, Kansas

KWIK SNACKS

1 pkg. buttermilk dressing mix	1 tbsp. lemon pepper
1 c. oil	2 12-oz. packages soup crackers
1 tbsp. dillweed	

Mix all ingredients except crackers. Pour over crackers in serving bowl; mix well.

Peggy Larrabee
Preceptor Delta, Belle Fourche, South Dakota

SEASONED OYSTER CRACKERS

1 tsp. each garlic salt, lemon-flavored pepper, dillweed	1 pkg. buttermilk dressing mix
1 c. oil	2 pkg. oyster crackers

Mix all ingredients except crackers. Pour over crackers in bowl; toss to coat. Let stand, tightly covered, overnight. Serve with soup, chili or stew.

Joan Gilman
Xi Alpha Beta, Council Bluffs, Iowa

CANDY CANE COFFEE CAKE

2 pkg. dry yeast	6 c. (about) flour
2 c. sour cream	1 1/2 c. finely chopped dried apricots
Butter	
1/3 c. sugar	1 1/2 c. finely chopped maraschino cherries
2 eggs	
2 tsp. salt	Confectioners' sugar glaze

Dissolve yeast in 1/2 cup warm water. Heat sour cream until lukewarm. Combine with yeast mixture, 1/4 cup butter, sugar, eggs, salt and 2 cups flour; beat until smooth. Mix in enough remaining flour to make soft dough. Knead on floured surface for 10 minutes. Place in greased bowl, turning to grease surface. Let rise, covered, for 1 hour or until doubled in bulk. Roll into three 6 x 15-inch rectangles. Place on 3 greased baking sheets. Make 2-inch cuts at 1/2-inch intervals on long sides. Spread mixture of apricots and cherries down center of each rectangle. Crisscross strips to cover fruit. Stretch dough to 22 inches; shape into candy cane. Bake at 375 degrees for 15 to 20 minutes. Brush with melted butter and drizzle confectioners' sugar glaze over top. Garnish with additional cherries.

Paulette Twast
Gamma Sigma, Fernie, British Columbia, Canada

MERRY CHRISTMAS COFFEE CAKE

Sugar	4 c. flour
1/3 c. shortening	1/4 c. butter, softened
1/2 tsp. salt	1/4 c. bread crumbs
1 c. scalded milk	1/2 c. finely chopped nuts
1 cake yeast	1 1/2 tsp. cinnamon
2 eggs, well beaten	30 candied cherry halves
1/2 tsp. vanilla extract	Confectioners' sugar glaze

Mix 1/3 cup sugar, shortening, salt and milk. Stir in yeast dissolved in 1/4 cup lukewarm water, eggs, vanilla and 3 3/4 cups flour. Let rise, covered, until doubled in bulk. Cut butter into mixture of 1/4 cup flour, 1/2 cup sugar, crumbs, nuts and cinnamon. Drop dough by tablespoonfuls into crumb mixture; roll into ball. Arrange 16 balls on each of 2 greased baking sheets in shape of tree, using 15 for each tree and 1 for base. Let rise until doubled. Bake at 350 degrees for 25 minutes. Decorate warm coffee cakes with cherries and glaze.

Dorothy Armstrong
Xi Gamma, Miles City, Montana

APRICOT-PECAN BREAD

1 6-oz. package dried apricots	1/4 tsp. soda
	1 tsp. salt
2 tbsp. butter, softened	1 egg
1 c. sugar	1/2 c. orange juice
2 c. sifted flour	1/2 c. pecans
2 tsp. baking powder	

Soak apricots in water to cover for 30 minutes; drain and chop. Cream butter and sugar. Mix in sifted dry ingredients alternately with mixture of egg, 1/4 cup water and orange juice. Stir in pecans and apricots. Let stand in greased and floured loaf pan for 20 minutes. Bake at 350 degrees for 55 to 65 minutes. Remove from pan immediately.

Helen L. Edwards
Xi Gamma, Lawrence, Kansas

GERMAN STOLLEN

1 pkg. dry yeast	1/4 c. each citron, candied cherries, chopped raisins
1/2 c. sugar	
1/2 tsp. salt	
4 eggs	2 tbsp. grated lemon rind
Butter, softened	1 1/2 c. confectioners' sugar
3 1/2 c. flour	
1/2 c. chopped almonds	1 1/2 tbsp. milk

Dissolve yeast in 3/4 cup warm water in mixer bowl. Add sugar, salt, 3 eggs and 1 egg yolk, 1/2 cup softened butter and 1 1/2 cups flour. Beat at low speed for 30 seconds. Beat at medium speed for 10 minutes. Stir in remaining flour, almonds, fruit and lemon rind. Let rise, covered, for 1 1/2 hours; stir down. Chill, tightly covered, for 8 hours. Roll into two 7 x 10-inch ovals. Spread 3 tablespoons softened butter over each. Fold in half lengthwise, sealing edges; place on greased baking sheet. Brush with mixture of beaten egg white and 1 tablespoon water. Let rise for 45 to 60 minutes. Bake at 375 degrees for 20 to 25 minutes. Frost warm loaves with mixture of confectioners' sugar and milk. Garnish with almond halves, additional cherries and citron to resemble poinsettias.

Lorraine L. Kirkpatrick
Xi Eta Kappa, Barstow, California

SPICED BANANA-RAISIN LOAVES

3 1/4 c. flour	1 1/3 c. sugar
1/4 c. toasted wheat germ	4 eggs
1 tbsp. baking powder	4 bananas
2 tsp. each cinnamon, ginger	1/4 c. milk
1 tsp. each salt, nutmeg	2 15-oz. packages light raisins
1/2 tsp. soda	6 oz. pecans, coarsely chopped
1 1/2 c. butter, softened	

Combine first 8 dry ingredients. Cream butter and sugar. Beat in eggs 1 at a time. Puree bananas with milk in blender. Add alternately with flour mixture to creamed mixture. Stir in raisins and pecans. Spoon into 6 greased and floured 3 x 5-inch loaf pans. Bake at 325 degrees for 45 minutes. Cool in pans on rack for 10 minutes. Cool completely. Store in freezer. Garnish with light corn syrup and candied fruits.

Photograph for this recipe on page 4.

FROSTED WALNUT ROLL

1 cake yeast, mashed	1/2 tsp. salt
1 1/4 c. sugar	1 tsp. vanilla extract
1 c. sour cream	1 lb. walnuts, finely chopped
5 eggs, separated	Confectioners' sugar
Butter, softened	
4 c. flour, sifted	

Mix yeast with 1 tablespoon sugar. Add sour cream. Stir into beaten egg yolks. Cut 2 sticks butter into sifted mixture of flour, 3 tablespoons sugar and salt. Blend in sour cream mixture. Chill overnight. Roll into three 1/4-inch thick rectangles. Spread with butter. Fold vanilla and mixture of 1 cup sugar and walnuts into stiffly beaten egg whites. Spread on rectangles. Roll as for jelly roll; flatten. Let rise on cookie sheet for 1 1/2 to 2 hours. Bake at 350 degrees until browned. Frost with icing made of 1 tablespoon butter, confectioners' sugar and water.

Sharon Pusz
Xi Beta Nu, North Canton, Ohio

BRAZIL NUT BREAD

2 c. flour	1 lb. Brazil nuts
1 1/2 c. sugar	1/2 lb. English walnuts
1/2 tsp. salt	1/2 lb. pecans
1 tsp. baking powder	1/2 c. cherry juice
2 lb. dates	1 tsp. vanilla extract
1 10-oz. jar maraschino cherries	4 eggs, well beaten
	3 tbsp. shortening, melted

Mix sifted dry ingredients, fruit, nuts, cherry juice and vanilla. Stir in eggs and shortening. Bake in 3 loaf pans lined with greased waxed paper at 300 degrees for 1 1/2 hours. Freeze for easier slicing. Yield: 3 loaves.

Connie Maher
Xi Delta Mu, Hawarden, Iowa

SPICED BRANDY-NUT LOAF

1 pkg. quick nut bread mix	Dash of cloves
1 tbsp. flour	1/2 tsp. nutmeg
Brandy	1/2 c. butter, softened
1 egg	1/2 c. confectioners' sugar
1/2 tsp. cinnamon	

Mix bread mix, flour, 2/3 cup water, 1/3 cup Brandy, egg, cinnamon, cloves and 1/4 teaspoon nutmeg until just moistened. Bake in greased and floured 5 x 9-inch loaf pan at 350 degrees for 40 to 50 minutes. Cool in pan for 15 minutes; remove to wire rack. Serve with butter blended with confectioners' sugar, 1/4 teaspoon nutmeg and 1 tablespoon Brandy.

Joan Stockman
Laureate Omega, Arvada, Colorado

STRAWBERRY JAM-NUT BREAD

1 c. butter, softened	1 tsp. salt
1 1/2 c. sugar	3/4 tsp. cream of tartar
1 tsp. vanilla extract	1/2 tsp. soda
1/4 tsp. lemon juice	1/2 c. buttermilk
4 eggs	1 c. strawberry jam
3 c. flour	1 c. chopped nuts

Cream butter, sugar, vanilla and lemon juice. Beat in eggs 1 at a time. Mix in sifted dry ingredients alternately with mixture of buttermilk and jam. Stir in nuts. Bake in 2 greased 5 x 9-inch loaf pans at 350 degrees for 55 minutes. Yield: 2 loaves.

Barbara Colvin
Xi Delta Delta, Russell, Kentucky

EASY ONE-RISE CARAMEL ROLLS

1 c. packed brown sugar	1 tsp. salt
1 c. whipping cream	1 egg
1 pkg. dry yeast	Margarine
3/4 c. sugar	2 tsp. cinnamon
3 1/2 c. bread flour	1 c. chopped walnuts

Mix brown sugar and cream in 10 x 14-inch baking pan. Dissolve yeast in 1 cup warm water. Stir in 1/4 cup sugar. Mix in half the flour, salt, egg and 2 tablespoons melted margarine. Knead in remaining flour until smooth and elastic. Roll on floured surface into 11 x 18-inch rectangle. Mix 1/2 cup sugar, cinnamon, walnuts and 1/2 cup softened margarine. Spread over dough; roll as for jelly roll. Cut into 12 rolls; arrange in prepared pan. Preheat oven to 200 degrees. Turn oven off. Let rolls rise in oven with pan of hot water on bottom rack until doubled in bulk; remove pan of water. Bake at 375 degrees for 20 minutes.

Gail Cassidy
Xi Lambda Iota, Cross City, Florida

Gourmet Food Gifts / 149

APRICOT FUDGE

2/3 c. whipping cream
1/4 c. light corn syrup
1 lb. confectioners' sugar
1/4 tsp. salt
1/2 c. marshmallow creme
3 tbsp. butter
1/2 c. dried apricots, chopped
1 tsp. vanilla extract
1 c. chopped walnuts

Cook cream, corn syrup, confectioners' sugar and salt over medium heat until sugar is dissolved, stirring frequently. Cook to soft-ball stage. Add marshmallow creme, butter and apricots. Do not stir. Let stand for 15 minutes. Add vanilla and walnuts. Beat until creamy. Spoon into 8 x 8-inch dish. Chill in refrigerator. Cut into squares.

Ann Neale
Laureate Alpha Delta, Amarillo, Texas

BOURBON BALLS

1 16-oz. package semisweet chocolate chips, melted
1/2 c. sugar
1/3 c. Bourbon
2 1/2 c. finely crushed vanilla wafers
1/2 c. finely chopped walnuts
Confectioners' sugar

Mix chocolate and sugar until smooth. Blend in Bourbon. Combine with mixture of crumbs and walnuts; mix well. Shape into 1-inch balls. Roll in confectioners' sugar. Store in airtight container for several days, sprinkling with additional Bourbon if desired. Yield: 1 1/2 dozen.

Gladys Koller
Laureate Beta, Salt Lake City, Utah

PECAN CARAMELS

2 c. packed light brown sugar
1 c. light corn syrup
1/2 c. margarine
1 pt. whipping cream
1 c. pecans

Bring brown sugar, syrup and margarine to a boil. Stir in cream gradually. Cook to soft-ball stage; remove from heat. Stir in pecans. Pour into buttered 8 x 13-inch dish. Cut into squares when cool. Yield: 5 dozen.

Sally Jo Marquis
Xi Delta Phi, Blue Springs, Missouri

CHERRY MASH BALLS

1 box confectioners' sugar
1 box cherry frosting mix
1/4 c. melted margarine
2 tsp. vanilla extract
1/2 can sweetened condensed milk
1/2 to 1 jar maraschino cherries, chopped
1 12-oz. package milk chocolate chips
1 to 1 1/2 oz. paraffin, chopped
1/2 lb. peanuts, ground (opt.)

Combine first 6 ingredients; mix well. Chill. Shape into small balls. Freeze. Melt chips and paraffin in double boiler. Stir in peanuts. Dip candy into chocolate to coat. Cool on waxed paper. Yield: 3 pounds.

Alice Keller
Laureate Delta, West Des Moines, Iowa

CHOCOLATE-COVERED CHERRIES

1 lb. bitter chocolate
1/2 oz. paraffin
1 16-oz. box confectioners' sugar
3 tbsp. evaporated milk
1 tsp. vanilla extract
1 lg. jar maraschino cherries with stems, drained

Melt chocolate and paraffin in double boiler; cool slightly. Mix confectioners' sugar, evaporated milk and vanilla. Shape into half-dollar sized circles. Wrap around cherry. Dip by stem into chocolate to coat. Cool on waxed paper for 2 hours. Yield: 5 dozen.

Marian Hart
Alpha Tau, Page, Arizona

VELVET CHOCOLATE FUDGE

4 1/2 c. sugar
1 tbsp. cornstarch
1/2 tsp. salt
1 lg. can evaporated milk
1/2 c. melted butter
1 16-oz. package marshmallows
1 8-oz. milk chocolate candy bar, broken
1 12-oz. package semisweet chocolate chips
2 tsp. vanilla extract
2 c. chopped walnuts

Mix sugar, cornstarch and salt in 5-quart saucepan. Stir in evaporated milk and butter. Bring to a boil over medium heat, stirring constantly. Boil for 8 minutes, stirring frequently; remove from heat. Stir in marshmallows, candy bar, chocolate chips and vanilla. Beat until smooth. Stir in walnuts. Pour into 10 x 15-inch pan. Cut into 1 1/4-inch squares when cool. Yield: 8 dozen.

Dee McBride
Nu Delta, Burlington, Kansas

CRYSTAL CANDY

2 c. sugar
1/2 c. light corn syrup
Dash of salt
Red or green food coloring
4 to 6 drops of oil of cinnamon

Cook first 3 ingredients and 1/2 cup water in heavy saucepan to 290 degrees on candy thermometer. Stir in food coloring and flavoring. Drop by teaspoonfuls onto cookie sheet. May substitute oil of peppermint or wintergreen for oil of cinnamon.

Donis Ruth Eisiminger
Xi Zeta Epsilon, Savannah, Missouri

PEANUT BUTTER FUDGE PINWHEELS

1 c. peanut butter-flavored chips
1 can sweetened condensed milk
1 c. semisweet chocolate chips
1 tsp. vanilla extract
1/2 c. chocolate sprinkles

Melt peanut butter chips in half the condensed milk over low heat, stirring occasionally. Spread into 10 x 12-inch rectangle on cookie sheet lined with greased foil. Let stand for 30 minutes. Melt chocolate chips in remaining condensed milk, stirring frequently; remove from heat. Stir in vanilla; cool slightly. Spread over peanut butter layer. Let stand for 30 minutes. Roll as for jelly roll. Coat with sprinkles. Store, tightly wrapped, in refrigerator for 2 weeks or less. Bring to room temperature before cutting into 1/4-inch slices. Yield: 4 dozen.

Ruth Fuller Lature
Xi Alpha Tau, Hopkinsville, Kentucky

PEPPERMINT FUDGE

3 c. sugar
3/4 c. margarine, melted
2/3 c. evaporated milk
1 12-oz. package semisweet chocolate chips
1 7-oz. jar marshmallow creme
1/2 c. crushed peppermint candy
1 tsp. vanilla extract

Bring sugar, margarine and evaporated milk to a boil in 3-quart saucepan, stirring constantly. Boil for 5 minutes, stirring constantly; remove from heat. Stir in chocolate chips until melted. Beat in marshmallow creme, candy and vanilla until well blended. Pour into greased 9 x 13-inch pan. Cool to room temperature and cut into squares. Yield: 3 pounds.

Linda Todd
Xi Alpha Beta, Coldwater, Michigan

MICROWAVE ALMOND TOFFEE

3/4 c. butter
1 c. packed brown sugar
3/4 c. finely chopped almonds
1/2 c. semisweet chocolate chips

Microwave butter and brown sugar in glass bowl on High for 1 minute; beat until smooth. Microwave for 4 minutes longer. Stir in 1/2 cup almonds. Microwave for 2 minutes or until thick. Beat with wire whisk. Pour into 8 x 8-inch dish lined with buttered foil. Sprinkle chocolate chips over top. Let stand, covered with plastic wrap, for 4 minutes. Spread melted chocolate over top. Sprinkle with 1/4 cup almonds. Chill until chocolate is firm. Peel off foil. Break into pieces. Store, tightly covered, in refrigerator. Yield: 1 pound.

Vonita Tast
Upsilon Psi, Lake Elsinore, California

DINNER MINTS

1 lg. can evaporated milk
4 c. sugar
1/2 c. margarine
2 tsp. mint extract
1 12-oz. package chocolate chips
1 7-oz. jar marshmallow creme

Cook evaporated milk, sugar and margarine for 6 minutes, stirring constantly; remove from heat. Stir in remaining ingredients. Let stand until thick. Drop by teaspoonfuls onto waxed paper. Store in refrigerator when set. May be frozen. Yield: 8 dozen.

Bernadine Nelson
Xi Gamma, Miles City, Montana

FOUR'S CANDY

1 c. dark corn syrup
1 c. sugar
1 c. packed brown sugar
2 sticks butter
2 c. evaporated milk
1 tbsp. vanilla extract
1 lb. pecans, chopped
Dipping chocolate, melted

Bring first 4 ingredients and 1 cup evaporated milk to a boil, stirring constantly. Add remaining evaporated milk gradually, stirring constantly. Cook to hard-ball stage; remove from heat. Stir in vanilla and pecans. Pour into buttered pan. Cut into squares; dip in chocolate. Yield: 5 pounds.

Freddie E. Thomas
Laureate Beta Delta, Odessa, Texas

ENGLISH TOFFEE

2 sticks butter
1 c. sugar
1 tsp. light corn syrup
1 c. finely chopped almonds
Salt to taste
1/8 tsp. soda
1 lg. chocolate candy bar, melted
1 c. chopped walnuts

Cook first 5 ingredients over medium heat to hard-crack stage; remove from heat. Stir in soda. Pour half the melted chocolate into greased 9 x 13-inch pan. Spread toffee over top. Spread remaining chocolate over top. Press in walnuts. Break into pieces when cool.

Marty Woodward
Alpha Beta, Rocky Ford, Colorado

CONFETTI CUTOUTS

2/3 c. butter, softened
1 1/2 c. sugar
2 eggs
1 1/2 tsp. almond extract
3 1/2 c. flour
2 1/2 tsp. baking powder
1/2 tsp. salt
1 tbsp. milk
1/4 c. shortening
1 1/2 c. M and M's plain chocolate candies

Combine butter and sugar; blend in eggs and flavoring. Beat in combined dry ingredients alternately with milk.

Gourmet Food Gifts / 151

Chill for several hours. Roll out 1/8 inch thick on floured surface. Cut with floured 2 1/2-inch cookie cutters. Cut out small design in center of half the cookies. Bake on cookie sheet at 400 degrees for 7 to 9 minutes. Cool. Melt shortening. Add candies. Cook over very low heat, stirring constantly, until chocolate is almost melted and pieces of color coating remain. Cool slightly. Spread solid cookies with warm filling; top with cutout cookies. Chill for 30 minutes. Yield: 3 dozen.

Photograph for this recipe on page 145.

CHOCOLATE CHIP COOKIE WREATH

1/2 c. margarine, softened	1 1/4 c. flour
1/2 c. packed brown sugar	1/2 tsp. each soda, salt
1/3 c. sugar	1 6-oz. package
1 egg	chocolate chips
1 1/2 tsp. vanilla extract	1/2 c. chopped nuts

Invert two 4-inch ovenproof bowls in centers of two 10-inch pizza pans lined with foil. Grease outside of bowls. Cream margarine, sugars, egg and vanilla. Blend in flour, soda and salt. Stir in chocolate chips and nuts. Spread dough in each pan to within 1/2 inch of bowl and edge. Bake at 375 degrees for 10 to 15 minutes. Remove bowls carefully. Cool in pan before removing. Decorate as desired.

Lorrie Spidel
Alpha Kappa, Angola, Indiana

CHOCOLATE CRUNCH COOKIES

1 c. butter, softened	1 tsp. salt
1 1/2 c. packed light brown sugar	3/4 tsp. soda
2 eggs	1 1/2 c. M and M's plain chocolate candies
1 1/2 tsp. vanilla extract	1/2 c. chopped nuts (opt.)
2 1/2 c. flour	

Cream butter and brown sugar. Blend in eggs with vanilla. Add combined dry ingredients; mix well. Add candies and nuts; mix well. Drop by rounded teaspoonfuls onto greased cookie sheet. Bake at 375 degrees for 9 to 11 minutes. Press 3 additional candies firmly into top of each cookie. Cool. Yield: 5 dozen.

Photograph for this recipe on page 145.

FESTIVE FUDGE-FILLED BARS

2 c. quick-cooking oats	1 16-oz. package
1 1/2 c. flour	M and M's plain
1 c. chopped nuts	chocolate candies
1 c. packed brown sugar	1 can sweetened condensed
1 tsp. each soda, salt	milk
1 c. melted margarine	1/2 c. flaked coconut
2 tbsp. shortening	(opt.)

Combine oats, flour, nuts, brown sugar, soda and salt; mix well. Stir in margarine. Reserve 1 1/2 cups; press remaining crumb mixture onto bottom of greased jelly roll pan. Bake at 375 degrees for 10 minutes. Melt shortening. Add 1 1/2 cups candies. Cook over very low heat until candies melt, stirring constantly. Remove from heat; stir in condensed milk. Spread over partially baked crust to within 1/2 inch of edge. Combine reserved crumb mixture, coconut and remaining candies. Sprinkle over chocolate mixture. Bake for 20 minutes or until light brown. Cut into bars when cool.

Photograph for this recipe on page 145.

RUSSIAN PEPPERNUTS

3 1/2 c. flour	2 eggs
1 c. packed brown sugar	3/4 c. shortening
1 c. sugar	3 tbsp. sour cream
Pinch of nutmeg	1 tsp. vanilla extract
1 tsp. soda	1 c. chopped peanuts

Combine dry ingredients in bowl. Stir in remaining ingredients. Shape into thick ropes 12 inches long. Chill in refrigerator. Cut into small pieces. Bake on cookie sheet at 350 degrees for 12 minutes.

Mildred O'Banion
Xi Preceptor, Baxter Springs, Kansas

SINFUL SESAMES

Graham crackers	1/2 c. sugar
1/2 c. each margarine, butter	1/2 c. chopped nuts
	1/4 c. sesame seed

Line cookie sheet with graham crackers. Boil margarine, butter and sugar for 2 minutes. Pour over graham crackers. Spoon mixture of nuts and sesame seed over top. Bake at 350 degrees for 10 minutes. Separate crackers; remove immediately to waxed paper to cool.

Donna C. Luse
Preceptor Alpha Sigma, Marion, Ohio

SPRINGERLE COOKIES

4 eggs, beaten	1/4 tsp. anise oil
2 c. sugar	4 c. flour
1 tsp. salt	4 tsp. baking powder
1 tbsp. butter, melted	

Mix eggs, sugar, salt, butter and anise oil. Add sifted flour and baking powder; mix well. Roll 1/4 inch thick on cookie sheet. Press design into dough. Let stand, uncovered, overnight. Bake at 275 degrees for 20 minutes. Store cookies in airtight container when cool.

Lois M. Yack
Preceptor Alpha Iota, Midland, Michigan

152 / Gourmet Food Gifts

NUT HORNS

1 lb. margarine, softened
1 lb. cream cheese, softened
3 egg yolks
Dash of salt
5 c. flour
1 c. milk
1 1/4 lb. ground walnuts
1 1/2 c. sugar
1 egg white, beaten

Mix first 5 ingredients until smooth. Shape into walnut-sized balls. Chill, covered, overnight. Roll on floured surface into 3 1/2-inch circles. Cook milk, walnuts and sugar until thick, stirring constantly. Spread 1 teaspoonful onto each circle; roll as for jelly roll. Brush with egg white. Bake on cookie sheet at 350 degrees for 20 to 25 minutes. Roll warm cookies in additional sugar.

Irene Williams
Preceptor Alpha Lambda, Tucson, Arizona

NUT ROLL COOKIES

1 c. butter, softened
2 c. sugar
3 eggs, separated
4 c. flour
4 tsp. baking powder
1/2 tsp. salt
1 c. milk
2 lb. nuts, ground
1 stick margarine, melted
1 tsp. vanilla extract
3 tbsp. (about) warm milk
Confectioners' sugar glaze

Mix butter, 1 cup sugar, egg yolks, flour, baking powder, salt and 1 cup milk until smooth. Reserve 2 cups nuts. Combine stiffly beaten egg whites, 1 cup sugar, margarine, vanilla and remaining nuts. Stir in enough warm milk to make of spreading consistency. Shape dough into small balls. Roll to 1/8 inch thick. Spread with nut filling; roll as for jelly roll. Cut into 1-inch pieces. Bake on greased baking sheet at 375 degrees for 15 minutes. Dip warm cookies in glaze and roll in reserved nuts. Yield: 10 dozen.

Linda Burchfield
Xi Iota Chi, Steubenville, Ohio

CANDIED BRANDIED CRANBERRIES

1 lb. fresh cranberries, mashed
2 1/4 c. sugar
1/4 c. Brandy

Combine cranberries and 2 cups sugar in 7 x 11-inch glass baking dish; stir until sugar is dissolved. Microwave, covered with plastic wrap, on High for 11 to 13 minutes, stirring twice. Cool. Stir in Brandy and 1/4 cup sugar. Store in refrigerator or freezer. Yield: 8 servings.

Loraine Steves
Laureate Alpha, Mesa, Arizona

BRANDIED FRUIT

1 12-oz. can sliced peaches
1 12-oz. can pineapple chunks
1 12-oz. can fruit cocktail
1 pkg. dry yeast
3 c. sugar

Combine all ingredients in glass container; mix well. Let stand, loosely covered, for 3 weeks, stirring each day. Serve over pound cake, ice cream or in cakes. Add 1 cup sugar and one 12-ounce can fruit every 2 weeks. Spoon 2 cups mixture, 1 cup sugar and one 12-ounce can fruit into jar for gift.

Ruth Heinaman
Alpha, Jacksonville, Florida

HOT PEPPER JELLY

1 1/2 c. ground hot peppers
2 1/2 c. cider vinegar
1 pkg. Sure-Jel
5 c. sugar

Bring peppers, vinegar and Sure-Jel to a boil. Stir in sugar. Cook for 5 minutes. Pour into small, hot sterilized jars; seal.

Myrtle Ropert
Preceptor Iota, Shreveport, Louisiana

WINE JELLY

2 c. Port
3 c. sugar
1 pkg. Sure-Jel
Paraffin, melted

Dissolve sugar in Port in double boiler, stirring constantly; remove from heat. Stir in Sure-Jel. Pour into hot sterilized jars. Let stand until set. Seal with paraffin.

Eleanor Collins
Preceptor Beta Tau, Broomfield, Colorado

CANDY SNOWBALLS

1 c. butter, softened
1/4 c. confectioners' sugar
1 tsp. vanilla extract
2 c. flour
1 c. chopped M and M's candies

Combine butter and confectioners' sugar; blend in vanilla. Add flour; mix well. Add candies; mix well. Chill for 30 minutes. Shape into 1-inch balls. Bake on cookie sheet at 350 degrees for 15 to 18 minutes. Press 1 additional whole candy into top of each cookie. Cool. Sprinkle lightly with additional confectioners' sugar. Yield: 4 dozen.

Photograph for this recipe on page 145.

SPRITZERS

1 c. butter, softened
2/3 c. sugar
1 egg
1/8 tsp. green food coloring
1 1/2 tsp. almond extract
3 c. flour
1/2 tsp. baking powder
M and M's plain chocolate candies, chopped

Combine butter and sugar. Blend in egg, food coloring and flavoring. Add combined flour and baking powder; mix well. Force dough through cookie press onto cookie sheet in desired shapes. Decorate with chopped candies. Bake at 400 degrees for 6 to 9 minutes. Do not brown. Yield: 6 dozen.

Photograph for this recipe on page 145.

BRANDIED FRUIT CAKE

3/4 c. canned peaches, drained	3 c. flour
3/4 c. crushed pineapple, drained	1 tsp. salt
	2 tsp. baking powder
3 c. sugar	1 tsp. cinnamon
1 pkg. dry yeast	1/2 tsp. each cloves, nutmeg
3 eggs	1 tsp. vanilla extract
1 1/4 c. oil	1 c. chopped nuts

Combine peaches, pineapple, 1 1/2 cups sugar and yeast in glass container. Let stand for 2 weeks, stirring 2 times each day. Add 1 additional cup fruit and sugar every 2 weeks. Beat eggs, oil and 1 1/2 cups sugar until smooth. Stir in sifted dry ingredients. Fold in 3 cups fruit mixture, vanilla and nuts. Bake in well-greased and floured 12-cup bundt pan at 350 degrees for 1 1/4 hours. This cake can be frozen up to 4 months.

S. Kathleen Wallace
Laureate Alpha Zeta, Jacksonville, Florida

SPICED ENGLISH FRUITCAKE

4 c. flour	1 15-oz. package light raisins
1 tbsp. cinnamon	
1 1/2 tsp. nutmeg	1 6 1/2-oz. jar glace cherries, halved
1 tsp. each mace, baking powder	
	1 c. mixed glace fruits
1/2 tsp. each salt, cloves	2 4-oz. cans slivered almonds
1 1/2 c. butter, softened	1/2 c. red currant jelly, melted
1 1-lb. package dark brown sugar	
	3 8-oz. cans almond paste
8 eggs	Confectioners' sugar
1/3 c. Brandy	2 egg whites
1 15-oz. package dark raisins	1/4 tsp. glycerin

Combine first 7 dry ingredients. Cream butter and brown sugar in mixer bowl. Beat in 4 eggs 1 at a time. Stir in remaining eggs alternately with about 1 cup flour mixture. Stir in Brandy and remaining flour mixture. Stir in raisins, fruits and almonds. Bake in greased and floured springform pan at 300 degrees for about 3 hours. Cool in pan for 30 minutes. Cool on rack. Brush top and side of cake with jelly. Roll out 2 cans almond paste on board sprinkled with confectioners' sugar into two 4 x 15-inch strips. Press onto side of cake; press seams together. Roll 1 can almond paste into 10-inch circle. Fit onto top of cake. Combine 1 pound confectioners' sugar with egg whites, 1 tablespoon water and glycerin. Beat until stiff. Spread over top and side of cake. Set cake aside until frosting is hardened. Let stand for 12 hours. Decorate with additional icing, ornaments or holly. Store, tightly covered, for 2 to 3 months.

Photograph for this recipe on page 4.

GRANDMOTHER NEWMAN'S DARK FRUITCAKE

1 lb. dates	4 c. flour
1 lb. each golden raisins, seedless raisins, currants	1 tsp. each cinnamon, cloves, allspice, mace
	1/2 tsp. ginger, nutmeg
12 figs, chopped	1 tsp. soda
1 c. mixed candied fruit	1 c. Sherry
1 c. maraschino cherries	1 tsp. vanilla extract
1/2 c. Brandy	1 c. strawberry jam
1 c. butter, softened	1 c. molasses
2 c. packed brown sugar	1/3 c. each walnuts, almonds, pecans
5 eggs, separated	

Soak dates, raisins, currants and figs in water and candied fruit and cherries in Brandy overnight; stir several times. Drain raisin mixture. Cream butter and 1 cup brown sugar. Add mixture of beaten egg yolks and 1 cup brown sugar; mix well. Beat in sifted dry ingredients alternately with mixture of Sherry and vanilla. Stir in jam, molasses, raisin and fruit mixtures and nuts. Fold in stiffly beaten egg whites. Fill greased 8-inch, 6-inch and 4-inch square cake pans lined with greased paper 3/4 full. Bake with pan of water on bottom rack at 275 degrees for 3 1/2 hours. Cool in pans on damp towel on rack for 10 to 15 minutes before removing. Wrap in foil when cool. Let ripen in airtight container for 1 week.

Ruth Elizabeth Newman Smith, President
Preceptor Theta, Athol, Nova Scotia, Canada

TINY SPICED CAKES

1 pkg. pound cake mix	1 c. coarsely chopped walnuts
1 tbsp. apple pie spice	
3/4 c. milk	2 c. confectioners' sugar
2 eggs	5 to 6 tsp. lemon juice
1 c. chopped apple	

Combine cake mix and spice in mixer bowl. Add milk and eggs. Beat, using package directions. Stir in apple and walnuts. Fill lined cupcake pans 2/3 full. Bake at 350 degrees for 20 to 25 minutes. Cool on wire racks. Blend confectioners' sugar with lemon juice. Frost cupcakes. Garnish with walnut halves and colored sugar. Store, tightly covered, for 2 weeks. Yield: 2 dozen.

Photograph for this recipe on page 4.

BOURBON POUND CAKE

1 1/2 c. raisins
2 c. mixed candied fruits
1/3 c. Bourbon
1 1/2 c. butter, softened
1 3/4 c. sugar
6 eggs, beaten
3 1/2 c. flour
1 1/2 tsp. baking powder
3/4 tsp. nutmeg
1/2 c. milk
1 1/2 c. chopped pecans

Soak raisins and fruit in Bourbon for several hours. Cream butter and sugar in mixer bowl. Add eggs; mix well. Beat in sifted dry ingredients alternately with milk. Stir in fruit mixture and pecans. Bake in greased and floured tube pan at 275 degrees for 2 hours and 10 minutes or until cake tests done. Store, wrapped in Bourbon-soaked cheese cloth, for 3 to 4 weeks.

Babs Donoho
Laureate Beta Upsilon, Chico, California

WHITE CHRISTMAS CAKE

2 lb. bleached raisins
1/2 c. white wine
1 lb. butter, softened
2 c. fructose
8 eggs
5 c. sifted cake flour
6 pkg. pineapple slices
2 lb. candied cherries
1/2 c. blanched almonds

Soak raisins in wine overnight. Cream butter and fructose. Add eggs 1 at a time with 1/4 cup flour, beating well after each addition. Coat candied fruit with 1/4 cup flour. Add raisins and 4 1/2 cups flour to creamed mixture; mix well. Stir in floured fruit and almonds. Pour into 2 loaf pans lined with waxed paper. Place pan of water on bottom rack in oven. Bake at 250 degrees for 3 hours.

Iris McVicker
Sigma, Lewisporte, Newfoundland

ZUCCHINI FRUITCAKES

3 eggs
1 c. oil
2 c. packed brown sugar
1 tbsp. vanilla extract
3 c. flour
1 tbsp. cinnamon
1 tsp. each soda, salt
1 tsp. each allspice, nutmeg, cloves
1/2 tsp. baking powder
2 c. coarsely shredded zucchini
2 c. coarsely chopped walnuts
2 c. raisins
1 c. currants
2 c. mixed candied fruit
1/2 c. Brandy (opt.)

Beat eggs, oil, brown sugar and vanilla in mixer bowl. Stir in combined dry ingredients. Fold in zucchini, walnuts and fruits. Bake in 2 greased 5 x 9-inch loaf pans at 325 degrees for 1 to 1 1/2 hours. Cool in pans on racks before removing. Spoon Brandy over warm loaves. Let ripen in refrigerator for 2 weeks before serving.

Janet Quarnstrom
Preceptor Lambda, Nanaimo, British Columbia, Canada

DELICIOUS MINCEMEAT

1/2 lb. shredded suet, finely chopped
1 1/2 lb. apples, peeled, finely chopped
1/2 lb. currants, finely chopped
1/2 lb. raisins, finely chopped
3/4 lb. brown sugar
1/2 lb. sultanas, finely chopped
1/2 c. sugar
1/4 oz. each nutmeg, allspice
Grated rind and juice of 1 lemon
1/4 to 1/2 c. dark rum (opt.)

Combine all ingredients; mix well. Spoon into glass jars; seal.

Sharon Leonard
Beta Nu, Kitimat, British Columbia, Canada

GREEN TOMATO MINCEMEAT

6 c. chopped apples
6 c. chopped green tomatoes
4 c. packed brown sugar
1 1/3 c. vinegar
3 c. raisins
1 tbsp. cinnamon
1 tsp. ground cloves
3/4 tsp. each allspice, mace
3/4 tsp. pepper
2 tsp. salt
3/4 c. suet

Simmer all ingredients except suet for 3 hours or until thick. Stir in suet. Pour into 3 hot, sterilized quart jars; seal.

Laurel Hadland
Preceptor Beta Alpha
Fort St. John, British Columbia, Canada

CHOICE ANTIPASTO

2 qt. dill pickles, chopped
3 jars pickled sweet onions, chopped
2 heads cauliflower, chopped
5 cans sliced mushrooms
1 can anchovies, chopped
1 c. oil
1 c. malt vinegar
2 bottles of chili sauce
2 cans each green, red pimentos
4 cans cut green beans
3 cans green olives, chopped
2 cans chopped ripe olives
5 cans oil-packed tuna
4 32-oz. bottles of catsup
2 green peppers, finely chopped
5 drops of Tabasco sauce
Salt and pepper to taste
2 cans artichokes, chopped

Combine all ingredients except artichokes in large soup pot. Bring to a boil over low heat. Simmer for 20 minutes. Spoon over artichokes in hot sterilized jars; seal.

Zeta Pi
Houston, British Columbia, Canada

Gourmet Food Gifts / 155

PICKLED ASPARAGUS

Fresh asparagus, trimmed
1/4 tsp. cayenne pepper
Garlic cloves to taste
Dillweed to taste
2 1/2 c. vinegar
1/4 c. salt

Pack asparagus into hot sterilized jars leaving 1-inch headspace. Add cayenne pepper, garlic and dillweed to each jar. Bring vinegar, salt and 2 1/2 cups water to a boil. Pour over asparagus; seal.

Debbie Helfrecht
Xi Alpha Zeta, Pendleton, Oregon

CINNAMON RINGS

2 gal. large cucumbers, peeled, seeded, sliced 1/4 in. thick
2 c. lime
3 c. vinegar
1 tbsp. alum
1 sm. bottle of red food coloring
9 c. sugar
8 sticks cinnamon
1 pkg. red cinnamon candies

Soak cucumbers in lime and 9 cups water for 24 hours; drain. Soak in cold water for 3 hours; drain. Pour mixture of 1 cup vinegar, alum and food coloring over cucumbers in large saucepan. Simmer for 2 hours; drain. Bring 2 cups vinegar, 3 cups water, sugar, cinnamon sticks and candies to a boil. Pour over cucumbers. Let stand for 24 hours; drain, reserving liquid. Repeat procedure 2 times. Pack into hot sterilized jars after heating liquid on 5th day; seal.

Nora Conyers
Epsilon, Fairbury, Nebraska

PICKLED MUSHROOMS

2 lb. mushrooms
2 tbsp. salt
1 sm. onion, chopped
1 clove of garlic, chopped
1/2 c. chopped parsley
1 bay leaf
1/8 tsp. pepper
3/4 tsp. thyme
2 c. white wine vinegar
2 c. vinegar
1/2 c. olive oil
3 tbsp. lemon juice

Soak mushrooms in 4 cups water and salt; drain. Add remaining ingredients. Simmer, covered, for 10 minutes. Let stand for 2 hours. Store, covered, in refrigerator. Yield: 4 quarts.

Pam Fairbanks
Epsilon Omega, Olympia, Washington

PICKLED SQUASH

2 c. sliced onions
1 c. pickling vinegar
1 3/4 c. sugar
1/2 c. chopped green pepper
1/2 tsp. each mustard seed, celery seed
1 tbsp. salt
8 c. sliced squash

Bring all ingredients except squash to a boil in large saucepan. Add squash. Boil for 1 minute. Spoon into 4 hot sterilized pint jars; seal.

Billie B. Cole
Preceptor Gamma Kappa, Victoria, Texas

BREAD AND BUTTER PICKLES

4 qt. thinly sliced med. cucumbers
6 med. onions, sliced
2 green peppers, chopped
3 cloves of garlic
1/3 c. coarse salt
Crushed ice
5 c. sugar
2 tbsp. mustard seed
1 1/2 tsp. each celery seed, turmeric
3 c. cider vinegar

Combine first 5 ingredients in large saucepan. Cover with ice; mix well. Let stand for 3 hours; drain well. Pour mixture of remaining ingredients over cucumbers. Bring to a boil. Spoon into 8 hot, sterilized pint jars; seal.

Linda Hicks
Beta Iota, Rawlins, Wyoming

SWEET PEPPER RELISH

12 green peppers, ground
12 red peppers, ground
15 med. onions, ground
4 c. vinegar
5 c. sugar
2 tbsp. salt

Pour boiling water over ground vegetables in saucepan. Let stand for 5 minutes; drain. Repeat and let stand for 10 minutes; drain. Bring vinegar, sugar and salt to a boil. Pour over vegetables. Boil for 25 minutes or until peppers are tender. Spoon into 7 hot, sterilized pint jars; seal.

Evelyn Lonas
Laureate Alpha, Cleveland, Tennessee

PRIZEWINNING ZUCCHINI PICKLES

16 c. sliced zucchini
8 onions, sliced into rings
1/2 c. pickling salt
1/2 tsp. cloves
2 tsp. celery seed
1/2 tsp. alum
4 c. vinegar
4 1/2 c. sugar
1 1/2 tsp. turmeric
2 tsp. mustard seed

Pour ice water over zucchini, onions and salt in large saucepan. Let stand for 3 hours; drain well. Bring remaining ingredients and 1 cup water to a boil. Pour over vegetables. Cook until zucchini is tender. Spoon into hot, sterilized jars; seal.

Debra Beeson
Pi Beta, Ontario, Canada

POPCORN CAKE

1 stick margarine
1 16-oz. jar marshmallow creme
1/2 c. oil
4 qt. popped popcorn
1 16-oz. bag M and M's
16 oz. peanuts

Melt margarine and marshmallow creme in oil in double boiler, stirring until blended. Pour over popcorn, M and M's and peanuts; mix well. Press into tube pan. Let stand for 1 hour. Invert onto serving plate. Garnish with cinnamon candies.

Sally Sutherlin
Delta Preceptor, La Mesa, New Mexico

POPCORN CON PESTO

1/2 c. melted butter
1 tbsp. basil
1 tsp. parsley flakes
1 tsp. garlic powder
1/3 c. Parmesan cheese
1/2 c. peanuts
5 qt. popped popcorn

Mix all ingredients except popcorn. Pour over warm popcorn in serving bowl; mix well. Yield: 5 quarts.

Peggy M. Reed
Xi Delta Kappa, Littleton, Colorado

POPPYCOCK

1 c. butter, melted
2 c. sugar
1/2 c. light corn syrup
1 tsp. salt
1 tsp. vanilla extract
1/2 tsp. soda
5 qt. popped popcorn
1 c. almonds
1 c. pecan halves

Bring butter, sugar, corn syrup and salt to a boil, stirring constantly. Cook for 5 minutes. Do not stir; remove from heat. Stir in vanilla and soda. Pour over popcorn and nuts; mix well. Bake in two 9 x 13-inch baking pans at 250 degrees for 1 to 1 1/2 hours, stirring every 20 minutes. Store in airtight container.

Xi Theta Sigma
Godfrey, Illinois

SPECIAL SPICED NUTS

1 c. sugar
1/2 tsp. cinnamon
1/8 tsp. cream of tartar
1 1/2 c. nuts
Raisins (opt.)

Cook sugar, cinnamon, cream of tartar and 1/2 cup water to 240 degrees on candy thermometer. Add nuts and raisins; stir to coat. Spread on sheet to dry; separate nuts and raisins. Store in airtight container.

Betty King
Delta Upsilon, Newman Grove, Nebraska

MICROWAVE PECANS WORCESTERSHIRE

1 tbsp. butter, melted
2 tbsp. Worcestershire sauce
Dash of Tabasco sauce
1 1/2 c. pecans
Salt and pepper to taste

Mix first 3 ingredients in glass bowl. Add pecans; stir to coat. Microwave on High for 5 to 6 minutes, stirring twice. Season with salt and pepper.

Martha Donaldson
Xi Gamma Rho, Columbus, Georgia

SPICED WALNUTS

2 1/2 c. walnuts
1 c. sugar
1 tsp. cinnamon
1/2 tsp. salt
1 1/2 tsp. vanilla extract

Bake walnuts at 375 degrees for 5 minutes, stirring once. Combine sugar, cinnamon, salt and 1/2 cup water in 2-quart saucepan with buttered side. Bring to a boil, stirring constantly. Cook to soft-ball stage. Do not stir. Remove from heat. Beat until creamy. Stir in warm walnuts and vanilla. Spread in waxed paper-lined 10 x 15-inch pan. Separate walnuts. Yield: 1 pound.

Agnes C. Tracy
Laureate Nu, Flint, Michigan

FAVORITE SPICED NUTS

1/2 c. sugar
1/2 tsp. salt
1 tsp. cinnamon
1/4 tsp. cloves
1/4 tsp. nutmeg
1/2 c. walnuts
1/2 c. pecans

Cook sugar, salt, spices and 2 tablespoons water to 236 degrees on candy thermometer, stirring constantly. Stir in nuts; remove from heat. Stir until mixture loses gloss. Spread on buttered sheet. Break into pieces when cool. Yield: 1 1/2 cups.

Linda Misfeldt
Delta Beta, Chippewa Falls, Wisconsin

SUGARED PECANS

Rind and juice of 2 oranges
3 c. sugar
1 tbsp. flour
1 c. milk
2 tbsp. butter
4 c. pecans

Cut rind into thin slivers. Combine with sugar, flour, milk and orange juice. Cook to soft-ball stage; remove from heat. Stir in butter. Pour over pecans; beat until creamy. Spoon onto waxed paper; separate pecans. Store in airtight container with waxed paper between layers. Yield: 8 dozen.

Margaret Dowling
Laureate Eta, Gadsden, Alabama

Recipe on page 170.

Special Occasions

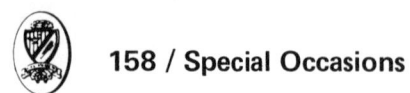

158 / Special Occasions

House Warming Soup Supper

COMPANY PUNCH BOWL

1 6-oz. can frozen limeade concentrate, thawed
1 6-oz. can frozen orange juice concentrate, thawed
1 46-oz. can red fruit punch, chilled
1 28-oz. bottle of club soda, chilled
1 28-oz. bottle of ginger ale, chilled

Combine concentrates and punch. Stir in club soda and ginger ale gradually. Add ice. Garnish with citrus slices. Yield: 20 servings.

Beverly Jean Lockman
Preceptor Laureate Zeta, Cheyenne, Wyoming

BETTY'S HOT SPICED WINE CIDER

2 qt. apple cider
4 cinnamon sticks
1 1/2 tsp. whole cloves
3/4 c. packed brown sugar
1/4 tsp. salt
2 c. Chablis
2 c. Burgundy

Heat first 5 ingredients for 30 to 45 minutes. Do not boil. Remove spices; add wines. Heat for several minutes longer. Yield: 16 servings.

Betty Cosgrove
Beta Nu, Joseph, Oregon

GREAT GAZPACHO DIP

1 15-oz. can whole tomatoes, chopped
1 sm. can chopped green chilies
1 sm. bunch green onions, chopped
2 tbsp. vinegar
3 tbsp. oil
1 sm. can chopped black olives
2 cloves of garlic, chopped
3 oz. Cheddar cheese, grated

Mix all ingredients together. Chill for 2 hours to overnight.

Barbara MacGillivray
Alpha Mu Zeta, Del Rio, Texas

PARTY CHEESE STRAWS

1 lb. Cheddar cheese, grated
2 sticks margarine, softened
2 c. sifted flour
1/4 tsp. each salt, cayenne pepper

Combine cheese and margarine. Add flour sifted with salt and pepper. Force through cookie press fitted with star tip into S shapes on baking sheets. Bake at 375 degrees for 12 to 15 minutes. Cool on wire rack. Store in airtight container. Yield: 8 dozen.

Martha Musgrove
Laureate Zeta, Gardendale, Alabama

EGGS BENEDICT

1/4 c. chopped onions
Butter
1 can cream of mushroom soup
4 eggs
4 slices baked ham, grilled
2 whole English muffins

Saute onions in 2 tablespoons butter. Stir in mushroom soup; heat through. Break eggs into soup mixture. Cook, covered, until eggs are set. Toast English muffins; top with butter. Place ham on muffins; top with eggs and mushroom sauce. Yield: 2 servings.

Carolyn Biossat
Beta Beta, Eureka Springs, Arkansas

STUFFED CUCUMBERS

2 lg. cucumbers
1 6 1/2-oz. can tuna, drained, flaked
2 tbsp. mayonnaise
1/2 tsp. grated onion
1/2 tsp. each lemon juice, Worcestershire sauce
1/2 tsp. each salt, paprika

Trim ends from cucumbers; remove centers with apple corer. Mix remaining ingredients. Stuff cucumbers; chill. Slice 1/2 inch thick.

Deana Stewart
Preceptor Tau, Memphis, Tennessee

MUFFIN CUP DAINTIES

1 c. butter
1/2 c. confectioners' sugar
1 tbsp. cornstarch
1 1/2 to 1 3/4 c. flour
Jelly
1 egg, well beaten
1/2 c. sugar
Several drops of vanilla extract
1 c. coconut

Combine first 4 ingredients. Shape into small balls. Press into greased miniature muffin cups with floured fingers. Add a small amount of jelly. Mix remaining ingredients. Spoon over jelly. Bake at 350 degrees for 10 to 15 minutes.

May L. Grainger
Xi Theta Epsilon, Riverside, California

Special Occasions / 159

CHEDDAR CHEESE SOUP

1/3 c. finely chopped carrots
1/3 c. finely chopped celery
1 c. finely chopped green onions
1 med. white onion, chopped
1/2 c. butter
1 c. flour
4 c. milk
4 c. chicken broth
1 15-oz. jar Cheez Whiz
Salt and pepper to taste
1/8 tsp. cayenne pepper
1 tbsp. prepared mustard

Cook carrots, celery and green onions in 2 cups water for 5 minutes; set aside. Saute white onion in butter. Blend in flour. Bring milk and broth to a boil. Stir briskly into sauteed onions with wire whisk. Add Cheez Whiz, seasonings and cooked vegetables with cooking liquid. Bring to boil. Serve immediately. Yield: 8 servings.

Donna M. Pickens
Xi Epsilon Mu, Cherokee, Iowa

CHICKEN NUGGET SOUP

1/2 lb. boned chicken breast, ground
1/2 c. dry bread crumbs
2 egg whites
1/4 c. chopped parsley
3/4 tsp. salt
1/2 tsp. pepper
Parmesan cheese
1 c. sliced mushrooms
1 c. sliced green onion
2 tbsp. olive oil
1 tbsp. lemon juice
1/4 tsp. oregano
4 13 3/4-oz. cans chicken broth
1 c. broken spaghetti

Mix first 3 ingredients with 2 tablespoons parsley, 1/4 teaspoon each salt and pepper and 1 tablespoon Parmesan cheese. Chill, covered, for 1 hour. Shape into 1-inch balls. Chill. Saute mushrooms and onion in oil for 3 minutes. Add lemon juice, 1/2 teaspoon salt, 1/4 teaspoon pepper, oregano and chicken broth. Bring to a boil. Add chicken balls and spaghetti gradually. Cook for 10 minutes, stirring occasionally. Top with 2 tablespoons chopped parsley and 1/4 cup Parmesan cheese. Yield: 2 1/2 quarts.

Betty Wells
Laureate Beta, Salt Lake City, Utah

SPECIAL BEAN SOUP

16 oz. dried beans
1 lg. onion, chopped
1 clove of garlic, minced
2 c. chopped celery
2 carrots, chopped
2 tbsp. oil
Ham, chopped
3/4 tsp. thyme
1 tbsp. salt
1/4 tsp. pepper
1/3 c. Parmesan cheese

Boil beans in 10 cups water for 2 minutes. Turn off heat. Let stand for 1 hour. Saute onion, garlic, celery and carrots in oil. Combine with beans, ham and thyme. Simmer for 2 hours. Puree 2 cups beans in blender. Stir into soup; add remaining ingredients. Heat to serving temperature.

Jane Friedman
Zeta Pi, Fulton, Missouri

CRAB-MUSHROOM BISQUE

1/4 c. finely chopped green pepper
1 scallion and top, chopped
1/4 c. finely chopped onion
2 tbsp. chopped parsley
1 c. sliced fresh mushrooms
6 tbsp. butter
2 tbsp. flour
1 1/2 c. milk
1 tsp. salt
1/8 tsp. pepper
1/4 tsp. mace
Dash of Tabasco sauce
1 c. half and half
1 1/2 c. cooked crab meat
3 tbsp. dry Sherry

Saute vegetables in 4 tablespoons butter. Blend 2 tablespoons melted butter and flour. Stir in milk gradually. Cook until thick, stirring constantly. Stir in seasonings, sauteed vegetables and half and half. Bring to a boil, stirring constantly; reduce heat. Add crab meat. Simmer for 5 minutes. Add Sherry just before serving. Yield: 4 servings.

Sharon Carlile
Lambda, Walla Walla, Washington

CORN CHOWDER

3 or 4 lg. potatoes, chopped
6 to 8 slices bacon
1 lg. onion, chopped
2 or 3 lg. cans cream-style corn
1/2 stick butter
1 qt. milk
1 pt. half and half
1 c. shredded Cheddar cheese

Cook potatoes in water to cover. Fry bacon until crisp; drain and crumble. Saute onion in bacon drippings. Add bacon and sauteed onion to potatoes. Add remaining ingredients except cheese. Cook for several minutes. Add cheese just before serving. Yield: 12 servings.

Dorothy Janie Hobbs
Preceptor Alpha Tau, Independence, Missouri

ONION SNACK BREAD

2 pkg. dry yeast
4 to 4 1/2 c. flour
1 c. process cheese spread
2 tbsp. sugar
10 tbsp. butter, softened
1 tsp. salt
1 pkg. dry onion soup mix

Dissolve yeast in 1 cup warm water in mixer bowl. Add 2 cups flour, cheese, sugar, 2 tablespoons butter and salt. Beat at medium speed for 2 minutes. Mix in remaining flour. Let rise in warm place until doubled in bulk. Roll into two 11 x 16-inch rectangles. Spread with soup mix blended with 1/2 cup butter; roll as for jelly rolls, sealing edges and ends. Place seam side down on baking sheet; cut half through lengthwise. Let rise, covered, until doubled in bulk. Bake at 350 degrees for 30 to 35 minutes.

Dottie Neher
Preceptor Zeta, Caldwell, Idaho

FAST FRUIT SOUP

1 11-oz. package dried mixed fruit
1/2 c. golden raisins
1 11-oz. package prunes
1 3 to 4-in. cinnamon stick
2 1/4 c. pineapple juice
1/4 c. sugar
2 tbsp. pearl tapioca, soaked
1/2 tsp. salt
1/4 c. currant jelly (opt.)

Combine all ingredients with 4 cups water. Simmer for 30 minutes. Serve warm or cold garnished with orange sections.

Sandra Borg
Delta Upsilon, Lindsay, Nebraska

SUGAR PLUM CAKE

1 3/4 c. sugar
3/4 c. butter
4 eggs
4 c. flour
3/4 c. orange candy slices, cut up
1 1/2-lb. package dates, chopped
1 1/2 c. chopped pecans
1 3 1/2-oz. can flaked coconut
1 tsp. soda
1 c. buttermilk
1 tbsp. lemon juice
4 tsp. grated orange rind
2 c. confectioners' sugar
1 sm. can frozen orange juice concentrate

Cream sugar and butter together until light and fluffy. Beat in eggs 1 at a time. Sift 2 cups flour over orange candy slices, dates, pecans and coconut, tossing together. Sift remaining flour with soda. Add alternately with buttermilk to creamed mixture. Stir in lemon juice and 2 teaspoons orange rind. Mix in candy and fruits. Pour into greased and floured 10-inch tube pan. Bake at 300 degrees for about 1 1/2 hours. Combine remaining ingredients, mixing until smooth. Prick warm cake with fork; spoon glaze over cake.

Margarie Nelson
Laureate Lambda, Alturas, California

Birthday Dessert Buffet

PINK CHAMPAGNE PUNCH

1 bottle of Champagne
1 bottle of pink Champagne
1 bottle of sparkling Burgundy
1 can frozen lemonade, thawed
1 lg. bottle of club soda
2 lg. bottles of 7-Up

Combine all ingredients in large punch bowl. Garnish with favorite fruit.

Sharon Schroeder
Alpha Iota, Gardnerville, Nevada

YELLOW ROSE PUNCH

15 oz. sweetened powdered lemonade mix
64 oz. pineapple juice
1 6-oz. can frozen lemonade concentrate
1 qt. ginger ale

Prepare lemonade mix according to package directions. Combine with next 2 ingredients in punch bowl. Add ginger ale just before serving. Garnish with lemon slices. Yield: 60 servings.

Melissa Barton
Sigma, Beckley, West Virginia

AMARETTO CHEESECAKE

1 1/4 c. almond cookie crumbs
1/4 c. ground almonds
Melted butter
Sugar
3 pkg. cream cheese, softened
3 eggs
1 tsp. almond extract
1 tsp. Amaretto
1 pkg. sliced almonds

Mix crumbs, ground almonds, 1/3 cup melted butter and 3 tablespoons sugar. Press into bottom and 3/4 inch up side of 10-inch springform pan. Beat cream cheese and 1 cup sugar at high speed until fluffy; beat in eggs 1 at a time. Fold in 1/2 cup melted butter, almond flavoring and Amaretto. Bake in prepared pan at 450 degrees for 15 to 20 minutes. Sprinkle sliced almonds over top. Bake for 5 to 10 minutes longer. Chill for 12 hours.

Margaret Russell
Epsilon Sigma, Ville Platte, Louisiana

ITALIAN CREAM CAKE

1 stick margarine, softened
1/2 c. shortening
2 c. sugar
5 eggs, separated
2 c. flour
1 tsp. soda
1 c. buttermilk
2 tsp. vanilla extract
1 sm. can flaked coconut
1/2 c. pecans
1 8-oz. package cream cheese, softened
1/2 stick butter, softened
1 lb. confectioners' sugar

Cream margarine and shortening. Beat in sugar until smooth. Add beaten egg yolks; beat well. Beat in flour sifted with soda alternately with buttermilk. Stir in 1 teaspoon vanilla, coconut and pecans. Fold in stiffly beaten egg whites. Bake in 3 greased and floured 8-inch cake pans at 350 degrees for 25 minutes. Beat cream cheese and butter until smooth. Mix in confectioners' sugar. Add 1 teaspoon vanilla; beat until smooth. Frost cake; garnish with additional pecans.

Betty Jane Orme
Preceptor Nu, Maysville, Kentucky

Special Occasions / 161

HEAVENLY ANGEL CAKE

40 maraschino cherry halves
1 1/4 c. cherry Brandy
2 env. unflavored gelatin
6 eggs, separated
1 tsp. grated lemon rind
1 8-oz. can whole cranberry sauce
1/2 c. sugar
1 10-in. angel food cake
1 16-oz. carton whipped topping

Marinate cherries in Brandy for several days; drain, reserving Brandy. Soften gelatin in 1/2 cup cold water. Beat egg yolks with 1 cup reserved Brandy and lemon rind. Cook over low heat until thickened, stirring constantly; remove from heat. Stir in gelatin until dissolved. Mix in cranberry sauce and cherries. Chill until partially set. Beat egg whites with sugar until stiff. Fold into cranberry mixture. Layer bite-sized cake pieces alternately with cranberry mixture in oiled 10-inch tube pan until all ingredients are used ending with cake. Chill, covered, until firm. Unmold onto serving plate. Frost with whipped topping blended with 1/4 cup Brandy.

Jeanette Azar
Preceptor Beta Zeta, Mt. Clemens, Michigan

PECAN-CREAM CHEESE POUND CAKE

1 1/2 c. chopped pecans
1 1/2 c. butter, softened
1 8-oz. package cream cheese, softened
3 c. sugar
6 eggs
3 c. sifted cake flour
Dash of salt
1 1/2 tsp. vanilla extract

Sprinkle 1/2 cup pecans in greased and floured 10-inch tube pan; set aside. Cream butter and cream cheese together. Add sugar gradually, beating until light and fluffy. Add eggs, 1 at a time, beating well after each addition. Add flour and salt, stirring until combined. Stir in vanilla and remaining pecans. Pour batter into prepared pan. Bake at 325 degrees for 1 1/2 hours or until cake tests done. Cool 10 minutes in pan. Cool on rack. This cake can be frozen for later use.

Lourine T. Davis
Preceptor Pi, Salem, Virginia

STRAWBERRY-ALMOND BOMBE

1 qt. vanilla ice cream, slightly softened
2 16-oz. packages frozen sweetened strawberries, thawed
1 can sweetened condensed milk
1 1/2 c. chopped toasted almonds
1 c. whipping cream
1/4 tsp. almond extract
1 tbsp. cornstarch
1/4 c. Amaretto
1/4 c. toasted sliced almonds

Line chilled 2-quart mold with ice cream. Freeze. Drain 1 package strawberries, reserving juice. Mix condensed milk, strawberries and chopped almonds. Whip cream with flavoring. Fold into strawberry mixture. Chill for 1 hour. Pour into prepared mold. Freeze, covered, overnight to 2 weeks. Bring 1 package strawberries to a boil. Stir in reserved strawberry juice blended with cornstarch. Cook until thick, stirring constantly. Chill, covered, for 3 days or less. Stir in Amaretto before serving. Unmold bombe on chilled serving plate. Press sliced almonds around side. Freeze for 3 hours or less. Serve with prepared sauce.

Sheila Russell
Delta Kappa, Ontario, Canada

LUSCIOUS LEMON ROLL

6 tbsp. lemon juice
2 1/4 c. sugar
1 1/2 sticks butter
Grated rind of 2 lemons
7 eggs
1/8 tsp. salt
1 tsp. baking powder
1/2 tsp. lemon extract
3/4 c. sifted flour
Confectioners' sugar

Blend lemon juice, 1 1/2 cups sugar, butter and lemon rind in double boiler. Add 3 well-beaten eggs. Cook until thick, stirring constantly. Beat 4 eggs, salt and baking powder until fluffy. Beat in 3/4 cup sugar gradually until very thick. Fold in lemon extract and flour. Pour into greased 10 x 15-inch baking pan lined with greased waxed paper. Bake at 375 degrees for 13 to 15 minutes. Invert on waxed paper heavily dusted with confectioners' sugar. Remove paper; cool slightly. Spread lemon filling on cake; roll as for jelly roll.

Jeanne L. Phillips
Xi Lambda Theta, Garland, Texas

FROZEN PEPPERMINT DESSERT

3 tbsp. butter, melted
30 vanilla wafers, finely crushed
3/4 c. crushed peppermint candy
3/4 c. chopped walnuts
2 c. miniature marshmallows
1 1/2 pt. whipping cream, whipped
1 1/2 c. sugar
Dash of salt
Pinch of cream of tartar
1 1/2 sq. baking chocolate, melted
1 c. evaporated milk

Combine butter and crumbs. Line bottom and sides of 7 x 11-inch dish, reserving 1/3 of the crumbs for top. Fold candy, walnuts and marshmallows into whipped cream. Spread over crumbs; sprinkle reserved crumbs on top. Freeze. Thaw for 30 to 60 minutes. Add combined sugar, salt and cream of tartar to chocolate. Stir in evaporated milk gradually. Cook to desired thickness, stirring constantly. Serve over peppermint dessert.

Myrleen Turner
Laureate Beta, Salt Lake City, Utah

162 / Special Occasions

ELEGANT MERINGUE TORTE

6 to 8 egg whites
2 tsp. vanilla extract
Dash of salt
1/2 tsp. cream of tartar
2 c. sugar
8 3/4-oz. Heath bars, crushed
2 c. whipping cream, whipped

Beat egg whites until frothy; add vanilla, salt and cream of tartar. Add sugar gradually, beating until stiff. Spread meringue into two 9-inch circles on baking parchment on baking sheet. Bake at 275 degrees for 1 hour. Turn off oven. Let stand in closed oven overnight. Fold candy into whipped cream. Frost meringue layers as for cake. Chill for 8 hours. Yield: 10 servings.

Mary Dunworth
Xi Alpha Beta, Coldwater, Michigan

PINEAPPLE TARTS

1 can crushed pineapple
Sugar
2 eggs, separated
2 tbsp. flour
1/4 tsp. salt
2 doz. baked tart shells

Drain pineapple, reserving juice. Combine 3/4 cup sugar, egg yolks, flour, salt and 1/2 cup pineapple juice; mix well. Add remaining juice and pineapple. Cook over medium heat until thickened. Cook for 1 minute longer. Fill baked tart shells. Whip egg whites until frothy. Beat in 4 teaspoons sugar slowly; beat until stiff peaks form. Top tarts with meringue. Bake in 350-degree oven until lightly brown.

Mrs. Lil Rennie
Preceptor Alpha Sigma
Surrey, British Columbia, Canada

CUSTARD CRUNCH MINCE PIE

1 c. sugar
2 tbsp. flour
1/8 tsp. salt
3 eggs, slightly beaten
1/4 c. melted butter
1/2 c. chopped nuts
1 c. mincemeat
1 9-in. unbaked pie shell

Combine sugar, flour and salt. Add slowly to eggs; mix well. Combine butter, nuts and mincemeat. Add to egg mixture. Pour into pie shell. Bake at 400 degrees for 15 minutes. Reduce temperature to 325 degrees. Bake 30 minutes longer.

Helen Horten
Alpha Theta, Brookings, South Dakota

MOCHA PEANUT CLUSTERS

1 c. semisweet chocolate chips
16 lg. marshmallows, quartered
1/3 c. butter
1 tbsp. instant coffee powder
2 c. salted peanuts

Melt first 3 ingredients in double boiler, stirring occasionally. Add instant coffee; remove from heat. Stir in peanuts. Drop by teaspoonfuls onto waxed paper; cool.

Juanita Lunn
Beta Alpha, Mount Vernon, Ohio

CHOCOLATE MINT CUPS

1 c. butter, softened
2 c. confectioners' sugar
4 sq. unsweetened chocolate, melted
4 eggs, beaten
1 tsp. peppermint extract
3 tbsp. vanilla wafer crumbs

Blend first 3 ingredients. Beat in eggs, 1 at a time. Stir in flavoring. Sprinkle 1/4 teaspoon crumbs into each of 36 miniature muffin liners. Fill with chocolate mixture. Freeze until firm. Garnish with whipped topping and cherry.

Marge Haggland
Laureate, Fairbanks, Alaska

CANDY BAR COOKIES

Butter, softened
Confectioners' sugar
2 tsp. vanilla extract
Evaporated milk
1/4 tsp. salt
2 c. flour
28 caramels
1 c. chocolate chips
Pecan halves

Cream 3/4 cup butter and 3/4 cup confectioners' sugar. Add 1 teaspoon vanilla, 2 tablespoons evaporated milk and salt. Blend in flour. Chill dough. Roll into two 8 x 12-inch rectangles on floured surface; trim sides. Cut into 1 1/2 x 3-inch rectangles. Bake on cookie sheets at 325 degrees until lightly browned. Melt caramels in 1/4 cup evaporated milk. Stir in 1/4 cup butter and 1 cup sifted confectioners' sugar. Spread 1 teaspoonful on each cookie. Melt chocolate chips in 1/3 cup evaporated milk. Mix in 2 tablespoons butter, 1 teaspoon vanilla and 1/2 cup sifted confectioners' sugar. Top each cookie with 1/2 teaspoon icing and pecan half.

Donna Taylor
Theta Nu, Spillville, Iowa

Fireside Picnic

HOT MADRILENE DRINK

1/2 lb. butter
2 tbsp. minced onion
4 cans beef broth
10 c. vegetable juice cocktail
2 bay leaves

Special Occasions / 163

Mix all ingredients. Simmer for 5 minutes; remove bay leaves. Yield: 25-30 servings.

Hazel Uren
Laureate Beta, Salt Lake City, Utah

STUFFED CHERRY TOMATOES

1 carton cherry tomatoes
1 8-oz. package cream cheese, softened
2 tbsp. mayonnaise
1/2 lb. bacon, crisp-fried, crumbled
4 tsp. chopped chives

Remove stem end of tomatoes; scoop out pulp. Blend cream cheese and mayonnaise until smooth; stir in bacon and chives. Spoon into tomatoes.

Reba Plaisance
Iota Epsilon, Baton Rouge, Louisiana

FRENCH ONION SOUP

4 lg. onions, sliced
2 tbsp. butter
4 cans beef consomme
2 bouillon cubes
1/2 consomme can cooking wine

Saute onions in butter until golden. Add remaining ingredients and 2 consomme cans water. Simmer for 30 minutes. Serve in soup mugs topped with cheese croutons.

Ruth A. Anderson
Xi Gamma Omega, Storm Lake, Iowa

FINGER STEAKS

1 lb. 1/2-in. thick round steak
2 tbsp. butter
2 tbsp. flour
1 egg, slightly beaten
1/3 c. fine dry bread crumbs
2 tbsp. Parmesan cheese
1/2 tsp. salt
1/4 tsp. onion salt

Cut steak into 1-inch strips. Melt butter in 9 x 13-inch baking pan in 400-degree oven. Coat steak strips with flour; dip into egg beaten with 1 teaspoon water, then mixture of bread crumbs, cheese and salts. Place in prepared pan. Bake for 15 to 20 minutes; turn. Bake for 15 minutes longer.

Patricia Reynolds
Alpha Chi, Pope AFB, North Carolina

COZY SANDWICHES

1 lb. Tillamook cheese, grated
2 sm. onions, grated
1 sm. cans green chilies, finely chopped
2 sm. cans chopped olives
2/3 c. oil
2 tbsp. vinegar
1 can tomato sauce
French rolls

Combine first 7 ingredients. Scoop out roll centers. Spoon cheese mixture into rolls. Wrap in foil. Bake at 350 degrees until heated through.

Sherie and Dorothy Hoid
Alpha Iota, Gardnerville, Nevada

BARBECUED CHICKEN

12 chicken pieces
1 pkg. dry onion soup mix
4 oz. apricot preserves
4 oz. pineapple preserves
2/3 bottle of Russian salad dressing

Place chicken, skin side up, in 8 x 14-inch casserole. Combine remaining ingredients. Spread over chicken. Bake at 350 degrees for 1 1/2 hours. Yield: 4-6 servings.

Sarah Sue Rathjen
International Alpha, Kansas City, Missiouri

BARBECUED SHRIMP

12 jumbo shrimp
1/2 c. flour
1 egg, well beaten
1 c. milk
Salt and pepper to taste
1 c. fine cracker crumbs
1 qt. cooking oil
1 pt. Hickory House Smoke Sauce

Peel and devein shrimp, leaving shell on tails. Dust shrimp with flour. Place egg in a bowl; add milk, salt and pepper to taste. Dip shrimp in egg mixture, then roll in cracker crumbs. Heat oil in deep saucepan to 350 degrees. Fry shrimp for 4 minutes to seal moisture in shrimp. Remove; saturate with Hickory Smoke Sauce. Place in shallow pan. Place under broiler for 5 minutes. Serve with mild barbecue sauce. Yield: 2 servings.

Nelda L. Haefs
Sigma Iota, Freeport, Texas

BUSY-DAY POT ROAST BARBECUE

2 lb. beef pot roast
2 tsp. salt
1/4 tsp. pepper
2 tbsp. lard
1 8-oz. can tomato sauce
3 med. onions, sliced
1/4 tsp. garlic powder
2 tbsp. brown sugar
1/2 tsp. dry mustard
1/4 c. lemon juice
1/4 c. vinegar
1/4 c. catsup
1 tbsp. Worcestershire sauce

Rub roast with salt and pepper. Brown in hot lard in Dutch oven. Add 1/2 cup water, tomato sauce, onions and garlic powder; cover. Simmer for 1 1/2 hours. Combine remaining ingredients. Pour over roast. Simmer for 2 1/2 to 3 hours or until tender. Yield: 6 servings.

Mary Miller
Alpha Nu, Bridgewater, Virginia

164 / Special Occasions

CHICKEN-STUFFED EGGS

6 hard-cooked eggs
3/4 c. chicken
1/2 c. chopped celery
1/2 tsp. salt
1/4 c. mayonnaise
Paprika

Cut eggs in half lengthwise. Remove yolks; mash. Combine chicken, egg yolks, celery, salt and mayonnaise; mix well. Stuff whites with mixture. Sprinkle with paprika. May be made with crab meat. Yield: 6 servings.

Nancy Jane Young
Xi Alpha Chi, Ripon, Wisconsin

LEA'S BARBECUE SAUCE

2 2-lb. packages brown sugar
2 lg. bottles of barbecue sauce
2 pt. vinegar
1 lg. bottle of lime juice
4 bottles of dried barbecue spices
1 to 2 bottles of cayenne pepper
2 bottles of liquid smoke
2 bottles of hot sauce
1 bottle of steak sauce
2 cans beer

Mix all ingredients in order given in saucepan. Simmer for 10 to 12 hours. Yield: 1 gallon.

Leona Hoy
Preceptor Gamma Tau
Oak Grove, Missouri

GLORIA'S BROWN BREAD

1 c. chopped dates
1 tsp. soda
3/4 c. sugar
1 tbsp. melted butter
1 egg
2 c. flour
1 tsp. baking powder
1 c. chopped nuts
1 c. maraschino cherries, chopped

Add dates to 1 cup boiling water; let cool. Add soda; mix well. Add remaining ingredients; mix well. Pour into greased and floured loaf pan. Bake in 325-degree oven for 1 hour.

Gloria Lott
Phi, Memphis, Tennessee

S'MORES CAKE

1 1/2 c. sugar
2 eggs
1 c. margarine, softened
2 tsp. vanilla extract
3 c. flour
2 tsp. baking powder
2 tsp. salt
2 5 3/4-oz. packages chocolate kisses
1 13-oz. jar marshmallow creme

Combine sugar, eggs, margarine and vanilla. Mix in flour, baking powder and salt. Spread half the mixture in buttered 9 x 13-inch baking pan. Press kisses into dough. Spread marshmallow creme over kisses. Flatten remaining dough by tablespoonfuls into circles. Arrange over top, sealing edges. Bake at 350 degrees for 30 to 35 minutes.

Lisa Winans
Beta Theta, Shreveport, Louisiana

Brunch-In-A-Basket

CHABLIS SLUSH

1 12-oz. can frozen pink lemonade concentrate
2 c. pink Chablis
1 46-oz. can pineapple juice

Combine all ingredients in punch bowl. Freeze overnight. Spoon into clear plastic 8-ounce glasses. Wrap in plastic wrap tied at top with pink ribbon. Thaw for 45 minutes before serving.

Debbie Evans
Gamma Alpha Gamma, Fairfield, California

CREME DE MENTHE GRAPES

1 lb. seedless green grapes
1/2 fifth Creme de Menthe
1 1-lb. box confectioners' sugar

Soak grapes in Creme de Menthe for 2 to 3 hours, turning frequently; drain on paper towels. Roll grapes in confectioners' sugar to coat. Let stand until dry. Reroll in confectioners' sugar. Refrigerate or freeze until serving time. Place in 4-ounce clear plastic glasses. Place each on plastic wrap. Tie at top with green ribbon.

Theresa Boley
Kappa Gamma, Columbia, Missouri

OLIVE AND PECAN FINGER SANDWICHES

1 8-oz. package cream cheese, softened
1/2 c. mayonnaise
1/2 c. chopped pecans
1 4 1/2-oz. can chopped salad olives
Dash of pepper
1 loaf sandwich bread

Mix first 5 ingredients. Chill, covered, for 24 to 48 hours. Toast bread; trim crusts. Cut in half diagonally. Spread half the triangles with cream cheese mixture. Top with remaining bread. Place in plastic sandwich bags; tie with brown ribbon.

Melanie P. Williams
Epsilon, Brigham City, Utah

HAM AND CHEESE BRUNCHWICHES

1 c. finely chopped ham
3/4 c. finely chopped Swiss cheese
2 green onions, chopped
1 1/2 tsp. prepared mustard
1 8-oz. can refrigerator crescent dinner rolls, separated
1 egg, beaten
1/2 tsp. poppy seed

Mix ham, cheese, onions and mustard. Place 2 heaping tablespoonfuls in center of each roll triangle. Fold tips to center to enclose filling; seal. Place on greased baking sheet. Brush with egg beaten with 1 tablespoon water; sprinkle with poppy seed. Bake at 375 degrees for 12 minutes. Pack in plastic deli sandwich containers. Tie with pastel plaid ribbon.

Johnann Allen
Xi Iota Delta, Denver City, Texas

GREEK SALAD

4 stalks celery, sliced diagonally
1 sm. cucumber, sliced diagonally
2 green peppers, coarsely chopped
1/2 c. whole black olives
1 med. onion, coarsely chopped
1/2 c. pimento-stuffed green olives
1 c. cubed Swiss cheese
2 tomatoes, cut into med. wedges
1 1/2 c. oil
3/4 c. vinegar
1 c. finely chopped onion
1 tsp. salt
1 tsp. minced garlic
2 tsp. rosemary leaves
1 tsp. each basil, oregano

Toss first 8 ingredients together. Mix remaining ingredients. Pour over salad. Chill for 24 hours. Spoon into plastic salad bowl. Wrap with plastic wrap tied at top with red ribbon. Yield: 10-15 servings.

Beverly Scott
Preceptor Gamma Epsilon, Elma, Washington

EASY LEMON SQUARES

1 c. flour
1/2 c. butter
1/4 c. confectioners' sugar
2 tbsp. lemon juice
2 eggs
1 c. sugar
1/2 tsp. baking powder
1/4 tsp. salt

Combine first 3 ingredients. Spread in 9 x 9-inch ungreased pan. Bake at 350 degrees for 20 minutes. Mix remaining ingredients together. Pour over crust. Bake for 25 minutes longer; cool. Cut into 2-inch squares. Wrap in plastic wrap; tie at top with yellow ribbon.

Cheri Musial
Lambda Psi, Marine City, Michigan

Spring Salad Luncheon

SANGRIA SLUSH

1 8 1/4-oz. can crushed pineapple
2 1/2 c. dry red wine
1 1/2 c. orange juice
1/2 c. lemon juice
1/2 c. sugar
2 tbsp. grated lemon rind (opt.)

Process first 5 ingredients in blender at High speed for 5 seconds. Freeze in 9-inch square pan. Thaw slightly before serving. Garnish with lemon rind. Yield: 10 servings.

Teresa M. Nurre
Eta Iota, Cedar Rapids, Iowa

KIDNEY BEAN AND EGG SALAD

6 hard-boiled eggs
1 20-oz. can kidney beans, well drained
1 c. chopped walnuts
1/2 c. sliced black olives
1 green onion, minced
1/3 c. mayonnaise
2 tbsp. milk
1 tsp. prepared mustard
Salt and pepper to taste

Crumble 1 egg yolk; set aside. Chop remaining eggs. Toss lightly with beans, walnuts, olives and onion. Chill for 30 minutes or longer. Add mayonnaise blended with milk and mustard; toss lightly. Season with salt and pepper. Serve in lettuce-lined bowl; sprinkle with reserved egg yolk.

Margo Boles
Xi Nu Psi, San Diego, California

ALMOND-CHICKEN SALAD

3 c. chopped cooked chicken
1 1/2 c. white grapes
1 1/2 c. chopped celery
1 to 2 tbsp. chopped onion
2 tbsp. lemon juice
1/2 to 2/3 c. mayonnaise
Salt to taste
1 c. roasted almonds
1 c. whipping cream, whipped

Mix first 7 ingredients. Chill. Stir in almonds and whipped cream just before serving. Serve on lettuce-lined plates with assorted crackers.

Wilma Sherrick
Laureate Alpha Epsilon, Effingham, Illinois

166 / Special Occasions

HOLIDAY SALAD

2 c. fresh mushrooms, sliced
1 head romaine lettuce
1 head iceberg lettuce
1 14-oz. can hearts of palm
2 6-oz. jars artichoke hearts, cut up
2 c. cherry tomatoes, quartered
3/4 to 1 c. Caesar dressing

Soak mushrooms in salted water for 2 to 3 hours; drain. Tear romaine and iceburg lettuce into bite-sized pieces. Slice heart of palm in 1/2-inch slices. Toss all ingredients except dressing together. Add Ceasar dressing; mix well. Yield: 10-15 servings.

Judy L. Rayburn
Zeta Delta, Greeley, Colorado

MIXED FRUIT SALAD

2 18-oz. cans pineapple chunks
1/2 c. lemon juice
Juice of 3 oranges
2 eggs
1 c. sugar
2 tbsp. cornstarch
4 bananas, sliced
4 oranges, sliced
Seeded red grape halves

Drain pineapple reserving juice. Heat reserved pineapple juice with lemon and orange juice and 1/2 cup water. Beat eggs with sugar and cornstarch. Stir into juices. Cook until thick, stirring constantly; cool. Mix with fruit. Chill in refrigerator.

Connie Mayfield
Sigma Omega, Key Largo, Florida

ORIENTAL SPINACH SALAD

1/2 c. oil
1 tbsp. sugar
1 tsp. paprika
2 tbsp. grated onion
1/3 c. catsup
1/4 c. rice vinegar
1 tbsp. soy sauce
2 bunches spinach, torn
2 c. fresh bean sprouts
8 slices crisp-fried bacon, crumbled
2 hard-boiled eggs, chopped
1 can sliced water chestnuts, drained

Combine first 7 ingredients. Chill. Mix remaining ingredients. Add dressing; toss to coat. Serve immediately.

Anne C. Fugit
Xi Pi Rho, Napa, California

STEWED TOMATO ASPIC

1 pkg. lemon gelatin
1 can stewed tomatoes
1 tbsp. instant onions
1/2 green pepper, chopped
3 stalks celery, chopped

Dissolve gelatin in 2/3 cup boiling water. Add remaining ingredients. Chill until set. Garnish with mayonnaise and paprika.

Ann Abney
Xi Alpha Kappa, LaFayette, Georgia

CHICAGO SUPER SUMMER SALAD

1 pkg. macaroni, cooked
1 c. chopped dill pickles
1 12-oz. can tuna
1 can mushrooms
2 lb. tomatoes, chopped
1 c. diced Cheddar cheese
1/3 c. chopped green pepper
1/2 c. Italian salad dressing
1/2 c. sour cream
1 tsp. seasoned salt

Mix first 7 ingredients. Blend remaining ingredients. Chill. Add dressing to macaroni mixture; mix lightly.

Julie Yemm
Tau Pi, Sterling, Illinois

TAHITI SALAD

4 c. cooked rice
1 8 1/2-oz. can mixed vegetables, drained
1 7-oz. can whole kernel corn with sweet peppers
1 c. mayonnaise
1/4 c. vinegar
2 hard-boiled eggs, chopped
Dash of garlic powder
Salt and pepper to taste
1/2 c. chopped celery
2 tomatoes, chopped
2 tbsp. chopped green pepper
2 tbsp. chopped onions

Combine all ingredients. Chill in refrigerator. Yield: 10-15 servings.

Dianne Causey
Texas Xi Pi Psi, Eagle Lake, Texas

CHERYL'S SALAD DRESSING

1 c. sugar
2 tbsp. flour
1 tbsp. salt
Dash of pepper
1 tbsp. dry mustard
1 c. milk
1 c. vinegar
3 eggs, beaten

Combine all ingredients with 1 cup water in top of double boiler. Cook over boiling water until thick.

Cheryl Brown
Gamma, Souris, Manitoba, Canada

KULP CRANBERRY RING

1 qt. whole cranberries, washed
2 c. sugar
2 env. unflavored gelatin
1 c. chopped walnuts
1 c. sliced peeled seeded grapes
1 c. crushed pineapple, drained

Special Occasions / 167

Cook cranberries in 2 cups boiling water until they burst. Grind cranberries in meat grinder. Add sugar to ground cranberries; bring to a boil. Dissolve gelatin in 1/2 cup cold water; add to cranberry mixture. Add remaining ingredients; mix well. Pour into 6-cup ring mold. Chill until set.

Phyllis Kulp
Pennsylvania Xi Delta Alpha, Bethlehem, Pennsylvania

CONGEALED SEAFOOD RING

3 tbsp. unflavored gelatin	1 can tiny English peas, drained
Hot chicken stock	1/2 c. finely chopped celery
1 c. mayonnaise	
1/2 c. lemon juice	
Minced onion to taste	1/2 c. chopped almonds
Salt, pepper, oregano and Tabasco sauce to taste	1/2 tsp. chopped stuffed olives
1 c. cooked shrimp	3 hard-boiled eggs, chopped
1 c. crab meat	
1/2 c. lobster	

Soften gelatin in 3 tablespoons cold water. Dissolve in 1 1/8 cups chicken stock; cool. Stir in remaining ingredients. Spoon into lightly greased ring mold. Chill until firm. Unmold on serving plate.

Debbie Carter
Xi Beta Upsilon, Clarkston, Georgia

FANCY FRESH FRUIT PIZZA

1 can sweetened condensed milk	1/4 c. packed brown sugar
1/2 c. sour cream	1 c. flour
1/4 c. lemon juice	1/4 c. oats
1 tsp. vanilla extract	1/4 c. finely chopped walnuts
1/2 c. margarine, softened	Assorted fresh fruit

Combine first 4 ingredients. Chill. Cream margarine and brown sugar. Mix in flour, oats and walnuts. Press into oiled pizza pan shaping rim. Prick with fork. Bake at 350 degrees for 10 to 12 minutes; cool. Spread sour cream mixture over crust. Arrange fruit over top. Garnish with mint leaves. Chill.

Janet Strouse
Xi Gamma Omega, Storm Lake, Iowa

COTTAGE CHEESE ROLLS

2 pkg. dry yeast	2 eggs, slightly beaten
2 c. cottage cheese	4 1/2 c. sifted flour
1/4 c. sugar	1 tsp. each dill, chives (opt.)
2 tsp. salt	
1/2 tsp. soda	

Dissolve yeast in 1/2 cup lukewarm water. Heat cottage cheese to lukewarm. Stir in next 4 ingredients and yeast. Stir in enough flour with dill and chives to make soft dough. Let rise in greased bowl until doubled in bulk. Shape into rolls in greased 9 x 13-inch pan. Let rise until doubled. Bake at 350 degrees for 20 minutes. Yield: 2 dozen.

Lynne Thomas
Alpha Omega Nu, Dayton, Texas

PEPPER-PECAN SANDWICHES

2 8-oz. packages cream cheese, softened	1/4 c. finely chopped onion
1 med. green pepper, finely chopped	1/2 c. sour cream
1 c. finely chopped pecans	1/4 c. mayonnaise

Combine all ingredients. Spread on trimmed rye or pumpernickel bread. Cut into fingers.

Melissa Stroud
Eta Rho, Covington, Louisiana

Wine & Cheese Promotion Party

PUNCHY SANGRIA

2 6-oz. cans frozen pink lemonade concentrate, thawed	1 lemon, thinly sliced
	1 orange, thinly sliced
	1/2 c. sugar
4 1/2 c. chilled Rose	1 28-oz. bottle of ginger ale
Juice of 1 lime	
2 c. chilled club soda	

Combine all ingredients. Chill. Yield: 24 servings.

Patsy M. Lynch
Xi Tau, Tuscaloosa, Alabama

WINE SPRITZER PUNCH

1 6-oz. can limeade concentrate, thawed	1 qt. club soda, chilled
	2 1/2 qt. 7-Up, chilled
2 fifths of Rose wine, chilled	1 orange, sliced
	1 lemon, sliced

Mix limeade concentrate and wine in punch bowl. Pour club soda and 7-Up down side of bowl; stir gently. Add orange and lemon slices.

Bonnie Harman
Xi Kappa Pi, O'Fallon, Illinois

PICKLED WIENERS

1 jar cocktail onions
1 qt. vinegar
1 tsp. liquid smoke
1 tsp. Worcestershire sauce
5 lb. wieners, cut into bite-sized chunks

Drain cocktail onions, reserving juice. Combine reserved juice and 1 quart water with next 3 ingredielts in saucepan bring to a boil. Place wieners and cocktail onions in gallon jar. Pour hot liquid over wieners. Refrigerate overnight. Serve on toothpicks.

Sue Kidd
Preceptor Laureate Alpha Psi, Odessa, Texas

ZIPPY CHEESE BALL

20 oz. cream cheese, softened
1 10-oz. package grated sharp Cheddar cheese
1 10-oz. package grated smoked Cheddar cheese
1/4 c. mayonnaise
1 tbsp. Worcestershire sauce
10 drops of Tabasco sauce
Onion and garlic salt to taste
Chopped walnuts

Blend first 8 ingredients. Shape into two 3-inch balls. Roll in walnuts. Chill until firm.

Renee Nichols
Gamma Kappa, Rockledge, Florida

FETA CHEESE PASTIES

1 8-oz. package cream cheese, softened
1/2 lb. feta cheese, crumbled
1 8-oz. carton large curd cottage cheese
3 egg yolks
2 tbsp. minced parsley
24 sheets phyllo
1/2 lb. butter, melted

Beat cream cheese, feta cheese, cottage cheese, egg yolks and parsley until smooth. Cut phyllo into 2 x 12-inch strips; brush each with butter. Place 1 teaspoon of cheese mixture on end of strip. Fold 1 corner over to make triangle. Fold remaining strip in like manner to enclose filling. Repeat with remaining phyllo and filling. Place on buttered baking sheet. Brush with butter. Bake at 350 degrees for 15 minutes. Yield: 4 dozen.

Christine L. Morrow
Preceptor Gamma, Smyrna, Delaware

CHEDDAR CHEESE CRISPS

1/2 c. butter, softened
2 c. shredded sharp Cheddar cheese
1 c. flour
1/4 tsp. paprika
Pinch of cayenne pepper
1 c. rice cereal

Beat butter and cheese together. Mix flour, paprika and cayenne pepper. Blend into butter mixture. Add cereal; mix gently. Roll into 1-inch balls; place on greased cookie sheet. Flatten slightly. Bake at 350 degrees for about 17 minutes. Do not brown. Yield: 3 dozen.

Paula M. Uhley
Preceptor Tau, Belleville, Illinois

ZINGY CHEESE RING

1 lb. sharp cheese, grated
3 tbsp. (heaping) mayonnaise
1 tbsp. grated onion
1 c. chopped nuts
1/4 tsp. red pepper
Garlic salt to taste (opt.)
Strawberry preserves

Mix first 6 ingredients. Chill in greased ring mold overnight. Unmold on serving plate. Fill center with strawberry preserves. Garnish with parsley. Serve with crackers. Yield: 20-25 servings.

Barbara S. Halaby
Xi Gamma Rho, Columbus, Georgia

CHEESE MOUSSE

2 env. unflavored gelatin
1 1/2 c. beef broth
1/2 to 1 clove of garlic, sliced
1/4 tsp. Worcestershire sauce
Dash of Tabasco sauce
12 oz. cream cheese

Soften gelatin in broth in saucepan. Heat over medium heat to dissolve gelatin; stir frequently. Do not boil. Cool. Pour into blender container. Add seasonings. Process for 30 seconds. Add cream cheese 1/3 at a time, processing constantly. Pour into 3-cup mold. Chill for about 3 hours. Serve with Melba toast.

Carolyn Yokley
Preceptor Alpha Epsilon, Brentwood, Tennessee

DUTCH CHEESE-SHRIMP PUFFS

1/2 c. butter
1 3/4 c. flour
6 eggs
2 cans sm. shrimp
2 c. shredded Gouda cheese
1 tbsp. finely chopped onion
Dash of Tabasco sauce
Salt and pepper to taste
Oil for deep frying

Bring butter and 1 cup water to a boil. Stir in flour. Cook until mixture forms ball; cool for 1 minute. Beat in eggs 1 at a time. Stir in shrimp, cheese, onion and seasonings. Drop by teaspoonfuls into hot oil. Deep-fry until golden brown. Drain on paper towels.

Linda E. Bauer
Alpha, Seoul, South Korea

PULL-APART ITALIAN BREAD

1 loaf Italian bread
1 med. onion, finely chopped
1 1/2 sticks margarine, softened
2 tbsp. mustard
2 tbsp. poppy seed
1 16-oz. package sliced Swiss cheese

Slice bread almost to bottom. Combine onion, margarine, mustard and poppy seed. Spread on bread slices. Place folded cheese slices in each cut. Wrap in foil, leaving top open. Bake at 350 degrees for 20 minutes or until cheese melts.

Joanne K. Mohr
Xi Alpha Beta, Brunswick, Georgia

COEURS A LA CREME

1 8-oz. package cream cheese, softened
1/2 tsp. vanilla extract
1/2 c. sifted confectioners' sugar
1 c. whipping cream, whipped
1/4 c. currant jelly
1 10-oz. package frozen raspberries, thawed, drained
2 tbsp. dry red wine

Blend cream cheese and vanilla in mixer bowl. Add confectioners' sugar gradually, beating at high speed until fluffy. Beat cream until soft peaks form. Fold into cream cheese mixture. Line six 3-inch coeur a la creme molds with moistened cheesecloth, allowing cheesecloth to overhang edges. Spoon mixture into molds. Chill, covered, for several hours to overnight. Melt currant jelly. Stir in raspberries and wine. Chill, covered, until serving time. Invert molds on serving plates; remove cheesecloth. Top with raspberry sauce. May substitute peach preserves for currant jelly, peaches for raspberries and orange liqueur for wine to make peach sauce. Yield: 6 servings.

Cheryl Miller
Preceptor Gamma, Concord, New Hampshire

RITZ CRACKER DESSERT

60 Ritz crackers
1/4 lb. margarine, melted
1 1/2 c. milk
1/2 gal. vanilla ice cream
2 sm. packages instant coconut cream pudding mix

Crush crackers; reserve 1/2 cup crumbs for topping. Combine margarine and cracker crumbs. Press in bottom of 9 x 13-inch pan. Combine milk, ice cream and pudding mix. Pour over cracker crumbs. Top with reserved 1/4 cup crumbs. Chill until serving time.

Sara Ann Charles
Xi Gamma Omega, Port Trevorton, Pennsylvania

Anniversary Celebration

LIQUID GOLD PUNCH

1 12-oz. can frozen orange juice concentrate
1 6-oz. can frozen lemonade concentrate
1 liter chilled ginger ale

Mix concentrates and 6 cups water; chill. Mix with ginger ale in punch bowl. Garnish with fruit ring made of strawberries, pineapple cubes, orange sections and mint leaves frozen in water in 1 1/2-quart ring mold.

Diana Field
Alpha Iota Tau, Cedar Park, Texas

SENSATIONAL CHAMPAGNE PUNCH

1 fifth Sauterne
1 6-oz. can orange juice concentrate, thawed
1 6-oz. can limeade concentrate, thawed
1 fifth Champagne, chilled
1 fifth club soda, chilled
4 oz. orange liqueur

Mix Sauterne, orange juice and limeade concentrates; chill. Combine all ingredients with decorative ice ring in punch bowl.

Barbara Arnold
Preceptor Beta Alpha, Sedalia, Missouri

SILVER CRAB DIP

6 oz. fresh crab meat
2 oz. Brandy
1 8-oz. package cream cheese, softened
2 to 3 tbsp. finely minced onion
1/8 tsp. pepper
4 or 5 drops of Tabasco sauce
1/3 c. slivered almonds
Paprika

Heat crab over medium heat until dry. Add Brandy. Cook until nearly dry. Beat cream cheese with remaining ingredients except paprika. Mix in crab. Spoon into baking dish; sprinkle with paprika. Bake at 350 degrees for 15 minutes. Garnish with parsley. Serve with cocktail rye bread.

Elma Gray
Preceptor Gamma Alpha, Castro Valley, California

ARTICHOKE DIP

1 1/2 13-oz. cans artichokes in water, drained, chopped
1 1/2 c. mayonnaise
1 6-oz can ortega chilis, chopped
6 oz grated Parmesan cheese

Combine all ingredients; mix well. Bake in 1-quart greased baking dish at 350 degrees for 20 minutes. Serve with corn chips or crackers. Yield: 20 servings.

Mary Ann Williamson
Preceptor Beta Pi, San Jose, California

CHAMPAGNE-FROSTED SANDWICH LOAF

1 1-lb. loaf unsliced white bread
1 c. chopped cooked chicken
2 tbsp. thinly sliced celery
2 tbsp. chopped pistachio nuts
5 tbsp. mayonnaise
3 tbsp. butter, softened
2 tbsp. chopped watercress
Dash of Worcestershire sauce
1 6-oz. package frozen crab meat, thawed, chopped
1/4 c. chopped cucumber
3 8-oz. packages cream cheese, softened
1/2 c. Champagne

Remove crust from bread. Cut horizontally into 4 layers. Spread mixture of chicken, celery, nuts and 3 tablespoons mayonnaise on first layer. Spread mixture of butter, watercress and Worcestershire sauce on second layer. Spread mixture of crab meat, cucumbers and 2 tablespoons mayonnaise on third layer. Stack layers on top of each other; top with remaining bread layer. Beat cream cheese until fluffy. Add Champagne; mix well. Frost top and sides of loaf. Decorate with remaining cream cheese mixture. Garnish with additional chopped pistachio nuts.

Photograph for this recipe on page 157.

SEAFOOD CASSEROLE

4 tsp. butter
1/4 c. flour
2 c. milk
3 tbsp. Parmesan cheese
1/4 c. white wine
1 lb. white fish
1/2 lb. crab meat
1/2 lb. lobster
1/2 lb. scallops
1 lb. med. shrimp
1/2 lb. mushrooms, sliced
Salt, pepper, garlic powder to taste
Ritz cracker crumbs

Melt butter; stir in flour. Add milk, stirring constantly until mixture is smooth and thick. Add cheese and wine. Layer seafood and mushrooms in greased 2-quart casserole. Season to taste. Pour white sauce over all. Top with cracker crumbs. Bake at 350 degrees for 1 hour. Yield: 8 servings.

Peg Bibby
Delta Delta Eta, Lake Isabella, California

GOLDEN PUFF PASTRY CHICKEN ROLLS

Flour
4 boned chicken breasts, skinned
Seasoned salt and herbs to taste
1 pkg. frozen puff pastry dough, thawed
1 3-oz. package cream cheese and chives, softened
1 egg yolk, beaten
1 can cream of chicken soup
1/2 c. mayonnaise
1/3 soup can milk

Brown flour-coated chicken in a small amount of oil; season to taste. Wrap in puff pastry spread with cream cheese; seal moistened edge. Place seam side down in baking dish. Brush with egg yolk beaten with a small amount of water. Bake at 400 degrees for 20 to 30 minutes. Heat soup, mayonnaise and milk to serving temperature. Serve with chicken rolls.

Rosalie R. King
Chi Phi, Lompoc, California

DIAMOND LOBSTER THERMIDOR

4 8 to 10-oz. lobster tails
14 tbsp. butter
1/4 c. oil
2 tbsp. minced shallots
1 c. white wine
2 tsp. each chervil, tarragon
1/4 c. flour
2 c. milk
1 slice onion
1 bay leaf
6 peppercorns
Pinch of mace
1/4 c. sliced mushrooms
1/4 c. heavy cream
1 tsp. Dijon mustard
6 tbsp. Parmesan cheese
1/4 c. Italian bread crumbs

Cook lobster tails in 1/4 cup butter and oil for 15 to 20 minutes; cool. Remove and chop lobster; reserve shells and pan drippings. Saute shallots in 2 tablespoons butter. Stir in wine, chervil and tarragon. Cook until liquid is reduced by half. Blend 1/4 cup melted butter and flour; stir in milk mixed with onion, bay leaf, peppercorns and mace. Cook until thick, stirring constantly. Remove onion, bay leaf and peppercorns. Stir in wine sauce, reserved pan drippings, mushrooms, cream, mustard and 2 tablespoons cheese. Cook over low heat for 10 minutes. Mix half the sauce with lobster. Spoon into reserved shells. Sprinkle with mixture of crumbs and 1/4 cup cheese. Drizzle with 1/4 cup melted butter. Broil until brown and bubbly. Serve with remaining sauce.

Jean B. Singman
Preceptor Kappa, Lutherville, Maryland

DELUXE MASHED POTATOES

5 or 6 med. potatoes
3 tsp. butter
1/2 c. milk
1 egg, beaten
1 tsp. parsley
1/4 tsp. onion
1 3-oz. package cream cheese, softened

Special Occasions / 171

Boil potatoes until tender; mash. Add butter and milk. Combine egg, parsley, onion and cream cheese. Add to potato mixture; mix well. Bake in buttered 2-quart casserole at 350 degrees for 20 minutes. Yield: 6 servings.

Carole Pipett
Xi Xi, Altoona, Pennsylvania

ASPARAGUS ALLA FONTINA

2 1/2 lb. thin asparagus, trimmed
1/4 c. butter
Salt, pepper and nutmeg to taste
1/3 c. grated Gruyere cheese
3/4 c. finely minced prosciutto
2 tbsp. minced parsley
3 eggs, beaten
3 to 4 tbsp. Parmesan cheese

Cook asparagus in boiling salted water for 7 minutes; drain and cut into 1-inch pieces. Cook asparagus with butter, salt, pepper and nutmeg over low heat, tossing to coat. Spread in lightly buttered 9-inch glass pie plate. Sprinkle with cheese, prosciutto and parsley. Pour eggs over top. Top with Parmesan cheese. Bake at 350 degrees for 35 minutes.

Kristina Scott
Gamma Gamma, Virginia Beach, Virginia

STAINED GLASS SALAD

1 lg. can pineapple chunks, drained
1 can mandarin oranges, drained
1 can peach pie filling
1 pkg. frozen strawberries, thawed
3 bananas, sliced

Mix all ingredients. Chill until serving time.

Linda Derrington
Xi Epsilon Kappa, Rush, Texas

ALMOND CREAM IN RUBY STRAWBERRIES

2 pt. large strawberries
1 sm. package vanilla instant pudding mix
1 c. milk
1 c. heavy cream, whipped
1 tsp. almond extract

Stem strawberries; cut deep X in top of each and spread apart to form petals. Prepare pudding according to package directions, using 1 cup milk. Fold in whipped cream and flavoring. Pipe cream into strawberries, using pastry bag.

Debbie Benson
Zeta Delta, Greeley, Colorado

ANGEL FOOD COOKIES

1 c. sugar
1 c. packed brown sugar
12 egg yolks
1 1/2 c. shortening
3 tsp. vanilla extract
3 1/2 c. flour
1/2 tsp. salt
1 tsp. soda
2 tsp. baking powder

Cream the sugars, egg yolks, shortening and vanilla in large bowl. Sift flour with salt, soda and baking powder. Stir into creamed mixture. Add small amount of flour for dough to be stiff enough to roll into walnut-sized balls. Roll in additional sugar. Place on lightly greased cookie sheet. Flatten with tines of fork to 1/4 inch thick. Bake at 350 degrees for 5 minutes or until light brown. Yield: 4 dozen.

Judy Bishop
Beta Upsilon, Dalhart, Texas

GLAZED PEAR PIE

1 1/2 c. finely crushed vanilla wafers
6 tbsp. melted butter
1 c. whipping cream
4 oz. cream cheese, softened
1/2 c. sifted confectioners' sugar
1 15-oz. can pear halves, drained
1 tsp. gelatin
1 1/2 tbsp. pear syrup
1/3 c. seville orange marmalade

Combine crumbs and butter. Press firmly into 9-inch pie plate. Chill. Whip cream until stiff; chill. Beat cream cheese until smooth. Add sugar gradually. Combine whipped cream and cheese mixture. Spread evenly over crust; chill. Arrange pears over cheese layer. Soften gelatin in pear syrup; melt over boiling water. Add marmalade; blend well. Cool slightly Spoon glaze over pears. Chill for several hours before serving.

Marion Harvey
Zeta Alpha, Revelstoke, British Columbia, Canada

MICROWAVE PETITS FOURS

1 lemon, strawberry, orange or yellow cake mix
1 can frosting to compliment cake mix

Mix cake using package directions. Fill Pam-sprayed styrofoam egg carton cups 1/2 full. Microwave 1 minute. Remove completely baked cakes. Bake any remaining cakes for 15 seconds. Place upside down on waxed paper. Remove aluminum liner from frosting container; microwave for 1 minute. Drizzle 1 to 2 teaspoons frosting over each petit four.

Emily Braden
Xi Alpha Mu, Owensboro, Kentucky

LEMON ICE SUPREME

1 1/2 c. sugar
2 tsp. grated lemon rind
1 c. lemon juice

Boil sugar dissolved in 2 cups water until clear. Stir in lemon rind and juice. Freeze in shallow pan. Beat in mixer bowl until thick and fluffy. Freeze, covered; serve in cantaloupe halves, on honeydew wedges or with strawberries drizzled with Cointreau.

Jana Howell
Xi Gamma Sigma, Waverly, New York

BAKED WATER CHESTNUTS

2 cans water chestnuts
Soy sauce
1 c. sugar
1 1-lb. package bacon

Marinate water chestnuts in enough soy sauce to cover for 1/2 hour. Roll water chestnuts in sugar. Wrap half slice bacon around each water chestnut; secure with toothpick. Place on cookie sheet. Bake at 400 degrees for 15 minutes. Drain. May be frozen.

Helen M. Montgomery
Xi Alpha Upsilon, Whitewood, South Dakota

HOT BUTTERED RUM BASE

1 lb. packed brown sugar
1 lb. confectioners' sugar
1 lb. butter, softened
1 qt. vanilla ice cream, softened

Blend sugars and butter until fluffy. Add ice cream gradually; blend well. Store in freezer. To serve use 1 heaping tablespoon base for each large mug. Add 1 jigger rum or whiskey. Fill mug with boiling water; stir well. Top with nutmeg. May be used with or without rum. Yield: 2 quarts.

Patricia G. Kopp
Xi Kappa, Pasco, Washington

A Movable Feast

STRAWBERRY SLUSH

1 c. sugar
1 16-oz. package frozen strawberries
1 12-oz. can frozen unsweetened orange juice concentrate
1 pkg. strawberry drink mix
1 2-liter bottle of 7-Up
1 c. vodka

Boil sugar dissolved in 3 cups water until clear. Add strawberries, orange juice and drink mix; cool. Add 7-Up and vodka. Freeze for several hours. Thaw slightly until slushy. Spoon into thermos for transporting.

Cheryl Ledger
Xi Kappa Beta, Wintersville, Ohio

MUSHROOM TURNOVERS

1 8-oz. package cream cheese, softened
Flour
11 tbsp. butter
1/2 lb. mushrooms, minced
1 med. onion, minced
1/4 c. sour cream
1 tsp. salt
1/4 tsp. thyme leaves
1 egg, beaten

Mix cream cheese, 1 1/2 cups flour and 1/2 cup butter. Shape into ball; wrap. Chill for 1 hour. Saute mushrooms and onions in 3 tablespoons butter over medium heat. Stir in sour cream, salt, thyme and 2 tablespoons flour. Roll dough 1/8 inch thick on floured surface. Cut into 2 1/4-inch circles with floured cutter. Spoon 1 teaspoonful mushroom mixture on each circle. Brush edge with egg. Fold over to enclose filling; press with fork to seal. Prick tops; brush with remaining egg. Bake at 450 degrees on baking sheet for 12 to 14 minutes.

Marcia Herman
Gamma, Laramie, Wyoming

TUNA MOUSSE

1 can tomato soup
2 env. unflavored gelatin
1 8-oz. package cream cheese
1 c. mayonnaise
1 c. finely chopped celery
1 onion, chopped
1 12-oz. can tuna
Salt and pepper to taste
1 tsp. Tabasco sauce (opt.)

Heat soup. Add gelatin; stir until dissolved. Combine cream cheese, mayonnaise, celery, onion and tuna. Stir into soup mixture. Season to taste. Grease mold with additional mayonnaise. Pour mixture into mold. Chill for several hours. Serve with crackers.

Xi Zeta Omega Sisters
Clairton, Pennsylvania

CHICKEN LIVER PATE

1 lb. chicken livers
1 can mushroom soup
1 med. onion
1/2 lb. margarine
1 tsp. thyme
Salt and pepper to taste

Process all ingredients in blender until liquified. Pour into baking dish. Bake, covered, in 1-inch deep water bath at 375 degrees for 1 1/4 hours. Chill overnight.

Margaret DuCasse
Preceptor Theta, Winnipeg, Manitoba, Canada

CREAMY SALMON PATE

1 7 3/4-oz. can salmon	1/4 tsp. dry mustard
1 8-oz. package cream cheese, softened	1 tsp. Worcestershire sauce
1 pkg. Ranch-style buttermilk salad dressing mix	1/4 tsp. dry mustard
	1 1/2 tbsp. lemon juice
1 tbsp. minced onion	1/4 c. finely chopped fresh parsley

Line 3-cup bowl with plastic wrap; set aside. Drain salmon; remove bones and skin. Combine all ingredients except salmon and parsley; mix well. Stir in salmon and parsley. Spoon mixture into lined bowl, pressing firmly; smooth top. Chill, covered, overnight. Invert bowl onto platter; unmold to serve. Garnish with parsley sprigs. Serve with crackers or fresh vegetable sticks. Yield: 8-10 servings.

Adrianne Loser
Gamma Gamma, Beach, Virginia

FAST CHICKEN AND RICE SQUARES

1 6 1/4-oz. box fast-cooking long grain and wild rice	6 whole chicken breasts, deboned
	4 6-oz. Swiss cheese slices
1 env. Shake 'N Bake	

Prepare rice using package directions. Sprinkle 1/2 package Shake 'N Bake in greased 9 x 9-inch baking dish. Flatten chicken breasts with side of small saucer. Layer half the chicken breasts, 3/4 cup rice and half the cheese in dish. Repeat layers. Top with remaining Shake 'N Bake. Bake, uncovered, at 400 degrees for 40 minutes. Yield: 4-6 servings.

Marilyn Manion
Xi Eta Eta, Greensburg, Pennsylvania

CHICKEN GARLICIOUS

4 whole chicken breasts, split, skinned, boned	1/4 c. minced fresh parsley
3/4 c. butter, melted	1 tsp. salt
2 to 4 cloves of garlic, pressed	1/4 tsp. pepper
	Juice of 2 lemons
1 c. fine dry bread crumbs	Paprika
2/3 c. Parmesan cheese	

Dip chicken breasts in butter mixed with garlic, then into mixture of bread crumbs, cheese, parsley, salt and pepper. Fold in half lengthwise. Roll up; secure with toothpick. Place seam side down in lightly greased baking dish. Sprinkle with lemon juice, remaining butter and crumb mixtures. Sprinkle with paprika. Bake at 350 degrees for 1 hour. Serve hot or cold.

Susie Ranager
Alpha Kappa, Pascagoula, Mississippi

PRIZEWINNING STUFFED MEAT LOAF

2 lb. mixed ground beef, pork and veal	1/2 c. Parmesan cheese
	2 hard-boiled eggs, sliced
1 c. bread crumbs	
2 eggs	1 6-oz. package Provolone cheese, sliced
1 tsp. pepper	
1/2 tsp. basil	
Grated rind of 1 lemon	1/4 lb. salami, diced
1 sm. onion, grated	2 tbsp. butter
1 clove of garlic, minced	1 c. bouillon

Mix meat mixture with next 8 ingredients. Pat into 10 x 12-inch rectangle on waxed paper. Arrange sliced eggs and Provolone lengthwise on top. Sprinkle salami over cheese. Roll as for jelly roll. Place seam side down in buttered baking pan. Pour bouillon over meat loaf. Bake at 350 degrees for 1 1/4 hours. Let stand for 10 minutes. Yield: 8 servings.

Rosalie Senuty
Preceptor Alpha Xi, Bellingham, Washington

TANGY ANTIPASTO SALAD

1/2 lb. hard salami	1 c. green olives
1/2 lb. pepperoni	1 lb. small shell macaroni, cooked
1/2 lb. provolone cheese	
2 med. green peppers	1 tbsp. oregano
3 stalks celery	1/2 tsp. salt
1 med. onion	1 tsp. pepper
3 tomatoes	1/2 c. vinegar
1 c. pitted black olives	3/4 c. oil

Cut meats, cheese and vegetables into bite-sized pieces; mix with olives and macaroni. Combine remaining ingredients. Pour over salad; toss well. Store, covered, in refrigerator. Keeps for weeks.

Pat Smith
Lambda Mu, Hughesville, Pennsylvania

WHEAT GERM-CHEESE WAFERS

3/4 c. grated sharp Cheddar cheese	1/3 c. flour
	1/2 tsp. salt
1/4 c. butter, softened	Sesame seed (opt.)
2/3 c. wheat germ	

Beat cheese and butter until blended. Stir in combined wheat germ, flour and salt mixture and 1 tablespoon water. Roll 1/2 inch thick on lightly floured surface; cut with small floured biscuit cutter. Sprinkle with sesame seed. Bake at 350 degrees on baking sheets until brown. Yield: 3 dozen.

Jene Yazel
Preceptor Gamma Upsilon, Gladstone, Missouri

174 / Special Occasions

CHEESE-PEPPER BREAD

1 pkg. dry yeast
2 1/3 c. flour
2 tsp. sugar
1 tsp. salt
1/4 tsp. soda
1 c. sour cream
1 egg
1 c. shredded Cheddar cheese
1/2 tsp. pepper

Dissolve yeast in 1/4 cup hot water in mixer bowl. Add 1 1/2 cups flour and next 5 ingredients. Beat at low speed for 1/2 minute then at high speed for 2 minutes. Stir in remaining flour, cheese and pepper. Pour into 2 greased 1-pound coffee cans. Let rise in warm place for 50 minutes. Bake at 350 degrees for 40 minutes. Remove from cans immediately to cool. Replace in cans for transporting.

Rose Bolen
Preceptor Gamma Upsilon, Kansas City, Missouri

TRIPLE-CHOCOLATE CAKE

Unsalted butter
1/4 c. unsweetened cocoa powder
3 eggs
3/4 c. sour cream
2 c. flour
2 c. sugar
1/2 tsp. salt
1 tsp. soda
1 6-oz. package semisweet chocolate chips
4 sq. unsweetened chocolate, melted
2 1/4 c. sifted confectioners' sugar
2 egg yolks

Bring 1 cup water, 1 cup butter and cocoa to a boil. Simmer for 2 minutes. Beat eggs with sour cream. Beat into mixture of flour, sugar, salt and soda. Stir in chocolate chips. Beat in hot mixture gradually. Pour into greased and floured 9 x 13-inch baking pan. Bake at 350 degrees for 40 to 50 minutes. Cool on wire rack. Blend melted chocolate, confectioners' sugar and 1/4 cup boiling water. Beat in egg yolks 1 at a time. Beat in 6 tablespoons butter 1 tablespoon at a time. Spread over cake. May substitute buttermilk for all or part of sour cream.

Patti Beldion
Xi Sigma Omicron, Beale AFB, California

LOU'S LOLLAPALOOZA

1/2 c. white rum
1/4 c. packed brown sugar
1 c. (real) sour cream
Seedless green grapes

Combine first 3 ingredients. Add grapes. Chill. Spoon into wide mouth thermos. Place grapes in stemmed glasses. Pour sauce over grapes. Do not cover completely.

Louise MacMillan
Preceptor Zeta, Nelson, British Columbia, Canada

SCALLOPED PINEAPPLE

1 1/2 c. sugar
3 eggs
1 c. margarine
1 No. 2 can crushed pineapple
4 c. bread cubes

Combine all ingredients in 9 x 12-inch casserole. Bake at 350 degrees for 1 hour. Yield: 12 servings.

Sherrie Blanchard
Texas Gamma Upsilon, Bedford, Texas

COCONUT PIE

2 eggs
3/4 c. sugar
3/4 c. milk
2 tbsp. butter, melted
2 c. shredded coconut, toasted
1 tsp. lemon extract
1 unbaked pie shell

Beat eggs and sugar together. Add next 4 ingredients; mix well. Pour into pie shell. Cover with foil. Bake at 350 degrees for 15 minutes; remove foil. Bake for 25 to 30 minutes longer. Cool.

Elizabeth M. Koenig
Precepter Kappa Kappa, Fairfield, California

OLD-FASHIONED RICE PUDDING

4 c. milk
1/4 c. sugar
1/4 c. long grain rice
1 tbsp. margarine
1/4 tsp. salt
1/4 tsp. nutmeg
1 tsp. vanilla extract
1/2 c. raisins

Mix first 7 ingredients. Bake in greased 1 1/2-quart casserole at 325 degrees for 2 hours. Stir frequently. Stir in raisins. Bake for 30 minutes longer or until rice is very tender. Yield: 6 servings.

Karen Ream
Zeta Beta, Phoenix, Arizona

PERSIMMON COOKIES

3/4 c. sugar
3/4 c. packed brown sugar
1/2 c. shortening
1 egg
2 c. flour
1 tsp. soda
1 c. persimmon
1 c. raisins or nuts
1 tsp. cinnamon
1/2 tsp. each nutmeg, ginger

Cream sugars and shortening until smooth. Add egg; mix well. Add flour and soda. Add persimmon, raisins and spices; mix well. Drop by teaspoonfuls onto greased cookie sheet. Bake at 350 degrees for 10 to 12 minutes. Yield: 3 dozen.

Janet Ridenour
Delta Delta Eta, Lake Isabella, California

Grand Tour Sampler

ALMOND TEA

2 c. sugar
Rind of 1/2 lemon
1 tsp. vanilla extract
1 tsp. almond extract
Juice of 3 lemons
2 c. strong tea

Boil sugar dissolved in 4 cups water with lemon rind for 5 minutes; cool. Mix with 2 cups water and remaining ingredients. Serve hot or cold.

Ruby Roberts
Alpha Alpha, Sapulpa, Oklahoma

ROSE PUNCH

3 12-oz. packages frozen strawberries
1 c. sugar
1 gal. Rose wine
4 6-oz. cans frozen lemonade concentrate
4 32-oz. bottles of club soda, chilled

Thaw strawberries with sugar in punch bowl for 1 hour. Stir in wine and lemonade. Add club soda just before serving. Yield: 64 servings.

Betty Henderson
Laureate Mu, Upland, California

SEVICHE

2 lb. fresh red snapper, boned, cubed
2 c. fresh lime juice
1/2 c. finely chopped onion
1 1/2 c. chopped peeled tomatoes
1/4 c. chopped fresh red hot peppers

Combine all ingredients in tightly covered glass dish. Chill for 3 hours to 2 weeks. Serve with crackers or tortillas.

Ginny Thomas
Xi Delta Phi, Merritt Island, Florida

ESCARGOTS IN MUSHROOM CAPS

2 tbsp. minced onion
1/2 lb. butter, melted
1/4 tsp. lemon juice
1 24 to 26-count can escargots, drained
24 to 26 fresh mushroom caps
2 tbsp. garlic powder

Saute minced onion in 1/4 cup butter. Add lemon juice. Place escargots in mushroom caps in individual escargot dishes. Spoon onion and butter over escargots. Sprinkle lightly with garlic powder. Let stand for 2 hours. Pour mixture of remaining butter and garlic powder over escargots. Bake at 350 degrees for 10 to 15 minutes. Serve with garlic toast.

Bonnie McIntosh
Alberta Xi Alpha Zeta, Leduc, Alberta, Canada

ITALIAN VEGETABLE TOSS

1 1/2 c. shell macaroni, cooked
2 c. broccoli flowerets
1 c. cauliflowerets
1 c. sliced fresh mushrooms
1 6-oz. can artichoke hearts, drained, rinsed, chopped
1 c. sliced pitted ripe olives
1/2 c. chopped green onions
2/3 c. Italian salad dressing
1 med. avocado, chopped
1 med. tomato, seeded, chopped

Mix macaroni with next 7 ingredients. Chill, covered, for several hours. Add avocado and tomato. Serve immediately. Yield: 12-16 servings.

Eva V. Easley
Xi Omicron, Bluefield, West Virginia

HAWAIIAN CHICKEN SALAD

2 c. chopped cooked chicken
1 1/4 tbsp. lemon juice
1/2 c. chopped celery
1/4 c. chopped onion
1 tsp. salt
1/4 tsp. pepper
1 tbsp. chopped pimento
1/3 c. mayonnaise
2 tbsp. slivered toasted almonds
1 c. seedless green grape halves
1/2 c. crushed pineapple, drained
1 cantaloupe, cut into 4 rings
Lettuce leaves

Sprinkle chicken with lemon juice. Add next 9 ingredients; toss to mix. Chill, covered, overnight. Mound salad in melon rings on lettuce-lined plates. Yield: 4 servings.

Lynda A. Guyer
Zeta Phi, St. Marys, Georgia

SOUTH PACIFIC CONCH SALAD

3 c. chopped fresh conch
1/2 hot pepper, mashed
1 c. chopped yellow onion
3 c. chopped firm tomatoes
1 c. each chopped celery, green pepper
2 c. lime juice

Mix first 6 ingredients; chill. Pour lime juice over salad just before serving.

Betty Hoke
Sigma Omega, Key Largo, Florida

CRAB PIZZA

1 12-oz. package cream cheese, softened
2 tbsp. Worcestershire sauce
1 tbsp. lemon juice
Garlic salt to taste
1 sm. onion, finely chopped
1 bottle of chili sauce
1 can backfin crab meat
Fresh parsley

Mix first 5 ingredients. Spread on serving plate; shape edge as for pizza crust. Spread with chili sauce and crab meat. Sprinkle with parsley. Serve with fish-shaped crackers.

Loretta Peacock
Xi Alpha Zeta, Laurel, Maryland

GREEK PASTICHIO

1 1/4 lb. elbow macaroni
1 tbsp. olive oil
6 green onions with tops, chopped
Butter, melted
2 1/2 lb. ground beef
1/2 6-oz. can tomato paste
1/2 c. white wine
Salt and pepper to taste
1 tsp. cinnamon
1/2 tsp. nutmeg
5 eggs
1 1/2 c. grated Greek Kaefaloteri cheese
5 tbsp. flour
4 c. milk

Cook macaroni according to package directions, adding 1 tablespoon olive oil. Do not overcook. Saute green onions in 2 tablespoons butter. Add beef. Cook until brown, stirring frequently. Stir in tomato paste, wine and seasonings. Simmer for 1 hour adding more wine, if necessary. Mix 1/2 cup butter, 3 beaten eggs and 1 cup cheese with macaroni. Layer half the macaroni, all the sauce and remaining macaroni in 9 x 13-inch baking dish. Blend 5 tablepoons butter with flour. Stir in milk gradually. Cook over low heat until thick, stirring constantly. Stir a small amount of hot mixture into 2 beaten eggs; stir eggs into hot mixture. Pour over layers. Sprinkle with 1/2 cup cheese. Bake at 350 degrees for 45 minutes. Cool slightly; cut into squares. May substitute Parmesan or Romano cheese for Kaefaloteri.

Patsy Christos Kandis
Laureate Alpha Omicron, Victoria, Texas

JAPANESE STACK-UP DINNER

Chicken broth
Cornstarch
1 can cream of chicken soup
2 c. cooked rice
1 lg. can chow mein noodles
1 lg. chicken, cooked, chopped
1 1/2 c. chopped celery
1 20-oz. can crushed pineapple, heated
3/4 c. chopped green onions
1 pkg. flaked coconut
1 c. sliced almonds
1 1/2 lb. longhorn cheese, finely grated

Thicken broth with cornstarch blended with a small amount of water to make gravy of desired consistency. Stir in soup. Place remaining ingredients in individual bowls for buffet serving. Layer rice and remaining ingredients in order given for each serving. Top with hot gravy. Yield: 10 servings.

R. Jeanette Elmore
Xi Delta Delta, Olathe, Kansas

SPAGHETTI CARBONARA

1/2 lb. bacon, chopped
6 tbsp. butter
1/3 c. dry white wine
1 lb. spaghetti, cooked
1/2 c. heavy cream
3 egg yolks
1 c. Parmesan cheese

Fry bacon until crisp; drain. Add butter and wine to skillet; deglaze. Cook until reduced. Add spaghetti; toss to mix. Beat cream and egg yolks. Add to spaghetti mixture; toss. Add cheese and 3/4 of the bacon. Garnish with remaining bacon. Serve on warm plate.

Gloria Newell
Preceptor Delta Chi, Key Largo, Florida

BRAZILIAN-STYLE BLACK BEANS

3 c. dried black beans
1 lb. dried beef, chopped
1 lb. Spanish-style sausage
1/4 lb. bacon, partially cooked
2 lb. 2-inch pork cubes
1 c. orange juice
1 c. red wine
Salt to taste
1 onion, chopped
2 cloves of garlic, minced
2 tbsp. olive oil
1/2 tsp. chili powder
3 c. cooked rice
3 oranges, sliced
3 baked acorn squash, peeled, coarsely chopped (opt.)

Soak beans and dried beef separately in water to cover overnight. Drain beans; add fresh water to cover. Cook over low heat for 2 hours. Drain dried beef. Add fresh water to cover. Bring to a boil; drain well. Add fresh water to cover sausage, bacon and pork, reserving several pieces of sausage. Cook over medium heat for 2 hours. Combine beans and meat mixture. Cook over very low heat for 2 hours or until beans are very soft. Stir in orange juice, wine and salt. Cook for 30 minutes longer. Puree 1 1/2 cups bean mixture in blender. Saute onion and garlic in olive oil for 10 minutes. Mash reserved sausage. Add sausage, chili powder and enough bean puree to make of thick gravy consistency. Cook over low heat for 15 minutes. Adjust seasonings. Add half the sauce to bean mixture. Spoon beans over rice in large deep dish. Arrange sliced sausages and meats on top. Pour remaining sauce over the top. Arrange orange slices around edge. Serve with squash.

Danna Lloyd-Black
Xi Kappa Tau, Dallas, Texas

SWISS MOUNTAIN-STYLE BAKED CAULIFLOWER

1/2 c. pumpernickel bread crumbs
2 3/4 c. grated Swiss cheese
1 1/3 c. light cream
3 egg yolks
1/4 tsp. nutmeg
1/2 tsp. salt
1/4 tsp. pepper
1 lg. head cauliflower
1/4 c. melted butter

Mix first 7 ingredients. Break cauliflower into flowerets. Cook in boiling salted water until tender; drain. Place in generously buttered shallow baking dish. Top with cheese mixture. Drizzle with butter. Bake at 350 degrees for 15 to 20 minutes.

Judy L. Hamel
Beta Iota, Sinclair, Wyoming

ONE-HOUR DINNER ROLLS ITALIANO

3 1/2 to 4 c. flour
2 pkg. dry yeast
2 tbsp. sugar
2 tsp. garlic salt
1 tsp. Italian seasoning
1 c. milk
4 tbsp. margarine
1 egg, beaten
3/4 c. Parmesan cheese

Mix 1 1/2 cups flour and next 4 ingredients in mixer bowl. Heat milk, 1/2 cup water and 2 tablespoons margarine to 120 degrees. Add to flour mixture with egg. Blend at low speed. Beat at medium speed for 3 minutes. Stir in 1/2 cup cheese and enough remaining flour to make firm dough. Knead on floured surface until smooth and elastic. Place in greased bowl turning to grease surface. Let rise, covered, in warm place for 15 minutes. Turn oven to lowest setting for 1 minute; turn oven off. Shape dough into balls. Dip tops into 2 tablespoons melted margarine and 1/4 cup cheese. Place in well-greased 9 x 13-inch baking pan. Let rise, covered, in warm oven for 10 minutes. Bake at 375 degrees. Remove from pan to cool.

Betty J. Friedrichs
Gamma Gamma, Herkimer, Kansas

LINZER TORTES

1 stick each butter, margarine, softened
2 c. sugar
3 eggs, beaten
1 tbsp. coffee Brandy
1 tsp. almond extract
1/2 tsp. lemon juice
4 c. flour
2 tsp. baking powder
1/2 tsp. salt
4 tsp. cinnamon
1/4 tsp. nutmeg
1/3 c. ground almonds
2/3 c. ground pecans
Black raspberry jam
Confectioners' sugar

Cream first 3 ingredients. Mix in eggs, Brandy, flavoring and lemon juice. Add sifted dry ingredients; mix well. Stir in almonds and pecans. Chill overnight. Divide into 4 portions. Pat 3 portions 1/2 inch thick over bottom and sides of three 8-inch pie plates. Spread lightly with jam. Cut remaining portion into strips; arrange lattice-fashion over tops. Bake at 350 degrees for 30 minutes. Fill spaces in lattice with jam. Sprinkle with confectioners' sugar.

Paula C. Dalton
Xi Iota Omega, Ozona, Florida

VIENNESE WALNUT BARS

3/4 c. margarine
1 3-oz. package cream cheese
1/4 c. sugar
2 1/4 c. flour
1 1/2 c. walnuts
1 c. chocolate chips
1/4 tsp. baking powder
1/4 tsp. salt
1 tsp. instant coffee
1 1/2 c. packed light brown sugar
2 eggs

Cream 1/2 cup margarine, cream cheese and sugar. Stir in 1 1/4 cups flour gradually; mix well. Pat evenly in 9 x 13-inch baking pan. Sprinkle 1 cup coarsely chopped walnuts over pastry. Sprinkle chocolate chips over walnuts. Combine 1 cup flour, baking powder and salt. Dissolve coffee in 1 tablespoon water. Beat 1/4 cup butter, brown sugar, eggs and coffee together, mixing well. Add flour mixture; mix well. Spoon over chocolate chips, spreading to cover evenly. Sprinkle with 1/2 cup finely ground walnuts. Bake at 350 degrees for 30 minutes. Cool; cut into 2 x 1 1/2-inch bars. Yield: 32 bars.

Gloria M. Kenney
Gamma Zeta, Camden, South Carolina

SWEDISH CRYSTAL NUTS

1 1/2 c. blanched almonds
2 c. walnut halves
1 c. sugar
Dash of salt
2 egg whites
1/2 c. butter, melted

Toast almonds and walnuts at 325 degrees until lightly browned. Fold sugar and salt into stiffly beaten egg whites; beat until very stiff. Fold in nuts. Spread nuts in butter in 10 x 15-inch pan. Bake at 325 degrees for 30 minutes, stirring every 10 minutes. Yield: 4 cups.

Ann Thorndike
Omega, Grand Island, Nebraska

BOURBON SLUSH

1 c. sugar
1 6-oz. can frozen orange juice concentrate
1 fifth of Bourbon
2 2-liter bottles of 7-Up
1 46-oz. can pineapple juice
1 jar cherries

Dissolve sugar in 1 cup water. Stir in orange juice concentrate and next 3 ingredients. Freeze for 12 hours; stir. Add cherries with juice. Freeze for several hours; stir. Serve in punch bowl. Garnish with additional cherries. Yield: 40 servings.

JoAnn Davis
Eta Rho, Mandeville, Louisiana

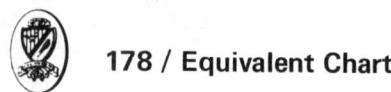

Equivalent Chart

	WHEN RECIPE CALLS FOR:	YOU NEED:
BREAD & CEREAL	1 c. soft bread crumbs	2 slices
	1 c. fine dry bread crumbs	4-5 slices
	1 c. small bread cubes	2 slices
	1 c. fine cracker crumbs	24 saltines
	1 c. fine graham cracker crumbs	14 crackers
	1 c. vanilla wafer crumbs	22 wafers
	1 c. crushed cornflakes	3 c. uncrushed
	4 c. cooked macaroni	1 8-oz. package
	3 1/2 c. cooked rice	1 c. uncooked
DAIRY	1 c. freshly grated cheese	1/4 lb.
	1 c. cottage cheese or sour cream	1 8-oz. carton
	2/3 c. evaporated milk	1 sm. can
	1 2/3 c. evaporated milk	1 tall can
	1 c. whipped cream	1/2 c. heavy cream
SWEET	1 c. semisweet chocolate pieces	1 6-oz. package
	2 c. granulated sugar	1 lb.
	4 c. sifted confectioners' sugar	1 lb.
	2 1/4 c. packed brown sugar	1 lb.
MEAT	3 c. diced cooked meat	1 lb., cooked
	2 c. ground cooked meat	1 lb., cooked
	4 c. diced cooked chicken	1 5-lb. chicken
NUTS	1 c. chopped nuts	4 oz. shelled
		1 lb. unshelled
VEGETABLES	4 c. sliced or diced raw potatoes	4 medium
	2 c. cooked green beans	1/2 lb. fresh or 1 16-oz. can
	1 c. chopped onion	1 large
	4 c. shredded cabbage	1 lb.
	2 c. canned tomatoes	1 16-oz. can
	1 c. grated carrot	1 large
	2 1/2 c. lima beans or red beans	1 c. dried, cooked
	1 4-oz. can mushrooms	1/2 lb. fresh
FRUIT	4 c. sliced or chopped apples	4 medium
	2 c. pitted cherries	4 c. unpitted
	3 to 4 tbsp. lemon juice plus 1 tsp. grated rind	1 lemon
	1/3 c. orange juice plus 2 tsp. grated rind	1 orange
	1 c. mashed banana	3 medium
	4 c. cranberries	1 lb.
	3 c. shredded coconut	1/2 lb.
	4 c. sliced peaches	8 medium
	1 c. pitted dates or candied fruit	1 8-oz. package
	2 c. pitted prunes	1 12-oz. package
	3 c. raisins	1 15-oz. package

COMMON EQUIVALENTS

1 tbsp. = 3 tsp.	6 1/2 to 8-oz. can = 1 c.
2 tbsp. = 1 oz.	10 1/2 to 12-oz. can = 1 1/4 c.
4 tbsp. = 1/4 c.	14 to 16-oz. can (No. 300) = 1 3/4 c.
5 tbsp. + 1 tsp. = 1/3 c.	16 to 17-oz. can (No. 303) = 2 c.
8 tbsp. = 1/2 c.	1-lb. 4-oz. can or 1-pt. 2-oz. can (No. 2) = 2 1/2 c.
12 tbsp. = 3/4 c.	1-lb. 13-oz. can (No. 2 1/2) = 3 1/2 c.
16 tbsp. = 1 c.	3-lb. 3-oz. can or 46-oz. can or 1-qt. 14-oz. can = 5 3/4 c.
1 c. = 8 oz. or 1/2 pt.	
4 c. = 1 qt.	6 1/2-lb. or 7-lb. 5-oz. can (No. 10) = 12 to 13 c.
4 qt. = 1 gal.	

Metric Conversion Chart

VOLUME

1 tsp.	=	4.9 cc
1 tbsp.	=	14.7 cc
1/8 c.	=	29.5 cc
1/4 c.	=	59.1 cc
1/3 c.	=	78.9 cc
1/2 c.	=	118.3 cc
3/4 c.	=	177.5 cc
1 c.	=	236.7 cc
2 c.	=	473.4 cc
1 fl. oz.	=	29.5 cc
4 oz.	=	118.3 cc
8 oz.	=	236.7 cc
1 pt.	=	473.4 cc
1 qt.	=	.946 liters
1 gal.	=	3.7 liters

CONVERSION FACTORS

Liters	X	1.056	=	Liquid quarts
Quarts	X	0.946	=	Liters
Liters	X	0.264	=	Gallons
Gallons	X	3.785	=	Liters
Fluid ounces	X	29.563	=	Cubic centimeters
Cubic centimeters	X	0.034	=	Fluid ounces
Cups	X	236.575	=	Cubic centimeters
Tablespoons	X	14.797	=	Cubic centimeters
Teaspoons	X	4.932	=	Cubic centimeters
Bushels	X	0.352	=	Hectoliters
Hectoliters	X	2.837	=	Bushels

WEIGHT

1 dry oz.	=	28.3 Grams
1 lb.	=	.454 Kilograms

CONVERSION FACTORS:

Ounces (Avoir.)	X	28.349	=	Grams
Grams	X	0.035	=	Ounces
Pounds	X	0.454	=	Kilograms
Kilograms	X	2.205	=	Pounds

Substitution Chart

	INSTEAD OF:	USE:
BAKING	1 tsp. baking powder 1 c. sifted all-purpose flour 1 c. sifted cake flour 1 tbsp. cornstarch (for thickening)	1/4 tsp. soda plus 1/2 tsp. cream of tartar 1 c. plus 2 tbsp. sifted cake flour 1 c. minus 2 tbsp. sifted all-purpose flour 2 tbsp. flour or 1 tbsp. tapioca
SWEET	1 1-oz. square chocolate 1 2/3 oz. semisweet chocolate 1 c. granulated sugar 1 c. honey	3 to 4 tbsp. cocoa plus 1 tsp. shortening 1 oz. unsweetened chocolate plus 4 tsp. sugar 1 c. packed brown sugar or 1 c. corn syrup, molasses, honey minus 1/4 c. liquid 1 to 1 1/4 c. sugar plus 1/4 c. liquid or 1 c. molasses or corn syrup
DAIRY	1 c. sweet milk 1 c. sour milk 1 c. buttermilk 1 c. light cream 1 c. heavy cream 1 c. sour cream	1 c. sour milk or buttermilk plus 1/2 tsp. soda 1 c. sweet milk plus 1 tbsp. vinegar or lemon juice or 1 cup buttermilk 1 c. sour milk or 1 c. yogurt 7/8 c. skim milk plus 3 tbsp. butter 3/4 c. skim milk plus 1/3 c. butter 7/8 c. sour milk plus 3 tbsp. butter
	1 c. bread crumbs	3/4 c. cracker crumbs
SEASONINGS	1 c. catsup 1 tbsp. prepared mustard 1 tsp. Italian spice 1 tsp. allspice 1 medium onion 1 clove of garlic 1 tsp. lemon juice	1 c. tomato sauce plus 1/2 c. sugar plus 2 tbsp. vinegar 1 tsp. dry mustard 1/4 tsp. each oregano, basil, thyme, rosemary plus dash of cayenne 1/2 tsp. cinnamon plus 1/8 tsp. cloves 1 tbsp. dried minced onion or 1 tsp. onion powder 1/8 tsp. garlic powder or 1/8 tsp. instant minced garlic or 3/4 tsp. garlic salt or 5 drops of liquid garlic 1/2 tsp. vinegar

Index

A

Antipasto
  choice 154
  Webb's 126
APPETIZERS
  anchovy stuffing for celery 108
  bacon poles, microwave 12
  beef
    corned beef
      mixture 38
      Reuben triangles 36
    ground beef
      meatballs
        cocktail, special 12
        sweet and sour 126
        teriyaki 13
      stuffed mushrooms, cheesy 13
  cereal party mix 146
  cheese
    and bacon strips 94
    and onion balls 12
    apple, ma's 146
    ball
      party 146
      zippy 168
    beer bites 125
    creamy cheese and crackers 82
    crisps, Cheddar cheese 168
    curry pate 11
    feta cheese pasties 168
    log, surprise 11
    mold, Easter 48
    mousse 168
    ring, zingy 168
    shrimp puffs, Dutch cheese 168
    straws, party 158
    wafers, wheat germ 173
  chicken
    chicken liver pate 172
    nuggets, golden 12
    nut puffs 12
    wings, Chinese 70
  cinnamon-raisin snack mix 83
  Creme de Menthe grapes 164
  dips
    artichoke
      anniversary 170
      hot 10
      microwave 125
      St. Patrick's day 36
    chalupa, microwave 10
    cheese
      chili con queso 71
      ginger-nut, crunchy 82
      spicy, hot 95
    crab, silver 169

    gazpacho, great 158
    passion pea dip 10
    salmon 125
    slow-ball dip 82
    spinach
      New Year's 11
      special 125
    taco dip 82
  escargots in mushroom caps 175
  ham
    balls 12
    wrapped apples 83
  Italian bites 12
  Jezebel sauce, firecracker 70
  koldtbord appetizer 125
  kwik snacks 146
  microwave
    bacon polls 12
    dips
      artichoke 125
      chalupa, Super Bowl 10
    stuffed mushrooms 126
      cheesy 13
  oyster crackers, seasoned 147
  pastry shells, curry-filled 95
  pizza, garden 83
  quiche appetizers 127
  salsa, Mike's 71
  sandwiches, see Sandwiches
  sausage-apple rolls 127
  scrambles 108
  seafood
    crab
      and spinach-stuffed mushrooms 13
      sesame rolls 13
      spread, overnight 125
    salmon
      log, holiday 11
      pate, creamy 173
      red salmon pate 11
    seviche 175
    shrimp
      cheese puffs, Dutch 168
      cocktails 127
      patties 127
      spread, dilled 11
    tuna
      garden wedges, creamy 71
      mousse 172
  sweet pickle ring 82
  tortillas, rolled 83
  turkey meatballs, tangy 126
  vegetable
    asparagus canapes, hot 36
    cherry tomatoes, stuffed 163
    cucumbers, stuffed 158
    mushrooms

182 / Index

marinated 127
spread, hot 11
stuffed
    baked 126
    cheesy 13
    crab and spinach 13
    microwave 126
    turnovers 172
snow pea pods, stuffed 13
spinach
    balls 37
    tortilla delight 37
    zucchini rounds, fried 95
water chestnuts, baked 172
wieners
    barbecued little smokies 82
    pickled 168
    tipsy hot dogs 83

Apples
cinnamon, mother's 26
see Desserts

B

Barley Casserole with Mushrooms 116
BEEF
and noodles 96
and rice, Sherried 96
barbecued, holiday 74
Brazilian-style black beans 176
brisket, Beta's best 74
chipped beef and egg casserole .. 15
corned beef
    and cabbage 38
    crusty casserole 38
    Dublin dinner 31
    whiskey-glazed 38
ground beef, see Ground Beef
kabobs
    dilly-bobs 62
    sirloin and corn 73
roasts
    pot roast
        barbecue, busy-day 163
    standing rib roast, elegant .. 49
see Appetizers
steaks
    London broil 14
    round steak
        and rice, simply elegant . 14
        Burgundy beef 25
        finger steaks 163
        pepper steak 62
        steak-on-a-stick 74
        top round aromatica 85
        with dressing 97
stroganoff 62
with broccoli, stir-fried 14

BEVERAGES
apricot slush 70
Bourbon slush 177
Chablis slush 164
Cheryl's hot spiced drink 10
cider, hot
    easy 94
    spiced 94
    wine, Betty's 158
cranberry
    cordial 146
    crush 124
daiquiris
    strawberry 24
        frozen 10
eggnog
    easy 124
    mocha 124
hot buttered rum 146
Irish cream, easy 36
kahlua 146
lemonade, picnic 70
lime cooler, merry 36
Madrilene drink, hot 162
orange blossoms 10
orange Julius 48
peppermint schnapps 146
pina colada 70
punch
    bubbling holiday punch 124
    Champagne 108
        pink Champagne 160
        sensational 169
    cherry-apple, spiced 94
    chocolate nog punch 10
    cider, hot 94
    cinnamon 94
    company punch bowl 158
    cranberry
        banger 124
        perky 125
    eggnog party punch 124
    hanging-of-the-greens punch . 36
    liquid gold 169
    open house punch 94
    party punch 24
    punchy sangria 167
    rose 175
    rum, hot 124
    shamrock punch 36
    sparkling fruit refresher 24
    St. Patrick's 36
    sweetheart 24
    wine 124
        spritzer 167
    yellow rose punch 160
rum, hot buttered 146
    base 172
sangria slush 165
strawberry slush 172
summer slush surprise 70
tea
    almond 175
    friendship tea 146
    spiced
        Gamma Theta 94
        mix 94
    super duper tea 82
twelve-o'clock cocktails 62
vodka
    slush 70

Index / 183

    lime ... 36
    wassail, English ... 125
    watermelon wine boat ... 70
BREADS
    apricot-pecan ... 147
    avocado ... 41
    banana-raisin loaves, spiced ... 148
    black walnut ... 134
    Brandy-nut, spiced ... 148
    Brazil nut ... 148
    breakfast bread ... 134
    brown bread
        Gloria's ... 164
        Irish ... 42
    buns, see Buns
    cheese
        cottage cheese-fruit ... 135
        pepper ... 174
    cherry-nut-cream cheese ... 26
    cinnamon twists ... 56
    coffee cake, see Coffee Cakes
    corn bread, see Corn Breads
    cranberry
        lemon-walnut ... 117
        sweet potato ... 135
    Danish ring, savory ... 90
    dill, casserole bread ... 118
    doughnuts, see Doughnuts
    egg bread, never-fail ... 118
    eggnog bread, Cassie's ... 134
    freckle bread, Irish ... 41
    herb
        easy ... 66
        New Year's ... 20
    Irish, holiday ... 41
    Italian, pull-apart ... 169
    muffins, see Muffins
    nut, Grandma Lunsford's ... 134
    onion snack bread ... 159
    persimmon, Brandied ... 118
    pineapple-carrot ... 55
    poppy seed ... 55
    rhubarb ... 56
    rolls, see Rolls
    sausage bread ... 75
    soda bread
        Irish, quick ... 42
        whole wheat ... 42
    strawberry jam-nut ... 148
    Swedish krinkla ... 55
    sweet potato-cranberry ... 135
    vegetable bread ... 67
    walnut Atlantic community's ... 117
    zucchini-nut ... 90
BUNS
    hocus-pocus buns ... 100
    hot cross buns
        Easter ... 56
        Lee's ... 56
Butter, fruit, holiday ... 130

C

CAKES
    angel cake

        frosted ... 67
        minted angel allegretti ... 42
    apple
        Crock-Pot ... 138
        fresh apple ... 91
    applesauce-nut ... 137
    baba au rum ... 21
    basket cake ... 58
    beet cake with cream cheese frosting ... 101
    blackberry jam ... 21
    carrot, Cover Mountain ... 120
    cherry
        gelatin cake ... 30
        maraschino cherry ... 29
        nut party cake ... 30
        pudding cake ... 27
    chocolate
        buche de noel ... 138
        cherry ... 29
        chocolate mousse-filled, heavenly ... 29
        cupcakes, see cupcakes
        custard devil's food ... 101
        German chocolate, easy ... 67
        jubilee ... 21
        triple-chocolate ... 174
    Coco Lopez cake ... 67
    coconut wreath ... 138
    cranberry
        holiday cake ... 138
        pudding cake ... 120
    Creme de Menthe cake ... 44
    cupcakes
        cherry ... 31
        chocolate
            filled ... 79
            goblin's delight ... 102
        muffin cup dainties ... 158
        spiced ... 153
        strawberry ... 31
    daffodil dessert ... 57
    Diamond Head crunch ... 67
    flag cake ... 79
    friendship cake ... 30
    fruit
        Brandied ... 153
        mixed fruit ... 139
    fruitcakes
        dark, Grandmother Newman's ... 153
        English, spiced ... 153
        spirited ... 138
        zucchini ... 154
    golden layer cake ... 58
    gumdrop cake
        Christmas ... 139
        Easter ... 59
    Italian cream cake ... 160
    lane cake ... 139
    lemon rolls
        luscious ... 161
        sponge ... 68
    microwave
        petits fours ... 171
    mint
        ice cream pie, frosty ... 46

184 / Index

    St. Patrick's day 44
neighbor cake 91
orange-cranberry torte 118
peach, fresh 92
persimmon 120
petits fours, microwave 171
pineapple, Hawaiian 91
pistachio
    St. Patrick's day 44
    Thanksgiving 121
poppy seed loaves 140
pound cakes
    Bourbon 154
    pecan-cream cheese 161
    pumpkin 121
    raisin-orange 21
pumpkin
    cake roll 102
    walnut-rum 121
red velvet 31
rhubarb
    fresh rhubarb 121
    quick 92
rum
    Italian 139
    New Year's 21
s'mores cake 164
strawberry
    Easter 59
    jam cake 102
    shortcut cake 29
    sour cream 31
sugar plum 160
sweetheart cake 30
walnut-cherry 30
white Christmas cake 154
white custard cake 31
yule cakes 139

CANDIES
apple
    bonbons 102
    cherry candy apples 103
caramels, pecan 149
chocolate
    Bourbon balls 149
    cherry mash balls 149
    chocolate-covered cherries 149
    fluted kiss cups 32
    four's candy 150
    fudge
        peanut butter pinwheels 150
        peppermint 150
        velvet 149
    toffee, almond, microwave 150
    truffles 32
cottontails 60
crystal candy 147
dinner mints 150
fudge
    apricot 149
    see chocolate candy
haystacks 102
microwave
    toffee, almond 150

mocha peanut clusters 162
orange balls, easy 105
rocky road Halloween squares 102
see Easter Eggs
spiders 103
strawberries
    Easter 60
    St. Valentine's day 32
toffee, English 150

CHEESE
and spinach strata 53
enchiladas 134
pierogis 134
rice casserole 89
sandwich, see Sandwiches
see Appetizers
soup, see Soups

CHEESECAKES
Amaretto 160
blueberry 68
cherry 32
chocolate lover's
    New Year's 22
    St. Valentine's day 32
cranberry 121
Irish cream 45
mandarin orange 144
peaches and cream 78
pistachio-almond 44
pumpkin, holiday 122

CHICKEN
and mushroom crepes 26
and ribs, honey-glazed 86
baked, cheesy 76
barbecued 163
breasts
    and rice squares, fast 173
    and shrimp grill 64
    and vegetable stir fry 18
    cheese rolls 98
    cheesy onion ring casserole 63
    cranberry chicken Michele 26
    delicious, easy 17
    garlicious 173
    golden crusty casserole 63
    love and kisses chicken 25
    low-calorie, with wild rice 63
    oriental chicken, shredded 17
    Parmesan 98
        special 110
    peachie 64
    puff pastry rolls, golden 170
    spaghetti, special 64
    Wellington 131
    with prosciutto 51
buttermilk 87
cacciatore, cheese-topped 98
country captain 64
crescent squares, savory 87
curried 87
fried
    oven-fried 76
    southern-fried, with squash 75
Japanese stack-up dinner 176

Index / 185

mandarin 18
maple 99
no-peekie 131
oven-barbecued 64
quiche noel 130
ruby chicken 130
sandwich, see Sandwiches
see Appetizers
soup, see Soups
St. Pat's 40
Chiles Rellenos Casserole, Margriet's 77
Chop Suey 17
Christmas 123-144
COFFEE CAKES
  butter pecan 54
  candy cane 147
  Easter egg braids 55
  German stollen 147
  harvest loaf 117
  merry Christmas coffee cake 147
  orange 100
  streusel 55
  walnut roll, frosted 148
  yogurt-poppy seed 20
COOKIES
  angel food 171
  animal cookies 105
  biscotti 60
  blarney stones 45
  butter cookies, valentine 33
  buttery gems, nutty 141
  candy bar cookies 162
  carrot
    bars
      Easter 60
      Halloween 103
    golden 104
  cheesecake cookies 33
  cherry bars
    maraschino cherry 32
    merry cherry bars 141
    St. Valentine's day 33
  chocolate
    brownies
      applesauce, favorite 79
      chocolate syrup 68
      mint swirl 46
    chocolate chip cookie wreath ..151
    Creme de Menthe bars 45
    crunch cookies 151
    fudge-filled bars, festive 151
    grasshopper squares 45
    snowballs 152
  Christmas cookies
    ball cookies 140
    company 140
  coconut chews 140
  confetti cutouts 150
  crackerjack cookies 104
  date and orange slice bars 103
  gingerbread boys 104
  gingersnaps
    favorite 104
    special 121

heart-shaped 33
honey 34
jack-o'-lantern tea cakes 104
kiss cookies
    crunchy 33
    Irish 44
    St. Valentine's day 34
lemon squares, easy 165
marvel bars 141
molasses crinkles 104
monster cookies 105
nut horns 152
nut roll cookies 152
pasquatas 140
peanut crackers 79
peppernuts, Russian 151
persimmon 174
pumpkin
    bars with cream cheese frosting ..103
    holiday cookies 104
Russian tea cakes 142
shamrock cookies, Irish 45
sinful sesames 151
springerle cookies 151
spritzers 152
sugar and spice snaps 142
sugar plum cookie tree 141
surprise bonbons 105
tassie cookies 141
valentine sweethearts 33
waffle cookes 140
walnut bars, Viennese 177
Corn Breads
  Mexican 77
  sour cream, scrumptious 67
  spoon bread, vegetable 100
Cornish Hens
  gourmet stuffed 40
  with mushroom stuffing 112
  with rice 112
Cranberry Casserole 134
Crock·Pot
  apple cake 138
  beans 76
  stew, Irish 39

D

DESSERTS
  almond puff 118
  amondrado 78
  angel cake, heavenly 161
  apple
    dumplings 90
    streusel-filled 105
    tarts, Grandma Bodin's 105
  bananas, flaming 78
  berry slump 90
  Brandy Alexander souffle 135
  cake, see Cakes
  candy, see Candies
  cheesecake, see Cheesecakes
  cherry
    cherries in the snow 136
    crepes 27

crunch ... 27
chocolate
  frozen delight ... 57
  mint cups ... 162
  mints, Russian ... 44
  mocha taffy dessert ... 135
  mousse
    Christmas ... 136
    strawberry ... 27
  pots de creme ... 27
coeurs a la creme ... 169
cookies, see Cookies
cranberries
  Brandied ... 22
    candied ... 152
crepes, grasshopper ... 42
date cups, Christmas ... 131
eggnog
  cup ... 136
  ring ... 136
fruit
  Brandied ... 152
  Brandy fruit supreme ... 20
  pizza, fresh ... 167
  refresher ... 78
heavenly hash ... 137
holiday wreath ... 144
ice cream, see Ice Cream
India House swans ... 118
Irish mint cream ... 43
Jell-O, party ... 58
lacy dessert baskets ... 28
lemon
  bisque ... 58
  frozen dessert ... 43
  whip ... 57
Lou's lollapalooza dessert ... 174
macaroon dessert ... 27
marguerites ... 28
meringues
  shells, valentine ... 28
mint
  frozen mint mallow ... 42
  Irish dessert ... 43
  Margo's marvel ... 43
noodle kugle ... 144
northern lights ... 58
Pavlova, Australian ... 140
peach delight ... 90
peppermint dessert, frozen ... 161
pie, see Pies
pineapple tarts ... 162
pizza, red-white and blue ... 78
pudding, see Puddings
pumpkin
  cake dessert ... 101
  crunch ... 119
  mousse, frozen ... 119
  squares ... 119
rhuberry kuchen ... 91
Ritz Cracker dessert ... 169
rum-raisin cream, festive ... 144
sherbet, see Sherbets
shortcake, autumn ... 120

snowballs ... 137
snowflake pudding with raspberry sauce ... 28
souffle, Brandy Alexander ... 135
strawberry
  almond cream in ruby strawberries ... 171
  delight ... 28
  pizza ... 29
tarts
  apple, Grandma Bodin's ... 105
  pineapple ... 162
tipsy pudding ... 21
Toronto pie dessert ... 79
tortes
  Bavarian, apple ... 56
  broken glass torte ... 57
  butternut squash-almond ... 120
  fudge mint ... 136
  ice cream, double-chocolate ... 57
  linzer tortes ... 177
  meringue, elegant ... 162
trifle
  Irish ... 43
  master's ... 91
  punch bowl trifle ... 58
  tipsy, mandarin ... 137
DOUGHNUTS
  buttermilk ... 100
  cherry ... 100
  funnel cakes ... 78
  spudnuts ... 100
DRESSINGS
  bread-pecan, for poultry ... 116
  corn bread
    favorite ... 116
    southern ... 116
  oyster-olive ... 116
  wild rice ... 116

Easter ... 47-58
EASTER EGGS
  butter cream ... 59
  magic ... 60
  nanaimo bars ... 59
  peanut butter
    marshmallow ... 59
EGGS
  and chipped beef casserole ... 15
  Benedict ... 158
  breakfast strata ... 51
  broccoli-ham casserole ... 65
  chicken-stuffed ... 158
  cup of gold ... 54
  deviled
    easy ... 77
    Rosie's ... 54
  Easter brunch eggs, gran's ... 50
  scrambled ... 20
Enchiladas, cheese ... 134
Equivalent Chart ... 178

F

Fettucini
  pasta primavera ... 54

Index / 187

FISH
    bass bake, Roxane's 75
    cioppino 18
    flounder, Ralf's favorite 65
    grilled 65
    microwave
        tuna wedges, Lenten 51
    salmon
        and cucumber casserole 64
        impossible seafood pie 87
    seafood casserole 170
    see Appetizers
    tuna
        baked tuna ring 87
        wedges, Lenten, microwave 51
Fondue, caramel 101

G

Goose
    glazed English roast goose with
        wild rice casserole 131
Gourmet Food Gifts 145-156
GROUND BEEF
    baird beans 39
    burgers, independence 62
    cavatini, baked 14
    chili
        crazy Mary's 86
        quick 97
    chimichangas, football special 15
    dinner-in-a-pumpkin 97
    hamburgers, baked 74
    lasagna, shortcut 15
    loaves
        cranberry 130
        ham 49
            upside-down 50
        stuffed, prizewinning 173
        Swiss 74
    pastichio, Greek 176
    pie, Halloween 97
    pigs in the blanket 86
    pizza
        spaghetti 15
        zucchini 86
    pumpkin dinner, holiday 97
    rolls, Spanish 85
    runzas 98
    see Appetizers
    stuffed cabbage rolls 39
    stuffed green peppers
        Italian 110
        St. Patrick's day 39
    tourtierre 16
    wild rice hot dish 116
    zita bake 15

H

Halloween 93-106
HAM
    breakfast casserole, Easter 50
    broccoli-egg casserole 65
    cranberry-glazed 110
    ham balls and sauce 50
    Hawaiian 63
    limerick ham dinner 39
    loaf 49
        upside-down 50
    New England casserole, favorite 133
    orange-glazed 50
    picnic-perfect 63
    sandwich, see Sandwiches
    Sheryl's spring bake 63
Hominy-Chili Casserole 77

I

ICE CREAM
    bombes
        holiday bombe with mincemeat 137
        strawberry-almond 161
    chocolate
        peppermint dessert 136
        roll 22
    homemade
        crowning glory 80
        Grandma Sevedge's 92
    ice cream crunch 67
    peach, fresh 80
    pistachio dessert 44
    six-three 92
    strawberry fantasy 79
Independence Day 69-80

J

Jelly
    hot pepper 152
    wine 152

L

Labor Day 81-92
Lamb
    leg of lamb with salsa 50
    riblets Monterey 17
    stew, see Stews

M

Macaroni
    shrimp a la Lorraine 73
Marinade, shish kabob 85
Memorial Day 59-68
Metric Chart 180
Mexican Casserole, marvelous 97
MICROWAVE
    appetizers
        bacon poles 12
        dips
            artichoke 125
            chalupa, Super Bowl 10
        stuffed mushrooms 126
            cheesy 13
    pecans Worcestershire 156
    petits fours 171
    pork, sweet and sour 98
    toffee, almond 150
    tuna wedges, Lenten 51

188 / Index

vegetables
- broccoli delish 52
- medley, zesty 66
- tomato casserole 88

Mincemeat
- delicious 154
- green tomato 154
- mom's 119

MUFFINS
- bran, quick 135
- carrot and pineapple 117
- cranberry, fresh 117
- gingerbread 90
- orange juicy muffins with honey spread 20
- orange streusel muffins 101
- pumpkin, Thanksgiving 117

Mustard, hot 41

N

New Year's 9-22

Noodles
- and beef 96
- noodle kugle 144
- with pesto 41

NUTS
- microwave
  - pecans Worcestershire 156
- pecans
  - sugared 156
  - Worcestershire, microwave 156
- spiced nuts
  - favorite 156
  - special 156
- Swedish crystal nuts 177
- walnuts
  - Chinese-fried 22
  - coffee 144
  - spiced 156

P

Pheasant
- delicious 112
- roast 112

PICKLES
- bread and butter 155
- cinnamon rings 155
- see Vegetables
- sweet hot 71
- zucchini pickles, prizewinning 155

PIES
- apple
  - cream 80
  - praline 80
  - sour cream 142
- apricot packable pies 68
- blueberry funny cake pie 92
- cantaloupe 80
- cheesecakes, cottage cheese 60
- chiffon, Peg's 106
- chocolate
  - black bottom 106
  - chocolate chip 22
  - German chocolate 106
- grasshopper, divine 46
- lime swirl 46
- pecan, southern 68
- coconut 174
- coffee 106
- cranberry-whipped cream 142
- daiquiri 46
- holiday, two-tone pie 106
- lemon, perfect 142
- macadamia mocha supreme 21
- mince, custard crunch 162
- peanut butter 68
- pear, glazed 171
- pecan, chocolate southern 68
- peppermint, pink 34
- pumpkin
  - cheese 122
  - sour cream 106
- raisin pies, French 142
- rhubarb, almost pie 22
- strawberry
  - chiffon 34
  - fresh strawberry 80
  - margarita pie 34
- very berry pie 92
- white Christmas pie 142

Pineapple, scalloped 174

POPCORN
- balls, fancy 101
- cake 156
- caramel corn, holiday 101
- con pesto 156
- poppycock 156

PORK
- bacon
  - breakfast strata 51
  - brunch lasagna, holiday 51
- barbecued 16
- Brazilian-style black beans 176
- ham, see Ham
- loaf, stuffed, prizewinning 173
- medallions with artichoke hearts
  - and apples 16
- microwave
  - sweet and sour 98
- roasts
  - cherry-almond 25
  - fruited 16
  - marinated 50
  - rib roast, fruit-stuffed 110
  - tenderloin, with cherry sauce ..130
- sausage
  - bread 75
  - hoppin' John 17
  - kraut pinwheel 17
  - pigs-in-the-blanket 86
  - ring
    - Christmas morning 130
    - rice ring 116
  - roll 86
- see Appetizers
- spareribs
  - and chicken, honey-glazed 86
  - barbecued, mama's 63

Index / 189

    dem ribs 75
    stuffed cabbage rolls 39
    sweet and sour 16
        microwave 98
    tourtierre 16
PUDDINGS
    almond-rice, Danish 143
    bread puddings
        Mexican 78
        old-fashioned, with everyday sauce 119
    cranberry steamed puddings
        and eggnog sauce 143
        Christmas 143
    plum, prize 143
    rice, old-fashioned .174
    suet pudding 143

Q

Quail, stuffed 112
Quiches
    noel 130
    seafood quiches 87
    see Appetizers

R

Relish
    beet and horseradish 54
    sweet pepper 155
RICE
    and chicken squares, fast 173
    and Sherried beef 96
    artichoke casserole 112
    cheese casserole 89
    Polynesian 89
    potluck cuisine 89
    sausage ring 116
    soup, see Soups
    wild rice
        casserole 131
        hot dish 116
        turkey casserole 111
    with Cornish hens .112
ROLLS
    butterscotch breakfast rolls 56
    caramel, one-rise, easy 148
    cinnamon yeast rolls 135
    cottage cheese 167
    dinner rolls Italiano, one-hour 177
    easy 67
    shamrock rolls 42

S

Salad Dressing, Cheryl's 166
SALADS
    antipasto, tangy 173
    bacon, hot 96
    beef
        corned beef 37
        ground beef
            taco salad 14
    Chicago super summer salad 166
    chicken
        almond 165

        Chinese 14
        fruited 73
        Hawaiian 175
        in melon rings 37
        rice 73
    deli salad, Italian 84
    egg salad, Aunt Nellie's 72
    fruit
        apple
            red cinnamon 24
            stuffed cinnamon apples 128
        apple cider 95
        apricot
            Easter 48
            layered 95
        cantaloupe gelatin salad 84
        chartreuse salad 128
        cherry, pink 24
        Christmas ribbon salad 128
        cranberry
            apple relish .108
            cream cheese 108
            creamy mold 108
            crunchy 108
            fresh cranberry salad 109
            frozen 128
            make-ahead 109
            relish mold .109
            ring, Kulp 166
        eggnog Christmas salad 128
        frosted 48
        frozen
            fruit cup 48
        grapefruit-avocado 38
        gumdrop salad 49
        lime-lemon gelatin salad 49
        mandarin orange
            almond 96
            rich 109
        mixed fruit 166
        mystery salad 129
        peach, pickled .109
        pears with fresh cranberry sauce 128
        pineapple
            Cheddar mold 71
            Easter salad 48
            mint 37
            spring party salad 49
        pretzel salad 24
        raspberry
            applesauce .109
            red 129
            St. Valentine's day 24
        red velvet salad 129
        red-white and blue delight 71
        sinful salad 129
        stained glass salad 171
        trick or treat salad 96
        twenty-four hour 129
        valentine salad 25
        with sour cream-fruit dressing 109
    ham, congealed 62
    macaroni, special 84
    rice

Index

and lentil salad 72
overnight 85
special 85
seafood
    bread salad 96
    conch, South Pacific 175
    crab, pineapple 62
    ring, congealed 167
    shrimp
        Carmen's 49
        party mold 129
    tuna
        hot-cold 73
        vinaigrette 84
spaghetti
    laborsaving salad 84
    overnight 72
    vermicelli 72
Tahiti salad 166
vegetable
    asparagus mold 13
    bean
        kidney bean 71
        and egg 165
    broccoli
        Cheddar cheese 83
    cabbage, Chinese 14
    carrot
        copper pennies 72
        Easter 48
    confetti salad 84
    Greek salad 165
    holiday salad
        luncheon 166
        red and green 128
    Italian toss 175
    pea, Grandma Wells' 84
    potato
        old-fashioned 72
        patio salad 72
        sour cream 83
    Russian vinaigrette salad 85
    simple summer salad 73
    spinach
        and strawberry 25
        oriental 166
        St. Patrick's day 38
    tomato aspic 166
    zucchini and orange 13

SANDWICHES
Champagne-frosted loaf 170
cheese
    and olive, curried 95
    cozy sandwiches 163
    party sandwiches 95
chicken-fruit 51
Diamond Head 132
ham
    and cheese
        brunchwiches 165
        Cheddar cheese, baked 86
        Swiss 74
    ham-filled buns 74
holiday sandwich wreath 126

olive and pecan 164
pepper-pecan 167
shrimp melts 51
veggie sandwich spread 37
SAUCES
almond 57
barbecue, Lea's 164
hot fudge, heavenly 46
onion-butter 77
tartar 89
Scent
Christmas, wonderful 144
holiday scent recipe 144
SHELLFISH
cioppino 18
crab
    imperial, Eastern Shore 75
    pizza 176
lobster
    Chinese, with noodles and vegetables 19
    thermador, diamond 170
oyster pudding 132
Pleasure Isle casserole 65
sandwich, see Sandwiches
scallops with vegetables 65
seafood casserole 170
seafood lasagna 26
seafood quiches 87
see Appetizers
shrimp
    a la Lorraine 73
    and chicken grill 64
    barbecued 163
    creole, easy 75
    garlic fried 65
    jambalaya 65
    scampi, Betty's 132
    super shrimp 18
soup, see Soups
tomato aspic 110
Sherbets
cranberry ice 119
lemon ice supreme 172
peach, fresh 92
SOUPS
bean, special 159
carrot bisque 99
cauliflower, fresh 127
cheese
    Cheddar cheese 159
    New Year's 19
chicken nugget 159
corn chowder
    buttermilk 132
    soup supper 159
crab-mushroom bisque 159
cream of leek, with Stilton 53
French onion 163
fruit soup, fast 160
Italian sausage 98
lentil 19
plum, Danish 82
potato
    mushroom 19

shoppers' lifesaver 133
St. Patrick's day 41
turkey, hearty 18
vegetable, creamy garden soup 115
wild rice 20
Spaghetti
carbonara 176
chicken spaghetti, special 64
Special Occasions 159-177
STEWS
beef
apple cider, Sue's 130
oven-baked, Halloween 96
lamb
Irish stew, Crock·Pot 39
St. Patrick's Day 35-46
Stuffings see Dressings
St. Valentine's Day 23-34
Substitution Chart 179

T

Thanksgiving 107-122
TURKEY
Chinese casserole 111
chow mein 111
divine 112
Florentine, saucy 131
goodbye turkey casserole 110
layered casserole 111
overnight turkey 111
pie, crusty 111
see Appetizers
soup, see Soups
wild rice casserole 111

V

Veal
meat loaf, stuffed, prizewinning 173
scallapini 16
VEGETABLES
artichoke-rice casserole 112
asparagus
alla fontina 171
pickled 155
beans
baird beans 39
baked, favorite 88
black beans, Brazilian-style 176
Crock·Pot 76
four-bean casserole 76
green beans, holiday 113
lima beans, barbecued 76
beets
with orange sauce 52
with pineapple 26
with sour sauce 88
broccoli
casserole 52
delish, microwave 52
ham-egg casserole 65
with Parmesan 40
Brussels sprouts provencal 52
cabbage

braised, Irish 40
Christmas cabbage 132
rolls, stuffed 39
carrots
and parsnips, orange-glazed 133
baked 99
cheese-scalloped 113
lyonnaise 132
nutty 52
ring 52
zucchini casserole 113
cauliflower
baked
Italiano 19
Swiss mountain-style 177
cheese casserole 114
tomato scallop 76
celery
holiday casserole 113
saucy casserole 52
connoisseur's casserole 115
corn
and sirloin kabobs 73
corn on the cob, herb-baked 76
custard fiesta 133
Fremont 53
fritters 88
hot corn, Millie's 88
pudding
baked 113
quick and easy 99
cucumbers
and salmon casserole 64
freezer slices 89
eggplant
Parmesan, layered 114
Parmigiana, favorite 88
stuffed, Doreen's 53
fresh vegetable jardiniere 133
garden medley 115
green peppers
stuffed 39
Italian 110
holiday casserole 133
Italian marinade 72
Italian vegetable toss 000
medley, zesty, microwave 66
microwave
broccoli delish 52
medley, zesty 66
tomato casserole 88
mixed vegetable casserole, special 115
mushrooms
pickled 155
pilaf, Vesta's 99
New England casserole favorite 133
onions, scalloped 115
pasta primavera 54
peas
green peas, Chinese 53
hoppin' John 17
pie, crustless 66
potatoes
Cheddar puff 53

192 / Index

colcannon 41
    chicken-flavored 40
company casserole 66
Delmonico potato casserole 54
hashed brown
    casserole 66
    scalloped 54
    mashed, deluxe 170
    Texas potatoes, cheesy 77
see Appetizers
soup, see Soups
spinach
    and cheese strata 53
    Gulliver's spinach 19
    Martello's casserole 114
squash
    pickled 155
    souffle 88
sweet potatoes
    bacon boats 114

crunch 113
    surprise, Beverly's 99
    yamboree bake, orange 114
tomatoes
    aspic 110
    casserole, microwave 88
vegetable casserole 40
vegetables en casserole 115
vegetarian lasagna 66
zucchini
    and tomato casserole 77
    carrot casserole 113
    crumb-topped casserole 114
    party bake 89
    something special 89

Z

Ziti Bake 15
Zowie Bars, meal-in-one 103

PHOTOGRAPHY CREDITS

Cover: United Fresh Fruit and Vegetable Association; Hershey Foods Corporation; Pepperidge Farms; American Spice Trade Association; McIlhenny Company; M&M Chocolate Candies; California Apricot Advisory Board; Best Foods, a Division of CPC International, Inc.; Pickle Packers International; National Cherry Growers & Industries Foundation; Ocean Spray Cranberries, Inc.; and Schieffelin & Company.

Library of Congress Cataloging in Publication Data
Main entry under title:
    The New Beta Sigma Phi Holiday Cookbook.
    Includes index.
      1. Holiday cookery. 2. Holidays. I. Beta Sigma Phi.
TX739.N37 1984   641.5'68   84-81115
ISBN 0-87197-177-1

Cookbooks available from Favorite Recipes Press are chock-full of mouth-watering, home-tested recipes that earn you the best compliment of all..."More Please!"

Every Favorite Recipes Press Cookbook includes:
- 128 to 232 pages.
- 300 to 500 delicious family pleasing recipes.
- color and black-and-white photos.
- lie-flat spiral binding.
- wipe-clean color covers.
- easy-to-read format.
- fully indexed.

To place your order, call our **toll-free** number **1-800-251-1520** or clip and mail the convenient order form.

☐ YES. Please send me the cookbooks I've checked below. I understand that if I'm not completely delighted I may return any book within 30 days for a full refund.

TITLE	Item #	Qty.	Retail Price	Total
The New Beta Sigma Phi Holiday Cookbook	40606		$6.95	
All-Occasion Casseroles Cookbook With Menus	28029		4.50	
Desserts and Party Foods Cookbook	25275		4.50	
The Golden Anniversary Cookbook	13706		5.95	
The Dining Room	13595		5.95	
Recipes From The World of Beta Sigma Phi	13692		5.95	
Dieting to Stay Healthy	13684		5.95	
Gourmet Cookbook	13617		5.95	
Party Book	13668		5.95	
Save & Win	13676		5.95	
Bicentennial Heritage Recipes	13560		5.95	
Postage and Handling	36579	1	$ .95	$ .95
TOTAL AMOUNT				

☐ Payment Enclosed.
☐ Please Charge My: ☐ Visa   ☐ MasterCard
Acct. No. _____ Expiration Date _____
Signature _____
Name _____
Chapter Name _____
Chapter Number _____
Address _____
City _____ State _____ Zip _____
Daytime Phone (___) _____

- No COD orders.
- Call our **toll-free** number for return information.
- Prices subject to change without notice.
- Books offered subject to availability.
- Call our **toll-free** number for information on **Creating Your Own Cookbook.**

Mail completed order form to:

FAVORITE RECIPES PRESS
P. O. Box 1408
Nashville, Tennessee 37202

BK